# Living Language
# and Literature

## 2nd Edition

Series editors
**Jane Bluett** and
**John Shuttleworth**

WITHDRAWN

**HODDER**
EDUCATION
PART OF HACHETTE LIVRE UK

Although every effort has been made to ensure that website addresses are correct at time of going to press, Hodder Education cannot be held responsible for the content of any website mentioned in this book. It is sometimes possible to find a relocated web page by typing in the address of the home page for a website in the URL window of your browser.

Hachette Livre UK's policy is to use papers that are natural, renewable and recyclable products and made from wood grown in sustainable forests. The logging and manufacturing processes are expected to conform to the environmental regulations of the country of origin.

Orders: please contact Bookpoint Ltd, 130 Milton Park, Abingdon, Oxon OX14 4SB. Telephone: (44) 01235 827720. Fax: (44) 01235 400454. Lines are open from 9.00am to 5.00pm, Monday to Saturday, with a 24-hour message answering service. Visit our website at www.hoddereducation.co.uk

**Series editors: Jane Bluett and John Shuttleworth**
**Author team: Susan Cockcroft, Sylvia Edmond, Mary Jay, John Shuttleworth**

© Susan Cockcroft, Sylvia Edmond, Mary Jay, John Shuttleworth 2008

First published in 2000 by
Hodder Education,
part of Hachette Livre UK,
338 Euston Road
London NW1 3BH

First edition published 2000
This second edition first published 2008

| Impression number | 5 | 4 | 3 | 2 | 1 |
|---|---|---|---|---|---|
| Year | 2012 | 2011 | 2010 | 2009 | 2008 |

Cover photo © Stan Laurel Productions/Hal Roach Studios

Typeset in Palatino and Helvetica Neue.
Editorial and production by Topics – The Creative Partnership, Exeter
Printed in Italy

A catalogue record for this title is available from the British Library
ISBN: 978 0 340 93954 3

# Contents

# Introduction

## Who are you?

If you are reading this book, then you probably

- already have some experience in studying and enjoying English Language at GCSE
- are studying English Language at either AS or A2 level
- are aware of some of the relevant ideas behind the subject and are familiar with ways of writing about it.

Obviously *Living Language* is primarily intended as an introduction to AS- and A-level English Language. However, it will also be useful if you are studying English Language & Literature.

In this introduction we explain

- the differences between GCSE and A level
- how this book relates to the Assessment Objectives for the English Language specifications.

## Bridging the gap: from GCSE to A level

You will find that moving from GCSE to A level is a big step, but not a step that you are unprepared for, nor one that will be too great. This is because there is an intermediate stage in A-level study which means that everyone has to sit an Advanced Subsidiary (AS) examination before proceeding to A level. Many people will take this examination at the end of the first year of their course, but it can be taken at other times, depending on how your course is organised. The AS exam is pitched at a standard in between A level and GCSE, so that, at the beginning of your A-level course, you are faced with less of a mountain to climb. You do not have to move on from AS to A level unless you wish to do so.

Your exams are now connected like this:

```
GCSE English ──┐
               ├──▶  AS English Language  ──▶  A-level English Language
GCSE English   │
Literature ────┘
     │                      │                          │
     ▼                      ▼                          ▼
end of course         end of course              end of course
```

| GCSE English | GCSE English Literature |
|---|---|
| Shakespeare | Shakespeare |
| Prose – one of these has to be pre-1914 | Prose |
| Poetry | Poetry |
| Non-fiction texts | Drama |
| Media texts | Comparisons between texts |
| A range of speaking and listening activities | Literary tradition |
| A range of writing activities | Cultural contexts |

### AS English Language

This requires you to show knowledge and understanding of

■ the key features of the following areas of language study:
  ◆ phonology (sound and intonation patterns of speech)
  ◆ lexis (vocabulary)
  ◆ grammar (of both spoken and written texts)
  ◆ semantics and pragmatics (the ways meanings are constructed and interpreted in both speech and writing)

■ the ways language varies according to whether it is written or spoken and according to the context in which it is produced

■ the ways language varies according to personal and social factors

■ the ways that variations in language can shape and change meanings and forms.

In addition you need to be able to

■ write appropriately and accurately for a variety of audiences and purposes and comment on what you have produced.

---

### A-level English Language (in addition to AS requirements)

This requires you to show deeper knowledge and understanding of

■ areas of language study
■ the ways in which historical and geographical variation shape and change meanings and forms in language
■ the ways in which human language develops. (This may be a requirement of AS study depending on the specification you are following.)

You need also to be able to

■ comment on and evaluate the usefulness of your application and exploration of these systematic approaches to the study of spoken and written texts, including texts from the past.

---

So how is GCSE different from AS and A level? Naturally, there is continuity with English Language GCSE, as you would expect. There you had to write pieces for different purposes and had to study a range of non-fiction and non-literary texts. These feature again at AS and A level, but in addition you will be studying some spoken texts. You will also be studying how spoken and written language is structured and organised.

In general terms, to succeed beyond GCSE you obviously need to enjoy studying language. You will also need to be prepared to study texts from outside your own time and culture, thus expanding your horizons. As you continue your studies, the methods you use will become as important as the content of the course. This is why how you approach a text is just as important as what you say about it. Above all, you will need to be able to make your own judgements about what you read and hear, coming closer to being an independent informed reader and listener as you progress through the course.

The course you are following is already an excellent one designed to test your knowledge, understanding and skills in English Language. However, the government has stipulated that there should also be a number of Assessment Objectives whose purpose is to assess whether you have achieved AS- or A-level standard and therefore whether you deserve an award in the subject. The mark you achieve in each component of the course depends entirely on how well you have demonstrated your ability to meet these Assessment Objectives, whether in coursework or in an end-of-module examination. It's as well, therefore, to know what these Assessment Objectives are.

Here they are in full for AS and A level. Below each objective is a user-friendly explanation of what exactly the objective requires.

## Assessment Objectives

> **AO1** – Select and apply a range of linguistic methods, to communicate relevant knowledge using appropriate terminology and coherent, accurate written expression.

Here you are being asked to show that you can write about language in a way that shows you have studied it at an advanced level. You must be able to use technical terms effectively and precisely and show your understanding of the areas of language study to which you have been introduced. Your own written language must also be effective. You should learn to apply your knowledge of language to your own writing. As a student of A-level English Language you need to show that you can use accurate and well-constructed sentences.

> **AO2** – Demonstrate critical understanding of a range of concepts and issues relating to the construction and analysis of meanings in spoken and written language, using knowledge of linguistic approaches.

Language concepts and issues are the ideas and opinions that surround the use of language in all its forms. You need to understand a range of theories about language use as well as the attitudes and values language expresses or provokes. You must show that you have engaged with these ideas in a critical way and are able to challenge them – for example, political correctness, how we acquire language, attitudes to accents.

> **AO3** – Analyse and evaluate the influence of contextual factors on the production and reception of spoken and written language, showing knowledge of the key constituents of language.

All language use, written or spoken, is dependent upon the context in which it occurs. Here you must show that you are aware of the contextual factors at work. These will always include audience and purpose as well as more specific contexts you may be asked to consider, such as gender, power, occupation.

> **AO4** – Demonstrate expertise and creativity in the use of English in a range of different contexts informed by linguistic study.

You will be expected to write effectively for a range of audiences and purposes. You need to explore the writing process and develop your own skills as a writer. You need to show that what you have studied in the course informs the writing you produce. Your creativity should be shown in the way that you can manipulate language in a variety of ways. For example, how would you present a complex idea to a non-specialist audience?

## Addressing the new specifications

Whichever English Language specification you are studying, you will be required to produce coursework and complete examination tasks that allow you to demonstrate the skills and understanding outlined in the Assessment Objectives. Each specification will ask you to do this in different ways. However, every A-level English Language student will be involved in the following activities:

- writing for different audiences and purposes
- analysing a wide range of written and spoken texts and data
- applying systematic approaches to the study of language
- exploring how language is used in a wide variety of social contexts
- evaluating theories and concepts to do with language use
- learning about the way language develops.

*Living Language* addresses each of these modes of study, providing you with a range of resources and activities designed to support you in your A-level course. As well as guiding you towards exam success, *Living Language* will help you develop your own ideas about language use and improve your skills as a language practitioner. We hope that you will find this book a practical and informative guide to your journey through the English language.

## Technical terms

Key technical terms are highlighted in blue the first time they occur in each chapter; these terms are defined in the Glossary at the end of the book.

# Key Concepts for Studying English

**At the end of this chapter you should be able to**

- select and apply a range of linguistic methods, to communicate relevant knowledge using appropriate terminology and coherent, accurate written expression (AO1)

- demonstrate critical understanding of a range of concepts and issues relating to the construction and analysis of meanings in spoken and written language, using knowledge of linguistic approaches (AO2)

- analyse and evaluate the influence of contextual factors on the production and reception of spoken and written language, showing knowledge of the key constituents of language (AO3)

- demonstrate expertise and creativity in the use of English in a range of different contexts informed by linguistic study (AO4).

For a more student-friendly version of these Assessment Objectives, turn to page vii in the Introduction.

## Introduction

One of the most irritating things when you start a new academic subject is that you don't know the words, you can't 'talk the talk', and you feel tongue-tied at best and totally mystified at worst. This can happen all too easily when you are introduced to the study of A-level English Language. Not only are you expected to know what people are talking about when they refer lightly to grammar, lexis and syntax, but alarming phrases like language concepts, diachronic change and phonological features may trip off the tongue of your teachers. How will you ever manage, you wonder? Maybe you should have taken AS Philosophy, Physics or PE instead?

The aim of this chapter is to create a sense of calm confidence in the face of any relevant concept, term or theoretical position associated with the study of English Language and Literature so that by the end of the chapter you can not only 'talk the talk' but understand and – when required – apply these concepts to real texts in English, whether they're literary or non-literary, spoken or written.

We start with the basic premise that language is either expressive (creative, conveying feeling and mood, literary) or functional (pragmatic, getting things done, non-literary) communication. (We shall be considering spoken and written English in this chapter, but most of the ideas, concepts and terminology can be recognised in all human languages.) Every language is structured in predictable patterns so that other speakers and writers recognise those patterns and can start to make sense of what is being spoken or written. (Babies learn from very early on to recognise the predictable patterns in the speech of their carers, initially of sounds, but soon of grammatical patterns as well as individual words.) These structured patterns or systems can be categorised as grammar, syntax, phonology and lexis. In order not to start off by creating the confusion we're anxious to avoid, here are some working definitions.

- Grammar and syntax are broadly interchangeable terms which describe the ways in which the sentence (written) or utterance (spoken) is organised into structures like words, phrases and clauses.
- Phonology means the individual sounds or phonemes which make up a particular language.
- Lexis is the vocabulary or word-stock of any given language

But patterns of words and predictable word order don't really convey meaning in themselves. A classic example of this is the following sentence cited by the American linguist Noam Chomsky:

'Curious green ideas sleep furiously.'

Can we make sense of this? The language is English, the patterning of words and the word order are recognisably English, the words are all part of our normal vocabulary – and yet the sentence doesn't mean anything! The simple explanation is that the words have meaning individually, but not when placed together in this particular sentence. Below we have taken each word from the Chomsky sentence and written a new sentence of similar length in which this word now makes sense.

**Curious** French children stare unblinkingly <u>at the visitors.</u>
Beautiful **green** trees sway rhythmically <u>in the wind.</u>
Exciting new **ideas** spread rapidly <u>through the company.</u>
Exhausted airline passengers **sleep** restlessly <u>on the benches.</u>
Busy financial traders chatter **furiously** <u>on their mobiles.</u>

In each new sentence the 'Chomsky word' is placed into a context where its meaning is relevant. The underlined phrase added to each sentence clarifies the specific context and elucidates the meaning further.

We can conclude that meaning does lie in the individual word (lexical item). But meaning is also determined by the word order (or patterned arrangement). Look what happens if we muddle up the order of the Chomsky sentence.

Furiously curious green sleep ideas.
Ideas green furiously curious sleep.
Sleep curious ideas green furiously.

Are you beginning to feel slightly disoriented? It's disconcerting to say the least to lose any ability to make sense of your own language because the word order is wrong and the grammar/syntax unguessable!

So where does meaning lie? Is it in the way language is visually represented on the page (graphemes)? Is it in the way in which the graphemes themselves represent the sounds of words (phonemes)? Is it linked with context, audience and purpose? These are urgent questions which will have to be addressed in this chapter. But before we bite the bullet and wade into the ocean of concept and theory (and we'll be talking about mixed metaphor a little later), let's look for a life-raft if not a life-boat.

The diagram on the facing page models the way we use language to communicate, whether in spoken or written modes. Two axes intersect: the horizontal or syntagmatic axis (representing the structure of language); and the vertical or paradigmatic axis or axes (representing language choices/variants available). The diagram uses the Chomsky sentence as a starting-point. Which of the sentences work in English?

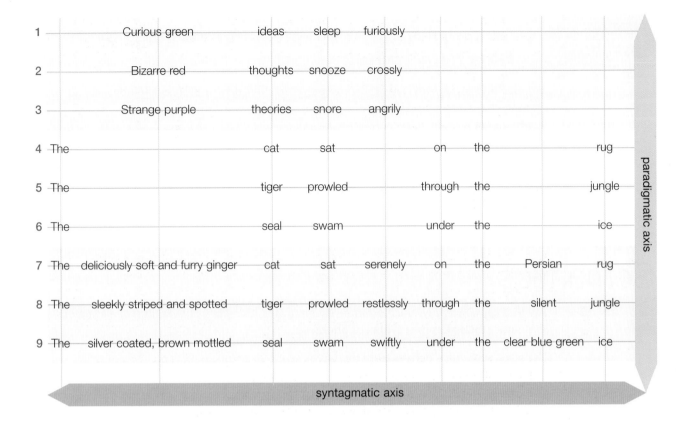

The Chomsky sentence (1) on the syntagmatic axis fails to convey meaning, despite its grammatical correctness, because it lacks context and relevance. Similarly, sentences 2 and 3 on the paradigmatic axis fail to work, because the alternative words also lack context and relevance. To create recognisable meaning, the paradigmatic choices have to be relevant and appropriate to context.

The next three sentences (4–6) demonstrate that the relationship between the syntagmatic and the paradigmatic axes can represent the communication of meaning in a sentence if the factors of context and relevance are in place. In sentence 4 the cat, a domestic animal, is sitting on the mat, a domestic item, hence the context is domestic. In sentence 5 the tiger, a predatory animal, is slinking through tropical terrain, hence the context is exotic. In sentence 6 the seal is exhibiting normal behaviour in a polar context. In other words, although sentences 4, 5 and 6 are as identical in form and structure as were sentences 1, 2 and 3, the former do communicate recognisable meaning whereas the latter don't. The reason is that the lexical choice on the paradigmatic axes for sentences 4, 5 and 6 is relevant to context.

What this model represents is the instantaneous nature of meaningful communication, whether spoken or written. All the time we are talking, we are making meaningful lexical choices according to context (and if people don't understand us, we have to choose again). What else it shows is that, however clear the structure of sentence/utterance, without communicating relevant meaning, nothing happens.

The last three sentences (7–9) show how meaning can be enriched by adding new descriptive and sound elements to the basic sentence structures in sentences 4–6. As you can see, the picture created in sentences 7–9 is becoming richer in detail and more powerfully imagined. What has happened is that words communicating sensuous detail (visual, tactile and aural) have been added, and the overall meaning enriched.

| Activity 1 | Exploring the structure of written language as it relates to meaning |
|---|---|
| **Pair work** | |

Working in pairs, make up a short sentence on the Chomsky model that is grammatically correct but doesn't mean anything.

Rewrite your sentence until you have turned it into a sentence of similar length and structure which does make sense.

What is the context of your new sentence? What kind of changes (paradigmatic choices) did you have to make before it had recognisable meaning?

# Semantics

The first key concept we shall examine is semantics (the study of meaning) conveyed via lexis rather than grammar, syntax or phonology.

The term 'semantics' derives from the Greek word '*seme*' meaning 'sign'. Meaning is communicated via verbal and non-verbal sign systems, and the study of meaning is called semiotics. Thus, whatever you chose today to wear (your favourite jeans, a T-shirt with a particular message, chunky jewellery, a woolly cap) all signalled to your friends, and to anyone else looking, something particular about you. Most of us, whatever age, try to communicate in our dress the person we want to be (professional lady, yummy mummy, absent-minded professor, cool media personality). These non-verbal sign-systems, such as codes of dress, convey meaning in exactly the same way that the Highway Code conveys meaning about our roads and motorways via another kind of semiotic system. The semiotics of verbal language utilise the sign-systems of speech and writing (phonemes in spoken language and graphemes in written texts) to convey meaning. In this section we shall only be looking at lexical semantics – the meanings of words – and leave the other systems till later.

There are two kinds of linguistic meaning conveyed in semantics – denoted meaning and connoted meaning. Denoted meaning is roughly equivalent to a dictionary definition of a word, but connoted meaning involves associated meaning, meanings based on points of similarity including metaphor. In the following edited examples from the *Chambers Dictionary*, the first part is the denoted meaning of each word (marked DM) and the second half is the connoted meaning (marked CM).

- **crocodile** noun. (DM) a large long-tailed tropical reptile … with powerful tapering jaws and a thick skin covered with bony plates; (CM) a double file of school pupils taking a walk; *crocodile clip* a clip for making electrical connections with serrated jaws that interlock; *crocodile tears* hypocritical grief, from the old story that crocodiles … shed tears over the hard necessity of killing animals for food …

- **crook** noun. (DM) a bend, or something bent; a staff bent at the end as in a shepherd's or a bishop's; (CM) a professional swindler, thief or criminal in general; a curved tube used to lower the pitch of a wind instrument: adj. (Austr. and NZ colloq.) ill; unfair; wrong, dubious; inferior, nasty, unpleasant …

Charles Dickens makes a famously grim joke about denoted (or literal) meaning in *Hard Times* (1854), a novel criticising the negative effects of the philosophy of utilitarianism and mechanical industrialism on society. The schoolmaster, Mr Thomas Gradgrind, asks a question:

> 'Bitzer,' said Thomas Gradgrind. 'Your definition of a horse.'
>
> 'Quadruped. Graminivorous. Forty teeth, namely twenty-four grinders, four eye teeth and twelve incisive. Sheds coat in the spring; in marshy countries sheds hoofs, too. Hoofs hard, but requiring to be shod with iron. Age known by marks in the mouth.'

Dickens is well aware that Bitzer's is an accurate definition for his day: however, he is making a point of contrast with Bitzer's inarticulate school fellow, Sissy Jupe, whose father is a circus equestrian and who actually knows about horses, their reality and their beauty, not just their teeth. The passage is a lesson in semantics!

## Activity 2 — Investigating denoted and connoted meanings

**Pair work**

Choose a good dictionary which includes a range of meanings and provides an etymology or word history, such as the *OED online* or the *Shorter Oxford Dictionary*, *Chambers Dictionary*, or *Collins Cobuild Dictionary*. (Avoid student dictionaries which may provide only basic definitions.)

Look up three words from the list below (or as many as you can) and in pairs discuss the differences between denoted and connoted meaning in each definition. You may also notice that your word has changed its meaning over time.

- apron
- wicked
- fox
- sinister
- barm
- villain
- doldrums
- career
- tart
- hilt
- silly
- wardrobe

## Semantics and society

Although it's interesting and useful to know that meanings of words change over time, what is really important is the reason why such changes happen. The explanation is that language reflects society. Communication between human beings, whether spoken or written, does not take place in a vacuum. Whatever we talk about today (the World Cup, the obesity crisis, politics, global warming, new clothes, iPods, flat-screen televisions, drugs, green issues, the post-code lottery, space travel, the war in Afghanistan, …) our lexis is up to it, and we have words available to construct and convey meaning. In the Middle Ages, when society was very different and no-one in Europe ate tomatoes or potatoes or drank tea and coffee or knew about DNA and the deep holes in outer space, the lexis was also different.

Social attitudes were different too, especially in relation to sex and gender, with significant effects on language, as we shall see. Overall, however, the point to remember here is that meaning in language is individually, socially and environmentally determined. A classic example is the fact noted by American linguist Benjamin Whorf that Eskimos have many different words for snow (they live in polar regions). Similarly in British English we have more words linked with rain and bad weather than with sunshine and clear skies, reflecting our different weather expectations. In other words, language reflects society, including the environment.

If the vocabulary of any language reflects the social practices and environment of that society, it follows that the vocabulary of individual speakers will reflect their personal circumstances (family, friends, education, occupation, region, etc.). Sociolinguists have come up with some useful terms to describe the ways people talk.

- Idiolect is an individual's unique way of speaking (comparable to style in written language).
- Sociolect describes the variety used by a speaker in his or her speech communities and social networks (friendship group, age group, occupation, social class, etc.).
- Genderlect has been coined to describe the lexical choices made by women or men.

Of course, spoken language is more than just vocabulary – grammatical choices also have to be made. In this section, however, the focus is on semantics and the way meaning is communicated via lexis. Indeed, whoever we're talking to, whether it's family or friends, people at work, people in shops, the bank, the supermarket, the surgery, the careers office or the travel agency, and wherever we go to seek information, exchange goods and services or just chat with friends, we must choose the right vocabulary to guarantee a successful interaction. Similarly when we are writing, whether it's a holiday postcard or a letter of application or an essay, the lexis we use will reflect our own lexical preferences or style, but also our sensitivity to context, audience and purpose. For example, a letter of condolence which uses trite clichés of 'sympathy' will mean less to the recipient than a few words reflecting genuine understanding of the person who has died, and empathy with how the recipient might feel.

## Activity 3
### Pair work

## Investigating lexical choice in spoken and written language

Working with a partner, imagine you have both been on holiday to the same destination at different times. One of you has had a good experience, the other less good.

Each describe your experience as if you were talking to a close friend at home.

Each write a postcard to a family friend who has paid your airfare describing your experience.

Discuss the different spoken and written lexical choices you used in relation to audience/purpose.

## Semantic field

An important aspect of semantics is the concept of semantic field. Semantic field means the range of vocabulary/lexis associated with a particular subject, topic, situation, profession, etc. For example, the semantic fields of education might include institutions (nursery, primary and secondary schools, college and university), the curriculum, the exam system, the inspection organisation (including Ofsted), teachers, pupils and teaching assistants, and physical equipment ranging from whiteboards to goal-posts. The list of possible areas within this enormous semantic field is mind-boggling.

## Activity 4

## Exploring the concept of semantic field

Choose five areas of education from the list above. Write down ten words from each semantic field. Are these semantic fields very different from each other or does each list 'run into' another?

Within a semantic field as broad as education, there are many separate discourses. The term 'discourse' has a range of meanings, but in relation to semantics, it is associated with more specialised lexis. So, for example, we might refer to the discourse of educational theory, the discourse of citizenship or pastoral care, as well as the discourses of history, physics or English studies. In the semantic field of medicine, examples of particular discourses might include the discourse of paediatrics, cardiology, geriatrics or sports medicine. In the semantic field of music, the discourse of reggae is very different from the discourses of world music, classical music, heavy metal and country and western. The discourse of journalism might include the subdiscourses of different ideological groups (right- and left-wing press), as well as the discourses of broadsheet and tabloid newspapers – all within the semantic field of publishing.

A final point. The examples given here of semantic fields are very broad: the term can also be applied to much smaller areas of specialisation, from skateboarding to surfing. So when can a semantic field be described as a discourse (and vice versa)? Katie Wales (in *A Dictionary of Stylistics*) suggests that this may happen when people are not only using similar lexis, but are also members of the same discourse community and 'engaged in the same communicative pursuit, united by common public goals'. There are real discourse communities like the world of advertising or the world of horseracing, where everyone involved is a confident user of the lexis. Ultimately applying the term 'discourse' to vast areas like education or medicine seems like putting a quart into a pint pot.

## Activity 5
### Pair work

## Identifying a range of semantic fields and discourses

Working in pairs, choose three or four topics from the list below and write down as many lexical items as possible associated with each one.

- sailing
- football
- fashion (clothing)
- tabloid journalism
- parliament

- cakes
- climate change
- cars
- percussion
- ICT

- rail travel
- fly-fishing
- weddings

As co-authors, write 150–200 words on one of the topics above to be published in a specialist journal. Compare your texts with those of others in the group, and decide which texts address specific discourse communities.

## Semantic change

Semantic change is the final aspect of semantics we need to address. We noted earlier that language reflects society, and that, as society changes, the lexis mirroring the physical, social, intellectual and cultural experience of its speakers will also change. A key factor here is the way social attitudes affect how people talk about basic human life experiences associated with gender, age and social hierarchy. For example, in country A, words like 'milk', 'bread', 'water', 'rock' may remain unchanged over centuries. But if country A is invaded by country B, and forced to use language B, a different lexis will be introduced which over time may lead to language A being lost.

Social attitudes within a country can lead to lexical change. Words in English whose meaning has changed in a negative way (pejorative change) tend be associated with women, age, folly and criminality, suggesting changing social attitudes over time. For example,

- 'hussy', derived from 'housewife', a former indicator of status, now means 'promiscuous woman'
- 'biddy', formerly a word for a hen or chicken, now means 'old woman'
- 'silly', originally 'sely', meaning 'happy', 'blessed' or 'innocent', now means 'foolish'.

Less frequently, change is ameliorative, meaning 'for the better'. Examples include
- 'mischief' – former meaning 'serious harm', current meaning 'playful misbehaviour'
- 'praise' – former meaning to 'judge, appraise', current meaning to 'express approval'.

| **Activity 6** | **Investigating some examples of semantic change** |
|---|---|

Look up the following words in a good dictionary (one providing an etymology or word history), and note, first, whether the changes are positive or negative, and, secondly, whether any words have either broadened or narrowed their meaning.

| | | | | |
|---|---|---|---|---|
| ■ harlot | ■ notorious | ■ fair | ■ girl | ■ spinster |
| ■ sinister | ■ enthusiasm | ■ boor | ■ egregious | ■ tart |
| ■ politician | ■ sophisticated | ■ lewd | ■ knight | ■ starve |
| ■ crafty | ■ annoy | ■ churl | ■ villain | ■ awful |

## Synonyms, antonyms and hyponyms

Here are three more useful terms associated with meaning.

Synonyms are words with the same or similar meaning (buyer/punter/customer; beautiful/lovely/glamorous; sad/miserable/fed up). We used synonyms earlier in this chapter when discussing the syntagmatic/paradigmatic axes (page 3). Which word we choose often depends on context and levels of formality (register). Thus 'punter' is informal, whereas 'beautiful' or 'miserable' are more formal choices.

Antonyms are sets of words with opposite meanings, either of degree (narrow/wide, strong/weak), of absolute contrast (alive/dead, true/false) or word pairs or converses representing two sides of a common semantic pairing or process (give/receive, husband/wife, borrow/lend).

Hyponyms are associated with the way we categorise meaning. The general or superordinate category 'animal' has subordinate categories such as 'cat' or 'bear'. These in turn have further subordinate categories like 'Siamese', 'Russian Blue, 'tabby', or 'grizzly bear', 'polar bear', 'brown bear'. Thus 'animal' is the superordinate hyponym of 'bear' and 'tabby' is the subordinate hyponym of 'cat'.

You may wonder whether it's remotely useful to know these terms – the answer is yes, absolutely. First, if you are a creative writer, the more you know about subtle variations of meaning the better; and secondly, any writer or speaker benefits from access to a wide range of lexical options, as well as being able to create better coherence and cohesion when they speak or write. (For more on this subject see pages 40–41.)

# Lexis or vocabulary

It's not a big jump to move from the meanings of words to the words themselves, whether we refer to them individually as lexical items, or to the lexis, the lexicon, vocabulary or word-stock of a language. English has an extraordinarily rich and ever-expanding vocabulary, recorded in dictionaries both online and on paper, enriched by borrowings from other languages, or loan words (pizza), and enlarged by neologisms (i-Pod), blendings (smog), clippings (fax), acronyms (NATO), compoundings (skinhead), affixations (healthwise) and back formations (burgle/burglar) – among other methods.

This huge lexicon provides a remarkable resource for people in all walks of life, whether they're novelists or nuclear scientists, cooks or CEOs, engineers or athletes, journalists or geologists, retailers or rose-growers. This vocabulary includes recently established colloquialisms as well as new scientific, technological and economic lexis. Usage is the criterion that determines entry into 'the dictionary' and lexicographers (dictionary writers) have access to corpora (computer 'banks' of recorded speech) as well as all published texts, as they observe the changes and developments in this amazing living entity, the English language.

## Content and function words

In English, by far the highest proportion of words in our vocabulary are content words (that is, nouns, adjectives, verbs and adverbs) which convey meaning. Function words on the other hand provide connections and maintain coherence and cohesion between content words. They are pronouns, prepositions, determiners (including definite and indefinite articles) and conjunctions, and they will be discussed in more detail in the section on grammar.

Now read Lewis Carroll's nonsense poem 'Jabberwocky' from *Through the Looking-Glass* (1871).

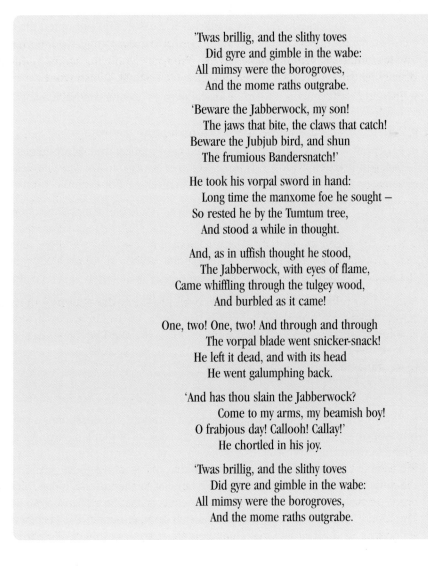

'Twas brillig, and the slithy toves
    Did gyre and gimble in the wabe:
All mimsy were the borogroves,
    And the mome raths outgrabe.

'Beware the Jabberwock, my son!
    The jaws that bite, the claws that catch!
Beware the Jubjub bird, and shun
    The frumious Bandersnatch!'

He took his vorpal sword in hand:
    Long time the manxome foe he sought –
So rested he by the Tumtum tree,
    And stood a while in thought.

And, as in uffish thought he stood,
    The Jabberwock, with eyes of flame,
Came whiffling through the tulgey wood,
    And burbled as it came!

One, two! One, two! And through and through
    The vorpal blade went snicker-snack!
He left it dead, and with its head
    He went galumphing back.

'And has thou slain the Jabberwock?
    Come to my arms, my beamish boy!
O frabjous day! Callooh! Callay!'
    He chortled in his joy.

'Twas brillig, and the slithy toves
    Did gyre and gimble in the wabe:
All mimsy were the borogroves,
    And the mome raths outgrabe.

9

This poem offers opportunities for many interesting activities, ranging from semantic investigation of Carroll's made-up or 'portmanteau' words like 'slithy' (slimy/writhing) to neologisms that have become part of our lexicon (burbled, galumphed, chortled). It also demonstrates very clearly that even if the lexis is unfamiliar, we can work out which are the content words and which the function words – in other words, the grammatical relationships.

**Activity 7**

**Pair work**

### Identifying the content words and function words in 'Jabberwocky'

Working in pairs, make two lists, one of content words, the other of function words in the poem. (Identify, if you wish, the individual parts of speech.)

Rewrite the poem as a short prose narrative, keeping to the story but replacing any content words you wish to.

How many conjunctions have you used to make your prose narrative flow smoothly (cohesion)? Another useful word to describe these words is discourse markers.

So far in this section we have looked at the richness and flexibility of English, touched on some of the ways in which its vocabulary is increased, and presented the lexical relationship between content and function words. To go further down that road at present would take us into grammar and syntax in more detail. Before we go there, here are a few useful terms you will encounter throughout your A-level course relating to lexis.

- Lexeme – this means a word or lexical item. A lexeme can have many different variants (dance/danced/dancing).
- Morphology – this means the structure or form of a word.
- Morpheme – this is the smallest viable grammatical unit. Morphemes that make independent sense (dog, car) are called free morphemes. Morphemes that don't make sense on their own are called bound morphemes (for example, prefixes like 'in-', 'un-', 'dis-', plural markers like 's').

**Activity 8**

**Pair work**

### Investigating the morphology of words

Look at the words below and list the morphemes in each word. Decide which are free and which are bound morphemes. You may find it helpful to look up the words in a good dictionary.

- conscience
- incomprehensible
- remarkable
- jejune
- frozen
- fight
- borrow
- seizure
- cart

Collocation is another word which needs explanation. A collocation is a group of words (phrase) which is readily recognised by most speakers of that language. It's not the same as a cliché (a worn-out expression like 'sick as a parrot', 'over the moon', 'at the end of the day', 'at this moment in time'). Collocations like 'cold front', 'soaring house prices', 'fish and chips', 'get the message', 'the mind boggles', though familiar, remain useful. Indeed, collocations are often used creatively by writers, poets, and comics to surprise the audience with unexpected insights. The Monty Python 'Pet Shop' television sketch reverses audience expectations using normal collocations and subverting them for comic effect. In this extract, collocations are underlined.

|  |  |
|---|---|
| **Praline** (John Cleese) | Hello, <u>I wish to register a complaint</u> … Hello? Miss? |
| **Shopkeeper** (Michael Palin) | What do you mean, <u>miss</u>? |
| **Praline** | Oh, I'm sorry, I have a cold. I wish to <u>make a complaint.</u> |
| **Shopkeeper** | Sorry, <u>we're closing for lunch</u>. |
| **Praline** | <u>Never mind that, my lad</u>. I wish to complain about this parrot what I purchased not half an hour ago from <u>this very</u> boutique. |

The audience laughs at the absurdity of this complaint (the parrot is 'stone dead', not 'resting', as the shopkeeper tries to assert) made more amusing by the comic seriousness of the opening conversation.

# Grammar and syntax

In this section we shall be looking at grammar and syntax from a rather different angle. Instead of investigating the detail of English grammar and syntax, we shall focus on broader principles, showing how understanding grammatical relationships helps us to make better sense of spoken and written texts. We hope this will transform the process of textual analysis into a creative exploration of language and literature, rather than a mechanical procedure in which you simply tick features from a checklist.

On pages 2–3 of the introductory section, grammar is linked with the concept of structure in language. Experience of learning a new language confirms to most people that different languages have very different grammatical structures and rules (never mind differences in vocabulary!). Although languages that belong to the same 'language families' may have some grammatical elements in common, each language has its unique grammatical system and structures. If you think about the Romance language family, which includes French, Italian, Spanish and Portuguese, there are numerous differences between these languages and not just in the lexis. Similarly, English, part of the Germanic language family, is significantly different from its 'relatives' Dutch, German, Swedish, Danish and Norwegian. Languages evolve according to what happens to their speakers socially, politically, economically and geographically. The grammar of a language spoken by a small number of speakers in a mountainous and inaccessible area will not change much over generations; indeed, grammar is always the slowest element in a language to be affected by change. Because English is so widely used by millions of first- and second-language speakers and has many different versions (Indian English, American English, West Indian English as well as Australian, Scottish, Irish and Welsh English!) its grammar *is* susceptible to some degree of change. Nevertheless, the basic grammar of English remains the same, and we shall be focusing on this.

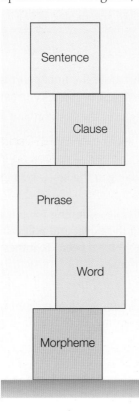

Rank order or hierarchy may seem a strange concept to apply to grammar, but if you think in terms of a tower of children's bricks, it should make more sense.

In the diagram, at the top we have the sentence, next down is the clause, next the phrase, then the word, and finally the morpheme. Obviously the sentence is the largest unit and the morpheme the smallest. The rank order is just the same in spoken language, except that utterance replaces sentence. Why is it relevant to talk about rank order at all? Our purpose here is to demonstrate that the term 'grammar' is a way of describing relationships between words, while 'syntax' is a way of describing relationships between different structures within the sentence/utterance. If you can remember the overall relationship between words and structures, it will help you to speak, write and analyse more effectively.

We have now established that for any writer/speaker, choices are not only lexical and content based (paradigmatic axis) but also order and structure based (syntagmatic axis). We'll look now at some aspects of grammar and syntax that students of language need to know about.

## Syntax

Under this heading we include structural features such as word order, phrase and clause patterning, right- and left-hand branching sentences, and the role of pronouns – all used by writers and speakers alike, according to context and circumstance.

### Word order
The normal word order in English, whether spoken or written, is SVO (subject–verb–object):

Mary (S) teased (V) the tiger (O).

However, for particular purposes, such as focus or emphasis, we sometimes invert subject and object:

That band (O) I (S) really hate (V).

This is called fronting. Samuel Pepys does something similar in his diary entry of 9 March 1666:

Music and women I cannot but give way to (OSV), whatever my business is.

So does Wordsworth in one of the mysterious 'Lucy' poems:

No motion has she now, or force (OVS, O)
She neither hears nor sees (SVV)
Rolled round in earth's diurnal course
With rocks and stones and trees.

### Sentence patterning
Sentences which pile up phrase and clause together until the final point is made are called left branching: the reader waits with increasing interest as more information is given. E.g.

Although we had watched the lightning playing over the horizon and seen the palm tree branches swooping violently in the gale, we were not prepared for that icy, solid curtain of rain.

Right-branching sentences, on the other hand, give you the key information quickly and then elaborate on it.

The car was packed, after we spent hours carefully positioning my pot plants and pictures so nothing would break, and squeezing the duvet and pillows round the boxes of books (not all read as thoroughly as they might have been) together with the carton of kitchen junk I hadn't managed to sort out in time.

Writers have the time to experiment with word order, but it's surprising how much variety there is in spoken language – worth listening for when people are chatting around you. Watch out for syntactic parallelism in speech or writing, from the simple 'Out of sight, out of mind' to the more complex

I could not love thee, Dear, so much
Loved I not honour more

(Richard Lovelace, 'To Lucasta, Going to the Wars')

## Activity 9
**Pair work**

# Creating different effects through word order and sentence structure

Working in pairs, choose one or two of the following options and write the opening paragraph, using a range of word-order variations/syntactic structures to create the appropriate effects for each genre:

- murder mystery
- tabloid news report
- children's story (age 7–11)
- space fiction
- broadsheet editorial or feature article

This example of a children's story is an extract from Roald Dahl's *The BFG* (1982).

> Sophie couldn't sleep.
>
> A brilliant moonbeam was slanting through a gap in the curtains. It was shining right on her pillow.
>
> The other children in the dormitory had been asleep for hours.
>
> Sophie closed her eyes and tried to doze off.
>
> It was no good. The moonbeam was like a silver blade slicing through the room on to her face.
>
> The house was absolutely silent. No voices came up from downstairs. There were no footsteps on the floor above either.
>
> The window behind the curtain was wide open, but nobody was walking on the pavement outside. No cars went by on the street. Not the tiniest sound could be heard anywhere. Sophie had never known such a silence.

Turn to page 48 for a commentary on this example. For more on the subject of writing in different genres, see pages 202–233.

# Grammar

Here (as an exemplar) we shall focus on a range of different grammatical verb forms including modality, tense and aspect, transitivity, mood and voice. But why choose verbs? Verbs constitute one of the most remarkable elements in English grammar because they can tell us so much, whether we are reading or listening.

At this stage you need to know only a few basic facts about verbs. They can tell us about what is happening to the 'subject' in a given situation, at a given time, who is taking action or receiving it, and how long that action lasted. Dynamic verbs describe action (running, walking, singing), whereas stative verbs describe states of existence (being, seeming, becoming).

### Tense and aspect
Tense and aspect tell us when something happened (past, present, future), and whether the action was completed (perfect aspect) or ongoing (continuous aspect). These two examples show the difference between tense and aspect.

- He <u>was</u> hungry, so he <u>turned</u> the left-overs into a giant Spanish omelette and <u>ate</u> it all himself.

Past tense – 'was', 'turned', 'ate'; third person singular – 'he'; perfect aspect – 'turned' and 'ate' are completed actions.

- She <u>was</u> <u>grilling</u> the steak when the smoke alarm <u>went</u> <u>off</u>.

  Continuous aspect – 'was grilling' is action continuing; perfect aspect – 'went off' is action completed.

Aspect is useful for the writer because it conveys further information about time to the audience without need for a more wordy explanation.

## Activity 10 — Practising the use of tense and aspect in creative writing

Choose two of these situations:

- a wedding
- climbing a mountain
- going out with friends
- an English lesson
- walking in the country

Describe one situation using the past tense and either perfect or continuous aspect. Describe the other situation using the present tense and either present or continuous aspect. What different effects are achieved by varying the use of aspect?

### Mood and modality

Mood and modality are not too hard to understand, because they relate to what verbs are doing: making statements (indicative mood); asking questions (interrogative mood); issuing commands (imperative mood). It's more difficult to understand the relationship between the grammatical subject and modality. Modal verbs themselves convey attitudes and express possibilities rather than certainties. For example:

- You <u>ought</u> to catch the train if you run.          (Obligation/expectation)
- You <u>should</u> get a high grade if you work hard.     (Obligation/logical necessity)
- You <u>might</u> pass if you put in some revision time.   (Possibility)
- You <u>would</u> enjoy that film.                          (Prediction/likelihood)
- You <u>must</u> go now or you'll get drenched.            (Obligation/compulsion)
- You <u>may</u> leave early for that dental appointment.   (Permission)
- You <u>will</u> be our first choice if Mary/Daniel resigns. (Prediction/insistence)
- You <u>can</u> be confident that we will support you.      (Are allowed to)

In literature, modal verbs are often used to reveal character, or provide more subtle description of a scene. In conversation, modal verbs tend to soften or mitigate comments, conveying politeness and protecting face ('Should you really be going out tonight when you've got such a terrible cold?'). There is an important relationship between the modal verb and the grammatical subject, whose subjectivity is thereby emphasised.

## Activity 11 — Investigating the literary use of modal verbs

**Pair work**

Read the following passage from *Macbeth* in which the murderous king sees that all is nearly lost. Identify the modal verbs and, with a partner, decide what effect Shakespeare might be seeking by using them.

> I have lived long enough: my way of life
> Is fall'n into the sear, the yellow leaf;
> And that which should accompany old age,
> As honour, love, obedience, troops of friends
> I must not look to have; but, in their stead,
> Curses, not loud but deep, mouth-honour, breath
> Which the poor heart would fain deny and dare not.

### Transitivity and voice

Verbs can tell us who did what to whom (SVO). If the grammatical subject (S) in a sentence is taking the action we call this a transitive verb. For example,

- The bird (S) ate (V) the worm (O).
- John (S) enjoyed (V) the walk (O) in North Yorkshire.
- The learner driver (S) narrowly missed (V) the low wall (O).

If the action of the verb is received by the grammatical subject (who is acted upon, not acting) we call this an intransitive verb. The verb has no object. For example,

- The worm (S) was eaten (V) by the bird.
- The sneezing child (S) was sent (V) home by the teacher.
- The weather forecast (S) was read (V) by a new presenter.

Voice is another important grammatical concept associated with transitivity. If the verb is in the active voice this means that the grammatical subject/real subject is taking the action. In literature (as well as in spoken interaction) sentences which convey information tend to use the active voice and have an object. The passive voice is when the action happens to the grammatical subject, who is acted upon. In literature, sentences which convey emotion or create mood tend to use the passive voice and have no object. The following sentence shows the use of transitive and intransitive verbs and therefore of active and passive voice.

> The exhausted detective trailed [transitive verb, active voice] the alleged suspect [object] for hours: then suddenly the man was surrounded [intransitive verb, passive voice] by a crowd of protesters and disappeared [transitive verb, active voice] from sight.

## Activity 12
**Pair work**

### Practising the use of transitivity

Working in pairs, take turns to tell each other the story of your day so far, using transitive verbs only. Then each write a shortened version of the other person's story, using intransitive verbs only. What kind of differences in effect did you observe?

## Activity 13
**Pair work**

### Investigating ways in which grammar conveys meaning in a poem

Read the following poem by W.H. Auden. He wrote it at the beginning of the Second World War, having seen Pieter Breughel's painting of the fall of Icarus at the Musées

Royaux des Beaux-Arts in Brussels. According to Greek legend, Icarus was the young son of the master craftsman Daedalus. His father crafted wings for them both, secured by wax, but Icarus flew too near to the sun, the wax melted and he fell to his death. The story has been used to symbolise the dangers of over-ambition, but Auden also points at human indifference to others' suffering.

Working in pairs, underline all the verb forms you can find in the poem. Look for one example of each of the following:

- past tense
- present tense
- perfect aspect
- modal verbs
- transitive verb
- intransitive verb

Try to work out together how his grammatical choices strengthen Auden's meaning.

Turn to page 48 for a commentary on this activity.

### Musée des Beaux Arts

About suffering they were never wrong,
The Old Masters: how well they understood
Its human position: how it takes place
While someone else is eating or opening a window or
Just walking dully along:

How, when the aged are reverently, passionately waiting
For the miraculous birth, there always must be
Children who did not specially want it to happen, skating
On a pond at the edge of the wood.
They never forgot
That even the dreadful martyrdom must run its course
Anyhow in a corner, some untidy spot
Where the dogs go on with their doggy
Life and the torturer's horse
Scratches its innocent behind on a tree.

In Brueghel's *Icarus*, for example: how everything turns away
Quite leisurely from the disaster; the ploughman may
Have heard the splash, the forsaken cry,
But for him it was not an important failure; the sun shone
As it had to on the white legs disappearing into the green
Water; and the expensive delicate ship that must have seen
Something amazing, a boy falling out of the sky,
Had somewhere to get to and sailed calmly on.

# Sound patterning and phonology

Every language has its own system of sounds represented by phonemes in speech and by graphemes in writing. This is what is meant when we talk about the phonology of a language. Every language has a unique set of phonemes, but each phoneme can be subtly varied according to where a speaker lives (accent and dialect). These slight variants are called allophones. For example, if you live in North Yorkshire some of your phonemes may be different depending on whether you live in the west of the county or the east. These allophones can be recognised and differentiated both by local residents and by linguists.

The technical study of speech sounds and how they are produced is called phonetics. The human articulatory structure (mouth, teeth, tongue, etc.) is the same worldwide, so the International Phonetic Alphabet (IPA) represents in graphic symbols the actual sounds made in whatever language is being spoken or studied. The phonemes of English include 24 consonants, 12 vowels and 8 dipthongs (double vowel sounds), as follows:

| Consonant sounds | | | | |
|---|---|---|---|---|
| /p/ as in *part* | /g/ as in *get* | /θ/ as in *thing* | /ʒ/ as in *measure* | /l/ as in *let* |
| /b/ as in *but* | /tʃ/ as in *chin* | /ð/ as in *this* | /h/ as in *has* | /r/ as in *red* |
| /t/ as in *too* | /dʒ/ as in *joke* | /s/ as in *see* | /m/ as in *mat* | /j/ as in *yes* |
| /d/ as in *did* | /f/ as in *food* | /z/ as in *zoo* | /n/ as in *not* | /w/ as in *will* |
| /k/ as in *kiss* | /v/ as in *voice* | /ʃ/ as in *she* | /ŋ/ as in *long* | |

| Vowel sounds | | | | |
|---|---|---|---|---|
| **Long vowels** | **Short vowels** | | **Diphthongs** | |
| /ɪː/ as in *each* | /ɪ/ as in *it* | /ʊ/ as in *put* | /eɪ/ as in *day* | /ɪə/ as in *near* |
| /ɑː/ as in *car* | /e/ as in *then* | /ə/ as in *again* | /aɪ/ as in *by* | /eə/ as in *there* |
| /ɔː/ as in *more* | /æ/ as in *back* | | /ɔɪ/ as in *boy* | /ʊə/ as in *truer* |
| /uː/ as in *too* | /ʌ/ as in *not* | | /əʊ/ as in *no* | |
| /uː/ as in *word* | /ɒ/ as in *much* | | /aʊ/ as in *now* | |

For more on the IPA, see pages 156–160.

Because sound is the first thing a baby responds to, it's no surprise that we all delight in patterned sound, from nursery rhymes to rap, rhythm and blues to Rachmaninov. Indeed, our everyday conversation is sound patterned much more than we realise ('I'm a poet and I didn't know it!'). Sound patterning is central to all literary genres, from lyric and epic poetry to fiction and drama, and in many non-literary genres too, like advertising and political speech-making. Indeed, as we shall see in the section on rhetoric later in this chapter (page 42), sound patterning lies at the heart of all persuasion.

## Some sound-patterning devices

One of the most accessible devices is onomatopoeia, when the sound of a word directly expresses its meaning (sizzle, bang, splash). A more general term for this is 'sound symbolism' or phonaesthesia. The poet Tennyson was particularly skilful with this kind of sound patterning, as you can see from the following texts. The first is an extract from 'Mariana', a poem imagining the situation of the deserted lover of Count Angelo in Shakespeare's play *Measure for Measure*. The second is from *Morte d'Arthur*, Tennyson's version of the death of King Arthur, whose loyal knight Sir Bedivere is seeking the death barge which will take the dying king to 'the island valley of Avilion'.

**Text A**

About a stone-cast from the wall
    A sluice with blackened water slept,
And o'er it many, round and small,
    The clustered marish-mosses crept.
Hard by a poplar shook always,
    All silver-green with gnarled bark:
    For leagues no other tree did mark
The level waste, the rounding gray.
    She only said, 'My life is dreary,
    He cometh not,' she said;
    She said, 'I am aweary, aweary,
    I would that I were dead!'

**Text B**

He heard the deep behind him, and a cry
Before. His own thought drove him, like a goad.
Dry clashed his harness in the icy caves
And barren chasms, and all to left and right
The bare black cliff clanged all around him, as he based
His feet on juts of slippery crag that rang
Sharp-smitten with the dint of armed heels –
And on a sudden, lo! the level lake,
And the long glories of the winter moon.

**Activity 14**    ## Investigating some poetic uses of sound patterning

In both extracts, look for examples of the following types of sound patterning:

- onomatopoeia, including phonaesthesia
- alliteration

- assonance
- consonance
- dissonance

**Reminder**
- Alliteration refers to repetition of the initial consonant (red rag).
- Assonance refers to repetition of a vowel sound with different consonants (fat cat).
- Consonance means repetition of a consonant group with different vowels (whistle/rustle/hassle/wrestle).
- Dissonance means use of clashing consonant sounds for dramatic effect.

What emotional and descriptive effects is Tennyson attempting to create in each extract? How successful is he?

# Rhyme and rhythm

The other major areas of sound patterning which must be considered are rhyme and rhythm. Rhyme refers to the repetition of a group of sounds or phonemes, while rhythm refers to the regular patterning of light and heavy beats (stressed and unstressed syllables). These repeated patterns usually are found in poetry, but can appear in prose, as well as in spoken language (formal or informal).

Initially lots of people find rhyme and rhythm confusing simply because of their awkward spelling (both words begin with the admittedly bizarre consonant cluster 'rhy-') and then lose heart. However, if you can master the spelling and remember the meaning, you will understand the powerful effects achievable by these types of sound patterning. Types of rhyme include end rhyme, internal rhyme, half-rhyme and eye rhyme; under the heading of rhythm we can include metre and metrical patterns.

### Rhyme

End rhyme is easily recognisable in this nursery rhyme, with an interesting non-rhymed variation in lines 4 and 5.

> Hey diddle <u>diddle</u>
> The cat and the <u>fiddle</u>
> The cow jumped over the <u>moon</u>
> The little dog laughed
> To see such fun
> And the dish ran away with the <u>spoon</u>.

Internal rhyme refers to 'phonetic echoes' within the poetic line itself (or the prose fiction sentence or even in conversation):

> The curfew <u>tolls</u> the <u>knell </u>of passing day,
> The <u>lowing </u>herd winds <u>slowly</u> o'er the lea.

Half-rhyme conveys a sense of rhyme and rhythmic patterning to the audience by using the same final consonant with different vowels and initial consonants (band/bind/found/wind).

Eye rhyme is visual rather than aural, in that the pattern is realised via graphemes, not phonemes. Examples include cough/bough/rough/slough.

You may also encounter the terms masculine rhyme and feminine rhyme, referring to end rhymes. This will make more sense when you've read the next section, but in brief, a poetic line ending with a strong stressed syllable is called masculine rhyme (Humpty Dumpty sat on a <u>wall</u>/Humpty Dumpty had a great <u>fall</u>), and an end rhyme which is weak or unstressed is called a feminine rhyme (Little Jack Horn<u>er</u>/Sat in a corn<u>er</u>). These terms are plainly sexist and reflect past attitudes. We use them simply for descriptive convenience.

### Rhythm

The word itself comes from the Greek *rhuthmos*, meaning flow, and refers to the patterning of sound not only in language but also in music. However, in terms of language, whether spoken or written, rhythm refers to the regular patterning of sound. We talk about certain languages being 'musical' and these tend to be languages from the Romance family like French, Italian and Spanish. Closer to home, people view certain regional varieties of English as being 'musical' or not (Newcastle/Liverpool, Welsh/Birmingham). People's individual idiolects also vary in their musicality. Nevertheless, poetry is the most obviously 'musical' or rhythmic literary genre, and metre is the name given to the regular patterning in verse of stressed and unstressed syllables.

Poets have a range of choices: they can choose to write in a regular metre, or an irregular metre (free verse). The choice seems to be partly a matter of individual preference, and partly poetic fashion. The most popular metre for English poets from Chaucer until the twenty-first century has been iambic pentameter or blank verse. This metre consists of 10 syllables, 5 of which are stressed and 5 unstressed. The reason for its popularity seems to be that it fits the ebb and flow of English speech. If you read aloud the lines on page 20 from Shakespeare's Sonnet 18, you can hear the way the voice (underlined) modulates the stressed/unstressed patterning. Stressed syllables are numbered in bold.

1 **2** 3 **4**   5 **6** 7 **8**  9 **10**
<u>Shall</u> I com<u>pare</u> thee to a <u>summer's</u> <u>day</u>?
1 **2**   3   **4** 5 **6**   7  **8**  9 **10**
<u>Thou</u> art more <u>lovely</u> and more <u>temperate</u>.
Rough <u>winds</u> do <u>shake</u> the <u>darling</u> <u>buds</u> of <u>May</u>
And <u>summer's</u> <u>lease</u> hath <u>all</u> too <u>short</u> a <u>date</u> …

Tetrameter (8 syllables, 4 stressed, 4 unstressed) is a metre which was popular with eighteenth-century poets. Here Dorothy Wordsworth writes about the cottage she and her brother shared at Grasmere in the Lake District.

1 **2** 3  **4** 5 **6**  7   **8**
Peaceful our valley, fair and green,
And beautiful its cottages,
Each in its nook, its sheltered hold,
Or underneath its tuft of trees

An example of trimeter (6 syllables, 3 stressed, 3 unstressed) is

**1**  2  **3**   4  **5** 6
Land of hope and glory
Mother of the free … .

Much less frequently encountered is dimeter (4 syllables, 2 stressed, 2 unstressed), the unwieldy hexameter (12 syllables, 6 stressed, 6 unstressed) and the even heavier fourteener (14 syllables, 7 stressed, 7 unstressed). Byron was a wonderfully inventive user of metrics, and this extract from 'The Destruction of Sennacherib' is hexameter at its most exciting.

1  **2** 3 **4**   5   **6**   7 **8** 9  **10** 11 **12**
The Assyrian came down like a wolf on the fold,
And his cohorts were gleaming in purple and gold;
And the sheen of their spears was like stars on the sea,
When the blue wave rolls nightly on deep Galilee.

The best way to be confident about metre is to try it out on poems you know, from nursery rhymes to Sylvia Plath. You may find that modern poets don't use as much regular metre as poets in the past, but there usually are patterns to be discovered. Watch out too for syllabic verse where the number of syllables in a line counts, rather than the number of stresses.

| Activity 15 | **Looking for sound patterns created by rhyme and rhythm** |
|---|---|
| Group work | Go back to the W.H. Auden poem on page 16. Half your group should focus on the broad area of rhyme and the other half on rhythm. Look for sound patterns and explore how effectively sound patterning enhances meaning. Share your findings. |

# Language functions

What are the functions of human language? Many theorists, in fields ranging from linguistics and philosophy to anthropology and sociology, have attempted to address this key question. For early humans the function of language was probably to exchange information and perhaps express feeling. The linguist Michael Halliday suggested that language has three overarching metafunctions:

- the ideational metafunction, by which information about the world is communicated
- the interpersonal metafunction, which concerns the personal relationships between speakers/writers in an exchange
- the textual function, which refers to the actual language mode used (spoken or written) and the genre chosen.

Looked at in more detail, these broad metafunctions can be linked with language functions identified by other theorists.

- The ideational metafunction includes the referential or descriptive function.
- The interpersonal metafunction includes conative, expressive and phatic functions.
- The metalingual or poetic function is part of the textual metafunction.

Halliday noted that when children talk, these metafunctions disappear. Instead we have separated functions:

- instrumental function – 'I want' ('Me want apple.')
- informative function – 'I've got something to tell you' ('Daddy home now.')
- imaginative function – 'Let's pretend' ('You be the engine driver.')
- regulative function – 'Do as I tell you' ('Granny fetch my book.')
- interactional function – 'Me and you' ('You and Henry my friends.')
- personal function – 'Here I come' ('I'm swinging higher.')
- heuristic function – 'Tell me why' ('What's that?').

As children's language develops, all these individual functions meld back together, and they ultimately acquire the metafunctions of adult language.

Having outlined the theoretical background of language function, we can turn to those aspects of language function particularly relevant to your A-level English course. We shall be looking at the pragmatic and expressive functions of spoken and written language, and in particular how they relate to the creative function in literary and non-literary language.

The pragmatic function of language is covered by the ideational metafunction, in that it is related to the world and its affairs, from shopping to cooking to climate change, school dinners, iPods, taxi-drivers, football and sausages. In other words, talking and writing about any aspect of the world is part of the pragmatic function of language, by which things get done, meals are prepared, conversations are concluded, doctor's appointments are made and kept, and service encounters of all sorts happen. Pragmatic language functions include

- to inform
- to advise
- to persuade
- to get something done (transactional)
- to argue (expository)
- to collaborate
- to socialise
- to evaluate

These purposes or functions tend to be associated with non-literary spoken and written language.

---

**Activity 16**

*Individual*

## Exploring a range of texts with pragmatic language function

List each spoken exchange you took part in during the course of one day (for example, talked to sister at breakfast, said hello to neighbour, bought bus ticket). Then identify each exchange in terms of its function from the list above.

The expressive function of language, included within the interpersonal metafunction, reflects the individual act of communication between speaker and audience or addressee, and writer and audience or reader. Its subfunctions are interactional, social and evaluative and convey feelings and emotions, express relationships and reveal attitudes and opinions. There is also the associated phatic function, which at the most basic level communicates human recognition of other humans as part of the same social world, thus creating a kind of social lubrication ('Hi, how are you?' 'I'm fine thanks. You OK?'). The expressive function appears in casual conversation as well as in more complex interactions, and it is a key aspect of literature. In literature the writer is

- expressing his or her emotions
- creating emotional response in the audience
- crafting and communicating emotion via a character, situation or description to affect the reader or audience
- exploring subjective and emotional experience via a particular literary genre, such as poetry.

## Activity 17 — Investigating a range of language functions

**Pair work**

In this activity we shall look at some examples of pragmatic and expressive language function in action across a range of text types. Text A is a transcript of a conversation in a shop. Text B comes from the *Times Educational Supplement* (October 2007). Text C is from Shakespeare's *Twelfth Night*. Text D is from 'At the Bay', by Katherine Mansfield (1932).

Working in pairs, look at each of the four texts in turn and decide

- how the ideational, interpersonal and textual metafunctions are realised in each
- which texts seem predominantly pragmatic and which expressive
- what other functions you can identify in each text (there will be several in each)
- how the creative function is demonstrated

### Text A
(.) indicates a short pause – a number in the brackets gives the length of a pause in seconds.

| | |
|---|---|
| Customer | er love (1.0) how come these in here are so cheap are they seconds or something |
| Salesperson | oh (2.0) it's just because they're white |
| Customer | what do you mean |
| Salesperson | well erm last year's stock summer (.) you know |
| Customer | oh I see so there's nowt wrong with them then |
| Salesperson | oh no |
| Customer | OK then I'll have this one please |
| Salesperson | thank you (.) there you go two ninety nine please thanks there's your receipt and your penny |
| Customer | thanks love |
| Salesperson | bye |

**Text B**

Conduct 'state of the nation research'

We invite experienced researchers, either individuals or consortia, to tender for a 'state of the nation' research project about teachers' continuing professional development (CPD). This project is intended to inform our strategy in this area.

The successful bidder will report on recent research that influences current CPD strategy. Using focus groups and surveys you will also gather and analyse teachers' experiences of CPD.

The contract will start on 7 January 2008 and will last 4–6 months.

**Text C**

**Orsino**    If music be the food of love, play on,
Give me excess of it, that, surfeiting,
The appetite may sicken and so die.
That strain again! It had a dying fall.
O, it came o'er my ear like the sweet sound
That breathes upon a bank of violets,
Stealing and giving odour.

**Text D**

A few moments later the back door of one of the bungalows opened, and a figure in a broad-striped bathing-suit flung down the paddock, cleared the stile, rushed through the tussock grass into the hollow, staggered up the sandy hillock, and raced for dear life over the big porous stones, over the cold, wet pebbles, on to the hard sand that gleamed like oil. Splish-Splash! Splish-Splash! The water bubbled round his legs as Stanley Burnell waded out exulting. First man in as usual! He'd beaten them all again. And he swooped down to souse his head and neck.

'Hail, brother! All hail, Thou Mighty One!' A velvety bass voice came booming over the water.

Great Scott! Damnation take it! Stanley lifted up to see a dark head bobbing far out and an arm lifted. It was Jonathan Trout – there before him! 'Glorious morning!' sang the voice.

'Yes, very fine!' said Stanley briefly. Why the dickens didn't the fellow stick to his part of the sea?

# Pragmatics

Pragmatics is an area of linguistics which is closely connected with language function or purpose, and with language in use. (This will lead us in the next section to consider another key concept, context.) Pragmatics is primarily associated with spoken language, and focuses on the ways in which people use language to 'get things done'. David Crystal (1987) puts it well: 'pragmatics studies the factors that govern our choice of language in social interaction and the effects of our choice on others'. Pragmatics theorists are therefore interested in how successful conversation works (for example, H.P. Grice's conversational maxims), and how direct and implied meanings are conveyed (for example, conversational implicatures). A further aspect of pragmatics is the way expectations work in the structuring of pragmatic interactions. (For more on how conversation works, see pages 163–169.)

Erving Goffman (1974) was an early exponent of frame theory applied to interaction. J.J. Gumperz (1982) argued that whilst we are talking, we pick up contextualisation cues (or frames) enabling us to recognise the situation and structure our responses appropriately. These mental frameworks help us to interpret the current situation and anticipate what is going to happen. Thus going to see the doctor or attending a job interview have particular frames leading to particular discourse structures. If these frames of expectation are disrupted (for example, the doctor insists on giving us an account of her symptoms, or the interviewer confides that the job isn't worth applying for) we are completely wrong-footed and don't know how to respond.

Schema theory develops the idea of the effect of expectations further. 'Schema' means a mental model or knowledge structure in the memory, with its own patterning of expectations, frames and assumptions. Deborah Tannen (1993) links frame theory with schema theory, and in the following extract from a fascinating case study demonstrates how conflicting frames can produce miscommunication between a paediatrician, a child patient who has cerebral palsy, her mother, and an unseen video audience of fellow doctors. Here each speaker uses different frames of communication. These range from a medical register (examination frame), a friendly register (paediatric consultation frame), and a register appropriate for addressing the mother (consultation frame). Each frame creates and fulfils its own discourse expectations – unless someone slips up and uses the wrong register (which is what happens). To make matters worse, in the same consultation, mother and doctor have totally mismatched schema. For the mother (mental schema: wheezing means illness) the child's noisy breathing at night is worrying; for the doctor (mental schema: wheezing signifies a specific medical problem, which is not present) noisy breathing at night is nothing to worry about. Result – mismatched schema and a significant problem of communication!

**Pediatric consultation frame**
| | |
|---|---|
| Doctor | Let me look in your ear. Do you have a monkey in your ear? |
| Child | [laughing] No |
| Doctor | No? let's see … I … see …a birdie! |
| Child | [laughing] No … |

**Consultation frame**
| | |
|---|---|
| Doctor | Her canals are fine, they're open, um her tympanic membrane was thin, and light … As you know, she does have difficulty with the use of her muscles. |

**Paediatric consultation frame plus examination frame**
| | |
|---|---|
| Doctor | [examining child's stomach] Okay? Okay. Any peanut butter and jelly in here? |
| Child | No |
| Doctor | No? Is your spleen palpable over there? |
| Child | No |

**Examination frame plus consultation frame**
| | |
|---|---|
| Doctor | Once more. Okay. That's good. She has very coarse breath sounds um … and you can hear a lot of the noises you hear when she breathes you can hear when you listen. But there's nothing that |
| Mother | That's the kind of noise I hear when she's sleeping at night. |
| Doctor | Yes. Yes. There's nothing really as far as pneumonia is concerned or as far as any um anything here. There's no wheezing um which would suggest a tightness or a constriction of the thing. There's no wheezing at all. |

## Activity 18

**Individual**

## Investigating the registers associated with different frames

How many registers are employed in these doctor-patient exchanges? Match the lexis with each register.

For more on frame and schema, see pages 175–176.

In most examples of pragmatics or language in use, the interaction works reasonably well, and if it doesn't there are obvious reasons why not, as in the Tannen case study described above. 'Language in use' encompasses many interactions of everyday life, often called service encounters (going to the supermarket, the bank, the hairdresser, student services or even the examinations office), where we tend to know what to expect. In Activity 17 we looked at an example of a service encounter in a shop. In the next activity there are two examples of pragmatic exchanges. One is entirely practical with only minimal phatic function, the other is more purpose driven and persuasive in function.

## Activity 19

## Comparing different kinds of pragmatic exchanges

Read both texts carefully. Identify the purpose(s) of each interaction, the participants and the situation. How did you reach your conclusions?

Compare the lexical choice in each text, including use of specialised jargon, evaluative lexis and any interpersonal language.

Assess the success/failure of each interaction, giving reasons for your decision.

**Text A**
A2    London afternoon MIDLAND 58 heading 335
ATC   MIDLAND 58 good afternoon climb flight level 180
A2    flight level 180 MIDLAND 58
ATC   SPEEDBIRD 32 GOLF contact London on 131.05 routing direct to Pole Hill
A3    131.05 direct Pole Hill SPEEDBIRD 32 GOLF
ATC   SHUTTLE 75 heading 340
A4    340 for SHUTTLE 75
A5    SHUTTLE 340 approaching flight level 200
ATC   SHUTTLE 40 thank you climb now flight level 280
A5    climb flight level 280 SHUTTLE 40
A1    AIRFRANCE 046 maintaining level 290
ATC   AIRFRANCE 046 roger
ATC   UK 618 continue present heading until advised
A6    continue present heading until advised UK 618 and heading 325
ATC   MIDLAND 58 climb flight level 280
A2    climb level 280 MIDLAND 58
[passage omitted]
ATC   AIRFRANCE 046 contact London 131.05 goodbye
[passage omitted]

A7    London good afternoon BRITANNIA 444B passing 260 descending flight level 200
ATC    BRITANNIA 44B thank you

ATC    UK 618 contact Manchester 124.2 goodbye
A6    124.2 goodbye
ATC    SHUTTLE 40 direct to Trent call London 128.05 goodbye
A5    128.05 direct to Trent SHUTTLE 40 bye
ATC    MIDLAND 58 contact London 131.05 goodbye
A2    131.05 MIDLAND 58 goodbye

**Text B**

Sarah    Mr A let me introduce you to Michael Smith (.) he's our customer adviser (.) he'll be looking after you this morning [pause] what would you like to drink (.) tea or coffee

Michael Smith    good morning Mr A (.) come through to my office (.) have a seat (.) I understand from Sarah that you've got some credit cards that you haven't managed to pay off in full (.) and I've noticed that you've got a small personal loan and you make a lot of use of your current account (.) is that correct

Mr A    yes it is (.) but I also owe some money to um Suite Ideas (.) who I got a three piece suite off recently

Michael Smith    how much are we talking about

Mr A    oh about two thousand two hundred pounds

Michael Smith    so apart from the things we've talked about already (.) and the money to Suite Ideas (.) what other outstanding debts have you got

Mr A    that's it (.) apart from my mortgage really

Michael Smith    so what we're going to do this morning (.) is to spend twenty minutes doing what we call a customer service review (.) and find out a bit of background information about you (.) and see if we can save you any money on a monthly basis (.) organise your overdraft (.) and make sure that if anything were to happen to you (.) all those debts were protected with insurance (.) how would that make you feel

Mr A    oh well that would be great (.) a big relief (.) I didn't think you'd be able to do that and save me money (.)

# Context

The importance of context in any written or spoken exchange should now be crystal clear. Without an understanding of the situation, events, participants and purpose of any spoken exchange we are lost. Without an understanding of the audience and purpose (and possibly genre) of any written text, whether literary or non-literary, it will be hard to make sense of it. Context is clearly of the utmost importance, as indicated earlier on pages 2–3.

## Context in spoken language

Whether we're talking with friends or strangers, almost the first thing to be established is the context of the discussion. Without contextual clues, we can feel excluded from the interaction, until someone helps out ('We're talking about the film that was released last week.'). Frame and schema theory can help, if we recognise a familiar situation ('Can I help you?' or 'I'm not trying to sell you anything but ...'). Once we've recognised the context, we can usually work out the audience and purpose.

In other situations, there are similar patterns of expectation, sometimes linked to the actual physical environment in which an interaction takes place (a bus stop, a train station, a supermarket, a classroom, the Strangers' Gallery in the Houses of Parliament, a public meeting, a travel agency or a bank). What can derail us in exchanges is if we have one set of expectations from an encounter and the reverse happens. Every situation has its own generic expectations, and if these are flouted or subverted, the end result is disturbing at best and disruptive at worst.

## Context in written language

Context is important to all written language, as many theorists have demonstrated over the last two decades. We also need to understand some different approaches to author, text and context which theorists have teased out. For example, there are clear differences between readerly and writerly texts and between reading and writing positions in relation to context.

- A readerly text is one where the reader and author share expectations, recognise the genre expectations and rely on them being present (for example, any detective story or romantic Mills and Boon novel).
- A writerly text is one where literary and generic conventions are violated, expectations are flouted and the reader has to work hard to understand the text (for example, James Joyce's *Ulysses*).
- Reading position refers to the fact that we all read from our own personal experience (including gender) as well as from our experience of society.
- Writing position refers to the individual author's desire to be creative, within the context of their personal life and their experience of society.

The concept of interrogating a text has also emerged. Although the word 'interrogation' has some negative overtones, the idea of vigorously asking questions of a text, rather than simply looking at it, gives the reader an active rather than passive role. Likely questions are predictable enough, however (Who wrote the text? For whom? When was it written? What was going on in the world at the time?).

The following constructed model is a useful and more developed way of approaching context. This breakdown of different contexts can be applied to any text, literary or non-literary, spoken/ heard or written. Where appropriate, the term 'listener/speaker' can be substituted for 'reader'.

- Context of immediate situation: Who is reading the text and from what position? Is it a text suited to objective reading or empathetic, creative reading? What other readings might be possible?
- Context of reception: Who were the first readers of the text and how would they have read it?
- Context of production: Who is/was the author/ producer of the text? How and why was it written? What is/was the author's own attitude?
- Context/larger cultural frame of reference: The social, historical, political and cultural environment in which the author wrote the text and readers read it.
- Context of text: What is the genre? What is the text about? Does it reflect the writer's individual and social experience? Does it appeal to the reader's individual and social experience? What literary influences or models are reflected in the text?

For practice in analysing these different contexts, see pages 28–31.

We shall now explore four texts, two literary and two non-literary, and apply the context model on page 27. Text A is a soliloquy by Hamlet. In Text B, from 'Mrs Midas' by Carol Ann Duffy, Midas's wife discovers that her husband's touch turns everything to gold. Text C is part of a speech by Martin Luther King (1963). Texts D, E and F are short extracts from Christmas circular letters from Simon Hoggart's collection *The Cat That Could Open the Fridge* (2004).

### Text A

**Hamlet**  To be, or not to be – that is the question;
Whether 'tis nobler in the mind to suffer
The slings and arrows of outrageous fortune
Or to take arms against a sea of troubles
And by opposing end them. To die, to sleep –
No more – and by a sleep to say we end
The heartache and the thousand natural shocks
That flesh is heir to. 'Tis a consummation
Devoutly to be wished ....

### Text B

He came into the house. The doorknobs gleamed.
He drew the blinds. You know the mind; I thought of
the Field of the Cloth of Gold and Miss Macready.
He sat in that chair like a king on a burnished throne.
The look on his face was strange, wild, vain. I said,
What in the name of God is going on? He started to laugh.
…
It was then I started to scream. He sank to his knees.
After we'd both calmed down, I finished the wine
on my own, hearing him out. I made him sit
on the other side of the room and keep his hands to himself.
I locked the cat in the cellar. I moved the phone.
The toilet I didn't mind. I couldn't believe my ears:

how he'd had a wish. Look, we all have wishes; granted.
But who has wishes granted? Him. Do you know about gold?
It feeds no one; aurum, soft, untarnishable; slakes
no thirst.

**Note:** Miss Macready was the narrator's history teacher. Henry VIII of England and Francis I of France had a magnificent but unproductive meeting in 1520. 'Burnished throne' is an intertextual and ironic reference to Cleopatra in Shakespeare's *Antony and Cleopatra*.

### Text C

I have a dream that one day this nation will rise up and live out the true meaning of this creed: 'We hold these truths to be self-evident; that all men are created equal.'

I have a dream that one day on the red hills of Georgia the sons of former slaves and the sons of former slaveowners will be able to sit down together at the table of brotherhood.

I have a dream that one day even the state of Mississippi, a desert state sweltering with the heat of injustice and oppression, will be transformed into an oasis of peace and justice.

I have a dream that my four little children will one day live in a nation where they will not be judged by the color of their skin but by the content of their character.

I have a dream. ...

## Text D

This year's stress has been my neighbour's wind chimes. I can hear them clearly in my bedroom, even with the window closed. It drives me mad. My neighbours do not respond to polite requests, they will not take part in mediation and they are merely indignant at letters from the Council. I am a Quaker and a pacifist, I have training in conflict resolution – well now I have first-hand knowledge too. I have discovered what hate is, and that I was blessed in not hating anyone for the first 33 years of my life.

## Text E

July and August were incredibly hot, and on the 21st, right on cue, the potato crisp hullabaloo broke out, since when the village has been at various times in an uproar, pitting brother against brother, and we still await a decision from the planning authority.

## Text F

This year Snugs (Mr Snugglekins, our cat) has kept us on our toes. He has learned to open the door of our new large fridge.

### Commentary on Text A

The extract comes from Hamlet's soliloquy after he has learnt that his father was murdered by his usurping uncle, Claudius. The text is currently read, studied and performed by actors and students worldwide; the tragedy of the protagonist, the Prince of Denmark, draws audiences into empathising with the witty but damaged hero (*immediate situation*).

The play was first published in the Quarto in 1603 and presumably performed at about the same time. Although we are short of contemporary evidence about its reception, there was a second Quarto edition 1604–1605, another in 1623, and many others since, so we can assume that the play's popularity has lasted (*reception*).

Our information about Shakespeare's life is limited, except that we know he had a grammar-school education, was an actor as well as a writer, and often wrote parts for fellow actors (*production*).

The play would have appealed to an audience keen on ghosts and familiar with Senecan tragedy, and to a society where the royal succession had only just ceased to be a burning issue, but where the murder of a king was truly shocking (*historical/cultural background*).

Contemporary audiences would have been aware of its sources in Jacobean revenge tragedy, as well as earlier historical texts which Shakespeare may have used, such as Saxo Grammaticus's twelfth-century *Historiae Danicae*, and Francois de Belleforest's sixteenth-century *Histoires Tragiques* (*text/genre*). Shakespeare's skilful reworking of his many sources has created a play where audiences, producers and readers can still find new ways of interpreting the character of Hamlet (see Tom Stoppard (1966) *Rosencrantz and Guildenstern are Dead*). The way Shakespeare uses powerful images of warfare, the sea and sleep to represent life and death, as well as the magnificent handling of iambic pentameter, and particularly the caesura and enjambement to convey Hamlet's mental struggle, are fruitful areas for further discussion.

### Commentary on Text B

'Mrs Midas' comes from *The World's Wife* (1999) by Carol Ann Duffy, in which the poet uses the voices of famous 'other halves' (Mrs Darwin, Mrs Aesop and Anne Hathaway) to provide a new perspective. The readership is contemporary, with perhaps particular interest from women. The construction of the poem makes it difficult, however, to read from any perspective other than that of the female narrative voice (*immediate situation/reception*).

In terms of the *production* of the text, Duffy has a strong interest in interpreting the world through a feminist perspective and exploring the breadth of women's experience. The collection, *The World's Wife*, and this particular poem represent a development in her work in that there is a common theme uniting the poems, namely women's relationship with men. Duffy is avowedly feminist; born in 1955, she grew up as feminism became politicised in the 1970s and 1980s (*larger social/cultural frame of reference*). The poem itself (*text*) is in relatively regular six-line stanzas, with variable line length. Duffy has a powerful ear for the rhythms of natural speech, so that the ironic voice of Mrs Midas conveys to the reader a kind of confessional, confidential quality, with allusions ranging from the mundane ('I moved the phone') to historic and literary allusions.

### Commentary on Text C

People who read or hear recordings of this speech today will respond differently depending on their national, political and personal attitudes both to the speaker and to his message. Most people who abhor slavery and its consequences will empathise completely with Martin Luther King's speech (*immediate situation*).

When the speech was given in August 1963 to celebrate the centenary of President Abraham Lincoln's emancipation proclamation, the supporters and members of the NAACP would have wholeheartedly supported King, as would other Americans who rejected segregation. Elsewhere in America, particularly in the South, very different views might have been held (*reception*).

The Reverend Martin Luther King (later a winner of the Nobel Peace Prize) was a well-known Civil Rights activist in the early 1960s, leading various demonstrations and marches in the Southern United States. In August 1963 he led a Freedom March from the Washington Monument to the Lincoln Memorial, and made this speech to an audience of over 200,000 marchers (*production, social/political/cultural frame of reference*). It is a masterpiece of rhetoric, and thought by many to be the greatest speech of the twentieth century (*text*).

### Commentary on Texts D–F

Hoggart selected these extracts as amusing examples of self-revelation (D), inadvertent mystification (E) and the climactic end to a narrative of family medical disaster (F). He seems fascinated by the combination of smugness, 'showing off', lack of self-awareness, and obsessive detail characterising this genre. The contexts of *immediate situation/reception* are complicated, in that the 'reader' is not the intended recipient (who disloyally sent the letter to Hoggart!). We can assume that by the time Hoggart's book was published many more people would have read the letters. We can only speculate about whether there might have been more sympathetic readings by other recipients.

The context of *production* is interesting here – why would the family/family representative write in such detail? The explanation seems to differ with each text. Text D is absurd and yet one sympathises with the writer, equally tortured by wind chimes and his conscience! Text E is funny because the imagination runs riot as to what the 'potato crisp hullabaloo' could possibly be about (the writer quite oblivious to a reader's mystification). Text F is comic within the context of the previous narrative of medical disaster. The bathetic image of the dextrous cat is unintentionally comic. The writing position in each text is entirely author focused, with zero awareness of audience. Egocentricity and one-upmanship prevail.

The *social/cultural frame of reference* is the social networking middle class. The genre of the round-robin letter (*text*) has become increasingly popular as a lazy way of telling people family news at Christmas. Hoggart tells of travelogues and medical histories 9000 words in length, as well as catalogues of spectacular achievement by the writer's children/ grandchildren. Readers find this genre appealing, appalling or a combination of guilty enjoyment, fascinated horror and straight embarrassment.

---

**Activity 20**  **Investigating context further**

Use the model on page 27 to write a contextual commentary.

Choose the first page of a short story or a 'coffee break' magazine story, and analyse the ways in which context is used to make the story appeal to the reader.

Select a one-page advertisement, with more text than image, and analyse how the use of context supports its persuasive purpose.

---

# Text and discourse

There is some discussion among linguists as to which is the superordinate category, text or discourse. The term 'discourse' can be applied to the specialised 'discourse of advertising' as well as to a passage of continuous written text beyond the sentence. The term also is used with general reference to spoken language, and the practice of discourse analysis explores stretches of spoken interchange, focusing in particular on the structures and patterns of interaction.

Text is a term also associated with the concept of structure. The word derives from the Latin noun *textum* meaning 'structure', which in turn derives from the Latin verb *texere*. This verb had four meanings:

- literal meaning 'to weave'
- transferred meaning 'to twine together, intertwine'
- 'to put together or construct'
- 'to compose speech or writing'.

It's not at all difficult to see how readily the word 'weave', associated with cloth, transferred its meaning to constructing spoken and written language into a web of words. Even today we use similar words to describe language, such as the 'fabric' of an argument or the 'texture' of the poem. So perhaps text is a superordinate category above discourse, both historically and philosophically?

Today the term 'text' is applied by linguists and post-modern theorists not only to written and spoken language, but also to graphic and multi-modal forms, such as film or installation art. In this section, however, we shall use 'text' to refer to any genre or form of spoken and written language. The transferred image of text as a woven structure remains useful, because all communication in language is in effect a woven structure of words, sound patterns, grammar, syntax and imagery. You may also have noticed that 'context' is related etymologically to 'text'. Both share the same root form, with the prefix 'con-' (together with) representing the extra information that context gives to a text.

## Activity 21 — Identifying audience, purpose and context

**Pair work**

Read the following texts carefully. Text A is a telephone conversation between friends. Text B is an extract from a twentieth-century American short story, 'New York to Detroit' by Dorothy Parker. Text C is a nursery rhyme. Text D is from the *Observer* newspaper (2007). Text E is a computer desktop message. Text F is an extract from a letter dated 1859 from a young woman (Sarah Ellen Gaukroger) to a young man who, she suspects, is trifling with her affections.

Working in pairs, identify audience and context for each text then consider how the language choices (including lexis, grammar, syntax and discourse features) match the purpose of the speaker or writer.

### Text A

| | |
|---|---|
| Stephen | Ian |
| Ian | Yes |
| Stephen | Hello |
| Ian | What did you do in English? |
| Stephen | We didn't do anything really. |
| Ian | Did you do your projects? |
| Stephen | No, because he was away. |
| Ian | Was he? |
| Stephen | Yes. |
| Ian | That was fortunate. |
| Stephen | Well I walked into the classroom and … |
| Ian | He's never away. |
| Stephen | No, but he's supposed to have a really bad cold or something |
| Ian | Oh that's a shame will he be there tomorrow? |
| Stephen | Er, well if he wasn't there today and he's got a really bad cold, I doubt it. But you've still got to go to the lesson though. |

### Text B

'All ready with Detroit,' said the telephone operator.

'Hello,' said the girl in New York.

'Hello?' said the young man in Detroit.

'Oh, Jack!' she said. 'Oh, darling, it's so wonderful to hear you. You don't know how much I –'

'Hello?' he said.

'Ah, can't you hear me?' she said. 'Why, I can hear you just as if you were right beside me. Is this any better, dear? Can you hear me now?'

'Who did you want to speak to?' he said.

'You, Jack!' she said. 'You, you. This is Jean, darling. Oh, please try to hear me. This is Jean.'

'Who?' he said.

'Jean', she said. 'Ah, don't you know my voice? It's Jean, dear. Jean.'

'Oh, hello there,' he said. 'Well. Well, for heaven's sake. How are you?'

'I'm all right,' she said. 'Oh, I'm not either, darling. I – oh, it's just terrible. I can't stand it any more. Aren't you coming back? Please, when are you coming back? You don't know how awful it is, without you. It's been such a long time, dear – you said it would just be four or five days, and it's nearly three weeks. It's like years and years. Oh, it's been so awful, sweetheart – it's just –'

'Hey, I'm terribly sorry,' he said, 'but I can't hear one damn thing you're saying. Can't you talk louder, or something?'

## Text C

Hickory dickory dock
The mouse ran up the clock.
The clock struck one,
The mouse ran down,
Hickory dickory dock.

## Text D

The BBC is being urged to appoint a language chief by critics who claim that its reputation as a bastion of the Queen's English is fading fast.

They claim that presenters and correspondents on both television and radio routinely misuse words, make grammatical mistakes and use colloquialisms instead of standard English.

Sir Michael Lyons, chair of the BBC Trust, will receive an open letter tomorrow calling for a 'democratic airing' of the proposals, which advocate the creation of a new post to scrutinise 'the syntax, vocabulary and style' of thousands of staff heard on air.

## Text E

Unable to connect you to preferred wireless network
Windows could not connect you to any of your preferred
wireless networks. Windows will keep trying to connect.
To see a list of all networks, including others you can
connect to, click this message

## Text F

I have heard (and from good authority) of your making an offer of your honoured self (not a month since yet) to a lady that I know would not deign to speak to you but no matter she has as you no doubt suppose plenty of the shining metal, and that leads me to think you are determined to have money, it is of more consequence to you by far than love affection and domestic happiness. And if you take a wife without money it will be the last recourse, I pitty [sic] the woman you get on that score, for you will ever repine at her want of <u>gold,</u> pardon me if I have said more than I ought but when we feel we have been slighted if we have any spirit we shew it, and I hope I am not without nor without common sense either. I think it a very serious matter talking of love and marring [sic] to much so to be trifled about; you need not think because you have got a <u>cage</u> you can have any woman for the asking for I would have you remember they don't all want you that looks at you …

# Intertextuality

The concept of intertextuality emerged in the 1960s, reflecting the interest of French critics in the theories of the Russian linguist and philosopher Mikhail Bakhtin. He regarded all language, spoken or written, as dialogic. He not only believed that spoken language reflected conversations between individuals but he saw our relationship with our society as dialogic. Bakhtin famously used the term heteroglossia (meaning 'multiple voices') to describe the rich texture of social and personal interaction.

Use of the term 'intertextuality' recognises the fact that all texts have links with each other over time, in subject-matter and in the lexis available. One American critic, Harold Bloom, coined the phrase 'the anxiety of influence' to describe this state of mutual indebtedness. He was trying to convey the burden of the past felt by many creative artists.

Since the 1960s, the idea of influence, of textual echoes, allusions and references in literature has broadened considerably. As recording technology has advanced, and corpora of spoken language become established, it has become clear that people use intertextual reference freely in their everyday conversations, and not just in literary high culture. We all see patterns of analogy and make connections as ways of understanding the world. Furthermore, as the concept of 'text' widens to include multi-modal and visual genres, we recognise other sorts of visual patterns and analogies, and intertextual links can be made between visual images in film and other art forms. One kind of powerful intertextual reference is the terrifying shower scene in Hitchcock's film *Psycho* – a visual echo which many subsequent directors have exploited to chilling effect.

Here are three examples of intertextual references in literature.

- In Shakespeare's sonnet the line 'My mistress' eyes are nothing like the sun' deliberately subverts the courtly love tradition of rosy lips and sparkling eyes.
- Aldous Huxley borrowed a phrase from the lines 'How beauteous mankind is! O brave new world/ That has such people in't', from Miranda's speech in *The Tempest*, as the title for his novel *Brave New World* (1932).
- T.S. Eliot made an intertextual reference to Enobarbus's magnificent description of Cleopatra in his portrait of a modern woman in 'A Game of Chess' in *The Waste Land* (1925).

## Activity 22 — Exploring how intertextuality enriches a text

**Pair work**

Text A is from Shakespeare's *Antony and Cleopatra*. Text B is from 'A Game of Chess', from T.S. Eliot's poem *The Waste Land*.

Working in pairs, read both texts carefully. Your task is to look for connections between them, to see what points Eliot might be making about twentieth-century society in his use of intertextual references. Here are some suggestions about aspects/features to consider.

- Compare the setting, situation and action in each text
- Lexis – try listing equivalent or semantically related words and phrases. For example, why does Eliot change 'burn'd' to 'glowed'?
- Syntax – look at comparable phrase and sentence structure, and word order
- Sound patterning – compare the metre and any other sound patterns.

**Text A**

The barge she sat in, like a burnish'd throne
Burn'd on the water: the poop was beaten gold;
Purple the sails, and so perfumed that
The winds were lovesick with them; the oars were silver,
Which to the tune of flutes kept stroke and made
The water which they beat to follow faster,
As amorous of their strokes …

**Text B**

The Chair she sat in, like a burnished throne,
Glowed on the marble, where the glass
Held up by standards wrought with fruited vines
From which a golden Cupidon peeped out
(Another hid his eyes behind his wing) …
In vials of ivory and coloured glass
Unstoppered, lurked her strange synthetic perfumes,
Unguent, powdered, or liquid – troubled, confused
And drowned the sense in odours …

(Note: 'Cupidon' is a variant name of Cupid, son of Venus and god of sexual love.)

# Narrative

Everyone can tell a story: narrative is part of everyday existence, whether it's an account of what happened at work, or a visit to yet one more university, or whether it's a funny story about friends or about a perfect stranger on the bus. We even narrate our symptoms to the doctor, and expect the diagnosis to provide a further explanatory narrative. Stories are told in travel journals or historical documents. Long-established genres like history, biography and autobiography are also narratives. As we tell our story, we are critically reassessing our social and physical environment and making new interpretations of the world. In other words, narrative combines both the ideational and the interpersonal metafunctions of language (see page 21). In the public context, news bulletins, journalism and advertising are all different kinds of storytelling. Some of these narratives are relatively impersonal and objective (national news broadcasting), others are full of 'human interest' and melodrama (tabloid press).

Storytelling or narrative in everyday life is universally recognised, but storytelling about imaginary or imagined characters and situations has an equally long tradition, going back to purely oral cultures when human beings made up stories to explain the mysteries of their terrifying world to each other, or told the adventures of tribal heroes. Many ancient cultures maintained written as well as oral versions of their history, stories and myths on vellum, papyrus, stone and even wood. We call this literature.

# Narrative voice

The narrative impulse is integral to human communication, but how does narrative actually work? We must start with the 'voice' of the storyteller. The concept of narrative voice is familiar to most people, and it is the voice that determines point of view or narrative perspective. In non-literary contexts like casual conversation, the narrative voice is first person, simply because the narrator is telling the story. However, the moment the narrator begins to tell someone else's story, the narrative voice becomes third person. In non-literary genres like advertising, second-person voice can be used as part of a strategy of synthetic personalisation (pretending friendliness to sell something – 'It's winter and you're fed up? Imagine yourself on a tropical beach …').

In literary genres like prose fiction and poetry, first- and third-person narrative voices are the norm. In drama, the situation is different, because dialogue between characters and the plot creates the overall narrative. Sometimes a character may step out of role to tell the audience more about the action. In *Henry V* and *Murder in the Cathedral*, Shakespeare and Eliot revive the Greek tradition of the chorus for their own purposes. In *Henry V* the audience is to imagine itself transported with the young king to France; in *Murder in the Cathedral* the women of Canterbury comment on events leading to Thomas Becket's martyrdom.

What are the advantages of first-person narrative voice? The reader benefits from insight into the character of the central narrator, as we can see in novels such as *Jane Eyre, Wuthering Heights, Huckleberry Finn* and *The Catcher in the Rye*. The reader also experiences events from the point of view of the narrator, the only disadvantage being that the narrator may not see the full picture or be reliable. Indeed, an author may exploit an unreliable narrator who holds back information, as Nellie Dean does in *Wuthering Heights*, to create suspense.

The third person or omniscient narrator is probably the most frequently used narrative voice because there is no intrusion of opinion or evaluation of events and character. The disadvantage is that the narrator is totally detached. A strategy counteracting this is the introduction of an authorial voice commenting on event, character or situation, and thereby drawing the reader into a more interactive relationship. Novels using third-person narrative voice include *Bleak House, Tom Jones, The Great Gatsby* and *Atonement*. Novels including an active authorial voice include *Middlemarch, Pride and Prejudice, Jane Eyre* and *North and South*.

For practice in identifying narrative voice, see pages 126–127.

# Point of view

It's also important to define 'point of view', which differs from narrative voice because it describes the 'angle of vision' through which plot and character are perceived and presented to the reader. It is not the voice speaking the narrative. A useful term which describes how point of view works is focalisation; the focalising eye of the narrator provides a crucial perspective for the reader. It is, of course, possible for an author to use a whole range of different points of view. If, alternatively, one point of view and one narrative voice are used throughout, this is called interior monologue or stream of consciousness. Every action, event and character is mediated through the direct words and thought of the focalised and subjective first-person narrator.

We can see how speech and thought are expressed in first-person narrative voice, but how are they represented in third-person narrative voice? These sentences illustrate the difference between how direct speech/thought and how indirect speech/thought are represented.

- The waiter said, 'Would you like to see the menu?' (Free direct speech – FDS)
- The waiter thought, 'I must remember that special order.' (Free direct thought – FDT)
- The customer said that she would prefer mineral water. (Free indirect speech – FIS)
- The customer thought that the service was excellent. (Free indirect thought FIT)

We have considered narrative voice, point of view and the representation of speech and thought mainly in relation to fiction. You should be aware that poetry can also use a range of narrative voices and different points of view.

## Narrative structure

The final aspect of narrative we need to explore is narrative structure. Although there have been other theorists, such as Vladimir Propp (1928) writing about structure in Russian fairy tales, we shall investigate William Labov's (1972) theory of narrative structure. Having done studies of oral narratives of Black New York teenagers, Labov defined narrative as a unit of discourse with clear boundaries, linear structure, and recognisable stages in its development.

| Labov's narrative stages | Key Stages 3 & 4 |
| --- | --- |
| abstract – summary | introduction |
| orientation – context | development |
| evaluation – point of interest in the story | complication |
| narrative – storytelling, involving a series of complicating events | complication |
| result – what finally happened | climax |
| coda – signals the end | resolution |

You can compare this model with the one you may be familiar with from Key Stage 3 and Key Stage 4, shown in the right-hand column. Another interesting similarity can be seen between Labov's stages and the ordering of arguments by Roman rhetoricians (see page 43 for comparison of models). Even more interesting is the fact that the narrative stages in Labov's model are not all obligatory – some features can be optional. This allows for the narrative flexibility needed by storytellers of all kinds and in all contexts. Here is an example of how the narrative structure model can be applied to a nursery rhyme.

| | |
| --- | --- |
| Jack and Jill went up the hill | abstract + orientation |
| To fetch a pail of water | evaluation |
| Jack fell down | narrative |
| And broke his crown | result |
| And Jill came tumbling after. | coda |

For more on Labov's narrative structure theory, see pages 174–175.

The relationship between reader and narrator/author is an interesting one, ranging from Jane Eyre's triumphant 'Reader, I married him' to Tristram Shandy's collusive invitation to the reader to 'Shut the door' whilst he tells the delicate story of his conception. Much thought has been expended by theorists on reader-response theory. Here are some of its basic principles in simplified form:

- There is more than one reader of a text.
- The implied reader means the reading audience the author expected; it can also mean the audience the text 'created' itself (because readers responded to it).
- The inscribed reader means the reader who 'fits' the text and who is comfortably at home with it.
- The intended reader is whoever the author says s/he wrote for.
- The ideal reader means the reader who will extract maximum value from a particular text.
- The informed reader is every writer's dream – s/he knows the language of the created text, understands its range of meanings as well as the relevant literary conventions.
- The empirical reader means someone capable of reading texts in a variety of ways.

## Activity 23

# Investigating theories of narrative and narrative structure

Here is a range of texts to investigate. Text A is from *Jane Eyre* (1848). Text B is a transcript of a conversation between a mother and her six-year-old child. Text C is an extract from Lawrence Sterne's *Tristram Shandy* (1760). Text D is an early version of a poem by Emily Dickinson. Text E is from Zadie Smith's novel *White Teeth* (2000). Text F is an extract from George Eliot's novel *Middlemarch* (1872).

Read these texts carefully, paying attention to the different kinds of narrative demonstrated.

Working with a partner, explore the ways in which the narrative functions in each text, using this list to help you:

- narrative voice
- point of view
- narrative structure
- authorial voice

What is the relationship between the reader and the narrator/author in each text?

### Text A

The next thing I remember is waking up with a feeling as if I had had a frightful nightmare, and seeing before me a terrible red glare, crossed with thick black bars. I heard voices, too, speaking with a hollow sound, and as if muffled by a rush of wind or water: agitation, uncertainty, and an all-predominating sense of terror confused my faculties.

### Text B

| | |
|---|---|
| Child | do you know what |
| Mother | (1.0) what |
| C | (3.0) I found (.) a fossil today |
| M | really |
| C | I mean a tooth |
| M | a tooth |
| C | yeah |
| M | wasn't one of yours was it |
| C | no (2.0) no it was off a dinosaur |
| M | a dinosaur where in school |
| C | no not inside |
| M | outside |
| C | erm |
| M | in the play area |
| C | yeah I saw a hole and then I looked in it and then I saw a (.) saw one |
| M | a tooth |
| C | yeah (.) and then I digged in with my finger (1.0) and then I saw one |
| M | are you sure it just wasn't a piece of stone |
| C | (.) no |
| M | why did you think it was a tooth |
| C | (3.0) because it was |
| M | (2.0) well sounds interesting enough to me |

## Text C

I wish either my father or my mother, or indeed both of them, as they were in duty both equally bound to it, had minded what they were about when they begot me; had they duly considered how much depended upon what they were then doing; – that not only the production of a rational Being was concerned in it, but that possibly the happy formation and temperature of his body, perhaps his genius and the very cast of his mind; – and, for aught they knew to the contrary, even the fortunes of his whole house might take their turn from the humours and dispositions which were then uppermost: –

## Text D

**The Chariot**
Because I could not stop for Death,
He kindly stopped for me;
The carriage held but just ourselves
And Immortality.

We slowly drove, he knew no haste,
And I had put away
My labor, and my leisure too,
For his civility.

We passed the school where children played,
Their lessons scarcely done;
We passed the fields of gazing grain,
We passed the setting sun.

We paused before a house that seemed
A swelling of the ground;
The roof was scarcely visible,
The cornice but a mound.

Since then 'tis centuries; but each
Feels shorter than the day
I first surmised the horses' heads
Were toward eternity.

(1891 version)

## Text E

For his second marriage [Archie] had chosen a mohair suit with a white polo-neck and both were proving problematic. The heat prompted rivulets of sweat to spring out all over his body, seeping through the polo-neck to the mohair and giving off an unmistakeable odour of damp dog. Clara, of course, was all cat. She wore a long brown woollen Jeff Banks dress and a perfect set of false teeth; the dress was backless, the teeth were white, and the overall effect was feline; a panther in evening dress; where the wool stopped and Clara's skin started was not clear to the naked eye. And like a cat she responded to the dusty sunbeam that was coursing through a high window on to the waiting couples. She warmed her bare back in it, she almost seemed to *unfurl*. Even the registrar, who had seen it all – horsy women marrying weasely men, elephantine men marrying owlish women – raised an eyebrow at this most unnatural of unions as they approached his desk. Cat and dog.

**Text F**

Nor can I suppose that when Mrs Casaubon is discovered in a fit of weeping six weeks after her wedding, the situation will be regarded as tragic. Some discouragement, some faintness of heart at the new real future which replaces the imaginary, is not unusual … That element of tragedy which lies in the very fact of frequency, has not yet wrought itself into the coarse emotion of mankind; and perhaps our frames could hardly bear much of it. If we had a keen vision and feeling of all ordinary human life, it would be like hearing the grass grow and the squirrel's heart beat, and we should die of that roar which lies on the other side of silence. As it is, the quickest of us walk about well wadded with stupidity. However, Dorothea was crying …

# Cohesion and coherence

These closely linked terms follow on well from the previous section on narrative structure. Labov's narrative-structure theory is plot based and sequenced. Texts which are less strongly narrative based are structured by other means. The question 'How?' is answered by the terms 'cohesion' and 'coherence'. Cohesion describes the specific means by which sentences and larger units of text 'stick together' and communicate meaning. Coherence looks beyond the sentence/utterance and describes the way in which a whole passage of speech or writing makes sense. We shall now look at the following range of cohesive devices:

- plot (in narrative genres)
- semantic and grammatical relationships in a sentence/utterance
- substitution
- anaphoric and cataphoric reference
- ellipsis
- repetition of lexis, syntax and sounds
- use of conjunctives and discourse markers.

**Plot:** Obviously events and action create the overall structuring of narrative, as we have already discussed.

**Semantic and grammatical relationships:** We have already looked in some detail (page 9) at the distinction between content and function words. The link between content words is semantic, creating basic cohesion, even if the function words are absent:

> hungry child eagerly ate red apple picnic asked.

We need the function words to create complete cohesion (and thus coherence):

> The hungry child eagerly ate my red apple at the picnic and asked for another.

So the content words provide coherent meaning and the function words explain the relationships.

**Substitution** is another cohesive device used in this example, where the pronoun 'another' substitutes for 'red apple'. Substitution occurs frequently in both speech and writing, without people being conscious of it. It's invaluable because it avoids unnecessary repetition and makes a sentence/utterance more fluent.

Anaphoric reference is a related cohesive device that 'looks back' to a previous noun. For example,

'Did you enjoy the film?' 'Yes, it was great, especially the car chase.'

'It' refers back to 'film', avoids repetition and provides cohesion and coherence.

Cataphoric reference is a cohesive device which 'points forward'. For example,

She just couldn't take it in. Her dream of being elected to Parliament had come true!

Ellipsis is another useful cohesive device also avoiding unnecessary repetition. For example,

James missed the bus, [he] arrived late and [he] spilt his coffee – but [he] got the job.

Repetition of lexical (L), grammatical (G), syntactic (S) and phonological (P) features is a frequently used cohesive device, both in spoken and in written language. Dickens is a particular master of this kind of cohesion, as we can see in the following extract from *Great Expectations* (1861). A commentary is provided on page 48.

> My first most vivid and broad impression of the identity of things, seems to me to have been gained on a memorable raw afternoon [S] towards evening. At such a time I found out for certain, that this bleak place overgrown with nettles [S] was the churchyard [S]; and that Philip Pirrip, late of this parish, and also Georgiana wife of the above, were dead and buried [L]; and that Alexander, Bartholomew, Abraham, Tobias, and Roger [L], infant children of the aforesaid, were also dead and buried [L]; and that the dark flat wilderness [S] beyond the churchyard, intersected with dykes and mounds and gates [L], with scattered cattle feeding [G] on it, was the marshes [S]; and that the low leaden line [S,P] beyond, was the river [S]; and that the distant savage lair [S] from which the wind was rushing [G], was the sea [S]; and that the small bundle of shivers [S] growing [G] afraid of it all and beginning [G] to cry, was Pip [S].

## Activity 24  Explaining how repetition creates cohesion

Reread the passage from *Great Expectations* and look at the suggested examples of lexical, grammatical, syntactic and phonological repetition. What effects does Dickens achieve by using these cohesive devices?

Conjunctives and discourse markers: These sound complicated but are easy to recognise and understand. They act as linking or listing devices (because, although, however, therefore, moreover, furthermore, firstly, secondly, next, finally, etc.). They clarify meaning, structure argument and create cohesion and coherence.

## Activity 25  Investigating conjunctives and discourse markers

Pair work

Find two editorials (opinion columns), one in a tabloid and one in a broadsheet newspaper. Underline the conjunctives and discourse markers.

Try reading the passages aloud to a partner, omitting the cohesive devices. Discuss what effect this has on the overall coherence of the text.

# Rhetoric

Rhetoric is the final section in this chapter and in many ways sums it all up. Until recently rhetoric was assigned to the dusty cupboard of out-of-date ideas and practices; it's only recently become better known and better understood as a vital tool in the study of spoken and written language.

The general public, if asked what they understood by the term rhetoric, would connect it with the discourse of politics, all flashy language or 'spin' and no real substance. This perception goes back to the times of Socrates, when rhetoric was condemned by some as the mother of lies. However, since people can lie in simple as well as sophisticated language, it seems rather unfair to condemn rhetoric out of hand as automatically dishonest. Indeed, the long fight back against this labelling began then, and continues today.

The etymology of 'rhetoric' is Greek (*techne rhetorike*) and it simply means 'the art of speech'. Developed in the fifth century BC by law-court orators, it was associated with public speaking as a means of persuasion. This association with the law was, in many ways, the undoing of rhetoric's reputation: because it is the duty of lawyers to defend the guilty as well as the innocent, they were obliged to use rhetoric (manipulation of language to persuade the jury) and were damned for it! Eventually, attitudes to rhetoric partially softened, and in medieval and renaissance times it became a major component of the classical curriculum, in which the art of speaking well (*bene dicendi*) was deemed essential.

Today, two perceptions of rhetoric co-exist: the traditional view (2500 years old) that rhetoric is (at best) suspect and (at worst) dishonest, and the current view held by linguists that rhetoric is simply the art of speaking and writing effectively. Unsurprisingly, this section adopts the second view!

A key word associated with rhetoric is 'persuasion'. It's not difficult to identify spoken and written genres with a strongly persuasive purpose (advertising, political speeches, even family arguments). However, persuasion is a powerful component in less overtly persuasive contexts. If you persuade a friend to come for coffee, go out clubbing with you or lend you a book, you have had an effect on them which should lead to your desired outcome. How did you persuade them? By rational argument? ('I really need that book for my essay – you could borrow my lecture notes tonight, and we could swap back tomorrow.') Or by affective arguments based on emotion? ('I'm really lonely since I broke up with … . Do come and keep me company!') Although your friend will use his or her own judgement in making their decision, they will have been affected by your persuasion.

The importance of what modern linguists call affect in language immediately broadens our understanding of the nature of rhetoric. It is no longer simply associated with politics, the law, or with that supreme world of artifice, advertising; it is a central aspect of every kind of text, spoken or written, which aims to affect or influence its audience. Even reference and information/fact-based texts, like scientific articles or instruction booklets, aim to have some kind of effect on their readership. We may conclude that persuasion (and hence rhetoric) is central to all human communication, with the persuasive element stronger or weaker, depending on the audience, genre and context. Hence the claim in the opening sentence of this section that rhetoric 'sums up' this chapter.

## But how does rhetoric work?

Some rhetorical strategies and techniques can be deployed across the whole spectrum of spoken and written texts. Our aim is to show you how to recognise these strategies when you are reading/listening and how to use them yourself when speaking/writing. These strategies include

- the marshalling and application of argument
- the ordering and structure of persuasive texts
- the application of a range of techniques from the persuasive repertoire (for example, lexical choice, sound patterning), from figurative language or trope, and from schematic devices (including syntactic effects).

## Marshalling and application of argument

This can only be mentioned briefly, because this chapter's overall focus is on method, not content. We therefore refer you to the Aristotelian concepts of rhetoric (*ethos* – personality and stance; *pathos* – emotional engagement; *logos* – the resources of reason), and suggest that you read these up for yourself if you are particularly interested in philosophy or critical thinking. The models of argument covered by the term *logos* are not difficult to understand, and are well used today. Here are some examples:

- definition model of argument – 'What it boils down to is …' or ' She's the kind of teacher who … .'
- oppositional model of argument – 'Don't blame the children, blame the parents.'
- place/function association model of argument – 'You don't come to school to stare out of the window! You come here to get on with your work.'

## Persuasive ordering

The way any text is structured and organised determines its effectiveness. When you add the element of persuasion (however strong or weak this might be), structure is even more important. In the table below, Labov's theory of narrative structure, with its obligatory and optional elements, is set beside the Roman rhetoricians' model of persuasive ordering.

| Roman rhetoricians | Labov |
| --- | --- |
| Introduction | Abstract |
| Narrative | Orientation |
| Determination of the point at issue | Orientation |
| Enumeration and summary of points | Complicating action |
| Proof or refutation of case | Complicating action |
| Conclusion (case proven) | Evaluation |
| Conclusion (response to points proved) | Result or resolution |
| Conclusion (call to action) | Coda |

Look at the optional and obligatory elements within the table. The function of evaluation or judgement must be an obligatory element in persuasion. For example, whether we are being persuaded to buy some magnificent car, or we are trying to write a convincing A-level essay, or telling our friends about a brilliant/appalling concert we went to, an expression of subjective opinion is inevitable. Other obligatory elements may include an opening statement of some sort ('The assertion that monetarism is an outmoded policy needs to be examined closely' or 'I thought … would be rubbish last night but actually she was fantastic!') or a closing statement ('I would argue that there is still room for monetarism in our economic policies' or 'and I was really glad that I wasn't put off by that terrible review in NME').

**Activity 26** | ## Investigating persuasive ordering in a range of texts

You can return to any of the passages already quoted in this chapter to investigate persuasive ordering. However, you will find it particularly interesting to look at the extracts from Martin Luther King's speech (page 29) and Sarah Gaukroger's letter (page 33).

## Persuasive repertoire

By now you should be well aware of the potential of lexical choice and sound patterning to create particular effects in a variety of texts. In the next activity you will see how two eighteenth-century writers, the playwright Richard Sheridan (Text A) and the poet Alexander Pope (Text B), harness these features to increase the persuasive effect they intend.

**Activity 27** | ## Exploring the persuasive effects of lexical choice and sound patterning

Read both passages carefully. Identify the lexical features selected to reveal the character of Sheridan's Mrs Sneerwell in Text A. Identify the phonological features selected to convey Pope's opinion of the named writers in Text B.

How persuasive are the authors?

Turn to page 48 for a commentary on this activity.

### Text A
Mrs Sneerwell | I confess, Mr Surface, I cannot bear to hear people attacked behind their backs; and when ugly circumstances come out against our acquaintance I own I always love to think the best. By-the-by, I hope it is not true that your brother is absolutely ruined?

### Text B

'Twas chatt'ring, grinning, mouthing, jabb'ring all,
And Noise, and Norton, Brangling, and Breval,
Dennis and Dissonance; and captious Art,
And Snip-snap short, and Interruption smart.

## Figurative language or trope

Although figurative language may be a familiar term, trope is unlikely to be. The latter is a rhetorical umbrella term that includes not only metaphor but also metonymy, synecdoche and irony.

## Metaphor

Metaphor is used when we want to explain something we see or imagine by comparing it with something different. Metaphor is an implicit comparison, unlike simile, which is an explicit comparison. To say 'She is a rose' is an implicit comparison; to say 'She is like a rose' spells out (makes explicit) that comparison. The attributes the woman shares with the rose, however, are the same in both metaphor and simile (beauty, softness, scent). Even so, the poetic power of Burns' use of simile in the following verse is as effective as the starker, more dramatic statement 'She is a rose'.

> O my Luve's like a red red rose
> That's newly sprung in June:
> O my Luve's like the melodie
> That's sweetly play'd in tune.

Modern theorists have shown that everyone uses metaphor in everyday conversation, without being aware of it. Cognitive linguists propose that there are certain basic metaphors (conceptual metaphors) that are rooted in our imagination. Some examples are

- Life is a journey – 'She'll go far!'
- Love is war – 'the battle of the sexes'
- Death is sleep – 'Night, night, grandma'
- Good is up – 'up-beat' or 'I'm really on top of the world'
- Bad is down – 'He's quite down in the dumps' or 'It's the pits'
- Anger is heat – 'It made my blood boil' or 'She blew her top'.

## Metonymy

Metonymy is based, not on semantic association as in metaphor, but on structural association. So we have 'The White House issued a denial' – the President's official residence stands for everyone who works there.

## Synecdoche

Synecdoche involves a relationship between an expressed idea, and an unexpressed one – so the part represents the whole. An example is 'I see a sail!' – the captain knows that it will be attached to a ship!

## Irony

Irony is one of the most frequently used tropes, not just in texts like fiction or journalism, but in everyday conversation – for example, saying 'You look as though you've had a miserable summer!' to a friend sporting a glorious rich tan.

# Schematic devices

Scheme is a classical rhetorical term, not to be confused with schema (discussed earlier in this chapter, page 24). Its meaning is more closely related to structure than to semantics. Use the table to explore a range of structural devices, including antithesis, listing, amplification, diminution and some other tricks and ploys. You already know more about schematic devices than you may think, since we all recognise the effectiveness of puns and wordplay (Beanz means Heinz) and earlier in this chapter (page 12) we examined the effects of syntactic parallelism and right- and left-branching sentences.

| Device | Explanation | Example |
|---|---|---|
| **Antithesis** | Contrasting directly opposed ideas and/or emotions | It was the best of times, it was the worst of times, it was the age of wisdom, it was the age of foolishness … (*A Tale of Two Cities* by Charles Dickens) |
| **Listing** | 'Heaping up' of detail which creates a powerful tension in an audience | All whom the flood did, and fire shall o'erthrow, All whom war, dearth, age, agues, tyrannies, Despaire, law, chance, hath Slaine … (*Holy Sonnets 4* by John Donne) |
| **Hyperbole** (amplification) | Exaggeration or overstatement; in drama, expresses strong emotion. Here Macbeth's emotion is pretended. | Here lay Duncan, His silver skin lac'd with his golden blood. (*Macbeth* by Shakespeare) |
| **Litotes** (diminution) | Understatement or playing down a situation for different reasons (politeness, modesty, not being unkind). Here down-playing is for ironic effect. | She was <u>not uninterested</u> in the prospect of a free trip to Australia accompanying his Stradivarius cello in economy class. |
| **Incrementum** (amplification) | Building up increment by increment | On his last skiing holiday not only did he miss the flight and arrive a day late, which was bad enough, but he also broke a ski, lost his expensive sunglasses and then, to cap it all, he slipped and fractured his leg near the ski-lift. |
| **Paradiastole** (whitewash) | Flattering vice and error by the use of neutral or positive terms | Using 'severe' instead of 'cruel', 'tired and emotional' for 'drunk and incapable', 'free spirit' for 'irresponsible person' |
| **Occultation** (passing over) | Saying you won't mention something, so actually drawing attention to it, often with comic effect | Don't mention the war! (*Fawlty Towers* by John Cleese and Connie Booth) |
| **Interrogatio** (rhetorical question) | Asking a question that does not require an answer from the reader/listener | If Winter comes, can Spring be far behind? (from Shelley's 'Ode to the West Wind') Isn't this a case in point? |
| **Pysma** | Asking a barrage of multiple rhetorical questions | Hath not a Jew eyes? Hath not a Jew hands, organs, dimensions, senses, affections, passions? … If you tickle us, do we not laugh? … and if you wrong us, shall we not revenge? (Shylock speaking in *The Merchant of Venice* by Shakespeare) |
| **Subjectio** | Asking a series of rhetorical questions and then answering them yourself | Do we know the solution to our problems? Yes, we know what to do, but will it be done? Yes, if we have the courage! |

## Activity 28
**Pair work**

## Investigating a range of texts from a rhetorical perspective

Working in pairs, select one or two literary and one or two non-literary texts or short extracts. Identify the genre, audience and purpose of each text. Identify the degree of persuasion in each (strongly persuasive to mildly persuasive). Assess how effectively the text structure, lexical choice and use of tropes/schematic devices work to support the persuasive purpose of each text.

## Activity 29
**Pair work**
**Group work**

## Persuading, using a range of rhetorical devices

Work in pairs or small groups. Select a genre, audience and topic from these lists.

| Genre | Topic | Audience |
| --- | --- | --- |
| speech | gangs | general public |
| newspaper editorial | socialising | teenagers |
| magazine article | political satire | left/right-wing supporters |
| facebook entry | being green | friends |
| blog | travel | parents/family |
| text message | old age | the Prime Minister |
| sketch | religion | Richard Branson |
| monologue | celebrity | outsiders/droppers out |

Write at least the opening section of your chosen genre (approximately 200–250 words). Your purpose is to persuade the audience, using whatever persuasive techniques and strategies seem appropriate.

Present your text to the group, asking them to assess its effectiveness on a scale of 1–5.

## Review

In this chapter you have been given the opportunity to

- discover how language is structured
- investigate how meanings are commmunicated via word choice, grammatical strategies and sound patterning
- explore the functions of language and some definitions of discourse
- discover the differences between text, context and intertextuality
- learn how to analyse stories and their structure
- investigate the story of rhetoric, past and present
- explore the role of persuasion in texts
- learn a range of persuasive techniques
- test out your own rhetorical skills.

**Commentary**

**Activity 9**

The focus of the passage keeps shifting from Sophie's voice, to her perspective on the scene, to the narrator's account. All the sentences are simple (one finite verb) or compound (two finite verbs linked with a conjunction, reflecting the child's view). The word order is SV, SVA or SVO throughout – again, reflecting the child as central consciousness. The repeated phrases 'No voices … no footsteps …No cars …Not the tiniest sound' all contribute to the extraordinary silence being conveyed before the initiating event – the arrival of the BFG!

**Commentary**

**Activity 13**

There are many examples of continuous-aspect verb forms – 'is eating … opening … walking … waiting … skating …disappearing … falling'. Auden uses continuous aspect to create a sense of suspended action for the reader, as the moment of tragic fall is caught by the artist (and no-one else, seemingly). The poignant contrast of continuous life with imminent death is suggested here by grammar.

**Commentary**

**Page 41**

This is the opening passage of the novel and the first cohesive feature is Dickens' introduction of the first-person narrative voice ('*My* first … impression … seems to *me* …', 'At such a time I found out …'). Immediately we recognise an adult perspective on the child's increasingly frightening experience in the graveyard. The lengthy compound sentence reaches a climax as the reader focuses on 'the small bundle of shivers …' and learns his name – 'Pip'. Dickens also creates a sense of threatening gloom by lexical and phonological repetition of noun phrases ('raw afternoon', 'bleak place overgrown with nettles', 'churchyard', 'dark flat wilderness', 'dykes … mounds … gates … marshes', 'low leaden line … the river', 'distant savage lair … the sea'). There is also the grammatical cohesion of features like past and present participles, differentiating between the grim past ('dead and buried') and the mournful present ('cattle feeding', 'wind rushing' and the child 'growing afraid …' and 'beginning to cry'). Overall the passage is skilfully constructed to create a sense of the central consciousness, adult or child, refracting the gloomy and frightening landscape of the churchyard in the marshes, and preparing the reader for worse.

**Commentary**

**Activity 27**

Richard Sheridan's comedy *The School for Scandal* (1777) shows the self-revealing hypocrisy of the outrageous gossip Mrs Sneerwell through her own word choice.

Similarly, Alexander Pope in his ferocious attack on foolish writers uses dissonance and a range of harsh consonants to persuade his readers of their individual folly.

# How Genres Work

2

Knowledge of genre will help you to recognise and categorise texts of different types.

In this section you will
- be introduced to a variety of texts from different genres, both spoken and written
- explore a number of texts to find out how they have been deliberately shaped and crafted
- develop your knowledge and understanding of literary and linguistic approaches.

As you learn to recognise how and why writers and speakers manipulate language you will also be subconsciously developing skills that you will be able to use in your own writing.

# What is a genre?

'Genres are kinds, categories or types of cultural product and process, including texts.'
(Rob Pope, *The English Studies Book*)

'Genre' is originally from the Latin word *genus*, meaning type or category.

- A genre is a type or a kind of something.
- A genre can be identified by a set of rules or conventions.
- Any text can be placed into a genre and will have a set of defining characteristics.
- Some writers or producers of texts deliberately break the rules to create particular effects.

A genre is not restricted to literature and the following list of examples will give you an idea of the variety of text types that can be placed in a specific genre:

- letters/diaries/journals
- reportage
- biography/autobiography
- travel writing
- speeches
- screenplays
- television programmes
- horoscopes
- personal problem pages
- reviews
- advertising
- obituaries

In order to recognise and analyse a genre you need to be able to see the similarities and differences between texts. Activities 1–3 will demonstrate this.

## Activity 1    Diaries – public or private reading?

Texts A–D are examples of diaries written in different ways.

- Text A is from *The Andy Warhol Diaries*.
- Text B is a weblog posted by Zoe, voted the Best European Blog of 2006.
- Text C is from the diary of a sixth-former which appeared as a regular column in *Guardian Education*.
- Text D is from the diary of Tracey Emin, artist, from a column in the *Independent* newspaper.

What are the clues that identify each text as a diary? Do you think they are intended for private reading or for a wider audience? Make a note of your findings.

Now read the commentary on page 87 and compare your list of features with those in the commentary.

### Text A

**1981**

We went to Sonny's (Bono) wedding in Aspen. We finally found the beautiful church and we had to stand, the ceremony was already on, and they were singing beautiful songs, and the preacher finally came on and said, 'I pronounce you, Sonny and Cherie' – he said Cherie instead of Susie – and the whole audience gasped and she said, 'My name isn't Cherie, it's Susie' and the preacher got very upset, he said he just knew he was going to do that, and then he said a million times, 'Sonny and Susie, Sonny and Susie' till the end of the ceremony. They had lighted candles and Chastity (daughter of Sonny and Cher) was the flower girl, she was kind of tall. And it was really beautiful, it was snowing outside and everybody had candles and Susie was all in white and Sonny was crying. We were invited to a party for Sonny but we went off to one of the halls to a New Year's Eve party instead.

### Text B

**Monday, March 27, 2006**

Nobody told me
'It's ten past ten', announced Todd yesterday as he took it upon himself to wake me up even though he should have been at his dad's.

'No it's not. The clock says ten past nine', I bleated and turned over for more shut-eye.

'Hahahaha – you forgot to turn your clocks forward'.

'Nobody informed me of this inconvenience, so of course I didn't. Let me sleep'.

'But Mama, it's ten past now. Get up'.

'Grrr, go away'.

Moving clocks backwards and forwards several times a year is annoying, to say the least. The first thing that comes to mind when the clocks go forward is 'thank god this only happens on a weekend – I'd be so late for work'. The second thought is 'where the hell did that hour go to? Space?'

You lose an hour, then you gain an hour so someone, probably Gordon Brown or that pesky Prime Minister, Tony Blair are probably pocketing all these hours. One goes in and another comes out later in the year, but why, oh why, can not someone inform me?

I'm off to write a letter to my MEP about this disgraceful behaviour towards the general public but I will be sure to end the letter nicely to thank him for the extra hour at the end of the day.

Daylight robbery, that's what it is.

## Text C

**September 19 2006**
It has been two weeks back at school, and I am officially stressed out. Just hearing the word Ucas makes me recoil into a childlike ball, not to mention the dreaded Personal Statement. We all feel under so much pressure to sell ourselves and achieve our predicted grades that we seem to have become worryingly uninspired when it comes to our studies this year.

Therefore, with the intention of self-motivation, I have thrown myself into all activities extra-curricular. I am directing a student-led drama production to be performed in seven weeks and producing the annual 'Stars in their eyes' talent show to be staged in less than 11 weeks. I am consequently running round the school like a headless chicken, permission forms, assembly notices, rehearsal registers in tow.

Needless to say, my new fitness regime has come to a halt. Acknowledging the need for some brief academic time, I have attempted to cut down my hours at the local supermarket where I work. After fierce persuasion my boss has agreed that this will be fine, providing I am willing to train on the meat and fish counter alongside my ex-boyfriend. Hurrah. Blood and guts and awkward silences on a Saturday morning. Bring it on.

## Text D

**Friday 5 Jan 2007**
Thank God it's 2007. Last year was so roly-poly. Strangely, being cradled in the two 0's, the 2 didn't seem sharp at all, and the 6 was totally bottom-heavy. Everything in 2006 seemed to be about waiting for it to happen, whatever the 'it' was. It was like 'we'll just sit here in 2006 until 2007 comes along', as though 2007 was the real year.

We have the 007 factor, the 2 + 7 = 9 thing, and best of all, the 2 and the 7 look like they're really good friends and could not care less about a couple of 0's to keep them apart. Plus, the 2's just happy to be there instead of the more glamorous (in the numeric world) 3. Yes, I feel it in my bones: 2007 is going to be a dynamic year.

Here are two definitions.

- Diary: daily record of events, especially those of personal concern to the writer.
- Weblog or blog: website where individuals or groups publish regularly updated accounts of their own or others' activities and interests. Items are displayed in reverse chronological order.

Some diaries are written purely as a personal record for private reading, whereas others may be written with the intention to publish. A weblog is clearly intended for a public audience.

| Activity 2 | Investigating the diary genre |
| --- | --- |

Now investigate Texts A–D on a deeper level to find out how they achieve an intimate, informal style. Read them again and think about what language techniques each uses to relate to the reader and to create the effect of spoken language.

Then read the commentary on page 87.

| Activity 3 | Similarities and differences in the same genre |
| --- | --- |

Texts A–D are all in the same genre. What differences between them have you noticed?

Note your ideas about the individual features of each text then turn to the commentary on page 88.

| Review | |
| --- | --- |

In this opening section you have

- been given a definition of genre and some examples of different genres
- done some investigation into the characteristic features of diaries and weblogs, noting how diaries can have either a public or private audience
- explored the similarities and differences between texts in the same genre.

This should have made you aware that although a particular genre may have certain characteristic features, the individual writer or speaker always creates their own distinctive style, so you need to look for variations of style within a genre.

# Understanding genre conventions

This short activity will help you to find out how much you already know about the conventions or accepted rules of writing in different genres.

| Activity 4 | Ten-minute texts |
| --- | --- |

Group work

1  Working in groups of three or four, choose one of the following genres and write a short text on any topic. Your text must include the words 'train', 'love' and 'courage'.

- diary/journal
- obituary
- horoscope
- travel writing
- mass-market newspaper article
- postcard
- text message

**Class work**

2  Exchange texts with another group. Try to identify the genre of the text you have been given. Check your answer with the writers of the text.

Discuss: how has each text followed the rules for its genre?

3  Now assemble all the text types you have explored and for each one make a list of the main conventions of each genre. How have the three given words been used in different ways and with different meanings? This should help you to see how the choice of genre influences the ways in which words are used.

To take this further you could now choose another of the genres listed and try writing a longer text, on your own or in pairs. Exchange your text with another member of your group and examine the texts to find evidence for classifying them in a particular genre.

If possible, share your findings with the whole group.

# Categories of non-literary genres

In this section you will explore a variety of different genre types. You will classify texts by identifying the characteristic features of texts in specific genres and you will be introduced to a systematic approach to analysing texts.

There are vast numbers of non-literary types of text. So where should you start your research?

Here is a list of types of genres and sub-genres. Use this as your starting-point. You will be able to add more types as you continue your exploration of genre.

### Travel writing
This can be divided into the sub-genres of

- the travel guide – for example, a *Rough Guide* or *Lonely Planet Guide* (informative with some description and opinion)
- the travelogue – for example, works by Bill Bryson, Paul Theroux, Jan Morris, William Dalrymple (more reflective, personal, autobiographical)
- travel journalism – for example, articles in weekend newspapers (containing elements of both travel guide and travelogue).

Historical travel writing would also be an interesting area for you to explore.

### Letters/diaries/journals
This genre also includes weblog diaries and e-mails.

### Biography/autobiography
Biography is an account of someone's life, often a historical or famous person's. Autobiography is written by the subjects themselves, although many celebrity autobiographies have a ghost writer, a professional writer who puts the story together.

This area could also include spoken texts such as television and radio interviews.

### Reportage

Reportage means a journalist's report/interpretation of events. Reportage can also include the genre known as popular science. This covers popular scientific writing from magazines, periodicals, collections of essays, books and transcripts of television programmes, such as Dava Sobel's *Longitude*.

### Spoken texts

Any of the genres identified above could also be in the spoken mode – transcripts or written records of speeches, television or radio documentaries, etc.

Be prepared for genres to appear in unexpected forms, such as a mix of food, travel and autobiography.

---

**Activity 5**

**Pair work**

## Researching genre

Each pair should select one genre and research the answer to these questions.

1   What are the main characteristics of the genre?
2   What are some good examples of the genre?

Then each pair should present their findings to the rest of the group, where possible giving specific examples from the genre.

---

### How to keep a genre bank

Collect a range of spoken and written texts and classify and file them according to genre (be aware that some texts may fit into more than one genre). You can do this as a whole class or individual activity.

You can continue to add to the genre bank at regular intervals throughout your course and use the texts for practice analysis.

You can also return to the genre bank to add more categories as you proceed through this chapter.

---

**Review**

You have now been introduced to further examples of different genres and also to the idea that they can be further divided into sub-genres. This should help you to become familiar with the variety and complexity of texts that you will meet throughout your Language & Literature studies.

---

# Analysing texts in different genres

In this section you will continue to explore and classify texts in different genres and you will be introduced to a systematic approach to analysing texts.

## Classifying texts

The boundaries between the various genres and sub-genres may be slightly fuzzy, but that need not concern you at the moment. It is worth noting, though, that genres are constantly evolving and borrowing from one another (this could be an interesting area for you to research later).

At this stage it is more important to appreciate the distinguishing features that each genre shares. Three significant features are theme (or subject-matter), voice (the particular perspective and tone of the writer or speaker) and structure (including grammatical and lexical choices and any visual features). This 'genre-tree' shows the relationship.

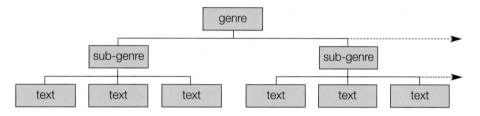

## How to analyse a text

This approach should help you to explore and discuss unseen texts.

Start with some of the more obvious features.

- What is the text about (theme/subject-matter)?
- Can you fit the text into a genre or sub-genre?
- Who do you think is the assumed audience?

Now start to identify the stylistic features that are unique to this particular text.

- Try to establish the voice – the tone and attitude of the writer/speaker.
- What is the register or degree of formality? Remember that this does not have to be a choice between formal or informal – there may be aspects of both. It is a common mistake to assume that a text must be either informal or formal. This can lead to over-stereotyping and means that you might miss some of the subtleties and implications in a text. It is often helpful to think of 'threads' of different types of register running throughout a text.

Next look closely at the language of the text at word and sentence level.

- Is there any use of specialist lexis or vocabulary drawn from a particular lexical field?
- Is there any use of idiom or colloquial language?
- Is there any use of idiolectal features? (Idiolect refers to an individual's personal language characteristics.)
- Is there any repetition or phonological patterning?

An important point to consider is how the text achieves cohesion. That is, what are the stylistic techniques that make the text progress logically and that give signposts for the reader/listener?

Having done some detailed work on language you can now consider these aspects.

- What does the writer/speaker reveal about themselves (consciously or subconsciously)?
- What does the writer/speaker reveal about their perceptions of their audience?

And for the final part of this exercise you might like to consider these personal questions.

- Would you include yourself in the target audience? Give reasons.
- How do you personally respond to the text?

| Activity 6 | Analysing a music review |
| --- | --- |

Practise the approach outlined on page 55 using the following text. It is an extract from a review of a Babyshambles concert in October 2006.

# Rock's pied piper of the apocalypse proves he's on a road to somewhere.

**First Night Babyshambles**
What to make of this Pete Doherty fellow? Is he moronic or Byronic, wan-faced pied piper of the apocalypse or a beautiful mess? Even without the endless procession of lurid 'drugs sham', red-top headlines, few in modern times have managed to combine squalid ruin with such glamour and romanticism.

Through Doherty's golden-brown tinted shades, he spouts dreamy Utopian references about Arcady and the good ship Albion, fusing them with Dickensian urchins, dispossessed, rude youth and heroic punk outsiders. But his poetic, shakily literate musings have never developed much beyond doodles on scraps of paper. Everything Doherty has produced, from the Libertine's four-year-old first single 'What A Waster', and the album, 'Up The Bracket', has been carelessly dragged out of the oven half-baked and semi-comatose, the misshapen pastoral muddle from his post-fallout group Babyshambles even more so.

Helped in no small part by his entanglement with Kate Moss, Doherty and his legions have bridged the gap between sartorial high fashion and the jumble sale.

When you have completed your analysis share with the rest of the group and add any extra points/ideas.

Compare your discussions with the commentary on page 88.

If you are interested in writing your own reviews, see the section 'Writing a review' on pages 202–204.

## Comparing texts

As part of your course you will probably be asked to compare texts in different genres. The texts may have a thematic link and you will usually be given details of where and when they were written.

The following grid should help you to identify quickly the initial features of each text. It is really important to remember that not every feature will apply to each text so you will need to select and be discriminating. If there are any technical terms that you don't recognise you will find explanations in the glossary at the end of the book.

| Model grid for analysing and comparing texts | | |
| --- | --- | --- |
| | Text A | Text B |
| Genre | | |
| Audience | | |
| Mode – spoken/written | | |
| Theme | | |
| Context – where/when was it produced | | |
| Register/formality | | |
| Lexis/semantics | | |
| Grammar/syntax | | |
| Figurative language | | |
| Tone/attitude | | |
| Phonological features | | |
| Rhetorical features – features used to involve the audience, often with the intention of persuading | | |
| Discourse features or cohesion – how a text is structured | | |
| Graphology/visual features | | |

## Activity 7    The death of John Lennon – comparing texts

Read Texts A and B on pages 58–59. The link between them is that they both concern the death of John Lennon, who was assassinated in New York on 8 December 1980, but they are in different genres and adopt very different approaches.

■ Text A is taken from the diaries of the playwright, Alan Bennett, who was in New York on the night of the murder.

■ Text B is an open letter from Yoko Ono, who was married to John Lennon. Her letter appeared in the *Independent* in Britain in December 2006.

**Individual**

Copy the model grid and use it to help you analyse and compare these texts.

1   Complete the genre boxes in your grid, then the rows for audience, mode and context.

2   Now look closely at the two texts to see what observations, if any, you can make alongside each of the other headings.

Pair work

3 Compare your investigation with a partner's then share your findings with the rest of the group. It will be interesting to see what similarities and differences there are. This may also help you to see that people perceive texts in different ways and that we all have our own way of approaching texts.

Individual

4 You now have an excellent starting-point for writing a longer analysis in continuous prose. Compare and contrast the literary and linguistic features of the texts, commenting on the attitudes of the writers.

Compare your response with the commentary on page 88.

## Text A

### 1980 (New York)

I am having supper at the Odeon when word goes round the tables that John Lennon has been shot.

'This country of ours', sighs my waiter. 'May I tell you the specials for this evening?'

The Chinese cook comes and stands at the door of the kitchen as a radio is brought to one of the booths.

At another table some diners call instantly for their check, hardly bothering to conceal their appetite for the tragedy (they are, after all, New Yorkers), and take a cab uptown to join what WNEW is already calling 'a vigil'. 'Would you describe the crowd outside the Dakota Apartment as a vigil?' asks Dan, our host. 'I would describe it', says the woman reporter, whose name is Robin, 'definitely as a vigil'.

In England this will mark New York down yet again as a violent and dangerous place, but I walk back up West Broadway, the street deserted except for a few drunks in doorways ('The slayer thought to be male, white') and feel perfectly safe. Already, though, there are candles burning in windows, and a girl weeps as she waits on this warm, windy night to cross Canal Street – 'Sixty-four degrees here on radio WNEW, the wind from the south-west', the wind and warmth making it possible for the male, white slayer to wait however long he had to wait in this unseasonable December night for the return of his victim.

## Text B

### FORGIVE US

December 8th is near again. Every year, on this day, I hear from many people from all over the world who remember my husband, John Lennon, and his message of peace. They write to tell me they are thinking of John on this day and how he was shot and killed at the prime of his life, at age 40, when he had so much life ahead of him.

Thank you for your undying love for John and also for your concern for me on this tragic anniversary. This year, though, on December 8th, while we remember John, I would also like us to focus on sending the following messages to the millions of people suffering around the world:

To the people who have also lost loved ones without cause: forgive us for having been unable to stop the tragedy. We pray for the wounds to heal.

To the soldiers of all countries and all centuries, who were maimed for life, or who lost their lives: forgive us for our misjudgments and what happened as a result of them.

To the civilians who were maimed, or killed, or who lost their family members: forgive us for having been unable to prevent it.

To the people who have been abused and tortured: forgive us for having allowed it to happen.

Know that your loss is our loss.

Know that the physical and mental abuse you have endured will have a lingering effect on our society and the world.

Know that the burden is ours.

As the widow of one who was killed by an act of violence, I don't know if I am ready yet to forgive the one who pulled the trigger. I am sure all victims of violent crimes feel as I do. But healing is what is urgently needed now in the world.

Let's heal the wounds together.

Every year, let's make December 8th the day to ask for forgiveness from those who suffered the insufferable.

Let's wish strongly that one day we will be able to say that we healed ourselves, and by healing ourselves, we healed the world.

With deepest love

**Yoko Ono Lennon**

New York City 2006

Here is an extract from a student's response to these texts followed by an examiner's comments.

### Student's response

We can tell that Text A is taken from a diary as it shows conventions of the diary form with references to time and place and use of the first person. In some ways it is a private text as the writer makes personal or deictic references to things that would not be understood by the reader ie, 'Dan, our host', and 'WNEW'. These features might suggest it was only intended to be read by the author but what is unusual for a diary is the amount of dialogue, which seems to make the event seem more realistic, almost as if we are reading a novel or play. His style is also very literary eg, he uses a metaphor to describe the other diners' 'appetite for tragedy' and he also uses descriptive writing eg, the candles burning and the alliterative effect of 'warm, windy', 'wind and warmth'. The use of lexis like 'victim', 'slayer', 'tragedy' increases the sense of drama.

Text B is very different. It is also about the death of John Lennon but Yoko Ono is reflecting on the past, rather than recording her initial impressions and she is writing to a very wide public audience. Her text is a letter but it really seems more like a speech. It is interesting linguistically as she makes it sound like a prayer with the opening imperative 'Forgive us' and the repetitions which are a bit like adjacency pairs in speech eg, 'To the civilians who were maimed, or killed, …', 'Know that your loss is our loss'.

There are some similarities with Text A as she also uses lexis which emphasises tragedy and suffering eg 'tragic', 'wounds', 'suffering', 'violence'. But, unlike Text A, there are also contrasting words such as 'undying love', 'healing'.

In terms of attitude Bennett is much more cynical as he comments on his fellow diners and he seems to have a low opinion of people in New York (they are, after all, New Yorkers). In contrast Yoko Ono has taken a more gentle approach and she seems to be concerned more with global issues not just with the death of John Lennon. She uses her personal tragedy to raise awareness of violence and suffering throughout the world so her text is much more emotive and abstract.

### Examiner's comments

There is some good discussion of lexical choices and the different attitudes and purposes of the writers are explored. The student refers to the linguistic feature of deixis, which is useful for identifying the personal and inclusive nature of texts. There is also understanding of the genre conventions of the diary and an awareness that Ono is using a style more often associated with a prayer. Use of frequent quotations helps to support the analysis.

**Review**

In this section you have
- done a significant amount of work on classifying and analysing texts.
- examined in detail the language of texts to identify their genre and to consider their audiences and purposes
- become increasingly aware of how the personal viewpoint and attitude of a writer plays an important part in their choices of language and literary devices.

### Suggestions for further work

1 Compare the review of the Babyshambles concert in Activity 6 (page 56) with one from a music magazine which approved of the performance of the Babyshambles group.

2 Try to find other examples of texts like Yoko Ono's which seek to persuade by adopting an unusual approach. This could be particularly useful in giving you ideas for your own writing or text production.

# Autobiography, biography and obituary

In this section you will
- explore the linked genres of autobiography, biography and obituary
- consider the effects of choice of narrative voice and examine the intentions and perspectives of the writers
- undertake activities that will help you to structure your own writing should this prove a genre that interests you.

### So, how do the approaches differ?

You can distinguish biography from autobiography by the writer's choice of pronoun: an autobiography will be in the first person and a biography in the third person. However, many 'autobiographies' of living celebrities are ghost written by a professional writer and could be classed as biographies presented in the first person.

A writer using first-person narrative appears to share information and a viewpoint with the reader: the reader in turn may then unconsciously adopt the position of the writer and accept uncritically what he/she says. In this way the writer is often said to 'position' the reader. A writer using third-person narrative often appears far more objective as the reader is less aware of a particular person's viewpoint, although both forms of writing can be persuasive in different ways.

Before you explore the next text, look at this brief explanation of how pronoun use is classified.

- **First person**     I (singular), we (plural)
- **Second person**   You (singular or plural)
- **Third person**    He/she/it (singular), they (plural).

## Exploring biography

Now you are going to examine the skills and approaches of biographers. The following text is an extract from the opening of a biography of the novelist Charles Dickens written by Peter Ackroyd (1990).

> Charles Dickens was born on the seventh of February 1812, the year of victory and the year of hardship. He came crying into the world in a first floor bedroom in an area known as New Town or Mile End, just on the outskirts of Portsmouth where his father, John Dickens, worked in the Naval Pay Office. He was born on a Friday, on the same day as his young hero, David Copperfield, and for ever afterwards Friday became for him a day of omen. Whether like his young hero he was born just before midnight when the tide was in, is not recorded; but this strange association between himself and his fictional characters is one that he carried with him always.

---

**Activity 8**

**Group work**

## Biography – fact or fiction?

Read the text then, working in small groups, identify the elements that are definite fact and those which might be speculation or opinion.

You may have noticed how Ackroyd uses a literary style which is sometimes a reflection of Dickens' own writing. What is the effect?

Compare your ideas with the commentary on page 89.

---

The next text is also an opening to a biography of a celebrated historical figure, Mary, Queen of Scots, written by the historian and novelist Antonia Fraser (1969).

> The winter of 1542 was marked by the tempestuous weather throughout the British Isles; in the north, on the borders of Scotland and England, there were heavy snow-falls in December and frost so savage that by January the ships were frozen into the harbour at Newcastle. These stark conditions found a bleak parallel between the political climate which then prevailed between the two countries. Scotland as a nation groaned under the humiliation of a recent defeat at English hands at the battle of Solway Moss.

| Activity 9 | Creating atmosphere |
|---|---|

Read the text on page 61 then consider how Fraser, like Ackroyd, has employed a mix of fact and elements of fictional writing to give her biography wide appeal.

Find examples of factual elements and those which are used to create atmosphere. Compare your findings with the commentary on page 89.

| Activity 10 | Narrative perspective |
|---|---|

**Individual**

To explore the effects of the choice of narrative perspective in more detail, choose one of the two biography openings and rewrite it using the first person.

**Pair work**

Working in pairs, discuss the effects of changing the narrative perspective to the first person. Make a note of your findings and discuss with the rest of the group.

Finally, discuss how effective you found the openings of these two biographies, giving reasons based on your analysis of the language used.

## Writing autobiography for different audiences

Adeline Yen Mah's family considered her to be bad luck because her mother died giving birth to her. They discriminated against her and made her feel unwanted. After the death of her stepmother she decided to write her story. She called this *Falling Leaves* (1997) and after it became a bestseller she wrote her autobiography in a different way for children. This version she called *Chinese Cinderella* (1999).

Here are the openings of each autobiography.

---

**Text A**

Falling Leaves
The true story of an unwanted Chinese daughter

At the age of three my grand aunt proclaimed her independence by categorically refusing to have her feet bound, resolutely tearing off the bandages as fast as they were applied. She was born in Shanghai (city by the sea) in 1886 during the Quing dynasty when China was ruled by the child emperor Kuang Hsu, who lived far away up north in the Forbidden City.

The pampered baby of the family, eight years younger than my grandfather, Ye Ye, Grand Aunt finally triumphed by rejecting all food and drink until her feet were, in her words, 'rescued and set free'.

---

**Text B**

Chinese Cinderella
The secret story of an unwanted daughter

Autumn 1941
As soon as I got home from school, Aunt Baba noticed the silver medal dangling from the left breast pocket of my uniform. She was combing her hair in front of the mirror in our room when I rushed in and plopped my schoolbag down on my bed.

---

'What's that hanging on your dress?'

'It's something special that Mother Agnes gave me in front of the whole class this afternoon. She called it an award.'

My aunt looked thrilled. 'So soon? You only started kindergarten one week ago. What is it for?'

'It's for topping the class this week. When Mother Agnes pinned it on my dress, she said I could wear it for seven days. Here, this certificate goes with it.'

I opened my schoolbag and handed her an envelope as I climbed onto her lap.

'We'll write today's date on the envelope and put it away somewhere safe.'

I watched her open her closet door and take out her safe-deposit box. She took the key from a gold chain around her neck and placed my certificate underneath her jade bracelet, pearl necklace and diamond watch – as if my award were also some precious jewel impossible to replace.

---

## Activity 11 — Autobiography and audience

**Pair work**

Read the two autobiography openings. Working in pairs, make a list of all the differences you have noticed in the two versions.

- What differences do you notice in the titles and subtitles of each text?
- What variations are there in the content and style of each text?
- What are the differences in choice of sentence structure and lexis?

Share your findings with the rest of the group. This should help you to see some of the differences between writing for adults and writing for children.

Note and discuss the techniques that Adeline Yen Mah has employed in the children's version of her autobiography. Compare your response with the commentary on page 90.

## Obituary

A type of writing which is linked to biography is that of obituary writing. An obituary is an announcement of a person's death which usually appears in a newspaper and is accompanied by a short biography. Obituaries written for newspapers concern famous people or those who were well known in a particular field.

Read the following text, which is an extract from an obituary for Sandy West, who was the drummer with a girl band called the Runaways in the 1970s. This obituary appeared in the *Independent* in October 2006.

In 1976, five teenage girls who called themselves the Runaways burst into the music scene with the single 'Cherry Bomb'. They were like the Ramones with added sex appeal and played a proto-punk style of music influenced as much by the hard rock of Led Zeppelin and Kiss as by the glitter sound of Slade and Sweet. Assembled by the musical Svengali Kim Fowley in Los Angeles the previous year, the band – Cherie Currie (vocals), Lita Ford (lead guitar), Joan Jett (rhythm guitar and vocals), Jackie Ford (bass) and Sandy West (drums) – released five albums between 1976 and 1979. With short, sharp songs like 'You Drive Me Wild', 'Born to Be Bad', 'Neon Angels on the Road to Ruin', and 'Wasted', they became cover stars, toured the world, appeared on 'The Old Grey Whistle Test' and played arenas in Japan before imploding after several line-up changes because of bad management.

She [Sandy West] was born Sandy Pesavento in 1960 in Long Beach, California, the most athletic of seven sisters, enjoying surfing and water-skiing. She briefly played the violin but took to drumming with gusto when her grandfather bought her a kit. Her early interest in classical music was soon replaced by an appreciation of Deep Purple, Black Sabbath, Queen and Aerosmith. She started playing live aged thirteen as the only female member of a local band. 'We played very loud music', she told 'Metal Maidens' magazine. 'I was aggressive and I was physical'. The most technically accomplished musician in the Runaways, West had often sung lead vocals on the group's cover of the Troggs' 'Wild Thing'. When she launched the Sandy West Band she sang as well as playing the guitar and drums. West dreamt of a Runaways reunion, which was often mooted but never happened. 'Now that I look back', said West, 'even the rough times were good. How many teenage girls get to do what we did in a lifetime? We used to stick together, go to bat for each other, support each other. A lot of people think all we did was fight with each other but that's not true. We had a lot of great times'.

Pierre Perone

*Sandy Pesavento (Sandy West), drummer, singer, guitarist: born Long Beach, California 10 January 1960; died San Dimas, California 21 October 2006.*

## Activity 12   Looking at obituaries

**Pair work**

1 In pairs, discuss the kind of material that is included in the obituary for Sandy West and the style in which it is written. Who do you think is the audience for this text? Give reasons based on the style and language. Make some notes on your findings and share with the whole group.

The following text offers a different perspective on obituary writing. It is a short extract from an obituary (published in the *Independent*) for Desert Orchid, a famous racehorse who died in November 2006.

2 Read the extract, noting any differences and similarities between the content and style of this text and the obituary for Sandy West.

Compare your responses with the commentary on page 90.

### The Grey Eminence
It wasn't just the colour of his coat that turned Desert Orchid into a racehorse whose popularity verged on the mythic. It was also that his virtues of strength, heart and courage were easily understood and struck a chord with the public at large.

*By Chris McGrath, Racing Correspondent*

### The death of a racing legend
Though he was granted the sort of retirement he deserved, Desert Orchid has for many years already been the Ghost of Christmas Past. Even as he pranced before the stand at Kempton on Boxing Days, paraded in the minutes before the King George VI Chase – skittish and spry as he was, shimmering in the winter sunshine – he had become a spectre. For in the history of jump racing he was long ago assured immortality. He might as well have been carved out of chalk downland.

In winning the race four times he lit up the shortest days of the year like an ancient pagan carnival. When he soared over the last fence, time after time, he was like a cold, white ray of sunshine dependably blazing into a narrow sporting shrine. After all, man has no more primitive need than something to clear his hangover on Boxing Day.

He started his career, and ended it, at Kempton – scene of seven of his 34 wins, and all his most celestial display.

Desert Orchid will be buried a few yards away, near his statue by the parade ring. 'He departed from this world with dignity and no fuss,' his trainer said. 'He did his dying in the same individual way he did his living. It was time to go'.

## Review

In this section you have

- experienced how biography and autobiography are constructed and you have also examined a genre that you may be less familiar with – obituary writing. You will no doubt have noticed that obituaries are like summarised biographies

- been made aware of the different effects achieved by employing different narrative voices.

It is worth remembering the brief explanation on page 61 of use of the first, second and third person as this will help you to identify the narrative voice in other texts.

# Reportage or writing about the real world

In this section you will be exploring

- what reportage means
- different ways of presenting information and of engaging with the audience
- variations in perspective and approach.

'Reportage' can be defined as a journalist's report on and interpretation of an event or problem. Different forms of reportage are

- an eye-witness account reported immediately after the event
- an account written retrospectively based on eye-witness accounts, interviews, etc.
- an account written after the event and based on research
- spontaneous spoken reports on television and radio news
- edited and recorded television and radio programmes.

The best form of reportage is often felt to be the first-hand eye-witness account because of its immediacy and spontaneity, but there are also excellent examples of retrospective accounts.

Reportage often concerns major events and issues that are of global interest. However, it does not have to be about important events. What matters is the quality of the writing and the observation/perception of the writer.

## Activity 13 Reporting on the real world

Text A is an extract from a first-hand account of life with the NATO troops in Afghanistan, written by a journalist who accompanied the troops for 10 days. He recorded his impressions in the form of a diary, published in *The Times* in March 2007.

Text B is an extract from *Imperial Life in the Emerald City* (2007), a book giving an account of life inside the American zone in Baghdad. It was written by a reporter who experienced life in the American zone and is based on interviews and documents.

Work in small groups of three or four. When you have read the texts, record and discuss your immediate impressions of the differences between them. Consider these issues:

- What kind of impact is each writer trying to achieve?
- What do you feel are their motives for writing?
- What can you judge about their attitudes to their subject?
- How is the reader made to feel part of the experience?

Annotate the texts and identify any sentences/phrases you think are particularly effective.

### Text A

**Afghanistan, Front Line**
Talking, waiting, joking, killing … ten days in the Taleban's sights

**Day 1**
Hidden eyes count out the patrol as it leaves J Company base in Geresk. There are few places in which the marines can escape the gaze of the Taleban in Helmand. The watchers will have noticed the armoured Vikings, the .50 calibre machineguns on the Land Rover weapon platforms, the recovery vehicles, the two 105 mm field guns. They will have seen the J Company emblem on the turret cupolas – a grinning death's head in a jester's cap. There are nearly 200 marines in more than 30 vehicles.

They carry with them thousands of litres of fuel and water, artillery shells, mortar bombs, boxloads of grenades and hundreds of thousands of rifle and machinegun rounds. Carried too are 'consent-winning packs': kites, footballs, pencil cases and coloured pens. The aim is to split the insurgent from the local population. The Marines are prepared to talk of peace, to express goodwill, to bid for hearts and minds. They are also ready for war.

I travel in the back of 'Beowulf', the Viking belonging to Corporal 'Tug' Wilson's section. The 12-tonne, all terrain vehicle with two tracked cabs is eulogised. It has survived strikes by mines, rockets and machine gun fire. Yet it is tiny. There are seven of us in the back cab.

**Day 10**
The Taleban are still shooting as the Marines return to their Vikings. As many as twenty insurgents are believed dead, but their rocket fire continues as J Company leaves the ridge. Inside 'Beowulf', the men assess the fight to have been in the 'top five' of those they have had since arriving in Afghanistan last autumn. Then they stop talking, and begin to doze off. Most are still asleep as the patrol returns to base.

'Yeah, that was hoofing in the end', Tug says cheerily, as his men wander away to their tents. 'Another good trip courtesy of Tug Wilson Travel.'

And I wonder whether J Company's luck will hold, whether they will all come back from the next mission.

### Text B

**Inside Baghdad's Green Zone**

Unlike almost anywhere else in Baghdad, you could dine at the cafeteria in the Republican Palace for six months and never eat hummus, flatbread or a lamb kebab. The fare was always American, often with a Southern flavor. A buffet featured grits, cornbread and a bottomless barrel of pork: sausage for breakfast, hot dogs for lunch, pork chops for dinner. There were bacon cheeseburgers, grilled cheese-and-bacon sandwiches, and bacon omelets. Hundreds of Iraqui secretaries and translators who worked for the occupation authority had to eat in the dining hall. Most of them were Muslims, and many were offended by the presence of pork. But the American contractors running the kitchen kept serving it. The cafeteria was all about meeting the American needs for high-calorie, high-comfort food.

When the Americans had arrived there was no cafeteria in the palace. Saddam Hussein had feasted in an ornate private dining room and his servants had eaten in the small kitchenettes. The engineers assigned to transform the palace into the seat of the American occupation chose a marble-floored conference room the size of a gymnasium to serve as the mess hall. They brought in dozens of tables, hundreds of stacking chairs, and a score of glass-covered buffets. Seven days a week, the Americans ate under Saddam's crystal chandeliers.

A mural of the World Trade Center adorned one of the entrances. The Twin Towers were framed within the outstretched wings of a bald eagle.

Each branch of the US military – the army, the air force, marines and navy – had its seal on a different corner of the mural. In the middle were the logos of the New York City Police and Fire departments, and atop the two towers were the words THANK GOD FOR THE COALITION FORCES AT HOME AND ABROAD.

The Kuwaiti sub-contractor had hired dozens of Pakistanis and Indians to cook and serve and clean, but no Iraquis. Nobody ever explained why, but everyone knew. They could poison the food.

When I asked one of the Indians for French fries he snapped: 'We have no French fries here, sir. Only freedom fries.'

The seating was as tribal as that at a high school cafeteria. The Iraqui support staffers kept to themselves. They loaded their lunch trays with enough calories for three meals. Between mouthfuls, they mocked their American bosses with impunity. So few Americans spoke Arabic fluently that those who did could have fitted round one table with room to spare.

Share your findings with the whole group. Then compare them with the commentary on page 91 and the students' responses below.

Here are some extracts from students' responses to these texts followed by an examiner's comments linked to the Assessment Objectives. For a student-friendly version of the AOs, turn to page vii.

### Student's response 1

Texts A and B are connected by the theme of war viewed from the perspective of someone who is not personally involved in the conflict but is there to observe and comment. However, the texts are very different in terms of attitudes and approaches. Both writers are professional journalists but whereas the writer of Text A is travelling with NATO troops in armoured vehicles in Afghanistan, experiencing at first hand the thrills and terrors of warfare, the writer of Text B is describing the routine of life that goes on behind the conflict in Iraq. Presumably the writer of 'Inside Baghdad's Green Zone' has had the opportunity to revise and edit the text as it is from a longer book which was obviously intended for publication. The writer of Text A is using the diary format to record immediate impressions.

In 'Afghanistan, Front Line', the focus is on the military capacity of the troops and the experiences of the soldiers. The writer's use of language choices and structural features reflect this. There is much specialist lexis to describe the weapons and their capability eg, '50 calibre machineguns', '105mm field guns', and numbers are used to make the reader aware of the scale of the operation '200 marines', 'more than 30 vehicles', 'thousands of litres' etc. There are some interesting contrasts and use of juxtaposition throughout the diary eg the troops have 'hundreds and thousands of rifle and machinegun rounds' and 'boxloads of grenades' but they also carry 'consent winning packs' containing children's toys and coloured pencils. I found this particularly moving and emotive. Also the use of abstract nouns like 'peace' and 'goodwill' create a shock effect when they are followed by 'ready for war'.

The reader is also made to feel part of the experience in Text B but this time in a very different way as the setting is the more familiar scene of a cafeteria. The lexical field of food (eg, 'cornbread', 'cheeseburgers', bacon omelets') might have created a comfortable, friendly setting but instead this is used to show divisions between groups in society and lack of cultural understanding. Racial identity is clearly important as the writer selects features of the scene which emphasise American dominance ('mural of the World Trade Center', 'the outstretched wings of a bald eagle') and their insensitivity to the people who live in Iraq eg, 'many were offended by the presence of pork', 'the cafeteria was all about meeting the American needs' all serve to emphasise cultural differences. This contrasts with the approach of the NATO troops in Text A whose mission is 'to bid for hearts and minds'.

The motives and attitudes of the two writers do appear to be very different. In Text A the journalist wants to raise awareness of the conditions in which troops work and to give a flavour of life on the front line with its dangers, fears and moments of humour and humanity eg 'Another good trip courtesy of Tug Wilson Travel'. The conclusion shows the journalist's personal concern for the soldiers he has spent time with 'I wonder whether J Company's luck will hold'.

The intention of the writer of Text B is to criticise the American regime and to show how people of different nationalities are living separate existences within the American zone. Pakistanis and Indians have been employed to cook for the Americans but ironically (it is their country), not Iraqis as 'They could poison the food'.

## Examiner's comments

The introduction makes thematic links and contrasts the approaches of the writers. The answer addresses AO2 by making comments about how ideas in both texts are organised and structured. The texts are compared in some detail and there is clear awareness of the circumstances in which they were written and how this affected the writer's approach, which is needed for AO3. Technical terms have been used appropriately, if economically. A wider range, and possibly more precise use of technical terminology could have given more depth to the analysis but the answer is well illustrated with frequent quotations which are integrated into the discussion.

## Student's response 2

Both texts have a strong impact on the reader. A sinister feeling and sense of tension is created in Text A with the lexical choices relating to surveillance eg 'watchers', 'gaze', 'few places in which the marines can escape'. The writer brings to the foreground the idea of military potential and strength by referring to the names and types of vehicles 'Viking' and 'Beowulf'. These names personify the vehicles and have connotations of aggressive, brutal warfare. The descriptions of the J Company emblem, 'the grinning death's head in a jester's cap', adds a touch of the macabre and a sense of threat. The contrast between 'death's head' and 'jester' seems like an oxymoron as usually a jester is associated with laughter and entertainment.

The writer of Text B is much more satirical (and possibly manipulative) as the writer seems keen to encourage the readers to accept his or her critical view of the Americans occupying Iraq. This is done by using the lexical fields of food and interior design and by making references to the American desire for comfort and prestige. A lot of asyndetic and syndetic listing is used to achieve this and the American sense of national identity is reinforced by the description of the mural with its military seals and logos.

### Examiner's comments
The response identifies some key techniques used to create impact (this is related to AO2 – the effect of the form of a text) and the answer begins to get into some detailed exploration of language, using some appropriate technical terms like 'oxymoron', 'connotations', 'asyndetic listing'.

Contrasts and juxtapositions are noted and commented on. Understanding of the different attitudes of the two writers and how they attempt to affect their readers is demonstrated (AO3).

### Student's response 3
I found Text A much more effective as the writer involves you with the use of present tense, quoted speech and straightforward declarative sentences to convey the scene and atmosphere. As a reader you feel that he or she is just 'telling it how it is', so maybe the writer is more sincere than the writer of Text B. The writer of Text B has a very different intention as he or she is really trying to persuade the reader to agree with a particular point of view. It is difficult to disagree with the writer's viewpoint when we learn that Muslims are 'offended by the presence of pork' and the fact that 'so few Americans spoke Arabic fluently', suggesting their lack of interest in being integrated.

But the writer of Text B must have had the opportunity to edit and re-write the work to create these effects, whereas in Text A the diary extracts seem to be a more spontaneous first impression.

### Examiner's comments
This is an evaluative, personal response which focuses on the relationship between writer and reader (AO3 – how the text is produced and how it affects the audience). The answer would also need to include developed analysis and use of appropriate technical terminology to give secure demonstration of subject knowledge and to gather evidence for AO1 and AO2.

Reading these responses by students should have helped you to see that many different approaches to analysis are possible. The key to a successful analysis of unseen texts is to keep in mind the Assessment Objectives and to read any questions very carefully.

## Historical reportage

Reportage is not a new form of writing: people have always been eager to record first-hand impressions of important events. In 1722, when the Great Plague hit London, Daniel Defoe wrote an eye-witness account of what he saw in his *Journal of the Plague Year*. Text C on page 70 is an extract from this journal.

## Activity 14

Individual

Pair work

### Analysing historical reportage

As you read the journal extract, consider how it is similar to and different from present-day reportage.

Discuss your findings with a partner and then share them with the whole group.

Finally read the commentary on page 91.

**Text C**

The face of London was now indeed strangely altered: I mean the whole mass of buildings, city, liberties, suburbs, Westminster, Southwark, and altogether; for as to the particular part called the city, or within the walls, that was not yet much infected. But in the whole face of things, I say, was much altered; sorrow and sadness sat upon every face; and though some parts were not yet overwhelmed, yet all looked deeply concerned; and as we saw it apparently coming on, so every one looked on himself and his family as in the utmost danger.

London might well be said to be all in tears; the mourners did not go about the streets indeed, for nobody put on black or made a formal dress of mourning for their nearest friends; but the voices of the mourners was truly heard in the streets. The shrieks of women and children at the windows and doors of their houses, where their dearest relations were perhaps dying, or just dead, were so frequent to be heard as we passed the streets, that it was enough to pierce the stoutest heart in the world to hear them. Tears and lamentations were seen almost in every house, especially in the first part of the visitation; for towards the latter end men's hearts were hardened, and death was so always before their eyes, that they did not so much concern themselves for the loss of their friends, expecting that they themselves should be summoned the next hour.

## Activity 15

### Comparing reportage texts

Using a grid with three columns, labelled Text A, Text B and Text C, list the features of the reportage genre for each of these three texts.

You should now be able to write a summary of the characteristic features of the genre of reportage.

Compare your summary with the checklist at the end of the chapter (page 92).

## Activity 16

Individual
Pair work

### Analysing spoken reportage

You can do this as an individual activity or you can carry out the activity in pairs and then share your findings with the rest of the group.

Record and transcribe a short extract from television or radio news. Identify the significant stylistic features of the text and compare with your analysis of written reportage. Make a note of any differences and suggest reasons.

# Popular science

Reportage also includes the type of writing known as popular science, which you are now going to explore.

| Activity 17 | Popular science – fact or fiction? |

The following text is an extract from *Panic Nation* (2005), a book which attacks popular misconceptions about food and health. This type of writing differs from the reportage texts you have just studied as the main concern of the writer here is to convey an argument and there is clear evidence of bias.

**Pair work**

Working in pairs, make notes on the methods used by the writer to convince the reader. You can use the same question prompts as you did for the eye-witness accounts:

- What kind of impact is the writer trying to achieve?
- What do you feel is his motive for writing?
- What can you judge about his attitude to his subject?

Did you find the argument persuasive or convincing? Give reasons based on your exploration of the literary and linguistic techniques used by the writer.

Now share your findings with the rest of the group. Try to establish how successful this text was in persuading members of the group as a whole.

This exploration of persuasive techniques could help you with your own persuasive writing.

Compare your response with the commentary on page 92.

### Junk Food
*by Stanley Feldman*

**The Myth:** A salad is better for you than a Big Mac.
**The Fact:** Many pre-packed salads have more calories than a Big Mac.

The term 'junk food' is an oxymoron. Either something is food, in which case it is not junk, or it has no nutritional value, in which case it cannot be called a food. It can't be both. Ask most people what they understand by the term and they think of McDonald's hamburgers. None of their explanations for why hamburgers are junk food make any sense; rather, they believe hamburgers are the cause of serious health problems because they have been told it is so.

Some rather ill-informed individuals have so convinced themselves of the dangers of hamburgers that they have suggested taxing them. Quite why hamburgers should be singled out as such a threat to out health defies reason. Why should mincing a piece of beef turn it from being a 'good food' into one that is such dangerous 'junk' that it needs to be taxed in order to dissuade people from eating it? What would happen if, instead of mincing the meat, it was chopped into chunks and made into boeuf bourguignon – should it be taxed at only 50 per cent? To try to justify this illogical proposal, these self-appointed food experts tell us that hamburgers contain more fat than a fillet steak. They fail to point out that the ratio of protein to fat in a hamburger is usually higher than in most lamb chops, and that most hamburgers contain less fat than a Sainsbury's Waldorf Salad.

But, that aside, why should the fat be bad? Would these same people like to tax the cheese offered at the end of the meal because, after all, it contains the same basic animal fat as the hamburger?

There is no such thing as junk food. All food is composed of carbohydrate, fat and protein. An intake of a certain amount of each is essential for a healthy life.

There is no doubt that snobbery and cost contributes to the perception of what is termed 'junk'. The term is associated with food originating in the fast food chains of America rather than those coming from 'foody France', home of the croque monsieur and foie gras. For a century, generations of Britons ate fried fish and chips, liberally doused in salt and vinegar, without becoming dangerously overweight. However, when the fish protein is replaced by the meat of the hamburger or Kentucky Fried Chicken, it suddenly becomes a national disaster.

## Activity 18

Group work

# Popular science – whose opinion?

Work in small groups. The writer of *Panic Nation* attempts to undermine the junk-food argument by calling its supporters 'ill-informed'. Does the writer himself provide any facts and figures or expert evidence for his viewpoint? Reread the text and identify any specific provable facts.

You might come to the conclusion that Feldman actually provides very few scientific facts. If so, and you found his argument appealing or convincing, then he must have achieved this by his language strategies.

This exercise should have helped you to consider techniques that you can use in your own persuasive writing.

## Activity 19

Individual

# Exploring spoken reportage

Now extend your exploration of popular science in reportage by reading and analysing the following text. It is an extract from a speech on climate change made by Sir David King, Chief Scientific Advisor to the government, in 2006.

In your analysis you should consider these aspects:

- What are the concerns of the speaker?
- What kind of effect does he intend to have on his audience?
- What are the language devices that he uses to achieve this?
- Remember to think about the cohesion of the text and any foregrounding of particular language features.

Write approximately 250 words for your analysis.

**Key:** Bold type indicates stressed words/phrases.

Climate change is the biggest single global challenge we face. The weight of evidence is now established beyond all reasonable doubt, and the implications for people across the planet will be profound.

We must act, and quickly, both to reduce the future impacts of climate change and to adapt to those impacts that cannot be avoided.

Governments are an **important part of** the solution. However, **everybody** is, in some way, part of the problem and must become part of the solution. We need to produce and consume in smarter ways. We need new and alternative sources of energy, better ways of working with the Earth's resources, more efficient transport of people and goods and a more inclusive **global society.**

**Activity 20**

Group work

## Sharing an investigation

Now work in small groups of three or four. Share your analysis of the text on climate change with other members of the group. You might want to exchange your written versions or even read them aloud.

Add to your own analysis any ideas you have gained by sharing your work.

**Activity 21**

## Comparing spoken and written texts on popular science

Explore further by comparing and contrasting the linguistic and literary techniques used by the writer of the text on junk food (page 71) and the speaker on climate change.

Before attempting any detailed analysis it is a good idea to prepare and plan your work. Start with careful reading and annotating of the texts.

Then collect and categorise your findings either in quick rough notes, a diagram, or using the model grid for analysing texts on page 57.

Here is a grid completed by a student in preparation for analysing the texts on junk food and climate change.

| Text | Junk food | Climate change |
| --- | --- | --- |
| Genre | popular science | popular science |
| Mode | written | spoken |
| Theme | healthy eating | climate change |
| Context | book on issues connected with health and lifestyles | not known |
| Register/formality | relatively formal with threads of informality | formal |

*table continued on page 74*

| Lexis/semantics | diet-food-cultural and lifestyle | the planet – global issues |
|---|---|---|
| Figurative language | metaphorical use of 'national disaster' | not used |
| Tone/attitude | satirical | emotive |
| Phonological features | punctuation used to indicate stress and emphasis | prosodic features – stressed words and phrases |
| Rhetorical features | questions to stimulate thought | forceful declaratives, repetition, listing, inclusive use of 'we' |
| Discourse features/ cohesion | argument and counter-argument, opposition of myth and fact | repetition of key terms, repeated references to climate, states problem then solution |
| Graphological features | layout features of heading and paragraphing | not relevant |

Remember that it may not be necessary to complete every part of the grid and you don't need to note the absence of features in a text unless this is surprising in some way. This type of preparation is intended to be helpful, not restrictive, so be brave and only choose for your full analysis the features that you consider to be relevant and significant.

## Activity 22 Write up your comparison

Using your grid, notes or diagram prepared in Activity 21, write up your comparison of the literary and linguistic approaches used in these texts. Use these questions to guide you:

- What does the use of language reveal about the apparent attitudes and values of the writer and speaker?
- Did you find either of the texts powerful and persuasive in any way? (Give reasons based on the use of language.)

To complete the activity read the commentary on page 92.

## Review

In this section you have

- been introduced to different types of reportage in both spoken and written modes
- explored historical reportage, and investigated the blending of fact and persuasion in reportage texts
- developed and extended your analytical skills by analysing and comparing texts and by reading the responses of other students

These activities should have increased your awareness of the complexity and diversity of the genre of reportage.

# Travel writing

In this section you will be looking at different types of travel writing and the possible approaches to the genre. Travel articles, travel guides and travelogues or travel journals are becoming increasingly popular as a genre both to read and to write. They often provide informative, entertaining reading and an insight into other people's lives and cultures.

**Activity 23**

**Pair work**

## The travel guide – informing and entertaining

Read the following extract from the *Rough Guide to New York City* (2002). Then work in pairs to make notes on

- the details that are factual
- the descriptive sections
- the parts that express the opinions of the writers
- the narrative voice.

Compare your notes with the commentary on page 93.

### SoHo

The grid of streets that lies between Houston and Canal streets, and roughly between Sixth Avenue and Lafayette Street, **SoHo** – short for South of Houston – has come to mean fashion, chic, urbane shopping, cosmopolitan galleries and cast-iron facades. High end chains attract hordes of tourists, making it difficult on weekends to navigate the neighbourhood; nevertheless, SoHo is a grand place to brunch at an outside café or for poking in and out of chichi antique art and clothes shops. Because SoHo is the place to see and be seen, people are decked out to the nines and some of the best people watching in the city is here.

Houston Street (pronounced Howston rather than Hewston) marks the top of SoHo's trellis of streets. Greene Street is as good a place to start as any, highlighted along by the nineteenth-century cast iron facades that in part, if not on the whole, saved SoHo from the bulldozers.

The #W, #Q and #F trains all go to the Broadway-Lafayette stop, the #6 stops at Spring Street, the #N and #R stop at Prince Street and the #1 and #9 stop at Houston.

**Activity 24**

## A sense of place

The next text is an extract from *At Home and Abroad* by V.S. Pritchett (1989), in which he describes his stay in the Brazilian port of Salvador.

**Group work**

Working in small groups:

- discuss the effect of the writer's use of the first person
- decide to what extent you feel this is a factual account or the writer's personal response to the atmosphere of the place
- discuss whether you would include the text in the guidebook sub-genre. Give reasons for your decision.

Groups should present their conclusions and then reach agreement on the primary purpose of the text.

Compare your responses with the commentary on page 93.

> Salvador is a town of churches and old doorways, of gramophone shops that blare out sambas and tangos all day while the crowd hangs round the doorways listening. The population is chiefly Negro or mulatto. It is a place of cotton frocks, beauty parlours, barbershops. White trousers, white shirts, white frocks, everywhere, give these places a littered appearance. In the superb blue and steaming bay, the steep-prowed fishing boats in the Portuguese style come in with their lateen sails; and the purple pineapples, the bananas, the mangoes, and the innumerable other fruits are heaped in the market and carried in baskets on yokes in the street. We never, in the north, eat pineapples like these, without acid or stringiness, as soft as scented water ices to the mouth. The Brazilian picks out his mango and smells it first, as if he were pausing to accept or reject the bouquet of a wine, making sure it has just the right, faint exhalation of the curious turpentinelike fragrance. In tropical countries, the scents and savours of the fruits are a refined pleasure of the senses. They are like wines in their vintages; indeed the fruit of South America is really the wine of the country, and the juices offered at the stalls belong to a world of natural soft drinks that is closed to palates hardened by alcohol. For myself, though I cannot drink the sweet Guarana which is consumed all over Brazil, I find the dry Guarana sold in the Amazon delicious. Most of the whiskey in South America, by the way, is a swindle, the gin deserves only to be drowned, the lager beer is excellent and the various vodka-like fire waters are for desperation.

By contrast with the V.S. Pritchett extract, here is an extract from *Holidays in Hell*, by an American writer, P.J. O'Rourke, in which he recounts his experiences of travelling in Europe.

### Among the Euro-Weenies
#### April–May 1986

The Europeans are going to have to feather their nests with somebody else's travellers cheques this year. The usual flock of American pigeons is crapping on statues elsewhere. Sylvester Stallone canned the Cannes Film Festival. Prince won't tour this side of the sink. The US junior Wimbledon team is keeping its balls on the home court. And transatlantic rubber-neck bookings have taken a dive. Some say it's fear of terrorism. Some say it's Chernobyl fall-out. Some say it's the weak dollar. But all of that ignores one basic fact. This place sucks.

I've been over here for one grey, dank, spring month now, and I think I can tell you why everyone with an IQ bigger than his hat size hits the beach at Ellis Island. Say what you want about 'land of opportunity', our forebears moved to the United States because they were sick to death of lukewarm beer – and lukewarm coffee and lukewarm bathwater and lukewarm mystery cutlets with mucky-coloured mushroom cheese junk on them. Everything in Europe is lukewarm except the radiators. You could use the radiators to make party ice.

The Europeans can't figure out which side of the road to drive on, and I can't figure out how to flush their toilets. Plus, there are ruins everywhere. The Italians have had over two thousand years to fix up the Forum and just look at the place.

I've had it with dopey little countries and all their pokey borders. Everything's too small. The cars are too small. The beds are too small. The elevators are the size of broom closets. Even the languages are itty-bitty. Sometimes you need two or three to get you through till lunch.

## Activity 25 — Points of view

In small groups compare the texts by Pritchett and O'Rourke. You may find it helpful to use the grid for analysing and comparing texts (see page 57).

- What contrasts do you detect in the level of formality and register?
- Do these differences seem to reflect any difference in the purposes of each text?
- How does each writer convey their attitudes to the reader?
- What would you say are the defining characteristics of the style of each writer?

Compare your grid or notes with the following extract from a student's response to these texts and read the examiner's comments. There is also a commentary on page 93.

### Student's response

Pritchett's text begins with the name of the place foregrounded, 'Salvador is a town of churches'. This immediately creates atmosphere and prepares us for a descriptive piece of writing. Pritchett draws heavily on lexis which has sensuous effects and connotations of abundance e.g. 'scents and savours', 'blare out sambas and tangos'. Colour is everywhere: 'blue and steaming bay'. Descriptions are enriched with pre- and post-modification and descriptive adjectives e.g. 'steep-prowed fishing boats in the Portuguese style', 'scented water ices', 'curious turpentine-like flavour'.

Asyndetic listing is used to accumulate detail and set the scene, which becomes almost like a painting e.g. 'the purple pineapples, the bananas, the mangoes'. There are many phonological effects, for example, the repetition of 'white' in 'white trousers, white shirts, white frocks' has a rhythmic effect, as does the soothing sibilance of 'scents and savours'.

Pritchett's style is mainly formal, with complex grammatical constructions and polysyllabic lexis but he does lower the formality and slips into a more colloquial register with 'the whiskey ... is a swindle'. He also shows his irritation, which contrasts with his earlier appreciative mood, with 'the gin deserves only to be drowned'.

Pritchett's text does not seem to be in the genre of travel guide as it does not provide any practical information. It is really a record of his impressions; the pace is leisurely and would take time to read so it does not have the quick impact of a travel guide like the Rough Guide series.

His writing is very literary with his use of adjectives and phonological effects. His purpose would seem to be to entertain and capture the imagination of the audience, almost as if he had painted a picture. This suggests that his book is in the genre of travel journals.

'Among the Euro-Weenies' has very little in common with Pritchett's text except that they are both records of personal experiences and impressions and are both written in the first person.

P. J. O'Rourke takes a completely different approach. He is describing a whole continent rather than one specific town so his comments are wide-ranging and over generalised. His purpose is clearly to entertain and not to be taken seriously as he adopts a humorous, satirical approach which relies on stereotypes of nationalities and cultures: 'The Europeans can't figure out which side of the road to drive on'. His intention is to amuse rather than offend as he presents himself as the stereotypically thick American tourist with his observations on Rome ie, 'The Italians have had over two thousand years to fix up the Forum and just look at the place'. O'Rourke's style is informal, colloquial and, at times, crude in contrast with Pritchett's poetic descriptions. He begins his article with a neologism in the headline, the 'Euro-Weenies',

'Weenies' suggests a derogatory term. He continues this approach in his listing of criticisms: like Pritchett he uses repetition but as a kind of refrain of complaint rather than for descriptive purposes ie, 'lukewarm beer', 'lukewarm coffee' 'lukewarm mystery cutlets'. He uses an expletive in 'crapping on statues' and an American colloquialism, 'sucks'.

Like Pritchett, he does use phonological effects, but to amuse and add humour e.g. 'canned the Cannes film festival'. He also uses the metaphor of the American tourists as pigeons. O'Rourke's style does resemble spoken language, rather like that of a stand-up comedian, e.g. there is a dramatic pause with 'Plus, there are ruins everywhere'.

O'Rourke's text is not useful as a guide book, even less so than Pritchett's, so it could also be classified as a travel journal, but really it is just a piece of satirical writing which takes travel as the theme.

### Examiner's comments
This answer targets all the Assessment Objectives.

There is an understanding of how literary and linguistic features are used to create effects and of how texts are organised (AO2).

There is some discussion of genre and 'literary' writing (AO1).

Technical terminology is used appropriately and where it helps the analysis (AO1), but notice that it is not used excessively or repetitively.

There is some comparison and contrast between the two texts (AO3) and a thoughtful discussion of the possible intentions of the two writers.

The audience for this response is, of course, the examiner, and the level of formality, tone and vocabulary are all suitable (AO4).

There is some discussion of phonological effects, which shows understanding of the differences between written and spoken forms of language. Short quotations are included at regular intervals to illustrate the argument.

Analysis always needs quotation to add support, to make a point clear or to illustrate a technique, but it is important to use short, apt quotations rather than lengthy sentences.

## Activity 26
**Pair work**

## Exploring the historical travel journal

In pairs, discuss what you think are the defining characteristics of the following extract from Charles Darwin's *The Voyage of The Beagle*. In what ways is his approach similar to or different from that of P.J. O'Rourke and V.S. Pritchett? Is this linked to his purpose?

Share your findings with the rest of the group.

A commentary on this text can be found on page 93.

### December 6

The *Beagle* sailed from the Rio Plato, never again to enter its muddy stream. Our course was directed to Port Desire, on the coast of Patagonia. Before proceeding any further, I will here put together a few observations made at sea.

Several times when the ship had been some miles off the mouth of the Plata, and at other times when off the shores of Northern Patagonia, we have been surrounded by insects. One evening, when we were about ten miles from the Bay of San Blas, vast numbers of butterflies, in bands or flocks of countless myriads, extended as far as the eye could range. Even by the aid of a telescope it was not possible to see the space free from butterflies. The seamen cried out 'it was snowing butterflies', and in fact such was the appearance. More species than one were present, but the main part belonged to a kind very similar to, but not identical with, the common English *Colias edusa*. Some moths and hymenoptera accompanied the butterflies; and a fine beetle (*Calosoma*) flew on board. Before sunset a strong breeze sprung up from the north, and this must have caused tens of thousands of the butterflies and other insects to perish.

## Review

After your exploration of the three texts in this section you should be aware of the many possible perspectives, purposes and styles of travel writing, the attitudes of writers to their subject and the different methods they employ to convey a sense of place to their readers.

The genre of travel also includes television and radio programmes, which tend to be a blend of information, personal experiences and travel tips.

Spoken texts in different genres are explored more fully in the next section.

# Spoken texts

Most of the genres you have explored can be found in the spoken as well as the written mode. In this section you will explore two different forms of spoken texts. The issues to consider are:

- To what extent are the texts spontaneous, edited, pre-planned or carefully crafted?
- What are the motives of the speaker?
- Who is the target audience?
- What effect is the speaker trying to achieve?

## The interview

## Activity 27 Investigating spoken texts

**Pair work**

Read the following two texts then, in pairs, explore them, using the questions above as your prompts.

- Text A is part of a transcript of an interview with the artist Andy Warhol which was part of a television documentary in 1973. The interviewer is David Bailey, a well-known fashion photographer.

■ Text B is an interview with the rap artist Snoop Dogg which appeared in a newspaper music supplement in 2007.

Share your findings with the rest of the group and try to establish the main differences between the two types of interview.

Compare your response with the commentary on page 94.

### Text A

| Key | W | Warhol | **Bold type** | stressed word/syllable |
|---|---|---|---|---|
| | B | Bailey | ..... | unfinished utterance |
| | (.) | micropause | [   ] | paralinguistic feature |
| | (3) | timed pause (in seconds) | | |

W  I was working on shoes (.) and (.) er (.) I got (.) er thirteen dollars a shoe (.) so (.) I could (.) I had to think in terms of thirteen dollars so everytime they (.) er (.) gave me a shoe (.) you know (.) every twenty shoes to do (.) that was thirteen times twenty

B  but (.) there wasn't some sort of **message** (.) I mean (.) there wasn't a message

W  no (.) there's no message

B  so (.) there's no (.) no social thing about suddenly choosing Elvis Presley

W  [shaking head] no (3) it could have been a shoe
[background laughter of female voices]

B  but why (.) why Elvis Presley (.) [female laughter] why did you suddenly pick on poor Elvis Presley

W  er (2) I'm trying to think [puts fingers to lips] (3) well (.) I didn't really pick on him

B  you did Marlon Brando also

W  I did Marlon Brando also

B  you did Elvis Presley first

W  er (.)

B  was it a childhood (.) I mean (.) when you were (.) say (.) six or seven (.) did you have fantasies about being......

W  no (.) I was more of an attorney [female laughter]

B  but (.) did you have fantasies (.) there's some questions here [consults sheet of paper] what were your fantasies when you were a child (.) was Elvis Presley your fantasy

W  no (.) I played with dolls

### Text B

#### Doggedly defiant

*As he works on his 15th album, Snoop Dogg is unfazed by his bad-boy image.*
*Matilda Egere-Cooper talks to the rapper*

Whoever said you can't teach an old dog new tricks obviously hadn't been introduced to Snoop Dogg. It's been an integral part of his surprisingly lengthy career – that is, the ability to evolve his music in an instant, branch out in new directions (Hollywood), and take on new ventures (marijuana-flavoured candy, anyone?).

At his small West Hollywood apartment, he's doing what he does best, with Teddy, a mild-mannered producer, who's fiddling around on a laptop, while, on another PC, there's a nerdy-looking kid.

A simple but catchy soul melody blasts from the speakers and Snoop rocks his head as he sings the chorus: 'It's the Hollywood night – it's gonna be crazy!' He starts to dance around in his seat. It's a track that may or may not be on his forthcoming album, *Ego Trippin*, which he feels makes a very timely statement.

'I'm at the point in my career where I'm just ego-tripping,' he drawls, with a little irony. 'I got an ego, I can do what I wanna do, and I can make the kinds of songs I wanna make. I don't have to do the regular or the normal. I can step out of the box and do it my way because I'm ego-tripping and it's just what I'm on right now'.

Who can blame him? Snoop has been making records for 14 years; he's been iconic since the moment his debut, *Doggystyle*, sold more than four million copies Stateside

Throughout that time, he has been heralded as one of the purveyors of gangsta-rap, spouting his grimy testimonials with a mesmerising drawl that's his own personal X-factor. As he puts it, some hits like Pharrell's *Drop It Like It's Hot* or Akon's *I Wanna Love You*, just wouldn't be that great if he wasn't in the mix.

## The political persuasive speech

In the next activity you will be examining cohesion: the means a writer or speaker uses to link a text together. Cohesion is achieved by deliberate choices of language to create patterns.

Cohesion is a key feature of any text which aims to inspire and motivate the audience. (See page 40 for more on cohesion.) A good example is the following text, which is an extract from a speech made by Winston Churchill in 1946 when he was the British Prime Minister. His speech features his concerns about the growing divisions between Western powers and the Soviet Union. It marked the beginning of the period that became known as the Cold War. Churchill delivered his speech in the United States.

The United States stands at this time at the pinnacle of world power. It is a solemn moment for the American democracy. For with this primacy in power is also joined an awe-inspiring accountability to the future. As you look around you, you must feel not only the sense of duty done, but also you must feel anxiety lest you fall below the level of achievement...

Opportunity is here now, clear and shining, for both our countries. To reject it or ignore it or fritter it away will bring upon us all the long reproaches of the aftertime.

It is necessary that constancy of mind, persistency of purpose, and the grand simplicity of decision shall rule and guide the conduct of the English-speaking peoples in peace as they did in war. We must, and I believe we shall, prove ourselves equal to this severe requirement.

I have a strong admiration and regard for the valiant Russian people and for my wartime comrade, Marshal Stalin. There is deep sympathy and goodwill in Britain – and I doubt not here also – toward the peoples of all the Russias and a resolve to persevere through many differences and rebuffs in establishing lasting friendships...

Last time I saw it all coming and I cried aloud to my own fellow countrymen and to the world, but no one paid any attention. Up till the year 1933 or even 1935, Germany might have been spared from the awful fate which has overtaken her and we might all have been spared the miseries Hitler let loose upon mankind.

There never was a war in history easier to prevent by timely action than the one which has just desolated such great areas of the globe. It could have been prevented, in my belief, without the firing of a single shot, and Germany might be powerful, prosperous and honoured today; but no one would listen and one by one we were all sucked into the awful whirlpool.

| **Activity 28** | **Rhetoric and persuasion** |
| --- | --- |

1   Work in small groups. One member of the group should read Churchill's speech on page 81 aloud while the others listen.

2   Make a quick note of your immediate impressions of the language Churchill uses to convey his message.

3   Read the text carefully and analyse it more closely to find the patterns of language. You will find it useful to divide your analysis under these headings:
   - patterns of grammar
   - lexical patterns
   - patterns of phonology in the sound and rhythm of the language
   - use of figurative and literary language.

4   When you have completed your group analysis share your findings with the rest of the class and add any additional features to your group work.

You should now have produced a substantial analysis of the text.

Compare your analysis with the commentary on page 94.

| **Activity 29** | **Investigating patterns of language** |
| --- | --- |

You can now extend your analysis of Churchill's speech by exploring the intended effect of its patterns of language. You should also evaluate whether or not you think the text is effective, giving reasons based on the language used.

Return to your small groups to carry out this evaluation and then share your ideas with the rest of the class.

### Suggestions for further work

To extend your analysis of rhetorical, persuasive speeches, here are two more extracts from speeches made by twentieth-century leaders.

- Text A is an extract from a speech made by Tony Blair at the Labour Party Conference in 1997 after winning the general election.

- Text B is an extract from a speech made in 1962 by John F Kennedy, President of the United States, on the American launch of a spacecraft to Venus.

**Text A**

A Beacon to the World

It has been a very long time waiting for this moment and all I can tell you is that after eighteen long years of Opposition, I am deeply proud – privileged – to stand before you as the new Labour Prime Minister of our country.

I believe in Britain. I believe in the British people. One cross on the ballot paper. One nation was reborn.

Today, I want to set an ambitious course for this country: to be nothing less than the model twenty-first-century nation, a beacon to the world. It means drawing deep into the richness of the British character. Creative. Compassionate. Outward-looking. Old British values but a new British confidence.

We can never be the biggest. We may never again be the mightiest. But we can be the best. The best place to live. The best place to bring up children, the best place to lead a fulfilled life, the best place to grow old.

**Text B**

## The Space Challenge

We meet in an hour of change and challenge, in a decade of hope and fear; in an age of both knowledge and ignorance. The greater our knowledge increases the greater our ignorance unfolds.

Despite the striking fact that most of the scientists the world has ever known are alive and working today, despite the fact that this Nation's own scientific manpower is doubling every 12 years in a rate of growth more than three times that of our population as a whole, despite that, the vast stretches of the unknown and the unanswered and the unfinished still far outstrip our collective consciousness.

And now if America's new spacecraft succeeds in reaching Venus, we will have literally reached the stars before midnight tonight. This is a breathtaking pace and such a pace cannot help but create ills as it dispels old, new ignorance, new problems, new dangers.

## Activity 30 | Analysing rhetorical speeches

Group work

Working in small groups, look back at the list of headings on page 82 that you used to guide your analysis of the speech by Winston Churchill in Activity 28. Use a similar approach to explore Texts A and B.

What are the features of rhetorical speaking that each speaker has used?

As in Activity 28, you might find it useful to have a member of the group read the texts aloud. Then read and annotate the texts individually. Share your findings with the rest of the group.

Turn to the commentary on page 95 for a checklist of rhetorical and stylistic features of spoken texts.

## Review

In this section you have explored in some detail spoken texts in two different genres:
- the interview
- the persuasive speech.

Remember that spoken texts do not form a separate genre but simply adopt a different mode from written texts. All of the genres you encounter in this chapter and in the course of your studies could easily appear as spoken texts.

# Subverting genre or texts with traps

In this section you will explore how and why producers of texts imitate other genres to create particular effects.

'Subvert' means to challenge accepted rules and ideas. Writers and speakers sometimes choose to challenge the accepted rules of a genre to attract the attention of their audience by presenting their message in an unexpected way. In the following activity you will examine how and why text producers subvert the accepted conventions of genre and you will consider the possible effects on their target audiences.

## Activity 31 — Misleading the reader

**Pair work**
**Group work**

Work in pairs or small groups. Read Texts A and B below then discuss these questions.

1 When you began reading the texts which genres would you have chosen to classify them as? Give reasons based on the genre conventions apparently followed by each text.

2 At what point in each text did you realise that the usual genre conventions were not being followed?

3 Why do you think that the text producers have chosen to subvert the genre conventions in this way?

Now read the commentary on page 95.

---

### Text A

**PRODUCT RECALL**
Due to the alarming number of incidents of sexual harassment of men, we have decided to withdraw batch 4379-4381. Lynx apologises to any men who have had their bottoms pinched or have experienced women making overly suggestive comments. However, if this kind of behaviour does not bother you, feel free to hold on to your can.
**THE LYNX EFFECT**

---

### Text B

**My Secret Affair**
*Last December we moved to a new house. Our milkman was very kind and helpful, making us feel most welcome. One day I invited him in, and we sat on the couch in the living room. Well ... one thing led to another, and before we knew it, that other thing led to something else. It's now being going on for over three months. Then last Thursday, as he was quietly leaving the house, the gate suddenly fell off its hinges, causing a terrific noise. All the neighbours heard the commotion and I'm sure the rumours are spreading already. What should I do?*

*Jayne*

Well, Jayne, there are two things you can do: either replace the old gate (any good local DIY store will have an extensive range of wood or wrought iron designs). Or why not try a lick of new paint? It's amazing how something old can be given a new lease of life. Or, there again, try a cup of 99 tea. It won't do your gate much good, but who cares anyway?

## Activity 32

**Pair work**

# Analysing texts with traps

Working in pairs, read and analyse the next two texts using the same method as you followed in Activity 31.

Compare your analysis with the commentary on page 96.

### Text A

### A postcard from Iceland

Glacial landscapes, volcanoes and geysers – Iceland is widely regarded as a beautiful country. But do you really think an agitated adolescent like me gives a monkey about such things?

Foreign journalists get over excited about the rural splendours of this land of ice and snow. And I could say the same thing about the local music scene. The story about the originality and purity of Icelandic music is the result of a misguided media frenzy. Before punk, Icelandic music was dull and sterile – in the Sixties, rock'n'roll bands mimicked the Beatles, and in the Seventies Pink Floyd.

In the Eighties there was an explosion of talent. Punk bands such as Peyr, Purrker Pilnick and Kukl felt like a breath of fresh air. Members of these groups formed Bad Taste Records and the Sugarcubes. I was only three when they split in 1992, but I gather there were lots of stories in the British press at the time about Icelanders eating puffin – as if that's weird. We think it's weird that the English eat fish and chips from a newspaper.

*Gunner Ragnarsson – lead singer with Jakobinarina*

### Text B

For Serefa, it was like prayer. She surrendered completely and was cured.

Serefa closed her eyes as Vijaya massaged the warm golden oil into her back in slow, rhythmic movements. Around her, flowers danced. The smell of the oil and ethereal fragrance of the incense were soothing. This was the last day of the fourteen day ayurvedic holiday. Fourteen delightful days of rejuvenating regimens, medicated baths and herbal diets. Fourteen days that wiped away a five-year-old backache. Put the confidence back in her stride. The dance back in her limbs. Youth back in her life. And a smile back on her lips. As Serena packed her bags she knew that Kerala had become an integral part of her life, where she would return year after year to revitalise her body, mind and soul.

Kerala – God's Own Country

## Activity 33

# Genre blending

The following text has many features of a travelogue yet it was included in a survey of Britain's motorways published in the *Guardian* (January 2007). Read the text and note the features that are reminiscent of a travelogue. You might find it helpful to review the texts you analysed in the travel-writing section (pages 75–79).

Share your findings with a partner.

### M11
### The Mysterious one

The M11 is like life. It starts mysteriously and ends at a crematorium. The M11 is a mystery because it doesn't start at Junction 1 like sensible motorways, but at Junction 4.

So, we start at Junction 4, sweeping majestically off the North Circular's multi-lane pomp into a near-death experience. Traffic from east London is soon trying to merge into us. A concrete mixer, twirling its Jim'll Mix It logo, overtakes us. The journey starts hopefully: only later will our spirits be crushed.

The flags are out and flapping at Birchanger services (the only place for legal pees and cups of tea on the M11). They advertise a new Sainsbury's outlet (goody!) and a £7.99 meal at KFC (I'd rather force-feed my children broken glass). The air is gag-makingly thick with Burger King beef fumes. We plump for the Coffee Primo concession where my blueberry muffin looks like underlay and tastes of nothing. The cappuccino is hot and may contain coffee.

Back on the M11, three lanes go down to two and as a result we get stuck behind lorries struggling up unexpectedly big hills. Unseen, there is a beautiful England out there. We will not see it today because we've made a solemn commitment to see the M11 through to the bitter end. At Junction 10, we cannot leave. Nor can we leave at Junctions 11, 12 or 13, even though we desperately want the civilization that Cambridge may offer. Then there is a sign to a crematorium and another to an immigration centre. The M11 has not died with a bang but with the promise of death or forced repatriation. We do a u-turn and head for Cambridge, for a decent lunch and to forget.

*Worst place to eat: Burger King*
*Best place to eat: in your car*
*Best place to stay: your only option is the services, best keep driving.*

## Review

In this section you have explored texts which subvert genre conventions or break the rules of genre in some way.

Many texts do blend elements of other texts and borrow from other genres in order to increase their appeal and to make them more accessible to their audiences. For example, travelogues frequently involve autobiographical elements, popular science and historical accounts draw on the conventions of storytelling, often adopting an approach which resembles a fictional narrative. A very popular approach in advertising is to use the mock-fiction genre (like Text B in Activity 32).

As well as being aware of subversions of genre you should also look out for texts which involve genre-blending.

**Commentary**

**Activity 1**

Features that place the texts in the genre of a personal diary:

- layout and graphology – dates, headings
- first-person pronoun creates personal perspective
- purpose mainly non-serious
- informality in style and situation
- elliptical – omits grammatical items
- time markers – date before diary entry (Text A), 'yesterday' (Text B), 'It has been two weeks' (Text C), 'Last year' (Text D)
- colloquial spoken effect – frequent use of commas and dashes (Text A), 'No it's not' (Text B), 'Hurrah ... Bring it on' (Text C), 'Thank God', 'Yes, I feel it' (Text D)
- topics concerned with everyday life or general observations
- assumption of shared knowledge – Sonny's wedding (Text A), 'announced Todd' (Text B)
- private references to people/situations known to the writer – 'we went', 'one of the halls' (Text A), 'Todd' (Text B)
- cultural/lifestyle references – 'MEP' (Text B), 'Ucas', 'Personal Statement' (Text C), 'Everything in 2006 seemed to be about waiting for it to happen' suggest on-going interaction.

**Public or private reading?**
All four texts seem to have been written for a wider audience. Text B, as a weblog, is clearly intended for a very wide public audience.

Texts A and C both show evidence of planning with structured and regular paragraphing and clear pointers to topic changes.

All employ interactive or rhetorical features to create effect – 'Chastity was the flower girl, she was kind of tall' (Text A), 'but why, oh why, can not someone inform me?' (Text B), 'Hurrah', 'Blood, guts and awkward silences' (Text C), 'Thank God it's 2007' (Text D) .

All try to establish a friendly rapport with their potential readers and assume shared understanding.

**Commentary**

**Activity 2**

Features that create the effect of spoken language:

- ellipsis – 'I've', 'I'm off'
- omission of grammatical items – 'Up at nine' (Text A), 'Just hearing the word' (Text C)
- non-standard expressions and clichés – 'to hang out' (Text A), 'Daylight robbery' (Text B), 'like a headless chicken' (Text C), 'It was like' (Text D)
- adverbs/adverbial phrases create a colloquial, spoken effect
- adjectives/adverbs used as intensifiers (words used deliberately to add emphasis)
- use of exclamations/questions
- use of minor sentences (sentences or utterances that omit one of the usual grammatical elements – 'Very odd!')
- imitation of dialogue.

**Commentary**

**Activity 3**

- Texts A and C are planned and structured with regular paragraphing and indications of topic shifts in a clear narrative framework.
- Texts B and D both give the impression of spontaneity and free association of ideas.
- All four texts attempt to develop a personal voice and to entertain the reader in some way – Texts A, B and C use personal anecdotes, Text D is more abstract and reflective.

**Commentary**

**Activity 6**

You may have found this review of the Babyshambles concert a surprisingly complex text as it is packed with literary and cultural references. This can be referred to as intertextuality, which means that the writer of a text refers either explicitly or by implication to other texts, genres, concepts, etc.

Doherty is compared with the poet Byron (notorious for his outrageous behaviour) and to the pied piper of the legend. Figurative language is used in describing his lyrics and music – cookery ('out of the oven half-baked'), fashion ('high fashion and the jumble sale') and a world after a nuclear war ('post-fallout'). The writer has mainly done this to give a satirical tone and (possibly) to demonstrate his own knowledge. The writer clearly assumes an educated, literate audience as the reader is expected to understand these references.

The language used reflects the writer's 'voice' and attitude to Doherty which is highly critical and suggests that he feels that Doherty's fame is not deserved – for example, describing his lyrics as 'doodles on scraps of paper'.

To set the text in context, it appeared in the *Independent*, which is regarded as a 'quality' newspaper.

**Commentary**

**Activity 7**

The genres of the texts are clearly different. So are their purposes as Bennett is recording his impressions of an event and the impact it had on him and the people around him immediately after it happened, whereas Ono is deliberately writing a persuasive text with a message some time after the event with the intention of raising awareness of wider issues.

If we explore the tone of the texts we can see that Bennett's diary extract is both personal and relatively informal: there are abbreviations, parenthetical statements for economy and some indication of assumed shared knowledge – 'the Odeon', 'WNEW'.

We can speculate about whether Bennett originally intended the diary to be published, although as he is a well-known playwright this is likely. There are also clues in the writing to suggest it is aimed at a wide audience – the inclusion of dialogue, the very atmospheric descriptive writing which creates the tension of the scene, such as the 'warm, windy night' and 'candles burning in windows'.

There are dramatic elements in the writing with the description of the 'vigil', the references to the 'slayer' and the quotations from news bulletins providing a background commentary. You may feel that these features relate to Bennett's profession as a playwright.

Bennett appears to be more interested in the reactions of others than in the murder itself and he conveys impressions of New Yorkers both explicitly '(hardly bothering to conceal their appetite for tragedy)' and more implicitly through the comment of the waiter 'This country of ours'.

The waiter's rapid shift of topic to 'May I tell you the specials for this evening?' adds a touch of bathos (the technique of moving rapidly from a serious tone to one which is more trivial).

In contrast Ono's text is an interesting sub-genre as it is a persuasive speech disguised superficially as a letter, which gives it a personal touch. This is an interesting text to analyse as a rhetorical text which, although written, captures the style of the spoken voice.

Ono has made her text sound like a prayer or litany by using the following features:

- syntactic parallelism or repetition of the same grammatical element to create patterning – 'To the people who have also lost loved ones', 'To the soldiers of all countries', 'To the civilians who were maimed'
- direct address to her audience
- inclusive use of 'Let's' and 'ours'
- use of imperative sentences.

It is reflective in tone and employs much emotive, abstract lexis – 'healed', 'suffered', 'forgiveness'.

**Commentary**

**Activity 8**

You may have noticed these features:

- factual details include dates, places, occupations
- the opinion and perspective of the biographer appear in the more colourful details such as 'He came crying into the world', and the speculation that Dickens had a strange association with his characters.

Ackroyd deliberately imitates Dickens' style of using parallel, antithetical grammatical structures to create effect in the phrase 'the year of victory and the year of hardship', which reflects the opening of Dickens' novel *A Tale of Two Cities*.

Ackroyd aims to make his narrative appealing by injecting moments of intrigue – 'Friday became for him a day of omen' and 'this strange association'. These features should encourage readers to continue as it is implied that there was something curious and fascinating about Dickens' own life.

**Commentary**

**Activity 9**

Like Ackroyd, Fraser grounds her narrative in fact by using dates and geographical locations but she also adds atmosphere by evoking extreme weather conditions and by linking these symbolically to the political feelings at the time. She uses literary devices of personification 'Scotland … groaned', and she creates vivid descriptions with her choice of adjectives – 'tempestuous weather', 'heavy snow-falls', 'stark conditions'. All of this creates a much more interesting read.

It may interest you to know that Antonia Fraser is also known for writing novels in the crime genre. As with Ackroyd's text, you will no doubt be able to identify features which are reminiscent of novel-writing.

**Commentary**

**Activity 11**

You may have been intrigued by the difference in the titles. Text A uses the words 'unwanted' and 'Chinese', reinforcing the autobiographical element, whereas Text B uses 'secret' and 'Cinderella', making a link with fairy tales.

Text A sets the story within the political, cultural and geographical context, using Chinese names which might be unfamiliar to a western audience, and looks back to an earlier generation in describing the story of the author's grand-aunt, which suggests a historical approach – 'She was born in Shanghai … in 1886 during the Quing dynasty'.

Text B, in contrast, focuses more specifically on the personal life of the author ('As soon as I got home from school') and describes an episode from her schooldays which is retold mainly through dialogue.

There is personal and domestic detail: children may find the descriptions of her aunt's jewellery box appealing – 'jade bracelet, pearl necklace and diamond watch'.

If you examine the sentence structure you will find that both versions use a variety of sentence types, including complex sentences. It is often assumed that texts written for children should concentrate on simple sentences but children's writing also needs some complexity in the sentence structure. In Text B the use of dialogue makes the event seem more immediate.

There is a contrast in Yen Mah's choice of lexical field: in Text A she uses lexis which is specific to the Chinese context ('Quing dynasty, 'Kuang Hsu, 'Ye Ye'), whereas in Text B the lexical choices create a domestic scenario and describe the precious stones and jewellery.

**Commentary**

**Activity 12**

You will have noticed that West's obituary concentrates on the highlights of her professional career and her achievements, with a chronological overview of her life. The style resembles that of a biography (third-person narrative, past tense) with a lexical field related to her career. Much of the lexis is context bound and specialist, which should have helped you to identify the potential audience. The inclusion of a quotation adds authenticity.

Desert Orchid is treated as a person and is given impressive human qualities with the use of abstract nouns – 'strength', 'heart', 'courage'.

Literary techniques are used to create the idea of a legend: for example, simile and metaphor, literary references and lexis related to the afterlife – 'ghost', 'spectre', immortality', 'shrine', celestial'.

These techniques add to the status of the subject and establish a reverential tone which is softened by the injection of humour with reference to the Boxing Day 'hangover'. Impact is added with the closing quotation, which ends with a simple declarative statement – 'It was time to go'.

**Commentary**

**Activity 13**

Both writers are bystanders who have the role of observing and commenting on what they see, but there are significant differences in their approach.

Text A was written very soon after the events happened and seems more immediate. The diary format makes it seem urgent, abbreviated and incomplete. The writer records a series of impressions, he uses the present tense and the emphasis is on quick observation of events unfolding around him. He is clearly fascinated by the workings of J Company. He gives detailed, technical descriptions of the weaponry and captures for the reader the shifting emotions and surges in tension.

The inclusion of quoted speech adds authenticity. He includes detail that shows the Marines' attempts to integrate and to engage with local people – the 'consent-winning packs' and the reference to the mission 'to bid for hearts and minds'.

The reporter suggests admiration for the work and efforts of the Marines and expresses concern for their future safety. There is a sense that he has bonded with them. The inclusion of humour lowers the tension.

His motive seems to be to provide the audience with an immediate insight into the situation and to show the human aspect of warfare.

Text B, written retrospectively, is more planned, organised and structured. The past tense is used to refer to regular routines and daily lives. The focus is domestic rather than describing details of combat.

The approach is satirical and the writer shows disapproval of the attitudes and practices of the occupying authorities. The descriptions are used to highlight the gulf between the local people and the Americans. The Americans are presented as being nationalistic and concerned with imposing their own values and customs – for example, the 'freedom fries'. The mural of the World Trade Center is symbolic and a constant reminder of the divisions between the occupying forces and the Iraqis.

Your reading and comparison of these two texts will have demonstrated how reporters select material carefully to offer a particular viewpoint or bias. All reporting is subjective – affected by the attitudes and values of the reporter. In both of these reports the bias is unconcealed but you also need to be aware of reporting (both written and spoken) where the bias may be less obvious.

**Commentary**

**Activity 14**

There are obvious differences in Defoe's style which reflect the conventions of the time in which he was writing – the formal register, some unfamiliar or out-dated grammatical constructions and formal use of punctuation with regular use of the colon.

Unlike the writers of the texts on Afghanistan and Baghdad, Defoe is not only an observer but very much a participant. Like them, he does attempt to present his impressions vividly: he writes in a very literary manner, using personification and abstract nouns, he recreates the emotions and reactions of the people and uses first-person singular and plural to show personal involvement.

**Commentary**

**Activity 15**

Here is a checklist of reportage features:

- eye-witness first-hand observation or a report based on eye-witness accounts
- the adoption of a particular angle or viewpoint
- presentation of a collection of impressions
- careful selection of detail to create a particular scenario
- use of figurative language such as metaphor
- emphasis on what it is like to experience the event/situation
- present or past tense depending on the immediacy of the reporting.

**Commentary**

**Activity 17**

The motive of the writer is to persuade his audience that the label 'junk food' is irrational because it is based on a false argument. He expresses disapproval (and even contempt) for those who proclaim the dangers of certain kinds of foods by describing them as 'ill-informed individuals' and 'self-appointed food experts'.

He uses parallel statements and juxtaposition to give cohesion to his argument, beginning with an initial juxtaposition in the subheading, where he contrasts 'The Myth' with 'The Fact'. He refers to the literary device of 'oxymoron' to demonstrate the contradictory nature of the junk-food argument and to develop his ideas he foregrounds the following language features:

- syntactic parallelism – 'in which case it is not', 'in which case it cannot'
- negative statements – 'None of their explanations', 'They fail to point out', 'no such thing'
- questions addressed to the audience – 'why should ...?', 'What would ...?'
- familiar examples such as 'Sainsbury's Waldorf Salad', used to connect with the audience
- impact created with the simple declarative 'There is no such thing as junk food'.

The writer appeals to the reader's sense of class-consciousness by referring to snobbery and by quoting French loan words which typically conjure images of expense and sophistication. He finishes with the use of hyperbole in the phrase 'national disaster'.

**Commentary**

**Activity 22**

The speaker attempts to appeal to his audience by using the technique of inclusivity to make them feel involved and responsible – he repeats the plural first-person pronoun 'We' and refers to 'everybody'. He makes firm declarative statements – 'beyond all reasonable doubt', 'will be profound'. The speech opens with a lengthy noun phrase which employs a superlative – 'the biggest single global challenge'.

He uses imperative forms – 'We must act', We need', 'must become'. Qualifying adjectives are used – 'smarter', 'better', 'more efficient', 'more inclusive'. He introduces parallel structures to provide a sense of balance to his argument – 'part of the problem', 'part of the solution'. He ends his speech with a list of aims ending with the concept of inclusivity.

Rhetorical features of repetition, imperatives, syntactic parallelism have all been foregrounded to create cohesion and rhythm with the intention of involving and persuading the audience.

**Commentary**

**Activity 23**

You probably noticed that the text has a good balance of information, description and opinion:

- factual – historical and architectural details, details of trains and geographical layout, pronunciation
- description – type of shops, the atmosphere
- opinion – comments which show the attitudes of the writers, such as 'hordes of tourists', 'a grand place to brunch'.

The text is written in the third person, which can be more distanced and formal than the first person, but be aware of how the writers of this text still convey a personal voice.

You can see that facts alone are not very interesting or meaningful so writers need to add some dressing-up or colour. The text can be woven in a number of ways by the writer, but these ways will be influenced by the writer's purpose and audience. Much dressing up involves an invitation, implied or explicit, to share a point of view. You can explore this in Activity 24, where you are given a text which employs a different approach.

**Commentary**

**Activity 24**

V.S. Pritchett's book is an example of a travelogue, an account of a personal journey that the reader is not expected to undertake. In such texts writers will recount to the reader what they experienced and how they reacted (although their reasons for doing so can vary).

**Commentary**

**Activity 25**

O'Rourke's text is more informal and casual, with its observations and anecdotal approach, in contrast with Pritchett's more elaborate, almost poetic descriptions. O'Rourke is aiming to amuse his readers with a satirical account. He achieves his effects by using ambiguous statements and by making ludicrous connections. He adopts the persona of the naïve American tourist encountering an unfamiliar culture and he undermines the European lifestyle by his use of incongruous images. His writing focuses on personal impressions and observations and gives little factual detail.

Pritchett aims to convey a strong sense of the flavour and atmosphere of Salvador, providing the reader with a cultural and geographic context. His descriptions are lengthy and detailed: you will have noticed the prevalence of the semantic field of fruit and the emphasis on sensory perceptions.

O'Rourke conveys his attitude with opinionated statements and a disrespectful approach – 'The Italians have had two thousand years to fix up the Forum'. Pritchett responds to the atmosphere and shows his appreciation through an accumulation of detail. He allows personal opinion to intervene in his assessment of the quality of the fruits and the alcohol.

**Commentary**

**Activity 26**

Charles Darwin's diary is a variation on the travelogue. His main intention is to record his observations as a naturalist and to communicate his experiences during his exploration of the South American coast in 1831–6. The register is more formal than that of O'Rourke and Pritchett and he uses technical Latinate lexis to identify the insects and butterflies.

Like O'Rourke and Pritchett, he does still convey his attitudes and feelings – his excitement at the discoveries and concern at the fate of the butterflies (notice his use of the word 'perish').

**Commentary**

**Activity 27**

Text A exhibits many features of spontaneous speech such as pauses, hesitations, repetition, unfinished utterances. It adopts the traditional interview question-and-answer format with adjacency pairs and regular turn taking. Bailey's role as the interviewer is to ask questions and to attempt to prompt Warhol into giving fuller responses but he does not offer his own comments and observations.

Text B has been written after the event and shows evidence of editing and reshaping. The subject of the interview, Snoop Dogg, is introduced by the journalist, who offers her own perspective and impressions. Snoop Dogg talks freely, presumably in response to questions posed by the journalist.

Warhol seems reluctant to offer any information and is unhelpful in his replies, possibly treating the interview with a mocking, satirical approach (indications of laughter in the background suggest that this is deliberate). Dogg is much more forthcoming about his motives and his attitude to his work.

The Warhol interview has an audience who are watching and listening so have the advantage of paralinguistic features, whereas Dogg's interview has been rewritten to be read so the words alone need to engage the reader.

As Warhol was a popular modern artist and Dogg is a rap singer we can assume that their audiences will mainly be people with a specific interest in their work. In a sense both speakers are attempting to create an image of themselves but whereas Warhol is being deliberately evasive in refusing to discuss the significance of his work, Dogg is open in his self-appraisal and at ease when discussing his career intentions.

You need to consider to what extent the crafting and reshaping of the Dogg interview by the journalist has affected the final text.

**Commentary**

**Activity 28**

**Grammatical patterns:** Many of the sentences have a similar balanced structure – 'primacy in power … awe-inspiring accountability', 'you must feel not only … but also you must', 'We must, and I believe we shall'. This technique can be described as syntactic parallelism.

**Lexical patterns:** Many of the words and phrases are in pairs or groups of three – 'clear and shining', 'rule and guide', 'sympathy and goodwill'. This device is known as a triadic structure and is a key feature of persuasive speaking.

**Figurative language:** Churchill uses metaphors and abstract nouns – 'the pinnacle of world power', 'let loose', 'the awful whirlpool'.

**Phonological patterns:** Many of the words and phrases are chosen to create a rhythmic effect – 'pinnacle', 'power', 'persistency of purpose'. You might have also noticed the number of modal verbs, used to express possibility or probability – 'you must', 'we must', 'we shall'.

**Conclusion:** By using carefully chosen patterns of grammar, lexis and phonology, Churchill's speech has rhythmic patterns which help to hold the attention of the listener and to create memorable phrases.

Traditionally the term used to describe skills in persuasive speaking was 'rhetoric'. Another useful term for describing specific linguistic and literary devices is foregrounding – that is, any use of language which is unusual or striking enough to attract attention.

This exercise should have directed you to make observations which form the basis of an analysis that describes textual features.

## Commentary
## Activity 30

**Checklist of rhetorical and stylistic features**
Both speakers employ the following techniques:

- syntactic parallelism
- repetition
- juxtaposition/balanced structures
- listing

- triadic structures
- qualifying adjectives
- phonological features
- figurative language.

Blair also uses a series of minor and short sentences (e.g. 'Outward-looking.' and 'I believe in Britain.') and Kennedy uses pairs of abstract nouns (e.g. 'change and challenge' and 'knowledge and ignorance').

## Commentary
## Activity 31

In each case the audience has been deliberately misled. The reader's expectations, given the format of the texts, would lead them to believe that Text A was an advertisement placed in the national press by a firm asking customers to return an unsafe product and that Text B was a letter to a problem page in a magazine.

**Genre conventions**
Text A has the heading 'PRODUCT RECALL' and refers to a batch number. The text begins with 'Due to' which suggests a problem. The lexis has connotations of danger – 'alarming number of incidents'.

Text B has the heading 'My Secret Affair', which suggests a confession and the writer gives her first name at the end (a typical problem-page convention which personalises the writer while maintaining anonymity). The text gives a brief narrative outlining the affair with the milkman and concludes by asking for advice.

**Subverting features**
In Text A you will have noticed the unexpected shift in tone with the use of bathos in 'bottoms pinched'. As this is usually associated with men harassing women it contradicts the reader's expectations and introduces a humorous approach. This is compounded by the relaxed instruction at the end 'feel free to hold on to'.

In Text B, the tone and content of the reply do not match our expectations of an agony aunt and by this point in the text you will have realised that you are being misled (you might have had suspicions earlier as an affair between a housewife and a milkman is an old cliché).

Summary

The texts rely for their impact on these stylistic features:

- ambiguity
- incongruity – juxtaposing two things in an unexpected way
- bathos
- humour.

Both are adverts for consumer products but they each masquerade as a different genre. By subverting the reader's expectations in this way they draw attention to the advert and could make people remember the product.

In Text A the realisation that this is an advert for Lynx reinforces the challenging nature of the text and the humour increases the advert's effectiveness.

Text B initially masquerades as a problem page, a genre which seems far removed from the advertising world, with the purpose again of amusing the audience and selling a product (99 tea). It is actually a parody – a satirical imitation of another genre. This works on your knowledge of other types of text and then plays around with them. This device of reference to other texts and text types is termed intertextuality.

There are other reasons for text producers wishing to subvert genres: it may be to persuade the target audience to adopt a particular cause or to change their behaviour. (Good examples are adverts for Amnesty International and government television campaigns against drink driving and smoking.) Or it may just be to intrigue the audience by presenting familiar material in new ways.

**Commentary**

**Activity 32**

Text A claims to be a postcard and begins like a travel guide but is, in fact, an article about Icelandic music from *Observer Music Monthly* (2006). This is apparent by the second sentence, when the tone changes to one that is much more informal and colloquial. There is a change in focus from the descriptive writing about the country to the opinions of the writer about the culture of the Icelandic music scene. As in the adverts in Activity 31, the writer uses bathos to signal this change.

Text B appears to be from the genre of romantic fiction – for example, Mills and Boon novels. It is in fact an advertisement from the *Tatler* magazine (2007) for a holiday in Kerala. The romantic-fiction genre is suggested by the narrative approach and the use of a female protagonist. The text uses sensuous lexis and words and phrases that have associations with pleasure and relaxation.

Indications that this is not simply a romantic novel creep in with the use of the specialist word 'ayurvedic'. Further references to holistic therapies add more evidence. However, the text does not acknowledge its real purpose until the signature line at the end: 'Kerala – God's Own Country'.

# Exploring and Comparing Texts

3

## Introducing an integrated approach

The primary purpose of this chapter is to help you explore how writers use prose in the rich and challenging art of storytelling in literature and to show you the range of possible approaches to study and the depth in which you should explore both set texts and unseen extracts. We understand that from the earliest times in human experience, people from every culture during every historical period have used storytelling as a way of sharing experiences and consolidating common values. This chapter shows you some of the ways in which this has been done in our own culture through works of prose. You will be offered guidance about your own writing and be given suggestions for practice pieces and coursework.

We shall be focusing mainly on what is generally termed literary fiction but, in addition, we shall be giving considerable attention to the works of writers whose narratives are fundamentally based on truth and actual events but who have used styles and strategies closely associated with literature in order to achieve their purposes. The commonly used term for this kind of writing is literary non-fiction.

### Linguistic and literary studies – an integrated approach

Throughout this chapter, you will find exercises and activities which will demonstrate to you how to adopt a consistently integrated approach in your analysis of texts, giving appropriate weight to both linguistic and literary aspects of all of the texts.

### Knowledge and skills

With regard to knowledge and skills, it is important for you to appreciate what exactly you are expected to know and what you are going to be asked to do. By the end of this chapter, you should be able to

- appreciate the meaning of a text and write about it accurately and confidently
- understand how a text has been constructed and be able to describe the technical aspects of its crafting

- construct an informed discussion of narrative approaches, including voice
- evaluate the success of a specific narrative approach
- establish a link between texts from different genres but with common themes
- compare works of writers who have common purposes while working in different contexts
- demonstrate your own writing skills.

# Crime writing – genre and sub-genres

The first section of this chapter introduces you to some of the core elements in the study of narrative prose, the most significant of which is genre. If you are at all representative of the reading population as a whole, you will be very much at home with the themes, conventions, narrative approaches and structures of the popular genre murder, mystery and suspense, with its various sub-genres, of which these are just a few:

- detective fiction
- courtroom drama
- real-life police stories
- psychological suspense novel
- crime reporting.

This prior knowledge of the genre will help you to navigate more readily through the technical challenges of critical understanding, especially as the variations and interweaving of genre features make this particular type of writing so rich in its potential. In addition to the many works of fiction that come under this heading, there are many texts which are loosely linked, though strictly speaking they do not belong to the same literary genre. There is a huge market for well-written and meticulously researched accounts of real crime. Criminals, both dead and alive, have become dubious celebrities. Others, wrongly convicted, have had their cases reviewed as a result of a writer's efforts to prove their innocence. The source texts for this section include both fiction and literary non-fiction, to show you how a genre such as crime fiction can be extended and developed.

In this section, we shall be aiming for three specific outcomes. When you have read through the selected extracts and completed the activities, you should be able to

- identify and describe features of genre
- present illuminating comparisons of writers' approaches
- discuss how writers make use of features from a range of genres – for example, mixing literary and journalistic approaches.

The fact that some of the writers make use of social and regional varieties of English provides us with the opportunity to study some features of linguistic interest associated with place and class.

### Source texts for this section
The source texts for this section are extracts from

- *Murders in the Rue Morgue* by Edgar Allan Poe, first published in *Graham's Magazine,* April edition, 1841; subsequently published with other short stories as *Selected Tales* (fiction)
- *In Cold Blood* by Truman Capote, published 1966 (literary non-fiction)
- *The Big Sleep* by Raymond Chandler, published 1939 (fiction)
- *The Mammoth Book of True Crime* by Colin Wilson, published 1973 (literary non-fiction)
- *The Lost Continent* by Bill Bryson, published 1989 (literary non-fiction).

# The writer in context

**Edgar Allan Poe (1809–49)** made his name as a writer by his extremely popular tales of mystery and horror. His particular brand of chilling story is usually classed as Gothic horror. His tale *The Pit and the Pendulum* is a good example for you to read as an easy way to check out the genre. His other claim to literary fame is that he was the first writer to create the fictional detective as the central character of murder and mystery stories. The character of C Auguste Dupin is particularly noted for his astuteness in dealing with criminal types, his perception in unravelling apparently conflicting evidence and his personal pride in getting at truths which are hidden from the authorities. Poe's creation lives on in many of the well-known names of crime writing – Sherlock Holmes, Hercule Poirot, Miss Marple and the numerous private investigators of paperback and screen. *The Murders in the Rue Morgue* is one of three Dupin stories and, as was the practice of the time, it was first published in *Graham's Magazine*. Thus the wider reading public was able to access Poe's works through the availability of modestly priced publications.

In this extract, Dupin's companion, who is also the narrator of the tales, describes how he and Dupin, having strolled around the area of Paris where they live, come across the newspaper account of the murders of a mother and daughter in circumstances which suggest the ferocity of a homicidal maniac with superhuman strength, not to mention the uncanny ability to get in and out of a locked room. The narrator provides the reader with the full verbatim account to set the scene for the challenge to Dupin's powers of detection.

## Extract from *Murders in the Rue Morgue* – a fictional newspaper account of a crime of horror within an apparently locked room

Not long after this, we were looking over an evening edition of the 'Gazette des Tribuneaux', when the following paragraphs arrested our attention.

'EXTRAORDINARY MURDERS. – This morning, about three o'clock, the inhabitants of the Quartier St. Roch were aroused from sleep by a succession of terrific shrieks, issuing, apparently, from the fourth storey of a house in the Rue Morgue, known to be in the sole occupancy of one Madame l'Espanaye, and her daughter, Mademoiselle Camille l'Espanaye. After some delay, after a fruitless attempt to procure admission in the usual manner, the gateway was broken in with a crowbar, and eight or ten of the neighbors entered, accompanied by two *gendarmes*. By this time the cries had ceased; but, as the party rushed up the first flight of stairs, two or more rough voices, in angry contention, were distinguished, and seemed to proceed from the upper part of the house. As the second landing was reached, these sounds, also, had ceased, and everything remained perfectly quiet. The party spread themselves, and hurried from room to room. Upon arriving at a large back chamber in the fourth storey, (the door of which, being found locked, with the key inside, was forced open,) a spectacle presented itself which struck every one present not less with horror than with astonishment.

'The apartment was in the wildest disorder – the furniture broken and thrown about in all directions. There was only one bedstead; and from this the bed had been removed, and thrown into the middle of the floor. On a chair lay a razor, besmeared with blood. On the hearth were two or three long and thick tresses of grey human hair, also dabbled in blood, and seeming to have been pulled out by the roots. On the floor were found four Napoleons, an ear-ring of topaz, three large silver spoons, three smaller of *métal d'Alger*, and two bags, containing nearly four thousand francs in gold. The drawers of a bureau, which stood in one corner, were open, and had been, apparently, rifled, although many articles still remained in them. A small metal safe was discovered under the *bed* (not under the bedstead). It was open, with the key still in the door. It had no contents beyond a few old letters, and other papers of little consequence.

'Of Madame L'Espanaye no traces were here seen; but an unusual quantity of soot being observed in the fire-place, a search was made in the chimney, and (horrible to relate!) the corpse of the daughter, head downward, was dragged therefrom; it having been forced up the narrow aperture for a considerable distance. The body was quite warm. Upon examining it, many excoriations were perceived, no doubt occasioned by the violence with which it had been thrust up and disengaged. Upon the face were many severe scratches, and, upon the throat, dark bruises, and deep indentations of finger nails, as if the deceased had been throttled to death.

'After a thorough investigation of every portion of the house, without further discovery, the party made its way into a small paved yard in the rear of the building, where lay the corpse of the old lady, with her throat so entirely cut that, upon an attempt to raise her, the head fell off. The body, as well as the head, was fearfully mutilated – the former so much so as scarcely to retain any semblance of humanity.

'To this horrible mystery there is not as yet, we believe, the slightest clew.'

## Activity 1

**Class work**

# Identifying and discussing features of genre

While making use of some features of the journalese (journalistic style) of the period, Poe overlays the account with hints of gruesome, unnatural brutality. In doing so, he has incorporated three genres: crime writing, crime reporting and Gothic horror. Collect together all the evidence for these categories. The following grid provides you with a starting-point. You will find that the categories overlap considerably.

| Crime writing | Gothic horror | Journalese |
|---|---|---|
| Fictional account of murders | Mutilated bodies | Sensational headline |
| Use of partly authentic locations to create a sense of realism | Macabre details of brutal attacks | Authoritative summary in the impersonal voice |
| Timeline of events in the discovery | Bloodstained weapon | Provides information of interest to local people |
| Vocabulary linked to crime and the law | Locked room | Gives most recent information |

## Activity 2

# Writing about genre

Write a short piece, approximately 500–600 words long, in which you discuss how the three genres contribute to the success of the newspaper account as an effective introduction to the mystery story.

## Writing in a different style

An optional activity which is potentially very rewarding is to rewrite the fictional article from the *Gazette des Tribuneaux* in a modern style. Refer to recent news reports of serious crimes to establish suitable style models.

## The writer in context

**Truman Capote (1924–84)** began his career in writing as a junior reporter. From there he graduated to serious journalism and novel writing. He was already recognised as a writer of considerable skill, especially noted for the clarity and freshness of his approach, when his eye was caught by a news story in the *New York Times* of 16 November 1959.

# Wealthy Farmer, 3 of Family Slain

A wealthy wheat farmer, his wife and their two young children were found shot to death today in their home.

They had been killed by shotgun blasts at close range after being bound and gagged. The father, 48-year-old Herbert W. Clutter, was found in the basement with his son, Kenyon, 15. His wife Bonnie, 45, and a daughter, Nancy, 16, were in their beds. There were no signs of a struggle and nothing had been stolen. The telephone lines had been cut. 'This is apparently the case of a psychopathic killer,' Sheriff Earl Robinson said. Mr. Clutter was founder of The Kansas Wheat Growers Association. In 1954, President Eisenhower appointed him to the Farm Credit Administration but he never lived in Washington. The Clutter farm and ranch cover almost 1,000 acres in one of the richest wheat areas. Mr. Clutter, his wife and daughter were clad in pajamas. The boy was wearing blue jeans and a T-shirt. The bodies were discovered by two of Nancy's classmates, Susan Kidwell and Nancy Ewalt ... Two daughters were away. They are Beverly, a student at Kansas University, and Mrs. Donald G. Jarchow of Mount Carroll, Ill.

Drawn towards the bizarre nature of the crime, in that isolated and peaceful community, he went with his childhood friend and fellow writer, Harper Lee (author of *To Kill a Mockingbird*) to explore the crime scene from the broadest possible perspective. In producing his groundbreaking work *In Cold Blood* he is credited with having invented the non-fiction novel. He and Harper Lee together interviewed friends, neighbours and officials associated with the enquiry and, finally, the convicted killers. Using for his source material only direct testimony, official records and his own observations he constructed a story of great power. The extract on page 102 is taken from the testimony of the classmate who discovered Nancy Clutter's dead body.

**Extract from *In Cold Blood* – Truman Capote restructures authentic evidence as neighbours describe their horrific discovery**

Susan, on this Sunday morning, stood at the window of this room, watching the street. She is a tall, languid young lady with a pallid, oval face and beautiful pale-blue-grey eyes; her hands are extraordinary – long-fingered, flexible, nervously elegant. She was dressed for church, and expected momentarily to see the Clutters' Chevrolet, for she, too, always attended services chaperoned by the Clutter family. Instead, the Ewalts arrived to tell their peculiar tale.

But Susan knew of no explanation, nor did her mother, who said, 'If there was some change of plan, why, I'm sure they would have telephoned. Susan, why don't you call the house? They could be *asleep* – I suppose.'

'So I did,' said Susan, in statement made at a later date. 'I called the house and let the phone ring – at least, I had the *impression* it was ringing – oh, a minute or more. Nobody answered, so Mr Ewalt suggested that we go to the house and try to "wake them up". But when we got there – I didn't want to do it. Go inside the house. I was frightened, and I don't know why, because it never occurred to me – well, something like that just doesn't. But the sun was so bright, everything looked too bright and quiet. And then I saw that all the cars were there, even Kenyon's old coyote wagon. Mr Ewalt was wearing work clothes; he had mud on his boots; he felt he wasn't properly dressed to go calling on the Clutters. Especially since he never had. Been in the house, I mean. Finally Nancy [Ewalt] said she would go with me. We went round to the kitchen door, and, of course, it wasn't locked; the only person who ever locked doors around here was Mrs Helm [the Clutters' housekeeper] – the family never did. We walked in, and I saw right away that the Clutters hadn't eaten breakfast; there were no dishes, nothing on the stove. Then I noticed something funny: Nancy's purse. It was lying on the floor, sort of open. We passed on through the dining-room, and stopped at the bottom of the stairs. Nancy's room is just at the top. I called her name and started up the stairs, and Nancy Ewalt followed. The sound of our footsteps frightened me more than anything, they were so loud and everything else was so silent. Nancy's door was open. The curtains hadn't been drawn, and the room was full of sunlight. I don't remember screaming. Nancy Ewalt says I did – screamed and screamed. I only remember Nancy's Teddy bear staring at me. And Nancy. And running....'

In the interim, Mr Ewalt had decided that perhaps he ought not to have allowed the girls to enter the house alone. He was getting out of the car to go after them when he heard the screams, but before he could reach the house, the girls were running towards him. His daughter shouted, 'She's dead!' and flung herself into his arms. 'It's true, Daddy! Nancy's dead!'

Susan turned on her. 'No, she isn't. And don't you say it. Don't you dare. It's only a nosebleed. She has them all the time, terrible nosebleeds, and that's all it is.'

'There's too much blood. There's blood on the walls. You didn't really look.'

'I couldn't make head nor tails', Mr Ewalt subsequently testified. 'I thought maybe the child was hurt. It seemed to me the first thing to do was to call an ambulance. Miss Kidwell – Susan – she told me there was a telephone in the kitchen. I found it, right where she said. But the receiver was off the hook, and when I picked it up, I saw the line had been cut.'

| Activity 4 | Crime reporting – comparing literary and authentic material |
|---|---|

Compare the two extracts from *The Murders in the Rue Morgue* and *In Cold Blood*. What similarities and differences do you find between them?

**Individual**

The best way of approaching a question of this kind is to construct a grid and map out a framework for investigation. Here is an example of a suitable framework grid but you may prefer to construct your own.

| Feature for comparison | *Rue Morgue* | *In Cold Blood* | Similar or different? |
|---|---|---|---|
| Text type – whole or extract | Features both text types. Fictional 'whole document' framed within a longer text, it appears complete but is likely to have important links to the rest of the story | Part of a longer text; not self-contained or discrete; conveys only a portion of the facts of the case | Different. A whole text is constructed to be independent of other material. Extracts and framed documents may rely on further reading to get the full effect |
| Recognisable genre | Journalism within a detective story | Literary non-fiction | |
| Themes | Discovery of murder by neighbours | Discovery of murder by close friends | Quite close but with one significant difference – emotional response |
| Attitudes presented | Shock and horror | Shock, horror, disbelief | Fairly similar |
| Structure and organisation | Timeline of events. Sequence logical | Sequence followed | Similar |
| Voices | Claims to be an editorial and impersonal summary from various sources but has a crafted touch | Authentic voice of Susan, other persons, and the editor Capote | Different, though both texts show some editorial interpretation and guiding of readers' responses |
| Naming conventions | Anonymous or generic except for victims' names | All actual persons named and identified | Different to a considerable degree |
| Scene setting | Extensive. Links to Paris and also provides links to the rest of the plot | Limited to important features | Different |
| Features of language<br>Lexis<br>Grammar<br>Syntax | | | |
| Language conveying period or class | | | |
| Phonology<br>What language sounds like | | | |
| Features of genre | | | |
| Achieving authorial purpose | | | |
| Meeting readers' needs | | | |

Group work

Another option, as a class exercise, is to get pairs or groups to look for one similarity and one difference and pool your findings. Then arrange the findings in a framework for oral discussion or writing.

If you attempt this activity as a writing exercise, you may be tempted to structure your answer in two sections, dealing first with similarities and then with differences. This approach is not likely to result in an illuminating comparison. It is better practice to select a feature for discussion and then cluster your evidence about the similar and/or different treatment in a single paragraph.

## Activity 5 — Writing about speech and contextual factors

Group work

1 Read aloud the testimony of Nancy Kidwell and Mr Ewalt. What evidence is there that this is naturally occurring speech and what features suggest planned utterances? Consider the circumstances in which the speech occurred. Consider the intervention of the writer in his role as editor.

Individual

2 Write a short piece in which you discuss the effectiveness of Capote's technique in using direct testimony as part of his narrative strategy. Consider the influence of contextual constraints and the writer's own contributions to the account.

## The writer in context

**Raymond Chandler (1888–1959)** first attempted crime writing in the form of short-story writing and for a short time he earned a successful living as a Hollywood screenwriter. He is widely recognised as the key writer of the cinema genre known as film noir and is credited with having rescued the private eye from third-rate pulp and B movies into the world of top-class literature with his creation Philip Marlowe. The fictional detective has become the gold standard of private investigators. He has come to embody the loner, relentlessly fighting crime and corruption, despite poor rewards and little gratitude. As a modern knight-errant, Marlowe has no equal for his blunt humour and caustic repartee. The strength of characterisation achieved in creating Marlowe was not matched by the writer's ability with plot management. A number of people, including the producers who struggled to put his works on screen, were mystified by who killed whom but, as the next extract shows, he excelled at creating character, atmosphere and tension.

Another term that aims to encapsulate the world of mobster sleaze that dominated crime fiction both before and after the Second World War is 'hardboiled'. This is amply demonstrated in the extract from *The Big Sleep*. Marlowe has agreed to negotiate with a small-time operator who claims that his girlfriend Agnes has crucial information worth $200 to anyone working for the Sternwood family. Feeling under a moral obligation towards General Sternwood, Marlowe agrees to meet Jones in the hope of saving his client further hassle from blackmailers, unaware that the situation is more complex than even Jones imagines and that organised crime, represented here by hardened hitman Canino, is taking an unhealthy interest in the case and has beaten him to the rendez-vous. From the cover of an adjacent office, Marlowe overhears as Canino, armed and dangerous, first intimidates Jones into revealing Agnes's whereabouts and then silences him by forcing him to drink cyanide.

Extract from *The Big Sleep* – the fictional narrator-detective witnesses the callous murder of a small-time hustler in a complex tale of murder and blackmail

A silence followed. I listened to the rain lashing the windows. The smell of cigarette smoke came through the crack of the door. I wanted to cough. I bit hard on a handkerchief.

The purring voice said, still gentle: 'From what I hear this blond broad was just a shill for Geiger. I'll talk it over with Eddie. How much you tap the peeper for?'

'Two centuries.'

'Get it?'

Harry Jones laughed again. 'I'm seeing him tomorrow. I have hopes.'

'Where's Agnes?'

'Listen —'

'Where's Agnes?'

Silence.

'Look at it, little man.'

I didn't move. I wasn't wearing a gun. I didn't have to look through the crack of the door to know that a gun was what the purring voice was inviting Harry Jones to look at. But I didn't think Mr Canino would do anything with his gun beyond showing it. I waited.

'I'm looking at it,' Harry Jones said, his voice squeezed tight as if it could hardly get past his teeth. 'And I don't see anything I didn't see before. Go ahead and blast and see what it gets you.'

'A Chicago overcoat is what it would get *you*, little man.'

Silence.

'Where's Agnes?'

Harry Jones sighed. 'Okey,' he said wearily. 'She's in an apartment house at 28 Court Street, up on Bunker Hill. Apartment 301. I guess I'm yellow all right. Why should I front for that twist?'

'No reason. You got good sense. You and me'll go out and talk to her. All I want to find out is she dummying up on you, kid. If it's the way you say it is, everything is jakeloo. You can put the bite on the peeper and be on your way. No hard feelings?'

'No,' Harry Jones said. 'No hard feelings, Canino.'

'Fine. Let's dip the bill. Got a glass?' The purring voice was now as false as an usherette's eyelashes and as slippery as a watermelon seed. A drawer was pulled open. Something jarred on the wood. A chair squeaked. A scuffling sound on the floor. 'This is bond stuff,' the purring voice said.

There was a gurgling sound. 'Moths in your ermine, as the ladies say.'

Harry Jones said softly, 'Success.'

I heard a short, sharp cough. Then a violent retching. There was a small thud on the floor, as if a thick glass had fallen. My fingers curled against my raincoat.

The purring voice said gently: 'You ain't sick from just one drink, are you, pal?'

Harry Jones didn't answer. There was laboured breathing for a short moment. Then thick silence folded down. Then a chair scraped.

'So long, little man', said Mr Canino.

Steps, a click, the wedge of light died at my feet, a door opened and closed quietly. The steps faded, leisurely and assured.

I stirred around the edge of the door and pulled it wide and looked into blackness relieved by the dim shine of a window. The corner of a desk glittered faintly. A hunched shape took form in a chair behind it. In the close air there was a heavy clogged smell, almost a perfume. I went across to the corridor and listened. I heard the distant clang of the elevator.

I found the light switch and light glowed in a dusty glass bowl hanging from the ceiling by three brass chains. Harry Jones looked at me across the desk, his eyes wide open, his face frozen in a tight spasm, the skin bluish. His small dark head was tilted to one side. He sat upright against the back of the chair.

A tramcar bell clanged at an almost infinite distance and the sound came buffeted by innumerable walls. A brown half-pint of whisky stood on the desk with the cap off. Harry Jones's glass glinted against a castor of the desk. The second glass was gone.

I breathed shallowly from the top of my lungs, and bent above the bottle. Behind the charred smell of the bourbon another odour lurked, faintly, the odour of bitter almonds. Harry Jones dying had vomited on his coat. That made it cyanide.

It will come as no surprise to you that Chandler was a very successful screenwriter and much of that skill is incorporated in his novel writing. In order to make his technique clearer to you, we are going to start by considering how this same scene could be conveyed in another medium.

## Activity 6
**Class work**

### Writing about the crime scene

As a class activity, present the extract in the form of a drama, in line with the following formula:

- use only the dialogue given in the extract to provide speech
- make notes for 'Canino' and 'Jones' to explain how you want them to convey aggression, threats, conflict and fear
- use Marlowe's account to provide a set of stage directions for the action
- follow Marlowe's guidance on sound effects
- produce a props list (tells the properties department what to provide to furnish the stage)
- produce a lighting score (explains to the lighting technicians how you want the stage to be lit at different points in the scene)
- draw a diagram of the set.

## Activity 7
**Individual**

### Writing about narrative technique

Armed with the information from Activity 6, write an extended piece (800–1200 words) on Chandler's narrative technique. You can use all the ideas you have gleaned from the drama activity because this will show you the extent of Chandler's detailed exposition. You must now include the following points

- Marlowe's unique contribution as the first-person narrator, which you were not able to use in the drama
- focused discussion about the ways in which speech conveys characterisation, including contextual factors such as social class and regional variation.

## The writer in context

**Colin Wilson (1931– ),** born in Britain, is a prolific writer who has established his name as one of the foremost contributors to the genre of non-fiction crime writing. Being an acknowledged authority on issues associated with criminal deviance and the workings of the penal systems, he has achieved a strong reputation on both sides of the Atlantic.

Extract from *The Mammoth Book of True Crime* – Colin Wilson uses social and historical evidence to suggest the causes of gun crime

The 1914 war was the first time that vast numbers of men actually handled guns. Before the war, most guns were owned by farmers or sportsmen; now everybody learned how to use them. An early Spencer Tracy film called *They Gave Him a Gun* put its finger on what happened: the servicemen came home from Europe, and found a new world that had already forgotten the war and the men who fought in it.

There were no jobs for the returning heroes; life was hard. So many of them decided to make use of what they had learned in the army, and suddenly, the police were faced with the greatest crime wave since 1720. But this time, it was not just in England, but in America, France, Italy and Germany.... The petty criminal who had never stolen anything larger than a watch discovered it was just as easy to walk into a bank and point a gun at the cashier.

And the Americans, with an innocence and an optimism that now seem stunning, decided to reform their country by banning all alcoholic liquor, and thereby produced an entirely new breed of social parasite called the mobster; seventy years later, in spite of numerous Acts of Congress and Commissions of Enquiry, America is still as securely in the mobsters' hands as it was in Al Capone's.

In most countries of the world, the authorities have achieved some sort of control by banning the sale of guns to private citizens. In America, financial interests – known as the 'gun lobby' – continue to prevent a measure that would probably cut the crime rate by 75%.

America's gun problem is not so much social as psychological. The past 50 years have seen an alarming increase in the numbers of mass murders committed with guns, and the majority of such cases have taken place in America. On December 30, 1950, a young psychopath named William Cook stopped a car driven by Carl Mosser; Mosser's wife, three young children and family dog were also in the car. Cook brandished a gun, and made the Mosser family drive around Texas for 72 hours; then, when the wife and children became hysterical, he killed them all.

On September 6, 1949, a 28-year-old ex-G.I. named Howard Unruh walked out of his house in Camden, New Jersey, carrying a German Luger pistol, and, in the next twelve minutes, killed thirteen people at random. Captured after a siege of his home, Unruh declared: 'I'd have killed a thousand if I'd had enough ammunition.'

In January 1958, Charles Starkweather took his girlfriend Caril Fugate on a murder rampage across Nebraska, and shot and killed ten people – mostly strangers – before he was captured a couple of days later. In Lathrup Village, Michigan, in August 1968, a family of six called Robinson were all 'executed' by an unknown killer with a .22 revolver.

In October 1970, John Linley Frazier 'executed' the family of Dr. Victor Ohta at his home near Santa

Cruz, California, and threw the five bodies into the swimming pool. On November 7, 1973, a family of nine – four adults, three teenagers and two young children – were all shot through the head by unknown killers at their home near Victor, California... .

It would be possible to list dozens – even hundreds – of such cases that have taken place in America – the only English parallel is the case of psychopath, Peter Manuel, who killed two families with a gun in late 1956 and early 1957 – but one more will suffice. On November 15, 1959, two ex-convicts named Perry Smith and Richard Hickock broke into the home of the Clutter family near Holcomb, Kansas, and slaughtered all four in the course of robbery.

In 1966, Truman Capote's reconstruction of the crime, *In Cold Blood*, broke best-selling records in America, although it failed to achieve the same success in other countries. Obviously, Capote had touched on some strange nerve in the American psyche. If we understood this, we would understand something important about the mysterious lure of gun violence in America. That lure can only be quashed by outlawing the gun.

## Activity 8 | Identifying features of informative and persuasive writing

As a starting-point, you might examine the ways in which Colin Wilson informs and persuades the reader of his theories concerning the rise of gun crime. If you look at the extract again, you will see

- discourse markers and a clear structure to signpost the chronology
- increasingly serious incidents involving guns
- authentic case references to support assertions
- lexical choices which shock
- repetition of paragraph structures to support the assertion of persistence in gun crime
- language and tone conveying implicit attitudes and explicit opinions.

Write a short appreciation of Wilson's style, offering your own opinions as to why crime writing is such a popular genre with the reading public.

## Writer in context

**Bill Bryson (1951– )** is probably best known for his witty and accessible travel writing but his interests are much broader. He has written knowledgeably about the English language and appears to enjoy experimenting with it, whatever the subject. Despite the apparently light-hearted tone of much of his work, he often uses humour to mask his very real concerns. In this extract from *The Lost Continent – Travels in Small Town America*, he reflects on the violence, prejudice, lawlessness, injustice and corruption within some sections of American society, giving the reader his quirky reminiscences of a time when he felt threatened even in his own country. He speculates how close he came to falling victim to the alienation that exists within American society and has in the past led to serious criminal acts.

### Extract from *The Lost Continent*

Just south of Grand Junction, Tennessee, I passed over the state line into Mississippi. A sign beside the highway said WELCOME TO MISSISSIPPI. WE SHOOT TO KILL. It didn't really. I just made that up. This was only the second time I had been to the Deep South and I entered it with a sense of foreboding. It is surely no coincidence that all those films you have ever seen about the South – *Easy Rider, In the Heat of the Night, Cool Hand Luke, Brubaker, Deliverance* – depict Southerners as murderous, incestuous, shitty-shoed rednecks. It really is another country. Years ago, in the days of Vietnam, two friends and I drove to Florida during college break. We all had long hair. *En route* we took a short cut along the back roads of Georgia and stopped late one afternoon for a burger at a dinette in some dreary little crudville, and when we took our seats at the counter the place fell silent. Fourteen people just stopped eating, their food resting in their mouths, and stared at us. It was so quiet you could have heard a fly fart. A whole roomful of good ole boys with cherry-coloured cheeks and bib overalls watched us in silence and wondered whether their shotguns were loaded. It was disconcerting. To them, out here in the middle of nowhere, we were at once a curiosity – some of them had clearly never seen no long-haired, nigger-loving, Northern, college-edjicated, commie hippies in the flesh before – and yet unspeakably loathsome. It was an odd sensation to feel so deeply hated by people who hadn't had a proper chance to acquaint themselves with one's shortcomings. I remember thinking that our parents didn't have the first idea where we were, other than that we were somewhere in the continental vastness between Des Moines and the Florida Keys, and that if we disappeared we would never be found. I had visions of my family sitting around the living room in years to come and my mother saying, 'Well, I wonder whatever happened to Billy and his friends. You'd think we'd have had a postcard by now. Can I get anybody a sandwich?'

That sort of thing really did happen down there, you know. This was only five years after three freedom riders were murdered in Mississippi. They were a twenty-one-year-old black from Mississippi named James Chaney and two white guys from New York, Andrew Goodman, twenty, and Michael Schwerner, twenty. I give their names because they deserve to be remembered. They were arrested for speeding, taken to the Neshoba County Jail in Philadelphia, Mississippi, and were never seen again – at least not until weeks later when their bodies were hauled out of a swamp. These were kids, remember. The police had released them to a waiting mob, which had taken them away and done things to them that a child wouldn't do to an insect. The sheriff in the case, a smirking, tobacco-chewing fat boy named Lawrence Rainey, was acquitted of negligent behaviour. No-one was ever charged with murder. To me this was and always would be the South.

| Activity 9 | Using language to evoke atmosphere |

**Class work**

Examine the ways in which Bryson uses language to convey his feelings in this extract. If you need a starting-point, you could first consider his choice of lexis to describe people. How effectively does he use register and slang?

| Activity 10 | Comparing extracts – constructing an agenda |

Choose any two extracts which you have particularly enjoyed and construct a framework for comparing them. You should aim for explicit comparison by structuring your answer around focus points, such as genre, voice, tone, purpose and reader satisfaction. Look again at the activities you have already completed for further examples of possible approaches.

**Review**

In this opening section you have been given the opportunity to

- describe features of genre
- identify common themes
- describe narrative voices
- link texts by genre and/or purpose
- construct frameworks for comparison of texts
- undertake independent critical reading
- become more confident in approaching unseen texts/extracts.

The rest of this chapter is divided into a series of sequences or study sections that will be helpful to you in your reading of a wide range of literary texts – both fiction and non-fiction – and in answering the types of questions that are likely to be set in examinations and in responding to coursework requirements. Within the sequences, you will find advice about how to analyse extracts. At the end of the chapter, there are some commentaries to provide you with exemplars of different ways of analysing narrative writing.

# The historical approach – 400 years of fiction

One of the skills which you will be expected to demonstrate during the course of your A-level studies in English is the ability to explore and compare texts belonging to different groups or genres. You will discover that there are a number of ways of approaching this task. This section focuses on three commonly used approaches

- thematic
- historical
- comparison of genre.

In the process, we shall have the opportunity to consider and compare different aspects of genre and features of composition.

## Thematic and historical approaches – chronology and genre

In this series of texts spanning 400 years, the linking factor is thematic – each text deals with a similar topic. Seafaring has played an important part in English history over many centuries. English ships travelled thousands of miles in search of trade and new lands to colonise. But these adventures were not without mishap and so the additional linking factor is that each text deals with shipwrecks and castaways.

In looking at these texts from a historical perspective, we take as our starting-point the fact that they were written over a period of time and may, possibly, provide evidence of some important features of development and change, both as regards the language that writers use and the style which they adopt.

In examining the extracts, you will have the opportunity to span a considerable period of literary time and become more confident in your discussion of

- different treatments of similar themes
- grammatical, syntactic, semantic and structural change

- changes and developments in narrative techniques, including voice
- writers' motives and approaches to moral and ethical issues
- variety and innovation in characterisation and presentation of events
- historical perspectives and readers' expectations
- use of commonly understood narrative conventions to extend the potential of the genre.

In addition to extending your knowledge and understanding of these issues, you will be introduced to the kind of terminology that you will need when you come to write about themes and narrative approaches in your essays and coursework. There will also be suggestions about your own creative writing tasks and the construction of coursework portfolios.

### Source texts for this section
The source texts for the first part of this investigation are extracts from

- *True Reportory of the Wrack,* a letter written by William Strachey, dated 15 July 1610
- *Robinson Crusoe* by Daniel Defoe, published 1719
- *The Beach* by Alex Garland, published 1997.

The common factor is that they deal with people who are on islands, away from their normal civilised life, and are in considerable danger.

## Writers in context

**William Strachey (1572–1621)** experienced at first hand the terrors of shipwreck and the challenge of survival on an uninhabited island. He was on board the flagship the *Sea Venture* when it was wrecked in a hurricane in 1609, while en route across the Atlantic from Plymouth to Jamestown, Virginia. The ship was owned by the Virginia Company, a trading enterprise, and was one of a fleet of nine supply vessels under the command of Admiral Sir George Summers. Under his direction, some of the ships managed to reach the shores of the Bermudas and were forced to stay there for another year until they could make the final leg of their voyage to the mainland.

Strachey was the appointed secretary to the company. In this capacity, he supplied reports to his employers which provided them (and later readers) with important evidence about conditions in the newly founded colony. Educated at Cambridge, he was one of the earliest English colonial historians and is best known for the letter from which the extract is taken. Though the text can be viewed as a private letter, we have evidence that it was widely circulated and was rewritten several times. It became known as the *True Reportory of the Wrack.* Some scholars believe that Shakespeare knew the letter and its contents well enough to use it as inspiration for his opening to *The Tempest,* in which a dreadful storm brings castaways to Prospero's island.

**Daniel Defoe (1660–1731)** earned his living both as a businessman and as a professional writer. His background was solidly middle class and his religious beliefs deeply rooted in the Puritan tradition. The most immediate difference between Strachey's letter and Defoe's novel *Robinson Crusoe* is that while Defoe presents his narrative of shipwrecked seafarer and long-term castaway as if the events were entirely authentic, readers understood the conventions of narrative and accepted that the events. while credible. were not necessarily true in the evidential sense of the word. *Robinson Crusoe,* for all that it is written as a real-life journal, is a fictionalised account. In the preface, Defoe states that he is the editor of Crusoe's writings. This allows him to present the story in the form of a first-person narrative within a frame which he as the author has created. The extract is from the opening section of Crusoe's 'journal'.

Alex Garland (1970– ) published his first novel at the age of 26. *The Beach* was an immediate success among young people who shared with Garland his passion for travel and adventure, specifically through the contemporary craze for backpacking in Asia. Set in Thailand, the story follows the progressively disturbing experiences of a group of backpackers who come across a remote island which has all the potential for paradise. The narrator, Richard, watches as the harmony of their relationship with the commune living there comes under pressure. As with many utopian experiments, this seemingly 'last place on earth' cannot be sustained. Garland presents the story, not as a celebration of backpacking, but as a criticism of a certain type of backpacker who believes that there is an Eden hidden away, waiting to be discovered, when in reality people bring their problems with them. It is themselves and not the land that destroys. The extract describes how the backpackers first became aware that they were intruding into a secret world.

## Extract from a letter written by William Strachey, dated 15 July 1610

East and by South we steered away as much as we could to beare upright, which was no small carefulnesse nor paine to doe, albeit we much unrigged our Ship, threw over-boord much luggage, many a Trunke and Chest (in which I suffered no meane losse) and staved many a Butt of Beere, Hogsheads of Oyle, Syder, Wine, and Vinegar ...

But see the goodnesse and sweet introduction of better hope, by our mercifull God given unto us. Sir George Summers, when no man dreamed of such happinesse, had discovered, and cried Land ... We were inforced to runne her ashoare, as neere the land as we could, which brought us within three quarters of a mile of shoare ...

We found it to be the dangerous and dreaded Iland, or rather Ilands of the Burmuda: whereof let mee give your ladyship a briefe description, before I proceed to my narration. And that the rather, because they be so terrible to all that ever touched on them, and such tempests, thunders, and other fearfull objects are seene and heard about them, that they be called commonly, the Devils Ilands, and are feared and avoided of all sea travellers alive, above any other place in the world. Yet it pleased our mercifull God, to make even this hideous and hated place, both the place of our safetie, and meanes of our deliverance.

And hereby also, I hope to deliver the world from a foule and generall errour: it being counted of most, that they can be no habitation for Men, but rather given over to Devils and wicked Spirits; whereas indeed wee find them now by experience, to bee as habitable and commodious as most Countries of the same climate and situation: insomuch as if the entrance into them wer as easie as the place it selfe is contenting, it had long ere this beene inhabited, as well as other Ilands. Thus shall we make it appeare, That Truth is the daughter of Time, and that men ought not to deny every thing which is not subject to their owne sense ...

Sure it is that there is to be no Rivers nor running Springs of fresh water to bee found upon any of them: when wee came first wee digged and found certaine gushings and soft bublings, which being either in bottoms, or on the side of hanging ground, were onely fed with raine water, which neverthelesse soone sinketh into the earth and vanisheth away ... A kind of webbe-footed fowle there is, of the bignesse of an English green Plover, or sea-Meawe, which all the Summer wee saw not ... Their colour is inclining to Russet, with white bellies (as are likewise the long feathers of their wings Russet and White) these gather themselves together and breed in those Ilands which are high, and so farre alone into the Sea, that the Wilde Hogges cannot swimme over them, and there in the ground they have their Burrowes, like Conyes in a Warren, and so wrought in the loose Mould, though not so deep ... and they were a good and well relished Fowle, fat and full as a Partridge ... The Tortoyse is reasonable toothsom (some say) wholsome meate. I am sure our Company liked the meate of them verie well, and one Tortyse would goe further amongst them, then three Hogs. One Turtle (for so we called them) feasted well a dozen Messes, appointing sixe to every Messe. It is such a kind of meate as a man can neither absolutely call Fish nor Flesh, keeping most what in the water ... .

## Activity 11
**Pair work**

### Considering change in language and style

Examine the differences between the English of Strachey's period, as demonstrated by this text, and modern English. You should use a dictionary which provides you with information about the origins of words and the changes in word usage. This branch of linguistic study is called etymology. Group your findings under the headings

- lexis and semantics
- grammar and syntax
- phonology/orthography
- punctuation.

## Activity 12
**Pair work**

### Continuity in language and style

Look at the Strachey text again and consider the things which have not changed. Make a list of textual references as evidence for your findings of continuity. Some of the things you should notice are

- word order
- types of sentences
- paragraphing
- function words
- conjunctions
- some pronouns.

Who is the narrator? Every narrative text has a 'voice', a term that is used to specify how we 'hear' the narrative. We all have a number of voices. We take roles according to our purpose and position. The voice through which a story is told has the power to influence our reception of it.

Strachey's letter is clearly written in a first-person narrative voice. This is a grammatical identification that also corresponds with the point of view because this is his eye-witness account. But there is more to it than that. When we examine the extract carefully, in the full knowledge of the context, we can detect that this is a structured account, intended for a specific audience. William Strachey was writing as company secretary. We should try to identify how this factor affected his writing choices

## Activity 13

### Writing accurately and confidently

Read the extract again very carefully. Then, using the following questions as a framework, consider how Strachey's voice comes over to the reader.

- In what capacity is Strachey writing?
- What motivated him to record his experiences in a letter?
- What aspects of the shipwreck and life on the island does he emphasise, and why?

- Did he write immediately or at a later date? What is the evidence?
- What moods did he want to convey?
- What impact did he want the letter to have on the reader(s)?
- What impression does he give of himself in the letter?
- Is it a public or a private document?

Write a short piece of about 700–800 words discussing Strachey's voice in this extract, supporting your ideas by specific examples from the text.

Compare what you have written with some of the ideas in the commentary on page 141.

Refer back to page 111 for background information on Daniel Defoe.

*Robinson Crusoe, saving his Goods out of the Wreck of his Ship.*

## Extract from *Robinson Crusoe* by Daniel Defoe

# The JOURNAL

*September 30, 1659.* I, poor miserable Robinson Crusoe, being ship wreck'd, during a dreadful Storm, in the offing, came on Shore on this dismal unfortunate Island, which I call'd the Island of Despair, all the rest of the Ship's Company being drown'd, and my self almost dead.

All the rest of that Day I spent in afflicting my self at the dismal Circumstances I was brought to, viz. I had neither Food, House, Clothes, Weapon, or Place to fly to, and in Despair of any Relief, saw nothing but Death before me, either that I should be devour'd by wild Beasts, murther'd by Savages, or starv'd to Death for Want of Food. At the Approach of Night, I slept in a Tree for fear of wild Creatures, but slept soundly tho' it rain'd all Night.

*October 1.* In the Morning I saw to my great Surprise, the Ship had floated with the high Tide, and was driven on Shore again much neare the Island, which as it was some Comfort on one hand, for seeing her sit upright, and not broken to Pieces, I hop'e, if the Wind abated, I might get on board, and get some Food and Necessaries out of her for my Relief; so on the other hand, it renew'd my Grief at the Loss of my Comrades, who I imagin'd if we had all staid on board might have sav'd the Ship, or at least that they would not all have been drown'd as they were; and that had the Men been sav'd, we might perhaps have built us a Boat out of the Ruins of the Ship, to have carried us to some other Part of the World. I spent great part of this Day in perplexing my self on these things; but at length seeing the Ship almost dry, I went on board; this day also it continu'd raining, tho' with no Wind at all.

*From the 1st of October to the 24th.* All these days entirely spent in many several Voyages to get all I could out of the Ship, which I brought on Shore, every Tide of Flood, upon Rafts. Much Rain also in these Days, tho' with some Intervals of fair Weather: But, it seems, this was the rainy Season.

*Oct. 20.* I overset my Raft and all the Goods I had upon it, but being in shoal Water, and the things being chiefly heavy, I recover'd many of them when the Tide was out.

*Oct 25.* It rain'd all Night and all Day, with some gusts of wind, during which time the Ship broke in Pieces, the Wind blowing a little harder than before, and was no more to be seen, except the Wreck of her, and that only at low Water. I spent this Day in recovering and securing the Goods which I had sav'd, that the Rain might not spoil them.

*Oct 26.* I walk'd about the Shore almost all Day to find out a Place to fix my Habitation, greatly concern'd to secure my self from an Attack in the Night, either from wild Beasts or Men. Towards

Night I fix'd upon a proper Place under a Rock, and mark'd out a Semi-Circle for my Encampment, which I resolv'd to strengthen with a Work, Wall, or Fortification made of double Piles, lin'd within with Cables, and without with Turf.

*From the 26th to the 30th,* I work'd very hard in carrying all my Goods to my new Habitation, tho' some Part of the time it rain'd exceeding hard.

*The 31st,* in the Morning I went out into the Island with my Gun to see for some Food, and discover the Country, when I kill'd a She-Goat, and her Kid follow'd me home, which I afterwards kill'd also because it would not feed.

*November 1.* I set up my Tent under a Rock, and lay there for the first Night, making it as large as I could with Stakes driven in to swing my Hammock upon.

*Nov. 2.* I set up all my Chests and Boards, and the Pieces of Timber which made my Rafts, and with them form'd a Fence round me, a little within the Place I had mark'd out for my Fortification.

*Nov. 3.* I went out with my Gun and kill'd two Fowls like Ducks, which were very good Food. In the Afternoon went to work to make me a Table.

*Nov. 4.* This Morning I began to order my times of Work, of going out with my Gun, time of Sleep, and time of Diversion, viz.: every morning I walk'd out with my Gun for two or three Hours if it did not rain, then employ'd my self to work till about Eleven a-Clock, then eat what I had to live on, and from Twelve to Two I lay down to sleep, the Weather being excessive hot, and then in the Evening to work again; The working Part of this Day and of the next were wholly employ'd in making my Table, for I was yet but a very sorry Workman, tho' Time and Necessity made me a compleat natural Mechanick soon after, as I believe it would do any one else.

## Activity 14   Considering change in language and style

Using the frameworks which you learnt in studying Strachey's writing, explain how this example of later English from Daniel Defoe differs from the earlier passage.

*Robinson Crusoe* is both an adventure story and a story of personal redemption, presented as an autobiographical diary. Towards the end of the seventeenth century the novel was beginning to emerge as a recognisable genre. Here there is an interesting integration of imagination and factual information to create this seemingly authentic tale of Crusoe's struggle against loneliness, privation and danger. In fact, there is a basis for the story in that Alexander Selkirk (1676–1721), a Scottish sailor, spent five years as a castaway on a desert island before being rescued. On his return to England, he managed to live off tales of his experiences and Defoe was certainly familiar with the facts of his case.

## Activity 15   Characterisation and voice

Group work

Using the material provided in the extract, draw up a pen portrait of Robinson Crusoe in his early days on the island.

**Activity 16**

## Where is the plot?

The story itself does not have a plot but it needs order and development. Crusoe himself provides these. Draw up a chart to list

- evidence that Crusoe's diary is real
- evidence that his diary is a piece of writing for an audience.

**Activity 17**

## Identifying the voice

Chart the progression of the passage to uncover the development from 'poor miserable Robinson Crusoe' down to 'made me a compleat natural Mechanick'. What voice emerges? Where do you identify

- Crusoe, the fictional character
- Crusoe, Defoe's fictional creation?

**Activity 18**

## Creating a main character

The most important feature of this extract by comparison with Strachey's account is the closeness of the reader to the narrator. Explain the ways in which Defoe engages the reader with Crusoe and his experiences. You may wish to include

- the use of the first-person narrator
- graphic description
- evocation of place
- expression of emotion
- changes in mood
- indications of character and personality.

You could also refer to the Strachey extract, using comparisons to extend your points.

Refer back to page 112 for background information on Alex Garland.

**Extract from *The Beach* by Alex Garland**

We set off immediately after breakfast: half a bar of chocolate each and cold noodles, soaked in most of the water from our canteens. There wasn't any point in hanging around. We needed to find a freshwater source, and according to Mister Duck's map, the beach was on the other side of the island.

At first we walked along the beach, hoping to circle the coast, but the sand soon turned to jagged rocks, which turned to impassable cliffs and gorges. Then we tried the other end, wasting precious time while the sun rose in the sky, and found the same barrier. We were left with no choice but to try inland. The pass between the peaks was the obvious goal so we slung our bin-liners over our shoulders and picked our way into the jungle.

The first two or three hundred metres from the shore were the hardest. The spaces between the palm trees were covered in a strange rambling bush with tiny leaves that sliced like razors, and the only way past them was to push through. But as we got further inland and the ground began to rise, the palms became less common than another kind of tree – trees like rusted, ivy-choked space rockets, with ten-foot roots that fanned from the trunk like stabilizer fins. With less sunlight coming through the canopy, the vegetation on the forest floor thinned out. Occasionally we were stopped by a dense spray of bamboo, but a short search would find an animal track or a path cleared by a fallen branch.

After Zeph's description of the jungle, with Jurassic plants and strangely coloured birds, I was vaguely disappointed by the reality. In many ways I felt like I was walking through an English forest, I'd just shrunk to a tenth of my normal size. But there were some things that felt suitably exotic. Several times we saw tiny brown monkeys scurrying up the trees, Tarzan-style lianas hung above us like stalactites – and there was the water: it dripped on our necks, flattened our hair, stuck our T-shirts to our chests. There was so much of it that our half-empty canteens stopped being a worry. Standing under a branch and giving it a shake provided a couple of good gulps, as well as a quick shower. The irony of having kept my clothes dry over the swim, only to have them soaked when we turned inland, didn't escape me.

After two hours of walking we found ourselves at the bottom of a particularly steep stretch of slope. We virtually had to climb it, pulling ourselves up on the tough fern stems to keep us from slipping down on the mud and dead leaves. Étienne was the first to get to the top and he disappeared over the ridge, then reappeared a few seconds later, beckoning enthusiastically.

'Hurry up!' he called. 'Really, it is amazing!'

'What is it?' I called back, but he'd disappeared again.

I redoubled my efforts, leaving Françoise behind.

The slope led to a football-pitch-sized shelf on the mountainside, so flat and neat that it seemed unnatural in the tangle of the surrounding jungle. Above us the slope rose again to what appeared to be a second shelf, and past that it continued straight up to the pass.

Étienne had gone further into the plateau and was standing in some bushy plants, gazing around with his hands on his hips.

'What do you think?' he said. I looked behind me. Far below I could see the beach we had come from, the island where our hidden rucksacks lay, and the many other islands beyond it.

'I didn't know the marine park was this big,' I replied.

'Yes. Very big. But that is not what I mean.'

I turned back to the plateau, putting a cigarette in my mouth. Then, as I patted down my pockets looking for my lighter, I noticed something strange. All the plants in the plateau looked vaguely familiar.

'Wow,' I said, and the cigarette dropped from my lips, forgotten.

'Yes.'

'... Dope?'

Étienne grinned. 'Have you ever seen so much?'

'Never ...' I pulled a few leaves from the nearest bush and rubbed them in my hands.

Étienne waded further into the plateau. 'We should pick some, Richard,' he said. 'We can dry it in the sun and ...' Then he stopped. 'Wait a moment, there is something funny here.'

'What?'

'Well, it is just so ... These plants ...' He crouched down, then looked round at me quickly. His lips had begun to curve into a smile, but his eyes were wide and I could literally see colour draining from his face. 'This is a field,' he said.

I froze. 'A field?'

'Yes. Look at the plants.'

'But it can't be a field. I mean, these islands are ...'

'The plants are in rows.'

'Rows ...'

We stared at each other. 'Jesus Christ,' I said slowly. 'Then we're in deep shit.'

## Activity 19 — Comparing the extracts

Draw up a framework for comparison of the three extracts by Strachey, Defoe and Garland. Write (or map out the structure of) an essay of 1000 words. Choose your own title and give yourself some freedom for developing your own focus. For example, you may wish to discuss

- the differences between those who had companions and Crusoe, who was alone
- the appeal to contemporary audiences
- the use of background detail
- evidence of plot or indications of likely development
- creation of mood
- narrative techniques
- use of sustained dialogue to further the narrative.

## Review

In this section you have been given the opportunity to

- examine extracts and compare them in speech and writing
- construct an introductory overview that establishes the common ground in texts and indicates areas of difference in theme and/or genre/treatment
- discuss and explain differences in writers' approaches according to context and purpose
- exemplify changes in language and style over time
- compare voices and other strategies for reader engagement
- demonstrate different purposes – information, persuasion, entertainment
- discuss the uses of speech in texts
- compare methods of characterisation.

### Key concepts

The art of effective critical appreciation takes us deeper into the mind of the craftsman. In creating narrative, writers make deliberate choices of theme, character, location and event. As students of language and literature, you need to appreciate these building blocks of narrative. A further step in understanding the narrative technique requires you to identify the voice of the storyteller. By taking both a thematic and a historical overview, it is possible to compare approaches and to consider how successive generations of writers have built on each other's achievements.

> **Writing skills**
> In the course of this section you have had the opportunity to practise your writing skills, using frameworks for comparison. The topics have included changes and continuity in written language and style over time and three examples of narrative approach – literary non-fiction, allegorical fiction and a hybrid of imaginative travel writing and utopian adventure.

# Values in literature – narrative and morality

Much early storytelling would have been associated with the passing on of received wisdom and the sharing of edifying accounts of bravery and virtue. A parallel strand of such narratives would certainly have been the cautionary tales of those who neglected good sense and went their own misguided way. The triumph of good over evil and of virtue over folly has provided the winning formula for many works of literature across all ages and cultures. It is the basis of the most common masterplots.

Some of the earliest examples of narrative to which we still have access are to be found in religious and moral works such as the parables of the Bible and Aesop's fables. These stories are generally unequivocal in their praise of the good and their condemnation of the wicked. Though neither parables nor fables had their origin in written English, both have contributed significantly to our literary history through the many translations which have been widely read throughout the centuries. In particular, these two genres of narrative have provided readers with an immediate recognition of archetypal figures and universal stereotypes, particularly through the use of animals and the connotations associated with them. This characterisation of animals, usually referred to as anthropomorphism, is the foundation of the beast fable.

As part of our study of the change and development in English narrative prose, we shall consider how this universal phenomenon, in which the art of storytelling is inextricably linked to the narrator's didactic purpose, has impacted upon our own literary history and how motives for writing have helped to shape genre. The best moralists have used satire, comedy and persuasion, indeed the whole raft of creative skills, to make their works more effective.

In this section you are going to investigate three examples of explicitly didactic writing and one in which the authorial intention is more subtly conveyed. In doing so, you will have the opportunity to span a considerable period of literary time and become more confident in your discussion of

- changes and developments in narrative techniques over time
- writers' motives and approaches to moral and ethical issues
- variety and innovation in characterisation and presentation of events
- historical perspectives and readers' expectations
- the impact of medium on the language of narrative.

In addition to extending your knowledge and understanding of these issues, you will be introduced to the kind of terminology that you will need when you come to write about themes and narrative approaches in your essays and coursework. There will also be suggestions about your own creative writing tasks.

**119**

Source texts for this section

The source texts for this investigation are

- *Of the Ant and the Sygalle* from Caxton's translations of Aesop's fables (1484)
- *The Judgment of Solomon* from the King James Bible (1611)
- an extract from David Kossoff's retelling of Bible stories, broadcast in the early 1960s on the BBC Light Programme (the most popular station at the time)
- an extract from *Oryx and Crake* by Margaret Atwood (2003).

# Writers in context

**Aesop:** Tradition has it that Aesop lived in Greece in or around the fifth century BC. Whether he was a real person is uncertain but his name has become synonymous with fables of wisdom and common sense. It is unlikely that any of the early fables were written down and certainly none have been handed down to us in their original form, but the genre has proved enduringly popular.

**William Caxton (*c.*1442–*c.*1491):** When Caxton published Aesop's fables in 1484 the material would have had a lot of appeal for those who could afford to buy his book. He translated his selected fables from the French version that was popular at the time. While it is true that the structure and narrative style of writing has undergone considerable evolution, we should be wary of approaching early texts at too simplistic a level. Writers have always sought to delight as well as challenge their readers. This is the work of a truly skilled writer who achieved a sound message within the framework of a pleasing structure.

**King James Bible:** The translation of the Bible commissioned during the reign of James I and first published in 1611 became known as the Authorised Version, as both the interpretation of the scriptures and the language used had the approval of the monarch and of leading churchmen of the day. It was not an entirely new piece of work, for the eminent scholars who were responsible for its production were heavily dependent on earlier translations. Their objective was to provide a translation that was both accessible and linguistically pleasing and that could benefit a wide range of people, many of whom would not be able to read the text for themselves but would be able to follow it easily as it was read out in church services. The King James Bible has achieved the status of a benchmark in the development of English, both for its clarity and for the richness of its vigorous prose. David Crystal examines its lasting influence on English in *The Story of English* (pages 271–7, Penguin 2004).

**David Kossoff (1919–2005)** was born in London, the son of immigrant Jewish parents. His humble origins and limited formal education, far from hindering him, made him determined to better himself, and he became an experienced actor and broadcaster. He is especially remembered for his retelling of well-known Bible stories on radio. He adapted the most memorable and accessible parts of the Bible, using skilful paraphrase which appealed to a very wide audience of listeners. His programmes were quite short, lasting approximately five minutes, and were presented as a daily series at five minutes to ten each morning of the week. His adaptations were later published by the BBC under the title *David Kossoff at Five to Ten*.

**Margaret Atwood (1939– )** is a Canadian writer, poet and critic who has achieved an international reputation as a novelist. While her narratives are remarkable for their inventiveness and incisive prose style, she manages to engage her reader in a profound debate about the nature of human dignity and her concerns for social justice and the future of the human race.

## Of the Ant and the Sygalle

It is good to purueye hym self in the somer season of suche thynges
wherof he shalle myster and haue nede in wynter season
as thow mayst see by this present fable of the sygalle whiche in the wynter tyme
went and demaunded of the ant some of her corne for to ete
And thenne the Ant sayed to the sygall
What hast thow done al the somer last passed
And the sygalle ansuerd
I have songe
And after sayd the ante to her
Of my corne shalt not thou none haue
And yf thow hast songe alle the somer daunse now in wynter
And therfore there is one tyme for to doo some labour and werk
And one tyme to haue rest
For he that werketh not ne doth no good
Shall have oft at his teeth grete cold and lacke at his nede

The word 'sygalle' carries the same sense as the modern French word 'cigale' meaning a cicada, though later versions of this story refer to a grasshopper. The layout of Caxton's original, in which there were no line breaks, has been modified so that the fable is easier to read.

Before the next two activities, which investigate meaning and narrative technique, we shall take the opportunity to consider changes in language since the time of Caxton. In deciphering this piece of late Middle English, you will find it helpful to read the fable aloud. You will have little difficulty in recognising most of the words which are still in common use. Two words – **purueye** and **myster** are glossed here to help you.

- In line 1, 'purueye' means 'purvey' or 'provide'; the word is still used in the context of a purveyor of foodstuffs, one who gathers together.
- In line 2, 'myster' means 'muster'; the word implies a gathering together, usually of men for the army; it is used here to suggest stockpiling food.

You will notice that the extract demonstrates changes in spelling, syntax and grammar that have taken place since Caxton's time. Lexis is surprisingly familiar, though the way in which words are used has changed. The most obvious differences concern spelling and orthography, some examples of which show variations even within this short extract. The letters 'i' and 'y' seem to be chosen at the discretion of the writer rather than by rule. The letters 'u' and 'v' were written identically unless they appeared at the start of a word.

The different emphasis between 'shall' and 'will' is shown here. You can also see inflectional endings on verbs – '-eth' – and the use of the now archaic second-person-singular pronoun 'thou' or 'thow'.

Punctuation, or lack of it, would now be considered incorrect. The most striking variation grammatically is the use of the double negative (lines 10 and 14), which still persists in some dialects but is not Standard English. If you check Caxton's choice of vocabulary in an etymological dictionary, you will see how many words have been borrowed from French. If you want to check word order within sentences and phrases, you should try to write a modern version.

Finally, you can see how the way people pronounced words has affected the way they are being written in this text. Remember that Caxton's own variety of English reflected the

English he was used to in the London area at the time he lived there. We cannot make broad assumptions about the wider use of English in the fifteenth century on the basis of this one piece of writing.

## Activity 20    Appreciating the meaning of the text

**Group work**

The challenges in terms of scope and depth shown in this fable are very limited, unlike the demands you will experience from the kind of novel you are required to study as part of your course. This activity will, however, help you appreciate which particular narrative skills Caxton has used even in so short a piece. It will also introduce you to some terminology that you will find helpful as well as reminding you of terms you already know.

Are these statements about the fable true or false?

1 The fable deals with the ant's moral dilemma.
2 The sygalle gets exactly what she deserves.
3 The narrator's commentary is longer than the action.
4 The reader is free to make a personal judgement.
5 The fable makes use of three voices.
6 The narrator is biased.
7 The sygalle is presented as a stereotype.
8 The narrator contextualises the fable for the reader.
9 The sygalle is given a rounded character.
10 The narrator presents the ant as being ungenerous.
11 The style is economical.
12 There is an assumption about the reader's response.
13 The narrator summarises and interprets.
14 There is a sense of closure.
15 The fable teaches the highest moral values.
16 This is a cautionary tale.
17 There is a single moral perspective.
18 The ant's experience is universal.
19 The sygalle attempts to exploit the ant.
20 There is no sympathy expressed for the sygalle.
21 The human types represented are easily recognised.
22 The sygalle's explanation presents her as feckless.
23 The dialogue is well shaped to convey character.
24 The opening statement sets the tone.
25 There is deliberate use of contrasting phrases.
26 The narrator is confident of the reader's agreement.
27 The ant's question is rhetorical.
28 The fable has a clear discourse structure.
29 The reader becomes involved in the sygalle's problem.
30 The narrator's contribution is redundant.

Look carefully at your answers and compare them with responses from other students in your group. What have you discovered? Use your findings for the next activity.

## Activity 21 Discussing the narrative approach

**Pair work**

The statements in Activity 20 are not in a logical order for discussing the narrative approach. Reorder the statements to make an outline for the piece of writing entitled 'Discussion of the narrative features that are characteristic of Caxton's fable'.

Use the newly ordered statements to produce your written discussion. You will find it helpful to cluster your ideas under these headings:

- theme
- voice
- characterisation
- language choices
- sentence types
- discourse structure.

This exercise gives you the chance to practise skills in organisation and analysis.

Turn to the commentary on page 143 so that you can compare your ideas with another version.

## Activity 22 Demonstrating your own writing skills

Write a short piece of prose which provides the opportunity to consider the problem from the sygalle's point of view. You can employ any type of genre or narrative approach which seems appropriate.

## Activity 23 Commenting on your own writing skills

Write a brief commentary on the piece you have written in Activity 22, explaining your choice of narrative devices.

- What devices have you incorporated that were not evident in Caxton's text?
- What changes have you made to ensure that the sygalle's point of view is prioritised?

You should include consideration of your choice of narrative voice, either first person or third person, and evaluate the success of your choice. How effective is your narrative in presenting a different perspective?

We now move forward in time to Early Modern English. The next text is an extract from the Bible, taken from the Authorised Version or King James Bible of 1611. It is another story in which justice is seen to be done. (The numbers in brackets are the verse numbers in the Bible.)

### The Judgment of Solomon

[16] Then came there two women, that were harlots, unto the king, and stood before him.
[17] And the one woman said, O my lord, I and this woman dwell in one house; and I was delivered of a child with her in the house.

[18] And it came to pass the third day after that I was delivered, that this woman was delivered also: and we were together; there was no stranger with us in the house, save we two in the house.

[19] And this woman's child died in the night; because she overlaid it.

[20] And she arose at midnight, and took my son from beside me, while thine handmaid slept, and laid it in her bosom, and laid her dead child in my bosom.

[21] And when I rose in the morning to give my child suck, behold, it was dead: but when I had considered it in the morning, behold, it was not my son, which I did bear.

[22] And the other woman said, Nay; but the living is my son, and the dead is thy son. And this said, No; but the dead is thy son, and the living is my son. Thus they spake before the king.

[23] Then said the king, The one saith, This is my son that liveth, and thy son is the dead: and the other saith, Nay; but thy son is the dead, and my son is the living.

[24] And the king said, Bring me a sword. And they brought a sword before the king.

[25] And the king said, Divide the living child in two, and give half to the one, and half to the other.

[26] Then spake the woman whose the living child was unto the king, for her bowels yearned upon her son, and she said, O my lord, give her the living child, and in no wise slay it. But the other said, Let it be neither mine nor thine, but divide it.

[27] Then the king answered and said, Give her the living child, and in no wise slay it: she is the mother thereof.

[28] And all Israel heard of the judgment which the king had judged; and they feared the king: for they saw that the wisdom of God was in him, to do judgment.

## Activity 24

**Class work**

# Examining the language and style of the text

Look carefully at the extract and identify aspects of language and composition practice which are different from our own modern practice. You could use this framework for your findings:

- lexis
- semantics
- grammar
- syntax
- idiom
- literary approach.

## Activity 25

**Group work**

# Examining narrative voices and characterisation

Read the extract out loud so that you can appreciate fully the four voices. Can you identify any characteristic language or idiolect? How does it compare, for example, with a play script, with a voice-over commentary? It might be interesting to see how easily it would adapt.

Turn to page 144 for a commentary.

The extract on page 125 shows you a version of the same story from the Bible but written especially for radio. While the meaning of the story has not changed, the method of presentation has been significantly altered to accommodate a listening audience, with particular attention to the needs of those who are unfamiliar with the character and reputation of Solomon. As a preface to the story, David Kossoff summarises earlier sections of the Book of Kings so that Solomon's wisdom and the source of his authority are more easily grasped.

### David Kossoff's Judgment of Solomon

Now, when King Solomon took over the throne of his father King David, he wasn't after all very old. Early twenties. He had a good head on him and a good education. He was interested in everything and possessed a marvellous memory. Strong-minded; like his mother Bathsheba. He was remarkable and rare. More sophisticated than his father, who'd begun life, you remember, as a shepherd-boy. Solomon for *all* his life had been the son of a *king*, the first great King of Israel, and maybe, the greatest.

The most important gift left to Solomon by David was a united and peaceful people. The twelve tribes close and happy together as never before. Missing their beloved King David but seeing in Solomon a new David. And Solomon was aware of the huge responsibility but not daunted by it. It's no fun being the son of a great man. People compare.

Not long after Solomon became king, during a big religious meeting, God appeared to him in a dream. A sort of vision-dream, and God asked Solomon how he could help.

Solomon was honest and told God how very much aware he was of his young shoulders and that he could do with a really wise head on them. 'An understanding mind,' he said. 'Clear knowledge of good and evil. This is a huge people. I don't know much.'

God was pleased. The humility and modesty pleased him. It always does. 'Right,' he told Solomon, 'you shall have wisdom and discernment as no one before you and as none who come after you. Also you shall have things you didn't ask for, honour, riches and possessions. Great power and peace.' And it was almost from the next day that Solomon began to be called 'wise'.

Part of this new God-given wisdom was a great knowledge of people and how they think. One day two women were brought before him for judgment. A nasty case. One woman accused the other of swapping her dead baby for her, the accuser's, live one. In the night. Both babies only days old.

Solomon listened. Both ladies very upset. Lot of screaming and crying. 'Bring a sword,' said Solomon. 'Cut the live baby in two. Each lady to have a half.'

Silence. Then the real mother begged it not to be done. 'Give her the baby,' she said. 'Don't kill my son!'

Solomon did nothing of the kind. 'Keep your son,' he said. 'Next case.'

---

**Activity 26** | ## Syntax in speech – writing for a listening audience

You may be tempted to describe the more modern language in this version of the Bible story as 'simpler'. Take a few minutes to analyse the style in detail before committing yourself. What exactly do we mean by 'simpler'? Read the text carefully. Try it again out loud and decide what language strategies make it suitable for its purpose.

There is something very different about the choice of style here. Look to see how many sentences are minor sentences (this means the main verb is not expressed). The omitted verb is usually the verb 'to be'. So, 'A nasty case' is a shortened form of 'It was a nasty case' or even 'What a nasty case it was'.

Write a short piece (500 words), identifying and describing the features of style that make this piece of storytelling particularly suitable for radio. You should consider

- discourse structure
- sentence construction
- presentation of character
- use of direct and reported speech
- reliance on the original
- creative approach

## Activity 27 Comparing texts

With reference to both accounts of Solomon's judgement on pages 123–125, identify and discuss the features of composition that make each text suitable for its purpose. By now, you should be able to construct your own framework for the piece. Look back at previous sections to remind yourself of the range of topics for discussing choices of language and style. In addition, you should consider

- context of production and context of reception
- suitability of the vehicle for conveying moral and ethical issues.

Refer back to page 120 for background information on Margaret Atwood.

### Extract from *Oryx and Crake* by Margaret Atwood

In this extract, Jimmy recalls what he knows about Oryx, the woman he loves. She guards the secrets of her past life quite closely but, from snippets of information, he eventually pieces together that she was sold into slavery by her widowed mother, who would otherwise have been unable to provide for the younger children. Her story encapsulates the plight of the impoverished peasantry of those Far Eastern countries in which bond labour, child prostitution and human trafficking are inescapable facts of life.

When Jimmy was seven or eight or nine, Oryx was born. Where exactly? Hard to tell. Some distant, foreign place.

It was a village though, said Oryx. A village with trees all around and fields nearby, or possibly rice paddies. The huts had thatch on some of the roofs – palm fronds? – although the best huts had roofs of tin. A village in Indonesia, or else Myanmar? Not those, said Oryx, though she couldn't be sure. It wasn't India, though. Vietnam? Jimmy guessed. Cambodia? Oryx looked down at her hands, examining her nails. It didn't matter.

She couldn't remember the language she'd spoken as a child. She'd been too young to retain it, that earliest language: the words had all been scoured out of her head. But it wasn't the language of the city to which she'd first been taken, or not the same dialect, because she'd had to learn a different way of speaking. She did remember that: the clumsiness of the words in her mouth, the feeling of being struck dumb.

This village was a place where everyone was poor and there were many children, said Oryx. She herself was quite little when she was sold. Her mother had a number of children, among them two older sons who would soon be able to work the fields, which was a good thing because the father was sick. He coughed and coughed; this coughing punctuated her earliest memories.

Something wrong with the lungs, Jimmy had guessed. Of course, they all probably smoked like maniacs when they could get the cigarettes: smoking dulled the edge. (He'd congratulated himself on this insight.) The villagers set the father's illness down to bad water, bad fate, bad spirits. Illness had an element of shame to it; no one wanted to be contaminated by the illness of another. So the father of Oryx was pitied, but also blamed and shunned. His wife tended him with silent resentment.

Bells were rung, however. Prayers were said. Small images were burned in the fire. But all of this was useless, because the father died. Everyone in the village knew what would happen next, because if there was no man to work in the fields or the rice paddies, then the raw materials of life had to come from somewhere else.

Oryx had been a younger child, often pushed to the side, but suddenly she was made much of and given better food than usual, and a special blue jacket, because the other village women were helping out and wanted her to look pretty and healthy. Children who were ugly or deformed, or who were not bright or who couldn't talk very well – such children went for less, or might not be sold at all. The village women might want to sell their own children one day, and if they helped out they would be able to count on such help in return.

In the village it was not called 'selling,' this transaction. The talk about it implied apprenticeship. The children were being trained to earn their living in the wide world: this was the gloss put on it. Besides, it they stayed where they were, what was there for them to do? Especially the girls, said Oryx. They would only get married and make more children, who would then have to be sold in their turn. Sold, or thrown in the river, to float way to the sea; because there was only so much food to go around.

## Activity 28

**Pair work**

### Creating the narrative voice

1 Consider how the voices of Jimmy, Oryx and the omniscient narrator are woven seamlessly into the account. Try to identify the contribution of each voice and justify your choice by reference to the actual wording of the text.

2 In what ways is this approach different from conventional dialogue?

3 How does the choice of language create a feeling of a thought process rather than of a writing process on Jimmy's part?

4 What ethical issue is being explored here? What conclusions are being drawn?

5 Is it possible to identify authorial opinion and if so, how?

## Activity 29

### Writing confidently about narrative technique

Using your findings in Activity 28, write a short piece (750 words) on the narrative style of the extract. You should look back over previous sections to draw up a focused agenda.

## Activity 30

### Coursework writing

*Either:* Refer to the complete text of *Oryx and Crake* to appreciate the whole of Oryx's story and the other aspects of the plot. Base your coursework around the multiple themes and the exploration of human failure. You should also consider the complex style of narrative for which, we hope, this section has prepared you.

*Or:* Using a text of your own choice, explore multiple themes and narrative techniques. This activity represents a greater challenge than any of the preceding exercises. It demands higher-level skills. You would need to take more responsibility for setting an agenda, for researching background and developing a personal approach.

**Review**

In this section you have been given the opportunity to

- identify ethical and moral issues in texts
- recognise the voice of narrator and fictional character
- appreciate perceptions and viewpoints
- explain how moral and ethical issues are presented through character and dialogue
- discuss the language strategies that deal with conflicting perceptions
- compare texts for their meaning and method.

## Key concepts

Writers throughout the ages have used narrative as a way of conveying moral and spiritual values and underpinning belief systems. Their approaches can be broadly divided between those whose purpose is certain and which meets with immediate recognition by the reader and those which explore a more complex and challenging dimension. It is a mistake to imagine that literature has developed along a simple continuum, from straightforward message to complex discussion, but it is true that writers have built on the work of their predecessors to create new and stimulating ways of presenting moral and ethical debates through narrative.

## Writing skills

You have had practice in writing about texts in a focused way. You should now understand the distinction between writing about themes and writing about the craft of composition. You should be able to identify and discuss the links between the writer's choice of theme and the literary and linguistic choices which are used. You have had practice in responding to set agendas in and creating frameworks for writing. You should have extended your knowledge of technical terms appropriate to the study of literature.

# Evocation of place – background and description in narrative

So far, we have been taking a chronological perspective on changes in English and we have been looking at works of literature in a way that suggests we expect to find solid evidence of language change as the years go by, because experience tells us that this is an inevitable development in the history of all living languages. When we compare the language and style in works of literature written several hundred years apart, we feel very confident of finding obvious differences in the choice and use of vocabulary and in some grammatical constructions. This was amply demonstrated when we compared the language of *Robinson Crusoe* with the speech of Alex Garland's characters. It would be true to say, however, that many of the differences that we have noted are surface features, such as changes in lexis, idiom and prose construction.

There are, however, some underlying differences to be considered, such as the writer's intentions and the choice of genre. These may be linked to developments in the art of writing and changes in readers' expectations, as well as appeal to a wider reading public. So, in this section, we will be considering how the study of more fundamental changes in language and style can be made clearer by looking at several extracts together. These changes may be linked to diachronic change or to synchronic change. We shall see. We shall also be looking more carefully at the relationship between literary works and literary non-fiction.

Works of literary non-fiction are becoming increasingly popular and are achieving status with the reading public. The specifications for English Language & Literature recognise the importance of this genre and provide students with opportunities to study this type of writing in greater depth. This section is designed to help you reach a high standard in these important Assessment Objectives, which require you to understand different forms of writing, and be able to discuss the differences knowledgeably. You must be able to use the terminology that is appropriate for literary and linguistic analysis. Above all, you have to appreciate how context and purpose may affect a writer's choice of language and/or style.

### Source texts for this section

The extracts for this investigation are from three source texts that are set in Africa:

- *Heart of Darkness* by Joseph Conrad, a short story (1899)
- *Congo Journey* by Redmond O'Hanlon, a travelogue (1996)
- *A Passage to Africa* by George Alagiah, an autobiography (2001).

Description of place has played a large part in the development of the novel and in other prose writings, such as travelogues, diaries, autobiographies and journalism.

By looking in detail at three extracts from books which have a common setting but which are very different in style and genre, you will be able to explore the kind of changes in language and style which you are likely to encounter in works of fiction and literary non-fiction in which background description and choice of environment play an important part. It is not intended that you should compare the extracts. It is more a case of examining each writer's approach to composition, given that Conrad was writing a short story while O'Hanlon's book is a travelogue. Categorising George Alagiah's book requires some thought. For now, we want to consider changes from one genre to another, rather than simply concentrating on surface features of genre and change over time.

## Writers in context

It will be useful to reflect briefly on the background of these three writers, and their works. It will help you to appreciate that they share a common backcloth for their writing. While having different authorial objectives and choosing different approaches to composition, they share a concern for the misunderstanding between races and the abuse of power.

**Joseph Conrad (1857–1924)** is widely recognised as one of the finest writers of English prose and as a master of storytelling. He had been a seaman and had travelled extensively, experiencing the hardships of foreign travel during the later years of the nineteenth century. He also gained first-hand knowledge of some of the darker corners of the globe, in particular of Central Africa, where he witnessed the injustices of colonialism. In his short story *Heart of Darkness*, the main character, Marlow, recounts to his friends the details of his dangerous expedition up the River Congo, as captain of a steamboat. As an employee of a Belgian trading company, he was on an ill-fated mission to bring assistance to a man called Kurtz who was in charge of an isolated trading post. Conrad knew the country and customs he incorporated into his story and made them an important part of the reader's experience. In the extract here, Marlow describes one of many unnerving encounters with the native peoples, on whose territory he and his companions are intruding. Marlow's use of the word 'pilgrims', in referring to certain other white men on the boat, is ironic. The god they worship is profit and they are on their way to exploit the riches of the jungle.

Redmond O'Hanlon (1947– ) is a scholar, explorer and journalist. He was natural history editor for the *Times Literary Supplement* and is widely recognised as one of the most intrepid travellers of our time as well as one of the most sensitive towards native peoples and their endangered environment. His travelogues are characterised by their offbeat, often very funny anecdotes but there is also a positively lyrical quality in many of his descriptions. He is master of a style that is broadly categorised as literary non-fiction. In the extract here, O'Hanlon and his companions, Lary Shaffer, an American professor of psychology, and Marcellin Agnagna, an expert in wildlife from the Ministry for the Conservation of Water and Forests (People's Republic of the Congo), have undertaken a daring expedition into the heart of the Congo jungle. On this occasion, they have been invited to accompany a hunting party. The pigmy people share with them the secrets of their ancient survival skills.

George Alagiah (1955– ), best known as the BBC presenter of the six o'clock news, is an acknowledged authority on African affairs. From his earliest years, he experienced racial and religious prejudice but nothing could prepare him for the shock of what he saw in post-colonial Africa. Born of Tamil parents in Sri Lanka (then known as Ceylon), at the age of five he emigrated with his family to the newly independent African state of Ghana, where his father believed the family would be free from the tensions between Ceylon's two communities – the Sinhalese, who were mainly Buddhists, and the Tamils, predominantly Hindus. Though George attended boarding school in Britain, he returned home regularly for holidays with his family, who continued to live in various African states for some years. He has travelled extensively in the course of his work and now lives permanently in the United Kingdom. His book *A Passage to Africa* gives an account of his personal experiences of Africa as he guides the reader through his journalistic missions and his interpretation of Africa.

As you read the following extracts for the first time, make a few notes to flag up anything you consider particularly important from the point of view of language and style, in preparation for the focused activities.

### Extract from *Heart of Darkness* by Joseph Conrad

'Towards the evening of the second day we judged ourselves about eight miles from Kurtz's station. I wanted to push on; but the manager looked grave, and told me the navigation up there was so dangerous that it would be advisable, the sun being very low already, to wait where we were till next morning. Moreover, he pointed out that if the warning to approach cautiously were to be followed, we must approach in daylight – not at dusk, or in the dark. This was sensible enough. Eight miles meant nearly three hours' steaming for us, and I could also see suspicious ripples at the upper end of the reach. Nevertheless, I was annoyed beyond expression at the delay, and most unreasonably too, since one night more could not matter much after so many months. As we had plenty of wood, and caution was the word, I brought up in the middle of the stream. The reach was narrow, straight, with high sides like a railway cutting. The dusk came gliding into it long before the sun had set. The current ran smooth and swift, but a dumb immobility sat on the banks. The living trees, lashed together by the creepers and every living bush of the undergrowth, might have been changed into stone, even to the slenderest twig, to the lightest leaf. It was not sleep – it seemed unnatural, like a state of trance. Not the faintest sound of any kind could be heard. You looked on amazed, and began to suspect yourself of being deaf – then the night came suddenly, and struck you blind as well. About three in the morning some large fish leaped, and the loud splash made me jump as though a gun had been fired. When the sun rose there was a white fog, very warm and clammy, and more blinding than the night. It did not shift or drive; it was just there, standing all round you like something solid. At eight or nine, perhaps, it lifted as a shutter lifts. We had a glimpse of the towering multitude of trees, of the immense matted jungle, with the blazing little ball of the sun hanging over it – all perfectly still – and then the white shutter came down again, smoothly, as if sliding in greased grooves. I ordered the chain, which we had begun to heave in, to be paid out again. Before it stopped running with a muffled rattle, a cry, a very loud cry, as of infinite desolation, soared slowly in the opaque air. It ceased. A complaining clamour, modulated in savage discords, filled our ears. The sheer unexpectedness of it made my hair stir under my cap. I don't know how it struck the others: to me it seemed as though the mist itself had screamed, so suddenly, and apparently from all sides at once, did this tumultuous and mournful uproar arise. It culminated in a hurried outbreak of almost intolerably excessive shrieking, which stopped short, leaving us stiffened in a variety of silly attitudes, and obstinately listening to the nearly as appalling and excessive silence. "Good God! What is the meaning–?" stammered at my elbow one of the pilgrims, – a little fat man, with sandy hair and red whiskers, who wore side-spring boots, and pink pyjamas tucked into his socks. Two others remained open-mouthed a whole minute, then dashed into the little cabin, to rush out incontinently and stand darting scared glances, with Winchesters at "ready" in their hands. What we could see was just the steamer we were on, her outlines blurred as though she had been on the point of dissolving, and a misty strip of water, perhaps two feet broad, around her – and that was all. The rest of the world was nowhere, as far as our eyes and ears were concerned. Just nowhere. Gone, disappeared; swept off without leaving a whisper or a shadow behind.

'I went forward, and ordered the chain to be hauled in short, so as to be ready to trip the anchor and move the steamboat at once if necessary. "Will they attack?" whispered an awed voice. "We will all be butchered in this fog," murmured another. The faces twitched with the strain, the hands trembled slightly, the eyes forgot to wink. It was very curious to see the contrast of expressions of the white men and of the black fellows of our crew, who were as much strangers to that part of the river as we, though their homes were only eight hundred miles away. The whites, of course greatly discomposed, had besides a curious look of being painfully shocked by such an outrageous row. The others had an alert, naturally interested expression; but their faces were essentially quiet, even those of the one or two who grinned as they hauled at the chain. Several exchanged short, grunting phrases, which seemed to settle the matter to their satisfaction.'

---

| Activity 31 | Exploring *Heart of Darkness* |
| --- | --- |

**Pair work**
**Group work**

Allocate one of the following tasks to each small group or pair in the class. Report findings in a plenary session, using an OHT where appropriate.

1   Plot the passage of time through the extract, using the time markers in the text. Don't forget to include both the man-made markers and the natural markers. Produce a chart to demonstrate your findings to the class. Generate a discussion about the framing and shaping of the extract.

2   Collect together all the words and phrases that could be considered technical terms in navigation or sailing contexts. Explain what they mean and what they contribute to the account. (Some of the words may have other meanings in different contexts.)

3   Draw a sketch of the steamboat's position in relation to other named physical features of the area, using the information in the extract. Explain the potential dangers to those aboard ship. How does the language of the passage convey this fear?

4   Collate references to plants and vegetation. Produce a chart that identifies generic terms and specialist botanical terms. Lead a discussion about Marlow's familiarity with the environment.

131

5 Collate all references to silence. Explain the effect on the reader and how it conveys a sinister mood.

6 Collate all references to noise – natural, mechanical or human – on a chart. Lead a discussion on the connotations of the most important words or phrases. Summarise the findings on the chart.

7 Summarise the reactions of the 'pilgrims' and the black crew. Select words or phrases that convey an idea of moral or spiritual values. Suggest how Marlow's character can be assessed by what he says here.

8 Present a brief written report on how Marlow conducted himself on this occasion, using the information in the text but adopting an assumed persona of a director in the trading company. Comment upon Marlow's suitability for further employment with the company.

## Extract from *Congo Journey* by Redmond O'Hanlon

So Marcellin, Lary and I set off in single file behind Beya, who in his right hand carried a long spear with a barbed iron point, and, suspended on split-vine straps from his shoulders, two huge bundles of liana-rope mesh hanging front and rear, a hunting net. The fearsome load had no effect on his habitual pace: I barely had time to notice the occasional spiky red flowers with no name seeming to hang disembodied in the gloom three feet above the jungle floor (waiting to be fertilized by what? Bees, butterflies, thrips?) and, beneath great buttressed trees, a scatter of fruit like giant puffballs (but they were green), before the sweat began to run into my eyes, my glasses steamed up every time I lowered my head, and it took all my energy to avoid the sudden tangle of lianas with inch-long thorns, the twist of surface roots across the path, and to concentrate on Lary's boots, the tallest, sturdiest pair of L.L. Bean.

An hour later, Beya stopped in a clearing, an opening made by the collapse of a massive tree, its surprisingly shallow root-mass (there was no tap root) jacked out of the ground at right angles, the top of its rough circumference three or four feet above Marcellin's head.

With a start I realised that the clearing was full of people: men and boys sitting silent, impassive, their arms on their knees, their dark-brown skins matching the brown of the fallen leaves, the soft shadows. Their spears were leaning, point up, against the surrounding trees: their nets, like inverted root-masses, hung from saplings cut off at pigmy head-height and trimmed into posts; and each net was crowned with phrynium leaves.

The women appeared behind us, mothers with toddlers slung to their sides, and the girls who had danced till dawn. The men and boys got up, swung their nets over their shoulders, collected their spears and moved off ahead; the women followed. A young boy, taking three attempts to lift a hunting net on to his head, was the last to leave. He looked out at us as he passed, his eyes big as an antelope's between the dreadlocks of the net, his forehead still with the convex curve of childhood. He walked up the rack (marked only by the odd bent-back twig or cut liana) in front of us, staggering slightly under his load. Lary said 'We should help that kid. I'll carry his net.' 'Quiet,' whispered Marcellin over his shoulder. 'We must now be silent. Besides, for you it would be impossible. It is difficult.' A thought struck him and he swung right round. 'You'd catch yourself in it!' he shouted, delighted with the joke. 'You'd catch yourself!'

The soil grew wetter, the canopy lower, the thickets denser, the thorns more predatory, and eventually everyone halted. Nobody spoke; the men, weaving between the trees, unrolled the nets with surprising speed; with wooden pegs already tied to the mesh the women fastened the bottom lines to the ground and hooked the tops to bushes and shrubs and saplings; a three-foot-high fence curved out of sight in both directions. Behind it, two or three yards back, the women sat and waited, half-concealed in the vegetation. Marcellin, Lary and I followed suit: fifteen yards away, on the other side of the net, a spearman stood almost invisible in the shadow of a thicket.

From the middle distance the sound of the beat reached us, a high-pitched yodelling; and ten minutes later a long-legged brown and white dog followed his muzzle out of the thicket, saw the net, realized he had overshot, wagged his tail apologetically and plunged back in; the beaters shouted sharp instructions to the waiting spearman; a line of leaves flicked fast across in front of us; a woman yelled from somewhere down the nets to our right.

'Mosomé! Mosomé!' sang a little boy, running past us.

'The Bay duiker!' said Marcellin. 'Quick'. And we ran after the little boy – which was not as easy as he made it look: by the time Lary and I had disentangled ourselves from a hanging net of thorned lianas the woman and two hunters were pulling the antelope out of the real net. About three feet long, its coat a dark-brown red (with a black strip from head to tail along its spine), its hind quarters bulky, its back legs longer than its front, in shape it was a tapered cylinder, an antelope evolved for moving low and at speed through thick vegetation. The men rolled it kicking onto its back, the woman held its head stretched out by the ears – elliptical ears that were longer than the two conical little horns set between them; one man gripped its fetlocks; the other, with a small knife, cut away the left front leg, then the right. The antelope made a deep snoring noise and died only when the hunter opened up its chest.

Shocked, I said 'You'd think they'd spear it first.'

The woman looked up and laughed happily.

'Yup,' said Lary, turning away from the blood on the ground, the division of the meat, the wrapping it in leaves. 'But I guess we were like that once. When our ancestors were hunter-gatherers. Before we took chickens seriously. Before farming arrived in Europe, 10,000 years before the present. Not that long ago. I don't think you care for animals, not as we might understand it, until you have to look after them, bring them up, treat them as surrogate children.'

Further down the line a small deer was struggling in the net, trying to stab down at the cords with little tusks in its upper jaw. Its body was about the same size as the duiker's, but its legs were shorter and its yellow-brown coat was spotted and striped with white, like sunlight on the floor of a thicket. I recognised it at once – the Water chevrotain or Mouse deer, not really a deer at all, but midway in form between deer and pigs and much older than either, almost unchanged from its fossils of thirty million years ago, looking much the same lying on the grasses at our feet as it did six million years before the grass itself evolved, 29.8 million years before *Homo sapiens sapiens* appeared.

## Activity 32 | *Congo Journey:* Stimulus for individual writing

**Group work**

Consider how O'Hanlon's relationship with the pigmy tribe is presented in this extract. Concentrate on the vocabulary he uses to identify and describe them.

Collate all the terms that suggest his knowledge of and enthusiasm for the natural world. What effect do they have on his writing?

Evaluate Lary's explanation for the difference between Western sensitivities towards animals and the hunter-gatherers' customs. What features of his speech make his reasoning particularly persuasive?

### Extract from *A Passage to Africa* by George Alagiah

In this extract, the journalist describes his feelings about Zaire at the moment when he and his cameraman enter the ruined palace of the deposed Zairian ruler, Mobutu, immediately after the dictator had fled for his life, having abused the country and its people for years. Mobutu's cancer was in an advanced state and had left him incontinent, hence the reference to the disposable nappies.

To write about Zaire, as it was still called when I first went there, is to deal in superlatives. There is nothing ordinary, nothing prosaic one can say about it. Whether you are talking about the huge potential locked up in its vast natural resources or the criminal waste of that God-given abundance by a thieving élite, you are led to the extremes. There is no middle ground.

Zaire is the heart of Africa. It lies dead centre, bordering nine other countries, each of them affected by the political vicissitudes of the giant next door. No country on the continent has such a contiguous relationship with so many others. Political convulsions have spread through the region like the tremors of an earthquake.

It is the size of Western Europe. The Congo River, which arches across the north of Zaire, acts as a highway in a country that has none overland. If you took a river steamer from the inland port of Kisangani (Joseph Conrad's 'Inner Station' in *Heart of Darkness*) to the capital Kinshasa, you would have travelled the distance between Moscow and Paris. At independence the Congo had 140,000 kilometres of roads. Today it has less than a tenth of that. There are some 200 different tribes in the country, each with its own distinctive language, and were it not for the river, the vast majority of people who live in the interior would be as isolated from the outside world and each other as they were 2,000 years ago, in the period just before the great Bantu migration to the south.

The river itself is the second largest in the world in terms of the amount of water it disgorges into the Atlantic Ocean. It crosses the Equator twice, the only river in the world to do so, as it progresses north from its source in eastern Zambia before curving west through the thick, dank, dense, lush rainforest, the largest in Africa. Further south, away from this life-force of vegetation, the land is blessed with the mineral deposits of primeval times. There's copper, zinc, diamonds, cobalt, uranium, gold, silver, tin, manganese and much more besides.

Zaire's people are among the most resourceful on the continent (you have to be to have survived under Mobutu Sese Seko). Their music is heard all over Africa and has influenced many an artist further afield. Call it Zaire, call it the Democratic Republic of Congo, as its current rulers prefer, the country still represents all that is possible in Africa and everything that is wrong about Africa. It is one of those pivotal states, like Nigeria in the west. If the DRC can be brought round, Africa will prosper. If it continues to sink into the quagmire of corruption and ethnically driven politics, there is little hope for the rest of the continent.

If Africa is to work, it must work in Congo.

Zaire's physical splendour, its natural opulence, is matched only by the mythical status it has acquired among those foreign travellers who have visited it. Ever since Conrad used the Congo River to take his readers on a journey through man's capacity for moral corruption, the country has held a fascination for writers. V. S. Naipaul, Ronan Bennett and Barbara Kingsolver have all explored the human condition against the backdrop of an outrageously fecund Congo.

A hundred years ago Conrad wrote of it: 'The great wall of vegetation, an exuberant and entangled mass of trunks, branches, leaves, boughs, festoons, motionless in the moonlight, was like a rioting invasion of soundless life, a rolling wave of plants, piled up, crested, ready to topple over the creek, to sweep every little man of us out of his little existence…'

But Congo's post-colonial years have been marked with even greater avarice than the Belgians ever exhibited. The big men who followed the imperial masters did not merely emulate the white men, they outdid them. And none more so than Mobutu.

'Yassus, man! Look at this! That's what I call being shit scared.' Glenn Middleton was pointing to the piles of disposable nappies on the floor of what had been the presidential living room. My cameraman, who was as much friend as workmate, often produced a flash of black humour when the going got a bit tense. Along with my producer, Hamilton Wende, we had sneaked into the presidential palace in Kinshasa, the first TV journalists to do so.

## Activity 33 | Analysing the writer's style

The following questions could be used as a framework to construct a piece of stylistic analysis. Some require you to take a literary approach while others require you to comment on linguistic features. This distinction has been made to help you focus more sharply but when you come to write your answer, aim for an integration of approaches. Some questions may seem to overlap.

You will find it helpful to search out the answers to all of the questions before beginning to write. It is likely that Questions 1, 2 and 3 will be easier to answer when you have a more complete sense of the writer's approach to composition.

1 **Authorial intention:** What exactly does the writer want to convey? What is his purpose for writing? How appropriate would you consider the term rhetoric?

2 **Discourse structure:** Examine the progress of the passage. What evidence is there of shape and direction? Is there evidence of an 'argument'?

3 **Content and agenda:** What information is provided by the extract? What is the rationale for the selection? Imagine a reader who knows very little about Zaire. What evidence is there that the extract is intended for the intelligent general reader? How accessible is it and how is that achieved?

4 **Lexical choice and description:** George Alagiah's opening assertion is that Zaire has to be dealt with in superlatives. How does he justify this by his choice of lexis? Consider all the ways in which size and excess are described or implied.

5 **Balance and contrast:** What devices of style are used here to convey the polarity between Zaire's potential and its condition?

6 **Voice:** How does the character of the writer come over in the extract? What values and ideals does he promote? From what perspective is the extract written? What emotions does he convey?

7 **Genre and register:** How would you define the genre of this work? Can you find any features of style that might suggest the writer's experience with both printed and spoken journalism?

8 **Characteristic features of style:** What effects are created by metaphor, simile, abstract nouns, euphemism, collocation?

9 **Syntax:** Analyse some of sentence types demonstrated in the extract. How suited are they to the writer's purpose?

10 **Focal point:** Who or what is the focal point of the extract? How is this managed? How effective is the extract?

Turn to page 144 for a commentary demonstrating one approach to this task. Notice in particular how each point made in the commentary is linked to some relevant aspect of theme and/or composition.

**Review**

In this section you have been given the opportunity to

- appreciate the significance of the writer's chosen context
- find evidence of the writer's political or social agenda
- identify ways of evoking atmosphere and a sense of place
- recognise the links between narration of events and description of the environment
- consider nineteenth-, twentieth- and twenty-first-century presentations of Africa
- comment upon the appeal of the modern travelogue
- comment on the effective use of authentic location
- categorise vocabulary
- comment upon uses of reported and direct speech
- collate aspects of imagery
- consider differences between narrative and account
- describe changes in register/demotic speech
- write accurately about relevant features of literary and linguistic interest
- consider diachronic changes in language and style.

### Key concepts

Choices of setting and background information are not arbitrary in works of fiction. Conrad's description plays an important part in creating the imagery of the story. Contemporary attitudes towards protection of the environment and fostering mutual respect between peoples are reflected in O'Hanlon's writing. By studying these two extracts, you have identified how these writers achieve their purposes.

### Writing skills

This section has given you an opportunity to extend your understanding of genre and style, as well as consolidating your knowledge of literary and linguistic features and the terminology that you need in order to describe these features effectively. You should be able to apply appropriate analytical approaches to any given pair of texts and produce a knowledgeable and well-organised discussion. This section should also have provided you with some food for thought and inspiration as regards your own creative writing.

# Comparing how writers present issues

By the time you are nearing the end of your two-year course, you will want to feel confident of your own independent approach, so this last section is designed to help you assess how effectively you have mastered the skills presented in the earlier sections of this chapter. If you are preparing for an examination, you will want to test your skills before the actual event. This section includes activities which reflect features of practice based on specifications from various examination boards.

When presented with a group of texts, you should be able to

- interpret the meaning of the texts, identifying the writers' intentions and appreciating their choice of genre/medium
- synthesise the common subject-matter of the texts, drawing conclusions about shared messages and significant differences (Here, 'synthesise' means give an integrated

summary of themes and ideas in the texts, providing the reader with an overview of the range of ideas.)

- make judgements about the meaning and tone of texts, defending your opinion by informed reference to literary and linguistic features
- identify and comment upon instances in which contextual factors have influenced the production and/or reception of texts
- provide evidence of critical insights by supporting or challenging the views of writers in the light of relevant historical and social development.

# Focused comparison

At this point it is important for you to appreciate that certain A-level assessments require you to produce a focused comparison. This phrase means that you are being asked to compare texts in relation to one or more central issues. In an examination, the focus will be set as part of the question. In a coursework task, you may be permitted to set your own focus, and obviously you will have to sustain it. But in either instance, you must avoid the trap of simply comparing features.

The information in this section deals specifically with examination questions but much of the advice is relevant to coursework assignments. If you are writing a coursework assignment, you will want to be sure that you are covering the higher-level skills that secure top grades. The main difference is that coursework is based either on material which is prescribed as a set text or on material you have selected for yourself, but if you are required to 'compare', then the quality of your comparison must be your first concern.

# Unseen extracts

As part of your essential preparation for writing examination answers, it is important to clarify a few fundamental technical points.

Some examination tasks will require you to deal with extracts that are entirely new to you. Extracts of this kind are usually referred to as 'unseen', as opposed to extracts from texts which are familiar to you because they have been selected from the prescribed set texts you have studied as part of your course. The thought of writing an examination answer on a group of unseen extracts can seem daunting but if you follow the steps that you have learned in this chapter, you will be able to draw up an agenda and feel confident of your approach.

Other tasks may be based on unseen extracts and selected material from prescribed texts. On the face of it, this mixture seems to provide an easier option but, when you plan your examination response, you must avoid the dangers of concentrating too much on the material you know, at the expense of the unseen. Your teacher will be able to advise you about the weighting of marks. It is likely that a significant percentage of the available marks will depend on your performance in relation to the unseen material. You cannot afford to neglect a part of the examination task that provides evidence of your independent skills and carries a lot of marks.

### Source texts for this section
The source texts for this section are all works of literature or literary non-fiction with an Australian theme:

- *The Fatal Shore* by Robert Hughes (1987)
- *True History of the Kelly Gang* by Peter Carey (2000)
- *Australia – A Biography of a Nation* by Phillip Knightley (2001)
- *The Secret River* by Kate Grenville (2005).

The writers were all born in Australia and have made their names as authors with a special interest in investigating the history of the former penal colony and charting its progress towards political and economic independence.

# Ensuring a focused comparison

The activities that follow Extracts A to D will give you hands-on experience in tackling examination tasks which require you to deal with groups of texts or extracts in a way that tests your ability to give an overview of common features and an informed, sustained comparison of significant differences. In accordance with common practice on examination papers, you will be given some contextual information about the extracts but nothing about the style or genre of the source texts. There are additional notes in the commentary section against which you can check your ideas when you have completed the activities.

## Extract A, from *The Fatal Shore* by Robert Hughes

In the early days of transportation to Australia, the assignment of convict labour to free settlers (those who had emigrated of their own accord and had received grants of land or trading rights) was a crucial factor in the economy and security of the young colony. Keeping men and women in prison was impracticable and unproductive, so it made sense to use them as a workforce. But convicts who were not under lock and key might be tempted to escape. Those who did became a most serious threat. Sir George Arthur (1784–1854), Lieutenant-Governor of Van Dieman's Land, the Australasian island later renamed Tasmania, instituted a system of convict management, in which the police played a key role in monitoring the movements of convict labour and the conduct of their masters, who were legally charged with keeping them under appropriate control.

The key to Arthur's scheme of surveillance was, of course, the quality of the police. 'It is extremely desirable,' he declared, 'that either through the Police or Principal Superintendent's Department, the most conclusive information should always be obtained of the character of the applicant [for] assigned labor and all circumstances.' To assure this, Arthur had to make sure that his police force was run by men who had no allegiance to either settlers or convicts and were responsible only to him; and that its rank and file had no reason to favor anyone either. He cunningly did both by appointing army men as district magistrates and by putting upward-moving convicts in the field police as a reward for good conduct and a step toward freedom. This was a bureaucratic master stroke. The convict constables were anxious to distinguish themselves, and could be kept in line by the merest threat of demotion, knew they had no second chances and doubtless took a certain pleasure in bossing the settlers around. One could expect dog-like obedience – and canine ferocity – from them. The army police magistrates might not know much about civil law; often they looked on the settlers with disdain and the convicts with contempt. But they were impervious to criticism from civilians and despised the press. Their background had trained them to handle the laborious, detailed paperwork of reports and to carry out every quillet of Arthur's copious, inflexible orders with military zeal. They believed in the chain of command as implicitly as Arthur did.

Not everyone resented the methods used by Arthur's police. They had cleaned out the bushrangers, destroyed the Brady gang and made the roads safe for trade; thousands of people could sleep easier because of them. Nevertheless, they poisoned the social air. Tempers had always been short in Van Dieman's Land, frictions magnified, manners gross. Bitching and backbiting were the favorite sports of Hobart society – as of Australian society in general. Among the 'dirty pack of unprincipled place-hunters' whom Arthur's auditor-general, the waspish George Boyes, saw occupying the upper rungs of Van Dieman's Land, 'lying, slandering, every hatred and malice are their daily ailment and their consumption is incredible.' Now the stew of ill-will was thickened by spying and the fear of denunciation.

### Extract B, from *True History of the Kelly Gang* by Peter Carey

In this extract recorded shortly before his death by hanging, the Australian outlaw Ned Kelly recalls his first encounter with the police when his mother attempted to bring a cake to her fifteen-year-old brother, imprisoned for the unlawful killing of cattle. Ned was three years old at the time.

We arrived at the Beveridge Police Camp drenched to the bone and doubtless stank of poverty a strong odour about us like wet dogs and for this or other reasons we was excluded from the Sergeant's room. I remember sitting with my chilblained hands wedged beneath the door I could feel the lovely warmth of the fire on my fingertips. Yet when we was finally permitted entry all my attention were taken not by the blazing fire but by a huge red jowled creature the Englishman who sat behind the desk. I knew not his name only that he were the most powerful man I ever saw and he might destroy my mother if he so desired.

Approach says he as if he was an altar.

My mother approached and I hurried beside her. She told the Englishman she had baked a cake for his prisoner Quinn [Jimmy Quinn her brother] and would be most obliged to deliver it because her husband were absent and she had butter to churn and pigs to feed.

No cake shall go to the prisoner said the trap[*] I could smell his foreign spicy smell he had a handlebar moustache and his scalp were shining through his hair.

Said he No cake shall go to the prisoner without me inspecting it 1st and he waved his big soft white hand thus indicating my mother should place her basket on his desk. He untied the muslin his fingernails so clean they looked like they was washed in lye and to this day I can see them livid instruments as they broke my mother's cake apart.

[*] trap – slang word for policeman

### Extract C, from *Australia – A Biography of a Nation* by Phillip Knightley

The author describes relationships between the early colonists and the Aboriginal peoples. The very first fleet of transported convicts to arrive in Australia was under the command of Governor Phillip.

The killing began early on. In December 1790, after Aboriginals had speared one of his servants, Governor Phillip decided on a punitive raid on the offending tribe 'in order to convince them of our superiority, and infuse an universal terror'. He ordered Captain Watkin Tench to take fifty men and capture two Aboriginals and to kill and cut off the heads of ten others. Tench convinced him to reduce the number to be captured to six, of which two would be hanged and four deported to Norfolk Island. But if none could be captured alive, then all six would be shot and beheaded.

This was not government policy. But as writer Padraic P. McGuinness asked 200 years later, 'What did the colonial authorities think would happen when they populated Australia initially with a mix of criminals and other desperates, especially those such as the Irish who themselves had a history of oppression and dispossession… In Australia, the poor and ignorant settlers were forced into close relations with the Aborigines, upon whose goodwill they depended while having no understanding of how they thought and no chance of comprehending them ever. So the most elemental accommodation of rape, abduction and violence were the only means of getting on.'

In many states in the early days these settlers cleared Aboriginals from their land as casually as kangaroos. They shot them, poisoned them and clubbed them. In Tasmania they succeeded in wiping them out entirely. In the rest of the country over a period of 150 years the Aboriginal population declined from an estimated 300,000 to about 75,000. Smallpox, tuberculosis and malnutrition took their toll, but many were murdered by white settlers.

### Extract D, from *The Secret River* by Kate Grenville

The novel is set in Australia during the early years of colonisation. It tells the story of William Thornhill's progress from convicted felon to prosperous landowner in the newly discovered Australia. In this extract, Thornhill, his wife Sal and their children are spending their first night on the land which has been granted to them. The plot comprises a hundred acres of virgin land deep in the territory and far away from the township of Sydney. (Para.8: a damper is made from flour and water.)

The shadow slid up the golden cliffs opposite and turned them to lead. As darkness fell the distorted trees went on holding the fraction of light in the air.

The Thornhills squatted around the fire listening to the night, feeling its weight at their backs. Beyond the circle of light, the darkness was full of secretive noises, ticks and creaks, sudden rustlings and snappings, an insistent tweeting. Shafts of cold air like the draught from a window stirred the trees. From the river the frogs popped and ponked.

As the night deepened they hunched closer around the fire, feeding it so that as soon as it began to die it flamed up again and filled the clearing with jerky light. Willie and Dick heaped on armful after armful until the light danced against the underside of the trees. Bub squatted close up to one side, pushing in twigs that flared brilliantly.

They were warm, at least on one side, and the fire made them the centre of a small warm world. But it made them helpless creatures too. The blackness beyond the reach of the flames was as absolute as blindness.

The trees grew huge, hanging over them as if they had pulled up their roots and crept closer. Their shaggy silhouettes leaned down over the firelit clearing.

The gun lay close to Thornhill's hand. By the last of the daylight, out of sight of Sal, he had loaded it. He had checked the flint, had the powder-horn in his coat pocket.

He had thought that having a gun would make him feel safe. Why did it not?

The damper was burned from being cooked too fast, but the steamy fragrance under the charred crust was a comfort. The small noises they made with their food seemed loud in the night. Thornhill could hear his tea travel down his gullet, and the exclamations of his belly as it came to grips with the damper.

He looked up at where even the light of the fire could not dim the stars. He looked for the Southern Cross, which he had learned to steer by, but as it often did it was playing hide-and-seek.

*Might they be watching us*, Willie said. *Waiting, like*. There was the start of panic in his voice. *Shut your trap, Willie, we ain't got nothing to worry about*, Thornhill said.

In the tent he felt Sal squeezed up against him under the blanket. He had heated a stone in the fire and had wrapped it up in his coat to warm her feet, but she was shivering. She was panting as quick as an animal. He held her tight, feeling the cold at his back, until at last her breathing slowed in sleep.

A wind had arisen out of the night. He could hear it on the ridges, although down in the valley everything was still. It was like the sound of surf breaking on the shore, the way it swelled and then travelled around the ridges, its whisper growing and then fading away. The valley was dwarfed by the ocean of leaves and wind.

To be stretched out to sleep on his own earth, feeling his body lie along ground that was his – he felt he had been hurrying all his life, and had at last come to a place where he could stop. He could smell the rich damp air coming in the tent-flap. He could feel the shape of the ground through his back. *My own*, he kept saying to himself. *My place. Thornhill's place.*

But the wind on the leaves up on the ridge was saying something else entirely.

**Activity 34**

## Taking an overview of a group of texts

Read through Extracts A to D and consider the range of information and opinions that is being presented and the variety of literary approaches, overall.

Turn to page 147 for a commentary on this activity.

**Activity 35**

## Model examination question requiring a focused comparison

Compare the ways in which the forces of law and order are presented in Extracts A and B. In your answer, you should refer to the ways in which these writers use language, genre, structure and form to achieve their purposes.

**Activity 36**

## Further examination question requiring a focused comparison

Compare the ways in which aspects of conflict and tension are presented in Extracts C and D. In your answer, you should refer to the ways in which these writers use language, genre, structure and form to achieve their purposes.

**Commentary**

**Activity 13**

The term 'voice' comes to signify the persona we present when we speak or write. In real texts, this voice is assumed to be the authentic voice of the writer but, as we have seen, certain adaptations may be made to accommodate purpose and context. This is the voice of the company secretary, the hardy traveller, the keen observer, the pious Englishman, the survivor, the optimist, writing for others of his own class.

In the years following Columbus's discovery of the New World, European countries competed with each other in opening up routes across the Atlantic to further their colonial and economic interests. England's ambitions in this direction were very strong. English colonies were set up along the east coast of what is now the United States of America. The colonists, however, were far from being self-sufficient. They relied on convoys of supply ships to keep them alive through the harsh winters. Strachey was part of such a voyage.

In writing this letter, Strachey was underlining his social and professional position. He was recording events from the point of view of an interested party. He was not just a passenger on the ship. He was secretary of the trading company. Though the address is to 'your ladyship', he did not intend it to be an entirely private communication. The register is formal, the tone is serious and the structure and style are considered and well crafted.

Strachey was very near the top of the social ladder on this ship for he was involved in the company at a high level and was used to being on a par with the Admiral and officers. He became conversant with seafaring terms. He identified closely with their dilemma. In the earlier part of the letter, he describes the frightening experience of being pounded by the waves. <u>By using the personal pronoun 'we', he identifies with the whole company – 'we steered away', 'we much unrigged' – though it is unlikely that any of this activity was literally undertaken by the writer</u>. Strachey puts himself over as actively involved. A true team player. He describes the desperation with which they lightened the vessel of personal belongings and valuable food stores. There is no hint of self-pity, despite recognition of his personal losses.

The question arises as to how reliable a narrator is Strachey. The style and structure suggest he wrote some time after the event and having given the matter considerable thought. He describes both events and feelings and expresses judgements and opinions with a literary skill that would have been difficult in a spontaneous document. Though there is no suggestion of deliberate misrepresentation, he has, nevertheless, managed the information for his purposes.

As regards impact, he wanted his readers to share his experiences of the storm, the danger, the landscape and wildlife of the islands, while providing sufficient assurance that the venture was blessed by God, well managed and a credit to the company. Some of his comments seem rather contrived. For their deliverance, his natural piety gives credit to God in the first instance with the skill of Sir George Summers following quickly in second place. This tells us something more about Strachey's selection process. We do not know the names of the crew or the passengers. Principles of inclusion and exclusion were entirely within the writer's control.

Apart from the Virginia Company, the letter would have been of interest to contemporary readers, providing a degree of vicarious excitement to some who may hardly ever have left London. We should remember that sea travel at that time was unpredictable and required strong nerves. However, Strachey needed to put over the more positive aspects. He did not want to run the risk of damaging the company's prospects by suggestions that transatlantic crossings were doomed. We should note how enthusiastically he writes about the Burmudas and takes the opportunity of putting the record straight.

As secretary to the company, Strachey wrote what he believed was a true report of the shipwreck and their subsequent recovery. He was part of a prestigious expedition to the New World in support of an English colony, desperately in need of supplies. Unfortunately, for a time it went badly wrong. He offered his readers an eyewitness account of events and some reassurance that the voyage was not a complete disaster. His letter would serve to remind everyone that he was there and would enhance his own standing. Throughout the text, we hear his 'voice'.

If you found Activity 13 difficult, you could try it again, using the items underlined in the first paragraph of this commentary as the basis for your agenda. The underlined sentence in the fourth paragraph shows you how exemplification may be used to support your discussion of voice.

Caxton's version of Aesop's fable raises interesting points about his authorial intentions and his chosen style, which we might conveniently consider under two broad headings – 'Meaning' and 'Method'. On one hand, the message of the fable underpins the values and opinions of his contemporary audience. At the same time, no one wants to read a dull message. Several centuries later, the poet Alexander Pope defined good writing as the successful expression of well-known truths in new and stimulating ways: 'What oft was thought but ne'er so well expressed' (Essay on Criticism). In analysing Caxton's narrative approach, we shall consider both of these factors.

The fable contrasts the different conduct of two creatures. The ant, characteristically a hard worker, lays up stores in the summer to provide for hard times in winter. The sygalle, having frittered away the summer months, begs for food, unsuccessfully. Anthropomorphism is a long-standing narrative convention, in which animals are given the characteristics of humans providing, by implication, an opportunity for comment on the behaviour of certain types of people.

The discourse structure for the fable is provided by the narrator's opening and closing commentaries, which frame the whole text. In the opening phrase, he presents his theme in a confident and assured voice. The word 'good' has a moral tone about it. People ought to make provision for themselves while times are good, so they can live comfortably during leaner days. This is an unequivocal statement which prepares us for the fable itself. The narrator directly addresses the reader, assuring us that the truth of his assertion will be made plain. As if to underline the application to human affairs, he says 'as thow mayst see' and in the closing sentences, he reinforces his judgement. There is a solemn warning about the dangers of idleness which he makes specific to people. He uses the masculine pronoun, 'he that werketh not', whereas in the fable, the two creatures were female. He uses contrast and symmetry to considerable effect. There is 'one tyme for to doo some labour' and 'one tyme for to haue rest'. A balanced work/leisure ethic leads to 'good'; he who does no work will face 'grete cold and lacke'. This contrast is reflected in Caxton's choice of language, as we can see in the central section, where the reader hears the voices of the ant and the sygalle.

The sygalle's request is presented as reported speech. Presumably, it is the fact of the request rather than the actual wording of it that is of interest. The narrator does say, however, that she 'demaunded'. At that time, the word would carry more or less the same connotation as the modern English 'asked'. The ant's question could be interpreted as being either rhetorical or neutral. What has the sygalle been doing all summer to leave herself in this state? Either way, the sygalle's naïve reply sounds very hollow and gets the response which the narrator believes it deserves. The idea of singing carries a connotation of time wasting in this context, certainly of thoughtlessness. The ant's refusal is definite and without apology. There is a neat balance between the thoughtless summer months and the fate that awaits the sygalle in winter. She contrasts 'hast songe alle the somer', with 'daunse now in wynter'. The juxtaposition within the almost parallel grammatical constructions conveys a dismissive attitude on her part. The imperative 'daunse' carries with it no sympathy. The double negative 'shalt not thou none haue' offers no room for negotiation. The fate of the sygalle is unknown but can be guessed at. The economy of the style does not allow for exploration of motive and attitude. Indeed, the genre of the fable does not require it.

This is a story which recognises the value of good sense, hard work and the responsible conduct of one's personal affairs – acknowledged social virtues. The narrator seems confident of the reader's agreement. The ant's reply is judgemental and might well be supported by everyone who has ever felt exploited by ne'er-do-wells. But the question remains, 'Are these the highest moral values? Is this a truly ethical position?' Whether or not the world would be a poorer place without the sygalle is no part of this discussion.

**Commentary**

**Activity 25**

In this extract, the demonstration of character, as well as interaction between characters, is more complex than in Caxton's fable and the reader has to wait until the end to get the authorial direction as to how to interpret the story.

King Solomon's wisdom and perceptiveness are demonstrated through the account of a serious case in which there were no witnesses but one person was certainly lying. The story reveals how he unmasked the wrongdoer. The narrative style allows for both women to speak for themselves. One woman describes how the other stole her baby. She frames her accusation in very direct terms. She tells how they both had babies, scarcely a few days old, and were sharing accommodation. The other woman's baby died in the night and she sneakily made a swap between this woman's living child and the corpse of her own lifeless one. She tells her story clearly and with conviction. The accused woman's denials are equally positive.

The object of the narrative is not the exploration of character or motivation in the two women, both of whom are anonymous and have no other part to play than to provide a scenario for demonstrating Solomon's perception.

The writer of the Old Testament story obviously wants the reader to be impressed by the King. He is shown as being impartial, allowing each woman her say. He made time for them even though they were prostitutes. He took them seriously and decided on a ploy to unveil the wrongdoer. He sent for his sword. In his judgement, they could each have half of the child. The real mother, shocked at the thought, was prepared to give up her child to the baby-snatcher, if only he could live. She was reunited with her child.

The name of King Solomon is immediately associated with wisdom and justice. He chose an unconventional method of getting at the truth. Solomon was the embodiment of the perfect ruler. He was fair, approachable and he understood people. But this was not all his own doing. Right at the end, the reader is assured that the wisdom of God was in Solomon. This is a text with religious associations. The story is rather like a parable. It has a number of interesting features of language and style that reflect the date of this early translation of the Bible into English. The intended audience would have been Christian people. The text is unconditional in its faith in God and its support for Solomon's ability as a judge.

**Commentary**

**Activity 33**

George Alagiah feels passionately about Africa and in particular about Zaire, which testifies to the worst effects of brutal colonialisation, followed by an even worse period of independence, during which the native peoples were exploited by their own leaders. In this extract he intends to explain for the reader the tragic irony that a country of such enormous potential should be ruined by rulers of the calibre of Mobutu. Having both an informative and a persuasive purpose, there is a

Authorial
intention

Contrast
Values

rhetorical quality about the extract which invites the reader to understand Africa more intimately and identify with his concerns.

Enough information is given in the extract to provide a good factual understanding of Zaire's geographical position within Africa but the writer does not stick at topographical detail. By the use of metaphors such as 'the heart of Africa', we are told more than that Zaire occupies a central location. Africa is a living body of which Zaire is its most vital feature. Alagiah supports his own interpretation of Africa's greatness by reference to other writers. This also demonstrates his assumptions about his readers but the quotation fills in the gaps for those unfamiliar with Conrad's original.

As regards structure, it is helpful to imagine this as a piece of visual art. Each paragraph moves the 'viewer' from 'wide-screen to close-up'. The extract opens on the panorama of Zaire's grand scale, and closes with the sordid account of detritus in the abandoned presidential palace. In between, the focal lens gradually narrows, first as the river is described, then the country's people, followed by the tributes of famous visitors. Alagiah integrates into the descriptive passages his hopes and fears for the future but in the final paragraph, the voice of the cameraman takes over in describing the mess that Mobutu has left behind. It seems in itself a metaphor for the way he has treated Zaire. The 'argument' would seem to be that the God-given abundance and the resourceful people should not be entrusted to men like this and that Zaire and Africa deserve something better. God certainly intended it to be so.

To convey a sense of the country's size and of its wealth, Alagiah makes continual reference to scale, either by adjectives – 'huge', 'vast' – or through comparisons which the European reader would readily appreciate – 'It is the size of Western Europe', 'the distance between Moscow and Paris' – without the need to specify what the size and distance might be. There is also the use of the negative (which is in itself a form of extreme) to underline the fact that only superlatives can convey the reality and that 'nothing ordinary', 'nothing prosaic', 'no middle ground' can do justice to the land or its people. These three phrases emphasise the idea that nothing average is to be found here, only 'extremes'.

Throughout the extract the writer presents evidence of what Zaire might be and Zaire as the plunderers have left her. The abstract nouns 'potential', 'resources' and 'abundance' contrast in their connotation of plenty with the 'criminal waste' of a 'thieving élite'. The focus in the premodification conveys the idea of dishonesty where one would least expect it, 'thieving élite' being a sort of sarcastic oxymoron. He uses extensive collocation to spell out the richness of the forest and of the mineral deposits. The rainforest is 'thick, 'dank', dense' and 'lush', words which convey the mass of vegetation in a list which combines alliteration with phonological impact. The list of minerals reads like a treasure trove. He describes the land as 'blessed' by nature but destroyed by 'avarice', a word which is often used to suggest excessive and sinful greed. This contrast between what nature intended and what man has imposed is at the root of his argument. If even the Congo cannot be made economically and socially viable, then the rest of Africa is doomed.

Empathy
Rhetoric

Agenda
Content
Metaphor

Allusions
References

Structure

Scale
Lens

Values
Relevance
Sub-text
Argument

Lexis

Comparison

Contrast

Polarity
Word classes

Descriptors

Literary
devices

Moral
overtones
Connotations
Argument

The voice of the writer comes over strongly. He is obviously well informed, being able to provide accurate and thought-provoking information about the country and the people, using facts and figures. He is in awe of Africa. He recognises the ancient inheritance from 'primeval times'; he agrees with Conrad that there is enough here to dwarf any man: 'to sweep every little man of us out of his little existence'. In the final paragraph, we are more aware of his professional life. The BBC's man in Africa has to take risks, be grateful for the support of friends and take pride in being part of the team that bring us the news each and every night. It would be difficult for a reader to resist agreeing with his interpretation.

The genre of the whole text is both autobiographic and journalistic. In this extract there is just enough of the second strand to give a taste of the way in which the reader is invited into Alagiah's experiences. The quality of the language changes in the final paragraph, with the inclusion of direct speech and its taboo terms. Alagiah's sense of Mobutu's absurdity comes over in his sardonic juxtaposition of 'presidential' and 'living room', the one so prestigious and the other so banal, just like the man himself. There are several words and phrases linked to TV journalism. The words 'cameraman', 'producer', 'workmate' are different from the lyricism of the earlier descriptions of Africa and are fairly recent introductions, not as words in themselves but in the way in which they are used and received by a modern reader. He seems to have aimed for as wide a readership as possible, though it is not practicable to reduce the material to an altogether simplistic level. As a journalist, it is his job to make difficult concepts easy to assimilate. For example, to be effective in conveying the troubled history of the area, surrounding countries are personified as 'giants next door' whose political problems create the sort of unease we associate with aggressive and noisy neighbours. These rather homely images alleviate the low frequency words which require the reader to be tolerably well-educated and reasonably conversant with current affairs. Words like 'vicissitudes' and 'contiguous' are not commonly used in speech but the context makes the meaning clear. In a lower register one might describe having to rub shoulders with unpredictable neighbours whose ups and down affected one's own well-being. There is a good smattering of commonly used idioms, like 'sneaking into ... the palace'. He makes no attempt to disguise the squalor of the piles of disposable nappies.

His choice of sentence type is a further help in making the prose accessible. He appears confident in his judgement. He avoids expressions like 'I think' or 'I suggest'. His statements are positive and the verbs he uses are in the indicative mood, mostly in the present or the past tense. This gives his words a forceful quality, free from the type of tentative suggestions which require the use of the subjunctive mood, for example 'Africa would be in a better position', 'Politicians might be able to rule wisely'. Only when he balances fear and optimism does he introduce a number of conditional clauses with the conjunction 'if', but these are followed by definite statements, 'Africa will prosper', 'there is little hope'. The minor sentence 'And none more so than Mobutu' is a

Voice

Attitude

Character

Rhetoric

Genre
Occupational
variety
Language
change

Semantics

Readership

Images

Register

Demotic
language

Verb classes

Syntax

Sentence
types

Writing

useful example of his unambiguous style. A number of important points are made in simple sentences (those which have only one clause) – 'Today it has less than a tenth of that'.

*strategies and syntax*

The focal point of the extract is Zaire itself, seen through the description of its vast proportions, the Congo River and the people who have been there for centuries. The purpose is to engage the European reader with an understanding of the place and with a sense of the tragedy of its condition. As a result of the way in which the extract has been edited, it achieves the former more effectively than the latter. Those who take the opportunity to read the whole of *A Passage to Africa* will be spared that imbalance.

*Evaluation*

## Commentary

## Activity 34

The issues that have haunted generations of people since the colonisation of Australia up to the present day cannot be summed up in a few words but they include the memories of physical hardship and the sense of injustice that many, if not all of those people transported as convicts between 1788 and 1868, must have felt at being exiled to so distant and so alien a land, especially those who were regarded as particularly dangerous and were consequently assigned to the island of Van Diemen's Land, now known as Tasmania.

On the other hand, some enterprising free settlers, along with convicts who had served their time, managed to survive and make good, encouraged by the British government, who actively promoted increased colonisation.

Those early settlers thought of Australia as being a newly discovered continent. This was only partly true. The Aboriginal people had been there for thousands of years and the coming of the white settlers provoked inevitable confrontations. The right of the white newcomers to exploit the natural wealth of the land has only recently been challenged, though sadly too late to save the once vibrant community of Aborigines.

Conflict was not confined to inter-racial tensions. The prejudice and snobbery that lower social groups suffered in Britain were intensified when they were transported either as convicted criminals or as political activists with criminal connections. One of the most despised groups was the impoverished community of Irish origin.

Drawing on a wealth of documents, Robert Hughes's book provides a detailed and thoroughly researched account covering the history of transportation and the country's progress from being the largest prison camp the world has ever known into a free society. Phillip Knightley takes up where Hughes leaves off. Both works make use of historical information and personal reflection. These approaches allow them to report facts, quote from sources, make use of statistical data, as well as offering an interpretation. They approach their subject with an authority which encourages the reader to have faith in their findings. In the main, they aim to provide an informed overview. The two works of fiction operate more closely with individuals. Carey shows us what it was like to be in the power of an uncompromising policeman. Granville recreates through her fictional family the terrifying experience of being out in the wild. Both Carey and Granville direct our sympathies not through facts and figures but by recreating the experiences of their characters, which we as readers can share.

# Talk in Life and Literature

4

---

**At the end of this chapter you should be able to**

- select and apply relevant concepts and approaches from integrated linguistic and literary study, using appropriate terminology and accurate coherent written expression (AO1)

- demonstrate detailed critical understanding in analysing the ways in which structure, form and language shape meanings in a range of spoken and written texts (AO2)

- use integrated approaches to explore relationships between texts, analysing and evaluating the significance of contextual factors in their production and reception (AO3).

For a more student-friendly version of these Assessment Objectives, turn to page vii in the Introduction.

---

# Talking about talk: theories and explanations

## The beginnings of communication: a literary perspective

Talking is what makes us all human. Animals, birds, insects, even plants communicate in a rich variety of ways – but only humans can communicate their most complex ideas, emotions and needs by means of the vast, global range of sound systems we call 'spoken language'. Just as remarkable is the way that, over the millennia, humans have discovered how to record these sound systems in symbolic forms, both visual and tactile, called 'written language'. Pictures, hieroglyphics, pictograms, characters, ideograms and alphabet letters have been the means of relaying information since the days of cave paintings and drawings scratched on rock.

Major writers, from Shakespeare to Mary Shelley and William Golding (*The Inheritors*, 1965), have been intrigued by the mystery of evolving human language. In *The Tempest* (1611), Shakespeare creates a strange figure named Caliban, part human, part savage, whom the magician Prospero has made his servant and taught to speak. The following exchange shows Caliban bitter about what learning to talk has done for him.

Prospero  ... I pitied thee
         Took pains to make thee speak, taught thee each hour
         One thing or other. When thou didst not, savage,
         Know thine own meaning, but would gabble like
         A thing most brutish, I endowed thy purposes
         With words that made them known.

Caliban  You taught me language, and my profit on't
         Is, I know how to curse. The red plague rid you
         For learning me your language.

In contrast, Mary Shelley's monster in *Frankenstein* (1818) is eager to speak to his appalled creator, Frankenstein, when they meet in the high Alps. Explaining how he gradually learnt to be 'human', the monster tells how he discovered speech and became literate by secretly observing a family of 'amiable cottagers'.

'By degree I made a discovery of still greater moment. I found that these people possessed a method of communicating their experience and feelings to one another by articulate sounds ... . This was indeed a godlike science, and I ardently desired to become acquainted with it. But I was baffled in every attempt ... . Their pronunciation was quick; and the words they uttered, not having any apparent connexion with visible objects, I was unable to discover any clue by which I could unravel the mystery of their reference. By great application ... I discovered the names that were given to some of the most familiar objects of discourse: I learnt and applied the words fire, milk, bread and wood. ... I discovered that [Felix] uttered many of the same sounds when he read as when he talked. I conjectured ... that he found on the paper signs for speech which he understood, and I ardently longed to comprehend ...'

Shakespeare and Mary Shelley present quite different responses by their characters to the acquisition of speech, determined by the specific roles Caliban and the monster play in each literary text. However, it is clear that for each writer (and created character) language is the marker for membership of human society. Caliban angrily rejects this enforced 'privilege', whereas Frankenstein's monster desperately longs for acceptance, which is denied him. The tragic consequences of this denial become clear in the rest of the novel.

## Activity 1
**Pair work**

## Investigating linguistic and paralinguistic modes of communication

In pairs, agree on a simple question/answer exchange in which one person asks a question (for example, 'Where is the nearest bus-stop?') and the other provides the answer. Repeat the exchange using

1  gestures only
2  vowels only
3  consonants only
4  vowels with gestures
5  consonants with gestures.

Which mode was most/least successful? Compare your findings with the rest of the group.

## Which mode has higher status – spoken or written communication?

Historically and culturally, written language was valued more highly in the past because 'it was the medium of literature … a source of standards of linguistic excellence … [which provided] language with permanence and authority' (David Crystal *Cambridge Encyclopedia of Language*, 1997). The pendulum swung the other way in the twentieth century, when scholars argued that 'speech is the primary medium of communication among all peoples [and] should therefore be the primary object of linguistic study' (Crystal *op. cit.*). The status of speech was elevated further by the technical revolution in sound recording and improvements in phonetic transcription (using the International Phonetic Alphabet or IPA). In the second half of the twentieth century there was a virtual explosion in the study of spoken language, ranging from discourse analysis and child language development to gender and power politics.

Much of this research has been made possible by the availability to scholars of huge collections of spontaneous and planned speech on computer databases or corpora (singular corpus). These are frequently established in universities, and are often associated with publishers of dictionaries. Important examples of corpora include COBUILD (Collins–Birmingham University International Language Database), which stores written and spoken English, and CANCODE (Cambridge–Nottingham Corpus of Discourse in English), which stores spoken language only. These corpora are similar in principle to libraries, though not of course comparable with the British Library, which stores copies of every book written in English (as well as books in many other languages). Scientists, neurologists and linguists are making equally important advances in the field of artificial intelligence – that is, teaching computers to replicate the immeasurable range of activities the human brain is capable of performing, including speech. Artificially produced voices still sound rather Dalek-like, but voice-activated and voice-responsive computers are becoming normal rather than futuristic as the processes of acoustic modelling (of sounds we produce) and linguistic modelling (of sounds interpreted as words) are developed and refined.

Other developments in new media such as e-mail, CMC and text-messaging often blur the boundaries between spoken and written language, whereas more conventional ways of recording information in spoken form include voicemail and answer-phones, as well as libraries of recorded sound, talking books and other sound archives. Spoken and written language are no longer positioned confrontationally. Crystal's view is that 'modern society makes available to its members two very different systems of communication, each of which has developed to fulfil a particular set of communicative needs, and now offers capabilities of expression denied to the other'.

All this has resulted in remarkable changes in the public perception and attitude towards spoken language. Instead of talk being regarded as ephemeral and of little value compared with written language (for example, in fields like law, government and politics, business, science, academia), corpus linguistics have shown us that spoken language is an equally complex and important system of communication. The grammar is different, the lexis is different, the structures are different – but its functions are as varied and as valuable (and as straightforward or challenging) as the situations and purposes of the speakers involved. Lists like Leech, Deuchar and Hoogenraad's comparison of spoken and written language – 'repetitiveness/non-repetitiveness; normal non-fluency/fluency; monitoring/interaction features/no monitoring/interaction features, …' (1982) – seem simplistic in the twenty-first century.

**Activity 2**

### Investigating the spoken and written nature of text messages

**Individual**

Select and transcribe six texts from your text-message inbox. Rewrite the texts as if each sender was talking to you, then rewrite them again as if each sender was writing to you.

**Pair work**

Compare your three versions with another student's three versions and note the changes you both made to the original texts. Are text messages closer to spoken or written language?

## Everything starts with spoken language

In this section so far, we have established that spoken language is central to the experience of being human, however challenging that experience may be. We have addressed the thorny old chestnut (a very mixed metaphor) of whether speech is superior to writing or vice versa, and have rejected this status war as unnecessary, irrelevant and out of touch with current realities of communication. Before addressing the very real differences that do exist between spontaneous and crafted speech (literary or non-literary), we need to look in more detail at everyday spoken language to understand its extraordinary range and variety. But first, a quick glance at where it all began.

Jean Aitchison (*The Seeds of Speech*, 1996) suggested that early humans had to develop what she called the naming insight in order to acquire language; young humans today (whatever their language) start to name objects and people around them as they begin to acquire language. Because of this link between early humans and children today, we can look at early stages of children's talking to understand how our speech developed as well as to help us imagine how *homo sapiens* may have learned to talk about the world he and she lived in. What triggers talking in children seems to be a combination of social and functional factors. Children have a need, and wish to communicate this need to care-givers. Michael Halliday's functional theory of language acquisition convincingly demonstrates that as children's needs grow more complex, so does their language, reflecting as it does their developing understanding of the physical and social world.

As talking adults, we all have our own idiolect or unique way of using spoken language. This individual idiolect reflects physical characteristics such as voice quality, pitch and tone, as well as inherited vocal features, such as a tendency to lisp, or sensitivity to high- or low-frequency sound. It will also reveal how rich our experience of language was in childhood. Gender can be a significant factor affecting idiolect development in the context of family and school, as can other factors such as social and economic status, peer-group pressure, occupational experience (our parents' as well as our own), location, ethnicity and cultural background.

Even body language can enhance or detract from our performance as speakers: good talkers who communicate their views effectively have learnt to maximise strong points like a clear voice, ability to look people in the eye, avoidance of hesitation and respect for others' personal space. Sometimes people deliberately change an aspect of personal idiolect: Margaret Thatcher, the former Conservative Prime Minister, allegedly lowered her vocal pitch to gain more powerful masculine tones; others have 'lost' their regional accent, replaced it with Received Pronunciation (RP), only to find that regionality has kudos today. Even vocabulary choice can be changed in certain circumstances. People who normally use taboo language all the time will drop it if the occasion warrants, such as a funeral or an interview.

**151**

Conversely people who would never normally use taboo language can turn the air blue at a football match! But apart from these few exceptions, most individual idiolects are set for life; indeed, most people relish the way their speech reflects their unique identity.

## Activity 3 — Investigating the idiolect of someone you know well

Choose an older friend or member of your family who is willing to talk about their language history (you could record the interview if they're happy about it). Prepare a list of questions as prompts, for example

- Where were you born and where did your parents come from?
- Have you moved house/jobs?
- Educational and occupational background?
- Other languages spoken/understood?
- Attitudes to SE (Standard English), RP?

You could present your findings under headings such as

- pronunciation (including regional accent)
- lexical choice (including regional and occupational variants)
- standard and non-standard grammar and syntax
- normal non-fluency features (use of hesitations, fillers, false starts, etc.)
- vocal quality (including pitch, tone, intonation range, volume and pace).

With this evidence you should be able to create an accurate and detailed profile of your subject's idiolect – which they may find interesting and even surprising!

## Talking together

The famous linguist Michael Halliday once described language as a 'social semiotic' – that is, a system of signs or symbols used by human beings to communicate with each other. Speech is the most important among many modes of human communication. Other modes include body language (paralinguistics), communication by touch (proxemics) and eye contact (gaze). All function together to enhance the power of the spoken word. We talk because we have needs to communicate (e.g. seeking information, asking for help, expressing feelings, describing people, objects or places, giving explanations, instructions or commands, socialising, persuading people).

Talking is nothing if not functional! Halliday's theory of metafunctions offers a convincing theory about the way language works (both spoken and written). The ideational metafunction relates to the world we talk about, live in and react with; the interpersonal metafunction refers to the way we relate to each other; and the textual metafunction means the mode of language used for communication.

We talk to people we know, people we don't know at all; we talk to ourselves, we talk in our sleep; we talk to pets, we talk to toy rabbits; we talk in public and in private. Sometimes we know in advance what we're going to say, sometimes we have no idea – 'How do I know what I think till I see what I say?' is a not unfamiliar remark. We talk one to one, to a few friends, to a doctor or lawyer, to a large group, to a public meeting, to a radio audience, to a television audience. We talk in different ways according to how well we know someone, or how we view their status – in other words, according to social distance. How we talk can also be affected by physical distance, whether we speak face to face, on the telephone, by voicemail or answer-phone, and even using a voice-activated computer with its multiplicity of personal, financial, media, geo-political and industrial applications, including video-conferencing and skype.

The context and purpose or function of talking varies enormously, and will always affect the dialogue or exchange, determining everything from lexical choice and use of interactional devices to length of utterance, frequency of non-fluency features and number of interruptions or overlaps. We constantly shift or accommodate our language choices (including accent) in conversation, to fit the context and purpose, sometimes unawares. Linguisticians differentiate between transactional spoken language (used to obtain goods and services, such as buying a pair of jeans) and interpersonal spoken language (used for socialising, in the common room or club, for example). Interestingly, some interactions can be both, depending on context. For example, if your doctor is a family friend, there may be some social chat as well as the normal transactional exchange about medical matters. Similarly, you may be paying at the supermarket checkout whilst chatting about social plans with the cashier.

## Are we all good at talking?

This may seem a ridiculous question – of course everyone is good at this first of human skills. Or are they? Some people find that putting their ideas (and especially their feelings) into words is incredibly difficult, and their conversation is inhibited by hesitation and other non-fluency features. Others may say a lot – never stop talking, it seems – but communicate very little of their real thoughts and feelings. A comic example of this is given by the 1950s schoolboy Nigel Molesworth (created by Geoffrey Willans and Ronald Searle in *Down with Skool*, 1953). The prep-school headmaster is greeting the boys at the beginning of term. Molesworth (who chooses not to spell properly) provides this footnote 'Crib to reel thorts'.

> *Clang clang bell All sour-faced boys exsemble in skool hall*
>
> Headmaster: (*with cheerful smile*) hullo basil hullo timothy hullo john did you hav a good hols? [1] How is your dear mother? [2] (*to all more cheerful than ever*) We hav twelve weeks ahead of us and I want you to cram [3] as much aktivity into them as you can in work and pla. This term we hav a new head of the skool graber ma. [4] (*Claps noone joins in*) You all kno the vertues we prize most loyalty and good influence. [5]
>
> *CRIB TO REEL THORTS*
> *1. So they are back agane the little beasts*
> *2. As if I cared give me young mrs filips every time*
> *3. All they will cram is my food and tuck*
> *4. His father a millionnaire enuff said*
> *5. Hem-hem hav to say that sort of thing you kno*

The joke here plays on the fact that people hide their real thoughts when they are talking – often just as well!

Skilled public speakers, like Winston Churchill or Adolf Hitler, used their remarkable ability to exercise power over others for widely different purposes. For the demagogue, talk can become a tool of dominanace or even destruction. Equally, some people lie, prevaricate, and use their language skills to manipulate others and exploit their verbal vulnerability. Others are terrible listeners and always have to chip in, anticipate or even rephrase the other speaker's words. Perhaps most frustrating of all, and most demoralising, is the person who never, never listens. They may allow you to speak, but everything you say will be referred back to their own experience. You become – quite literally – a sounding board.

Successful talk is when the participants in an exchange feel that there is mutual co-operation, when their primary purpose has been fulfilled and when each speaker has been able to communicate without inappropriate interruption. We shall look in more detail at the theory of successful conversation shortly.

| Activity 4 | Comparing successful with unsuccessful conversations |
|---|---|

Select one day in the week when you are likely to be involved in or listening to a wide range of conversations. At the end of the day, list as many of the conversations as you can remember (gossip with a friend, tutor session, job interview, making weekend arrangements, negotiating family chores). Rate the success of each conversation on a 0–5 scale and suggest reasons for this. Compare your findings with those of other people in the group.

## Writing it down: crafting speech for different audiences

We have looked at the crucial role speech plays in human communication. Once human beings moved beyond writing systems like pictograms which provided basic factual information ('herd of deer near water'), the human desire to tell stories as a way of explaining the world emerged (What is thunder? Who makes it happen?). As a result we have early narratives on cave walls about animist spirits and gods. Later, when literacy was still confined to the powerful minority in a society, narratives of success in battle and of the adventures of the gods were carved on wood and stone, painted on walls or inscribed on long-lasting papyrus for the people to 'read'. Almost all religious buildings, whether temples or churches, included visual narratives in paint or mosaic for the benefit of the non-literate majority.

So how was speech represented? Perhaps not unexpectedly, rather as it is in cartoons today. It's quite a leap to see a medieval painting of the Angel Gabriel's annunciation to the Virgin Mary with the equivalent of speech balloons coming from the mouth of each figure (usually in the form of a narrow banner with the words inscribed on it; see left). Much earlier, in Greek and Roman times, the spoken exchange might be written below the visual image. Go to any medieval church today and you will be likely to find some kind of visual representation of speech, either as a wall painting, or in the stained glass, or on some tapestry.

We can thus be confident that the representation of spontaneous speech in written form is a longstanding tradition. However, the crafting of speech into a range of genres, both literary and non-literary, is a much more recent and complex phenomenon. It is closely linked with the growth of literacy and the change from the oral and secular literary genres like ballads, epic poems, folk tales and mystery plays, to the written literary genres of poetry (Geoffrey Chaucer, *The Canterbury Tales*, 1399), fiction (Thomas Nashe, *The Unfortunate Traveller*, 1594) and drama (Shakespeare, *Love's Labour's Lost*, 1598). Each of these genres is familiar today, and in each early text the writer has crafted language to represent spontaneous speech.

Once established, the crafting of speech – as part of a wide range of literary genres – became commonplace and predictable. Moreover, other forms of planned speech which had evolved from traditions other than oral literature emerged, such as rhetoric. The planned skills of pleading a case in court to create the desired effect on judge and jury constituted a further example of planned or scripted talk. More recently, other examples of scripted talk have emerged as a result of the 'media explosion' of the last century. These range from film scripts to television comedy sketches, soap opera on radio and television, television plays, docu-drama, news broadcasts, political discussions and even chat shows. If you want to see the dramatic difference between spontaneous, unplanned speech and crafted speech, just compare an episode of *East Enders* with an equivalent length of time on *Big Brother*! Nor is it only professional script-writers who craft speech.

We all craft speech in written form for particular occasions, and usually without any literary purposes in mind. As we shall see later, planned talk can differ in form, structure and lexical choice from spontaneous speech, and the contexts in which it occurs are often different from those of everyday talk. Moreover, the idea of planning ahead to speak in public can be uncomfortable, even alienating, for most spontaneous speakers, who do it with varying degrees of grace. (If the audience is familiar, it might help – but it could make matters worse!) Examples of planned speech include speeches at family celebrations (weddings, special birthdays), oral presentations in a work/professional context, and speaking on behalf of community groups (sports or social clubs, voluntary organisations like Neighbourhood Watch). Some people plan every word they say (even the jokes), whereas others speak from notes and improvise. Ironically, the highest praise for any public speaker is that he or she sounded 'completely natural' (that is, unplanned). Like virtuoso musicians, the most eloquent speakers in the public arena must appear to speak effortlessly – even though they may have learnt their speech by heart. Interestingly, technology today makes it possible for senior politicians to read their speech from a discreet monitor screen, thus seeming even more confident, fluent and persuasive.

A final question to consider – how 'natural' is natural-sounding speech? When you analyse different kinds of unplanned or spontaneous talk later in the chapter, you will see not only wide variation in form and structure, but also the effect of individual speakers' personality quirks. Indeed, we all have our own idiolect (including non-fluency features). Should a public speaker include such quirks in order to appear natural? The answer has to be 'No' – an audience doesn't want to hear too many **hedges**, stumblings and hesitations. They want to hear speech as they think they speak themselves – fluent and articulate, without ums, erms or pauses!

Planned or scripted talk then, whether in life or literature, must accomplish two things, one positive, the other negative. It must be so polished or seemingly accurate in its reproduction of naturally occurring talk that the audience is totally convinced, and it must not reproduce any of the muddle of normal exchanges such as non-fluency features, except very occasionally, for a warming touch of realism, or to create character in a literary text. These criteria will provide a valuable yardstick for evaluating and exploring scripted talk in a variety of public contexts and genres, ranging from legal and political speeches, lectures and sermons to entertaining genres like soap opera or comedy sketches, and informative genres like news broadcasts and radio or television documentaries.

## Activity 5 | Crafting a short speech

Write a short speech (3–5 minutes) to be given by you at a family celebration. You can choose what sort of celebration it is (brother's or sister's wedding, parents' anniversary, grandparent's birthday, birth of nephew or niece, uncle's or aunt's visit from abroad). You can also choose the format – it could be a regular speech or even a poem!

Perform your speech to the class/group and invite their comments about whether it matched your intended audience and whether it fulfilled its celebratory purpose.

**Activity 6**  **Writing a short script**

Write a script for a short extract from a radio or television soap opera of your choice (no more than 5 minutes in length) which can then be read out or acted by members of your group.

Choose a maximum of four characters you are familiar with to participate in this exchange. You may include one new character if you wish. Remember that this is crafted speech, so you will need to consider whether hedges, vague language and non-fluency features are required in the script.

**Review**  In this section, you have been given the opportunity to
- explore linguistic and paralinguistic modes of communication
- investigate spoken and written modes of one form of communication
- consider what makes a successful conversation
- craft a short speech in written form
- write a short script.

# Representing talk: sounds, signs and transcripts

## Studying the sounds of speech: phonetics and phonology

First things first! In this section we shall look briefly at the way human speech is produced, transmitted and heard or received by our amazing vocal-auditory system.

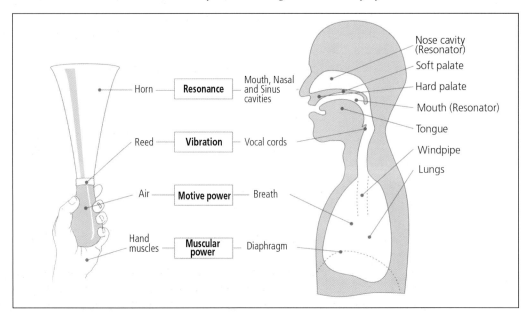

Phonetics refers to the study of the whole process of speaking and listening. Within phonetics, there are specialised areas of study: articulatory phonetics analyses the way sounds are produced by the vocal organs when we speak; acoustic phonetics analyses the physical properties of all the actual speech sounds; auditory phonetics analyses the way speech sounds are received when we hear them (Crystal 1994).

Phonology refers to the study of the sound systems of any one language – here we are studying the phonology of English. Within English, there are characteristic units of sound called phonemes which all L1 speakers acquire from birth, and L2 speakers learn later.

But before we look in more detail at English phonology, we need to be aware that other languages have very different phonemes, though some are similar to ours. The International Phonetic Alphabet (IPA) (created in the late nineteenth century, most recently revised in 2005) was devised in order to represent any human language in transcribed form. We can use it to represent visually any unit of sound (phoneme) made by any human speaker anywhere in the world and it is correspondingly complex as you can see on page 158.

Even so, when we listen to a language we don't speak ourselves, problems begin. The phonemes are different from English phonemes, the syllable and word boundaries (created by consonants and consonant clusters) are unrecognisable, word stress and intonation patterns are completely unfamiliar and everyone talks too fast. The stream of sound rushes by us, until suddenly it stops – help! Somebody has asked us a question. It's natural to try to reply (turn taking being our earliest experience of human language) – but how? In despair we resort to paralinguistics (gesture, including pointing; facial expression; body language). Trying to communicate without words (phonemic units) is at best difficult and frustrating, and at worst virtually impossible. The conclusion is that when learning any language other than our mother-tongue we need to learn not only the phonemes and phonology but also its prosody (intonation, pitch, stress patterning, tone, volume and pace). When we study sound patterning in literary/scripted texts later in this section, understanding English prosody will be of great importance.

## The units of sound

We can divide the sounds humans produce (whatever the language) into several groups – consonants, vowels, diphthongs and less common sounds (such as the 'ch' sound in the Dutch word *gracht,* meaning canal, or the click sounds in Xhosa). How you produce the sound makes all the difference: in most languages air is expelled from or drawn into the lungs, and depending on its route out of or into the mouth, different sounds are made. It also makes a difference whether the vocal chords are being vibrated (voiced) or not. For example, in English 'b' is voiced, whereas 'p' is unvoiced.

### Consonants in English
There are 24 consonants in English and they are produced by air being expelled at the front of the mouth, with the positioning of the lips, teeth, tongue and alveolar ridge (bone behind the teeth) changing the sound produced.

- Consonants made with the lips are called bi-labial (for example p, b, m).
- Consonants made with lips and teeth are called labio-dental (for example f, v) or dental (th).
- Consonants produced by the tongue on the ridge behind the teeth are called alveolar (t, s, n) and palato-alveolar (sh, j).
- Consonants produced by the tongue and hard palate are called velar (k, g, j, ch, ng).
- Consonants that sound like vowels are called approximants (w, y).
- A consonant that passes through the mouth unaltered is called an aspirate (h).

David Crystal identifies four ways in which these consonants are produced

- by complete closure of the vocal tract, followed by release (plosives – p, t, g; nasals – m, n, ng; affricates – ch, j)
- by intermittent closure and single tap on uvula or alveolar ridge, depending on regional pronunciation (trilled r)
- by partial closure – air passes on either side of tongue (lateral l )
- by narrowing, where two vocal organs are so close that air can be heard passing between them (fricatives – f, v, h; sibilants – s, z, sh )

## Vowels in English

There are 24 vowels in English and they also pass through the mouth cavity relatively unrestricted. The way we hold our mouth determines whether the sound is sustained (long vowel) or of brief duration (short vowel). The mouth is widest for 'a' and narrowest for 'o'. The other parts of the mouth that move, apart from the lips, are the tongue and the soft palate (uvula), and vowels are produced at the front, centre and back of the vocal cavity. English vowels can be

- monophthongs (single pure vowel – 'cat', 'net')
- diphthongs (two vowels together – 'hope', 'hate')
- triphthongs (three vowel qualities – 'player', 'fire', 'tower').

Vowel variation shows up particularly clearly in regional accents – an example is the famous Northern 'flat a' as opposed to the Southern long vowel in 'bath' or 'grass'.

The following list is an accessible description of English consonants and vowels.

### Consonant sounds

| | | | | | | | | | |
|---|---|---|---|---|---|---|---|---|---|
| /p/ | as in part | /g/ | as in get | /θ/ | as in thing | /ʒ/ | as in measure | /l/ | as in let |
| /b/ | as in but | /tʃ/ | as in chin | /ð/ | as in this | /h/ | as in has | /r/ | as in red |
| /t/ | as in too | /dʒ/ | as in joke | /s/ | as in see | /m/ | as in mat | /j/ | as in yes |
| /d/ | as in did | /f/ | as in food | /z/ | as in zoo | /n/ | as in not | /w/ | as in will |
| /k/ | as in kiss | /v/ | as in voice | /ʃ/ | as in she | /ŋ/ | as in long | | |

### Vowel sounds

| Long vowels | | Short vowels | | | | Diphthongs | | | |
|---|---|---|---|---|---|---|---|---|---|
| /ɪː/ | as in each | /ɪ/ | as in it | /ʊ/ | as in put | /eɪ/ | as in day | /ɪə/ | as in near |
| /ɑː/ | as in car | /e/ | as in then | /ə/ | as in again | /aɪ/ | as in by | /eə/ | as in there |
| /ɔː/ | as in more | /æ/ | as in back | | | /ɔɪ/ | as in boy | /ʊə/ | as in truer |
| /uː/ | as in too | /ʌ/ | as in not | | | /əʊ/ | as in no | | |
| /uː/ | as in word | /ɒ/ | as in much | | | /aʊ/ | as in now | | |

## The International Phonetic Alphabet (revised to 2005)

### Consonants (Pulmonic)

| | Bilabial | Labiodental | Dental | Alveolar | Post alveolar | Retroflex | Palatal | Velar | Uvular | Pharyngeal | Glottal |
|---|---|---|---|---|---|---|---|---|---|---|---|
| Plosive | p b | | | t d | | ʈ ɖ | c ɟ | k g | q ɢ | | ʔ |
| Nasal | m | ɱ | | n | | ɳ | ɲ | ŋ | N | | |
| Trill | ʙ | | | r | | | | | R | | |
| Tap or Flap | | ⱱ | | ɾ | | ɽ | | | | | |
| Fricative | ɸ β | f v | θ ð | s z | ʃ ʒ | ʂ ʐ | ç ʝ | x ɣ | χ ʁ | ħ ʕ | h ɦ |
| Lateral fricative | | | | ɬ ɮ | | | | | | | |
| Approximant | | ʋ | | ɹ | | ɻ | j | ɰ | | | |
| Lateral approximant | | | | l | | ɭ | ʎ | ʟ | | | |

Where symbols appear in pairs, the one to the right represents a voiced consonant. Shaded areas denote articulations judged impossible.

### Consonants (Non-pulmonic)

| Clicks | | Voiced implosives | | Ejectives | |
|---|---|---|---|---|---|
| ⊙ | Bilabial | ɓ | Bilabial | ʼ | *Examples:* |
| ǀ | Dental | ɗ | Dental/alveolar | pʼ | Bilabial |
| ǃ | (Post)alveolar | ʄ | Palatal | tʼ | Dental alveolar |
| ǂ | Palatoalveolar | ɠ | Velar | kʼ | Velar |
| ǁ | Alveolar lateral | ʛ | Uvular | sʼ | Alveolar fricative |

### Other symbols

| ʍ | Voiceless labial-velar fricative | | ɕ ʑ | Alveolo-palatal fricatives |
|---|---|---|---|---|
| w | Voiceless labial-velar approximant | | ɺ | Voiced alveolar lateral flap |
| ɥ | Voiceless labial-palatal approximant | | ɧ | Simultaneous ʃ and x |
| ʜ | Voiceless epiglottal fricative | | | |
| ʢ | Voiced epiglottal fricative | Affricates and double articulations can be represented by two symbols joined by a tie bar if necessary. | k͡p t͡s | |
| ʡ | Epiglottal plosive | | | |

### Vowels

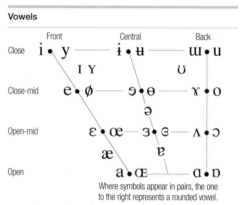

Where symbols appear in pairs, the one to the right represents a rounded vowel.

### Suprasegmentals

| ˈ | Primary stress | |
|---|---|---|
| ˌ | Secondary stress | ˌfoʊnəˈtɪʃən |
| ː | Long | eː |
| ˑ | Half-long | eˑ |
| ˘ | Extra-short | ĕ |
| ǀ | Minor (foot) group | |
| ǁ | Major (intonation) group | |
| . | Syllable break | ɹi.ækt |
| ‿ | Linking (absence of a break) | |

### Diacritics

Diacritics may be placed above a symbol with a descender, e.g. ŋ̊

| ̥ | Voiceless | n̥ d̥ | ̤ | Breathy voiced | b̤ a̤ | ̪ | Dental | t̪ d̪ |
|---|---|---|---|---|---|---|---|---|
| ̬ | Voiced | s̬ t̬ | ̰ | Creaky voiced | b̰ a̰ | ̺ | Apical | t̺ d̺ |
| ʰ | Aspirated | tʰ dʰ | ̼ | Linguolabial | t̼ d̼ | ̻ | Laminal | t̻ d̻ |
| ̹ | More rounded | ɔ̹ | ʷ | Labialised | tʷ dʷ | ̃ | Nasalised | ẽ |
| ̜ | Less rounded | ɔ̜ | ʲ | Palatalised | tʲ dʲ | ⁿ | Nasal release | dⁿ |
| ̟ | Advanced | u̟ | ˠ | Velarised | tˠ dˠ | ˡ | Lateral release | dˡ |
| ̠ | Retracted | e̠ | ˤ | Pharyngealised | tˤ dˤ | ̚ | No audible release | d̚ |
| ̈ | Centralised | ë | ̴ | Velarised or pharyngealised | ɫ | | | |
| ̽ | Mid-centralised | e̽ | ̝ | Raised | e̝ | (ɹ̝ = voiced alveolar fricative) | | |
| ̩ | Syllabic | n̩ | ̞ | Lowered | e̞ | (β̞ = voiced bilabial approximant) | | |
| ̯ | Non-syllabic | e̯ | ̘ | Advanced tongue root | e̘ | | | |
| ˞ | Rhoticity | ɚ a˞ | ̙ | Retracted tongue root | e̙ | | | |

### Tones and word accents

| Level | | Contour | |
|---|---|---|---|
| e̋ or ˥ | Extra high | ě or ˄ | Rising |
| é ˦ | Extra high | ê ˅ | Falling |
| ē ˧ | Mid | e᷄ ˧˦ | High rising |
| è ˨ | Low | e᷅ ˨˩ | Low rising |
| ȅ ˩ | Extra low | e᷈ | Rising-falling |
| ꜜ | Downstep | ↗ | Global rise |
| ꜛ | Upstep | ↘ | Global fall |

# Transcribing spontaneous speech

### How do you set about it?

First you record an exchange in whatever context is most convenient (casual conversation, service encounter, radio phone-in); then you write down (transcribe) everything that has been said, including the hesitations, false starts, overlaps, latchings and other non-fluency features. Transcription takes a great deal of time (always longer than you think) so start off by transcribing a few minutes of conversation only. You also need to be aware of a potential problem, which is that speakers are often uncomfortable if they know they are being recorded and speak in a stilted and awkward way. This has been described by the American linguist William Labov (1981) as the Observer's Paradox. The best way to avoid the problem is to record a lengthy session and start transcribing about 10–15 minutes after the start of the conversation, when the speakers have forgotten they're being recorded. (To keep your original data safe, it's wise to make a duplicate and keep it labelled, dated and secure.)

### How do you write it down?

Spoken language can be transcribed in graphemes (normal letter type) or in phonetic symbols (see diagrams on pp. 158–159).

- Graphemic transcriptions are not normally punctuated (no capital letters, commas, full stops, exclamation or question marks). Don't be thrown, however, if you encounter some punctuation in a graphemic transcript.
- Phonetic transcription indicates word divisions by /.../ ( /kat/ = cat; /sez/ = says; /fiːld/ = field). Punctuation, apart from capitals for proper nouns and first-person pronouns, is normally omitted.

The following conventions are used regardless of whether you transcribe into graphemes or phonetic symbols.

- Pauses can be marked by (.), meaning indeterminate length, or in minutes and seconds, for example (1.20).
- Overlaps (when one speaker starts before the previous speaker has finished) can be marked with elongated square brackets [ ].
- Latching (an immediate follow-up from the previous speaker without overlap) is signalled by =.
- Minor and major boundaries in conversation (equivalent to commas, semi-colons, colons and full stops in punctuation) can be marked by / (minor) or // (major).
- It's also possible to represent prosodic features like intonation patterns in speech: / means rising tone; ` means falling tone; /` means falling/rising tones; ^ means rising/falling tones.

## Activity 7 Transcribing in graphemes

Select a recording of conversation you have already made. Transcribe the first 2 minutes using normal graphemes and mark the overlaps, pauses, latching and boundaries.

## Activity 8 Transcribing using phonetic symbols.

Transcribe another 2 minutes from a different part of the recording into IPA. Mark the major and minor boundaries and falling and/or rising intonation.

**Practising reading transcribed speech**

Collect as much transcribed material as you can find (for example, A-level English Language or English Language & Literature past papers, transcriptions made by members of your group). Select one unseen transcribed passage and read it aloud (as fluently as possible) to your group. Without any discussion ask the group to guess:

- Who are the speakers and what is their gender?
- What is the context?
- What is the purpose and/or function of the exchange?

## Sound and sound patterning: spontaneous and crafted texts

Ordinary speech is as patterned as crafted speech – it's just that people don't notice! From infancy, children delight in nursery rhymes and songs, and especially in stories where there is pattern and repetition. As adults, we sometimes find ourselves rhyming unintentionally as we speak – and then someone jokes 'I'm a poet and I didn't know it!' (A very obvious place to look for patterning in non-spontaneous speech is the jingling world of advertising.) That human beings take pleasure in rhythmic speech as well as music is clear when you recall proverbial expressions beloved by grandparents such as 'A stitch in time saves nine' – a classic example of assonance. Listen for sound patterning in the speech around you every day – you may be surprised how much you find.

We are going to look, however, at a single poem as an example of sound patterning in literature – a particularly poignant choice because the poem is about deafness. Before we consider the poem below, here is a brief list of sound-patterning strategies you need to know about.

- Alliteration – repetition of initial (first) consonant in group of words
- Assonance – repetition of vowel in medial position (middle of words)
- Dissonance – deliberately discordant sounds grouped together
- Consonance – repetition of consonant in medial or final position
- Onomatopoeia – sound suggesting meaning of word
- Full rhyme – identical sequence of sounds (vowel and final consonant)
- Half-rhyme – variation in vowel, repetition of final consonant
- End rhyme/end stopping – rhyme at end of poetic line
- Pun/wordplay – repetition of same sound or similar sound
- Metre – classical in name (iambic pentameter or blank verse, tetrameter, trimeter, etc.) but accentual in form (strong /light stress)
- Caesura – break mid-line emphasises change of topic, mood, or prepares for smooth transition to next line, called enjambement or 'run-on' lines, creating flowing sound.

> ### *One Deaf Poet* by Walter Nash
> Small garden – voices gossiping on their stems,
> the chaffinch's pebble of song, are lost to me;
> my ears are closed to intricate device;
> somewhere aloft, the lark is dropping stitches,
> but I miss the click of needles. Music shrinks.
> Listening hard, I grasp only the gross
> purport of the notes; the delicate
> harmonics flutter briefly and elude me.

Audition's edifice crumbles. Bricks and bats,
wreckages of dry consonants, high vowels,
tumble out of my belfry, and the chimes
ring tinnily for vespers; grumpy, I lurk
suspiciously in the neighbourhoods of whispers.
 'You have to shout', visitors are instructed.
The more they shout the less I am informed;
shouting is amplifying formlessness.

How common talk distorts to comedy!
'Another slice of bread' reaches me as
'an overflight of dread', and 'aftermath'
as 'have to bath'. I hear a garbled text
by Peter Snug, filtered through Wonderland:
affable salesmen say 'a marbler's aid
offers a cistern with your healing problem'.
Cisterns and marbles will not heal me much.

But what of that? Neighbours, I am a poet,
I am an auditorium to myself.
Hooped in the strict confinement of my skull
elated wings of rhythm lunge and dart;
rustles within, shape the sonorities
of forms, measures, sounds in permutations
and patterned mazes, seeking, endless, endless,
a resurrection and the hope of heaven.
I nurture words of comfort that may yet
foster the Word. I wait in isolation
in this dark temple, murmuring 'Speak, Lord,
and thy servant will hear'.
          I am not deaf, after all.

The poet is cross and miserable at his loss of hearing, and the first two stanzas show this in their sound patterning: the alliteration and consonance of the sibilants in line 1 are contrasted with the hard consonants of the 'pebble' and the 'dropped stitches'. Further harsh alliteration 'bricks and bats' plus the repetition of 'shout' complete the cacophonous picture. The transition to comic versions of language lightens the poet's mood and in the final stanza he celebrates his vocation within the 'auditorium' of his mind where the music of poetry flows and resonates. Like the biblical figure Simeon in the Temple of Jerusalem, he can joyfully face the future, including death, having experienced revelation. Simeon was granted a vision of the child Jesus; the deaf poet expects to 'hear' his Lord calling.

There is more for you to find for yourself, but this is a start.

## Review

In this section, you have been given the opportunity to
- examine how humans produce speech and analyse it
- practise the methods for transcribing speech
- consider the importance of sound patterning in everyday and crafted speech.

# Talking with a purpose

## What makes a conversation successful?

A simple response might be that an exchange has succeeded if all participants have achieved their primary purpose, if every speaker felt able to communicate their meanings without inappropriate interruption, and if there was co-operation between participants. A more detailed analysis might investigate the use of politeness strategies; terms of address; facework; management of social distance and social solidarity; conversational maxims and implicatures. We shall offer a brief account of all these terms.

## Why is politeness important when we talk to each other?

Politeness means showing respect for the person you're talking to, whether the exchange is formal or informal. Robin Lakoff, in an article engagingly titled 'The logic of politeness: or minding your *p's* and *q's*' (1973), was a pioneer in the field of linguistic politeness, and since then scholars have become increasingly interested in this area of research. Indeed, a serious academic journal dedicated to the subject of linguistic politeness (*Journal of Politeness Research: Language, Behaviour, Culture*) has recently been established, and the whole area described (Harris 2007) as 'a significant and challenging field of research, much of which is cross-cultural and [involves] researchers on a global scale'. Although cultural difference is hugely important, our focus in this chapter has to be on predominantly English-speaking cultures. Nevertheless, one of the most recent angles on linguistic politeness associates politeness with power, a universal rather than culturally defined concept. More of this shortly.

One of the earliest and most influential researchers in the field of linguistic politeness was E. Goffman (1967), who introduced the idea of face and face-threatening acts. He argued that in talk we need to respect the other person's face needs. 'Positive face needs' means that we want to be liked and approved (hence greetings, compliments and appropriate terms of address). 'Negative face needs' means that we wrap up unpleasant requests or orders by using hedges ('It's sort of difficult but…') and apologies ('I'm sorry but would you mind if…'), thus avoiding face-threatening behaviour. We also need to respect the relative status, social distance and social solidarity between participants in a conversation, and be responsive to the social and cultural context (don't call an interviewer by her first name unless she asks you to, don't use taboo language with a head teacher, don't call your best friend by their full name if they prefer a nickname, etc.). Goffman (1981) also introduced the idea of footing in connection with the way people align themselves with what they are saying (in other words, their stance). Your footing in talking to a university admissions tutor, for example, might be as a would-be participant and you would adjust your language appropriately.

Brown and Levinson in *Politeness* (1978, 1987) go further in their detailed descriptions of positive and negative politeness in conversation. Positive politeness means that you claim common ground with other speakers and convey your assumption that all participants wish to be co-operative. Negative politeness means that you don't presume or assume anything about your relationship with other speakers, are direct, and neither force your own point nor impinge on others.

Some positive politeness strategies are

- pay attention to the other speaker(s) – show interest, sympathy, approval
- seek agreement – choose safe topics
- avoid disagreement – pretend to agree, use white lies, hedge your own opinions
- presuppose or assert common ground
- make jokes
- assume or assert reciprocal agreement – and there are more!

Some negative politeness strategies are

- be indirect
- question and hedge
- be pessimistic
- give deference
- be apologetic
- go on record as being indebted.

## Activity 10 | Identifying politeness strategies in use in the public domain

Record a radio or television one-to-one interview or radio phone-in. Select and transcribe a short extract (2–3 minutes only) then analyse your data to see what kind of politeness strategies are being used.

## Activity 11 | Examining the use of politeness strategies in drama to create character

Record an episode of a television or radio soap opera. Listen carefully to the taped episode (remember that it is scripted and not naturally occurring conversation) and select one character who plays a significant role. Listen again, noting to what extent politeness strategies are being used by the writer to reveal character.

## Successful/unsuccessful conversation: theory and practice

In 1975, a little later than Lakoff's pioneering article on politeness, another American theorist, H.P. Grice, proposed four basic conversational maxims or rules for successful conversation. (The links between linguistic politeness and successful conversation are fairly obvious.) They are

- be relevant – don't wander off the topic (maxim of relevance)
- be truthful and have enough evidence for what you say (maxim of quality)
- speak appropriately – don't talk too much or too little (maxim of quantity)
- speak in a clear, coherent and orderly way (maxim of manner).

These maxims or rules for successful conversation remain valid today, and are built into our everyday exchanges as unrecognised but basic assumptions about talk. They can be readily identified in a wide range of spoken registers and genres, from casual conversation to more formal speaking. Moreover, in written literary genres like fiction, drama or poetry – wherever talk is crafted into dialogue – it's equally possible to identify these maxims, even though they originated in Grice's theorising about spoken language. For example, in literature the author's purpose is to create character, describe a scene or further the plot. In order to do this, conversation or dialogue which is convincing to a reader or listener must be created. Consequently, if a writer's literary purposes are to craft successful conversation or dialogue, the maxims will be present. Conversely, if the writer wishes to create dialogue between characters who are unsuccessful communicators, then some or all of the maxims will be ignored or 'flouted' – to use Grice's own term.

**Activity 12** | **Identifying conversational maxims in casual conversation**

Record *either* a conversation with friends or between family members *or* a conversation in a work situation. Listen carefully to the tape several times (unless you have time to transcribe it). Decide whether the speakers fulfil or flout the conversational maxims.

### Saying what you mean

When we speak, we don't always say what we really mean. Conversational implicature is the technical description of inference in conversation. Implicatures or implied meanings are premised, of course, on the assumption that conversational maxims are being followed in any particular exchange. For example, if someone says 'I'm hungry!' the reply 'The Cat and Fiddle's over there' carries the implicature or inference that the speaker's hunger can be satisfied at the Cat and Fiddle pub nearby (also neatly fulfilling the maxims of quality and relevance). Another example would be the statement 'It's cold in here', the implicature being 'Please shut the window/door'.

**Activity 13** | **Considering the comic use of conversational implicature in fiction**

**Pair work**

Conversational implicature is often used with comic effect in fiction. Trace the use of this conversational tool and assess its effectiveness as a comic device in the following extract from *Pride and Prejudice* by Jane Austen (1813). Mr Collins, a foolish clergyman, has proposed marriage to his clever and appalled cousin, Elizabeth Bennett.

It was absolutely necessary to interrupt him now.

'You are too hasty, Sir,' she cried. 'You forget that I have made no answer. Let me do it without farther loss of time. Accept my thanks for the compliment you are paying me. I am very sensible of the honour of your proposals, but it is impossible for me to do other than to decline.'

'I am not now to learn,' replied Mr Collins, with a formal wave of the hand, 'that it is usual with young ladies to reject the addresses of the man whom they secretly mean to accept, when he first applies for their favour; and that sometimes the refusal is repeated a second or even a third time. I am therefore by no means discouraged by what you have just said, and shall hope to lead you to the altar ere long.'

'Upon my word, Sir,' cried Elizabeth, 'your hope is rather an extraordinary one after my declaration. I do assure you that I am not one of those young ladies (if such young ladies there are) who are so daring as to risk their happiness on the chance of being asked a second time. I am perfectly serious in my refusal. – You could not make *me* happy, and I am convinced I am the last woman in the world who would make *you* so.'...

'When I do myself the honour of speaking to you next on this subject I shall hope to receive a more favourable answer than you have now given me; though I am far from accusing you of cruelty at present, because I know it to be the established custom of your sex to reject a man on the first application, and perhaps you have even now said as much to encourage my suit as would be consistent with the true delicacy of the female character.'

'Really, Mr Collins,' cried Elizabeth with some warmth, 'you puzzle me exceedingly. If what I have hitherto said can appear to you in the form of encouragement, I know not how to express my refusal in such a way as may convince you of its being one.'

'You must give me leave to flatter myself, my dear cousin, that your refusal of my addresses is mere words of course...'

## Politeness and power: new theories about linguistic politeness

The key emphasis in linguistic politeness theory has been on face (Brown and Levinson *et al.*, 1987), focusing predominantly on politeness (supporting face). Within this framework power has always been part of the relationship between speakers/interactants.

A recent and interesting research development has been the focus on impoliteness (Mills 2003, 2004; Locher 2004). Their conclusions are important for the study of power in relation to politeness. Mills (2003) argues that impoliteness is 'an assessment of someone's behaviour rather than a quality intrinsic to an utterance'. If power is viewed as behaviour, then it is not a 'static component of particular interactive situations' or 'an inherent attribute which certain individuals possess' but is 'a complex, multi-faceted and dynamic force', and 'something people do to each other' (Harris 2007). Holmes and Stubbe (2003) suggest that 'people *do* power and politeness throughout the day in their talk at work'. If power is a kind of behaviour, then politeness is also behaviour rather than a set of precepts or rules. Moreover, when people talk to each other, whether at work or not, the context of the interaction (gender, age, education, status, identity, etc.) will affect these behaviours. Even more interesting, this interpretation of politeness and power in spoken exchanges convincingly explains so-called cultural differences in politeness in different social/ethnic and national groups. Hence, linguistic politeness exists as communities of practice (Mills 2004) rather than as individually chosen linguistic/cultural behaviours.

This all sounds very complicated! In fact the key words to pull out are

- politeness/impoliteness
- behaviour
- power
- context.

Although we've ended up in a rather different place from where we began (talking about positive and negative face), in no way should we be rejecting previous research on politeness and throwing the baby out with the proverbial bathwater! There is room for both approaches, and indeed the former is so well structured, systematised and theorised that we might be just tempted to stay with it. However, we need to keep up with new developments because they will help us to gain greater insights into the mysteries of human politeness.

| Activity 14 | Investigating the linguistic behaviour of speakers |
|---|---|

**Pair work**

The transcript extracts here are taken from an interview which took place in the 1950s between a 103-year-old male resident of Tunbridge Wells (Mr C) and a female interviewer (I) (cited in Langford 1994).

Working in pairs, see if you can apply to this text any of the theories about and explanations of linguistic politeness described in this section.

Key    (.) micropause        = indicates an utterance is cut short
       (1) timed pause (in seconds)

I    well now Mr C (.) you tell me (.) about Tunbridge We - lls =
Mr C    = I don't know anything about ... Tunbridge Wells
I    but you've lived here (.) I believe (.) since you were 18 =
Mr C    = that's right
I    and has it changed much in all that time
Mr C    yes (.) we had a lotta changes
I    what's what's the biggest change do you think
Mr C                   well er (.) lotta building an (1.5) 's all I know about it (.) about Tunbridge Wells (0.5)
I    what's the nicest thing about Tunbridge Wells =
Mr C    = what's what
I    what's the nicest thing (.) about Tunbridge Wells
Mr C                          I don't know
I    don't you know anything nice about it
Mr C    no
I    nothing at all
Mr C    no I know nothing about Tunbridge Wells
I    but it must be a healthy place
Mr C    mm
I    it must be a healthy place =
Mr C    = oh it's a healthy place cos you can go back (.) to the fif -(.) fifteenth and sixteenth century can't you (1.0)
I    yes (.) I know any
Mr C           bet you don't know that (0.5)
I    oh yes (.) I knew that (.) but any ways
Mr C              oh
I    it must be healthy (.) for you to be (.) looking so wonderful (.) at this age
Mr C    well why shouldn't I look wonderful (1.0)
I    mm (.) well erm that of course comes from the inner spirit I know
Mr C    mm
I    that comes from the inner spirit (1.0)
Mr C    mm

|       |                                                                                                                              |
|-------|------------------------------------------------------------------------------------------------------------------------------|
| I     | well from your own inner spirit                                                                                              |
| Mr C  | (2.5) I don't know what you want me to say (.) if I can say anything to please you I will but                                 |
| I     | what you're saying delights me (.) I                                                                                         |
| Mr C  |                                    mm |
| I     | I want you to tell me something about living in Tunbridge Wells                                                               |
|       | [passage omitted]                                                                                                            |
| I     | erm and (.) can you tell me anything (.) about changes in transport there (.) I suppose once upon a time there were horses where now there are motorcars |
| Mr C  | no I can't tell you anything about that (0.5)                                                                                 |
| I     | you don't remember that                                                                                                      |
| Mr C  | well I dare say I could remember but I didn't have any business in it (.) that's the thing makes you remember when you got some money in it |
|       | [passage omitted]                                                                                                            |
| I     | Just to finish off would you tell us your full name (.) and how old you are now                                             |
| Mr C  | true name my name                                                                                                            |
| I     |                your full name                     |
| Mr C  | my full name (.) Alfred Cranwell (1.5)                                                                                        |
| I     | and how old are you (1.0)                                                                                                     |
| Mr C  | born in eighteen fifty one (.) first o'January and you can work that out for yourself can't you |

## Activity 15   Comparing a crafted interview with a spontaneous interview

The extract below is taken from the play *Top Girls* by Caryl Churchill (1982). Marlene (M), who owns an employment agency, is interviewing Jeanine (J), who wants to join the agency. Compare this with the transcript of the spontaneous interview in Activity 14.

|     |                                                                          |
|-----|--------------------------------------------------------------------------|
| M   | So you want a job with better prospects                                  |
| J   | I want a change                                                          |
| M   | So you'll take anything comparable?                                      |
| J   | No, I do want prospects. I want more money.                              |
| M   | You're getting –?                                                        |
| J   | Hundred                                                                  |
| M   | It's not bad, you know. You're what? Twenty?                             |
| J   | I'm saving to get married.                                               |
| M   | Does that mean that you don't want a long term job, Jeanine?             |
| J   | I might do.                                                              |
| M   | Because where do the prospects come in? No kids for a bit?               |
| J   | Oh no, not kids, not yet.                                                |
| M   | So you won't tell them you're getting married?                           |
| J   | Had I better not?                                                        |
| M   | It would probably help.                                                  |
| J   | I'm not wearing a ring. We thought we wouldn't spend on a ring.          |

M  Saves taking it off.

J  I wouldn't take it off.

M  There's no need to mention it when you go for interview. Now Jeanine do you have a feel for any particular

J  But what if they ask?

M  kind of company?

J  I thought advertising.

M  People often do think advertising. I have got a few vacancies but I think they're looking for something glossier.

J  You mean how I dress? I can dress different. I

M  I mean experience.

J  dress like this on purpose for where I am now.

M  I have a marketing department here of a knitwear manufacturer. Marketing is near enough advertising. Secretary

J  Knitwear?

M  to the marketing manager, he's thirty-five, married, I've sent him a girl before and she was happy, left to have a baby, you won't want to mention marriage there. He's very fair I think, good at his job, you won't have to nurse him along. Hundred and ten so that's better than you're doing now.

J  I don't know.

**Review**

In this section, you have been given the opportunity to

● consider the role of politeness strategies in spontaneous and crafted talk
● examine the theories behind successful and unsuccessful conversation
● analyse transcripts showing the linguistic behaviour/social practices of the speakers.

# The structure of talk

As we have seen, talk and the literary 're-creation' of talk are more complicated than we might have expected. Most people are unaware of the multi-voiced, multi-faceted and multi-purpose nature of human communication. In the first sections of this chapter we have moved from an introduction to key ideas about speech in spontaneous and crafted forms to some exploration of what makes conversation or spoken exchanges successful, moving finally into the field of linguistic politeness and power relations.

Power relations in spoken language are of interest not only to politeness theorists, but also to discourse theorists such as Norman Fairclough (*Language and Power* 1989, 2001). This section will guide you through basic definitions of the term/concept 'discourse', through explanations of how spoken discourse is structured, how it functions, and how discourse analysts can provide valuable insights into our understanding of speech and its representations in literature.

## What is discourse?

According to Schrifflin, Tannen and Hamilton (*The Handbook of Discourse Analysis,* 2003), discourse has been defined by many linguists as anything 'beyond the sentence'. A more complicated version of the same definition is 'a unit of language greater than any individual sentence, clause or utterance'. A second and broader category (Jaworski and Coupland 1999) describes the study of discourse as 'the study of language in use'. A third category favoured by critical theorists as well as linguists looks even wider and uses the term 'discourse' as a 'count noun' (a noun which can be either singular or plural, e.g. discourse) referring to more general social and linguistic practices.

We shall be focusing in this section on the second category, language in use, and particularly on spoken rather than written language. However, because we are also interested in the crafting of speech in literary genres, there will be occasions when the other two categories will be relevant to the analysis/discussion.

Because talk (spoken discourse) is something most of us are not only rather good at, but also hugely enjoy, we tend not to question how, as mature speakers, we learnt to use and recognise the enormous range of patterns and structures within speech. In fact, these adult interactional skills – which we take for granted – were established from birth when we learnt turn taking. Before any kind of vocalisation (apart from the birth cry), a baby learns to respond to the carer's voice by moving his or her eyes, tongue, hands and feet or smiling. Thus taking turns is the beginning of structured spoken discourse.

We use these discourse structures in adult talk to achieve a wide range of purposes in everyday communication. (They are also replicated or represented in literature, according to a writer's particular purposes.) We need a methodology for analysing these patterns, structures and purposes in spontaneous and crafted speech (talk in life and talk in literature).

## Discourse analysis

Discourse analysis ('the linguistic analysis of naturally occurring **connected** spoken and written discourse' – Stubbs 1983) is one hugely important methodology which includes a variety of interesting and useful theoretical approaches. A major area of focus is spoken language, which includes speakers in a wide range of social contexts from casual conversation, to service encounters and court-room exchanges, to answer-phone messages, classroom talk and transcribed texts such as interviews and talk in parliament.

Some important theories of discourse analysis include

- speech act theory (Austin and Searle 1969)
- exchange structure theory (Sinclair and Coulthard 1975, 1992)
- pragmatics (Grice 1975, Levinson 1987)
- ethnography of communication (Hymes 1974)
- conversation analysis (Sacks, Schegloff and Jefferson 1973, 1984)
- frame and schema theory (Minsky 1974, Chase 1977)

Other theorists who focus on discourse analysis include Gumperz (1982), Stubbs (1983), Brown and Yule (1983), Halliday (1985), Biber (1988) and Schriffrin (1994).

It's also important to recognise that all talk has a purpose or function, which will affect its structure. As we shall see, this can vary according to the situation, context and audience.

Spoken discourse is either *transactional* or *interactional* in purpose (Brown and Yule 1983). Transactional language is used when the participants are exchanging goods and services (buying bread, visiting the doctor, seeing a financial adviser). Interactional language is when speakers are engaging in socialising/casual conversation.

In spoken discourse, *given* information precedes *new* information (Halliday 1967, Prince 1992). What follows in an exchange depends on the conversation topic, the shared knowledge of speaker and hearer, and the predictability of the next piece of information.

For example

    **A** Mum said you were very late last night [*given*].
    **B** How does she know? [B knows he was late but seeks *new* information.]
    **A** It was Dad who told her [*new*]; he woke up and heard you come in [*new*].

In spoken discourse the individual units of speech are described as 'utterances'. Utterances are context-defined units of language; hence, as Schriffrin (1994) says, discourse as utterances 'sits at the intersection of structure and function' (combining form with use).

# Theories of discourse analysis: structure and function

## Speech act theory

Speech act theory derives from the work of philosophers Austin (1962) and Searle (1969). Speech acts are the actions performed when we say something (Cutting 2004). A speech act can be described at three levels

- the words themselves – the locutionary act
- what is being done with the words – the illocutionary force
- the result of the speech act on the hearers – the perlocutionary effect.

These speech acts can be informative ('My eyes are blue') or performative (using performative verbs – 'I welcome you', 'I demand that...').

Illocutionary speech acts have been divided by Searle into five types

- representative – when the speaker believes in the truth of the proposition ('I believe...', 'I conclude ')
- directive – when the speaker tries to get the listener to do something ('I request...', 'I order...')
- commissive – when the speaker is committed to a course of action ('I promise...', 'I agree...')
- expressive – when the speaker expresses a personal attitude ('I deplore...', 'I congratulate...')
- declaration – when the speaker alters a situation by their action ('I dismiss you, 'I pronounce you man and wife', 'The court sentences you to ten years in prison').

According to speech act theory, successful speech acts must fulfil certain criteria, known as felicity conditions (although self-evident, people are not necessarily aware of them, and it is useful to identify possible reasons for conversations going wrong). Felicity conditions mean that

- you must have authority to perform the speech act (promise or baptise or arrest someone)
- you must perform the speech act correctly (welcome someone pleasantly, introduce a visitor appropriately)
- you must perform the speech act sincerely (don't apologise if you're not sorry, don't pretend to believe or agree if you don't).

Not only do speakers assume that felicity conditions have been met when talking to each other, but they also assume they can interpret indirect speech acts. For example, 'I'm boiling hot!' might be a simple statement of fact, but (depending on the context) it could mean something quite different ('Please open the window', 'Please fetch me a drink' or 'Why did you tell me to wear my coat?') to a listener. This is not dissimilar to the use of conversational implicature discussed on page 165.

*What is useful about speech act theory* is that it enables us to identify and describe in sequence different communicative functions within utterance units (Schriffrin 1994). Because individual speech acts can be illocutionary as well as perlocutionary (and indirect as well as direct), we can get a sense of the optional and unpredictable nature of talk. Moreover, being able to recognise felicity conditions helps us to understand more about what makes for successful conversation.

| **Activity 16** | **Identifying illocutionary and perlocutionary speech acts** |
|---|---|

Try comparing illocutionary and perlocutionary speech acts in an everyday conversation and in a literary text. Listen to a conversation over a meal (could be with friends or family) and observe whether individual speakers are more likely to be informative or performative (illocutionary or perlocutionary) in their exchanges. Did you notice any indirect speech acts/conversational implicatures? Compare your observations with those of others in the group.

Reread the passages from *Pride and Prejudice* and *Top Girls* on pages 165 and 168. Would it be reasonable to describe the former as mainly perlocutionary in effect and the latter as mainly illocutionary? Support your opinion with two or three quotations from each text.

## Exchange structure theory

Exchange structure theory was developed by Coulthard, Sinclair and Brazil (1975 onwards) as a result of their investigation into classroom interaction. Today it is less representative of teacher–pupil exchanges, and is not much used in analysing classroom interaction. Nevertheless it is worth examining. Note that the purpose of each exchange is transactional and that the power balance is very much in the teacher's favour.

Coulthard *et al.* found that whatever the subject, every lesson had the same *interactional* structure, with each move consisting of one or more speech acts. After an opening remark (framing move) such as 'Right', there was an initiating move, followed by a response followed by teacher feedback/evaluation. Another way of representing the exchange would be

| Move 1: ask question | *initiation*  (I) |
|---|---|
| Move 2: answer question | *response*  (R) |
| Move 3: comment | *follow-up, (F)* |

or IRF. This three-part exchange represents what happens in classroom interaction. Each new set of opening and closing framing moves provides exchange boundaries before the next three-part exchange begins. Here is an example.

| Teacher | Where was Shakespeare born? | *initiation/opening move* |
|---|---|---|
| Pupil | Warwickshire | *response* |
| Teacher | Yes, but can you be more precise? | *follow-up/initiation* |
| Pupil | It's Stratford, isn't it? | *response* |
| Teacher | Yes, that's right. | *evaluation/feedback* |

The two-part exchange or adjacency pair is a familiar pattern of exchange/turn taking, reminding us of our earliest interactions (baby/carer). This structure of conversation is found in doctor–patient interviews and many other service encounters. Again, the power balance tends to be in the hands of the initiator or questioner. Some variations on the basic pattern are

- question/answer ('What's the time?'/'Six o'clock')
- inform/acknowledge ('The train's late again'/'Yes, I'm really fed up')
- introduction/greeting ('John, this is Mary'/'Hi John, how are you?')
- complain/excuse ('I've a splitting headache'/'No wonder you lost your temper with him').

Adjacency pairs can be separated by insertion sequences (one or more intervening utterances), for example

'How much did those jeans cost?'/'Do you really want to know?'/'Yes I do – don't be mean!'/'Are you sure?'/'Yes – I might get some for my birthday'/'Well, they were a bargain – twenty-two quid.'

What is useful about exchange structure theory is that it provides a flexible model of discourse structure with wide-ranging applications far removed from the initial classroom discourse situation.

| Activity 17 | Investigating the use of exchange structures |

**Individual**

1 Record (with permission) part of or a whole lesson. Listen to the recording carefully, and select an extract which provides an example of three-part exchange structure. Identify each move in your example and describe its function.

**Group work**

2 Look at the following extract from Lewis Carroll's comic poem 'You are old, Father William' from *Through the Looking Glass* (1871) and see if you can identify the way in which Carroll uses two-part exchange structure for his comic purposes:

'You are old, Father William,' the young man said
'And your hair has become very white;
And yet you incessantly stand on your head –
Do you think, at your age, it is right?'

'In my youth,' Father William replied to his son,
'I feared it might injure the brain;
But, now I am perfectly sure I have none,
Why, I do it again and again.' ...

'You are old,' said the youth, 'and your jaws are too weak
For anything tougher than suet;
Yet you finished the goose, with the bones and the beak –
Pray, how did you manage to do it?'

'In my youth,' said his father, 'I took to the law
And argued each case with my wife;
And the muscular strength, which it gave to my jaw,
Has lasted the rest of my life.'

'You are old,' said the youth, 'one would hardly suppose
That your eye was as steady as ever;
Yet you balanced an eel on the end of your nose –
What made you so awfully clever?'

'I have answered three questions, and that is enough,'
Said his father; 'don't give yourself airs!
Do you think I can listen all day to such stuff?
Be off, or I'll kick you down-stairs!'

# Labov's theory of narrative structure

Labov's theory of narrative structure is based on his research into personal experience narratives (PEN). In the late 1960s he was investigating the ways in which social variables (class, gender, age, etc.) affected speech and particularly vernacular speech among the islanders of Martha's Vineyard and gang members from Harlem, New York City (Labov 1972). His conclusions confirm the centrality of narrative to human experience, providing psychologists, historians, educators, rhetoricians as well linguists and students of literature with ample opportunities for in-depth investigation.

Narrative, according to Labov, can be defined as a unit of discourse with clear boundaries, linear structure, and the following recognisable stages in its development

- abstract (summary)
- orientation (context)
- evaluation (point of interest in the story)
- narrative (storytelling, involving a series of complicating events)
- result (what finally happened)
- coda (signals the end).

*What is useful about narrative structure theory* is that it recognises storytelling as a discrete part of everyday spoken interaction with a unique capacity to hold the hearer's (or, in another context, the reader's) attention. Labov's identification of its structural features and differentiation between them (some features can be optional, others remain obligatory) confirms the integral nature of the relationship between form and function in spoken language.

| Activity 18 | Applying narrative structure theory to spoken and written narratives |
|---|---|

**Individual**

1  Record one of the following narratives

- a friend telling you about a family celebration
- a parent, teacher or babysitter telling a fairy story or nursery tale to one or more young children
- an adult telling a shaggy-dog story.

Listen to it several times. Can you identify the narrative stages Labov describes?

**Pair work**

2  The following extract is from the opening scene of Shakespeare's *Hamlet*. It is set on the battlements of Elsinore castle in Denmark, where the soldiers on guard duty tell Prince Hamlet's friend Horatio what they have seen at midnight.

Read the extract and then try to apply Labov's narrative structure theory. Remember that the story is being unfolded by all the speakers.

| | |
|---|---|
| Barnado | Welcome, Horatio. Welcome, good Marcellus. |
| Marcellus | What, has this thing appeared again tonight? |
| Barnardo | I have seen nothing. |
| Marcellus | Horatio says 'tis but our fantasy, |
| | And will not let belief take hold of him |
| | Touching this dreaded sight twice seen of us. |
| | Therefore I have entreated him along |
| | With us to watch the minutes of this night, |

|  | That, if again this apparition come, |
|---|---|
|  | He may approve our eyes and speak to it. |
| Horatio | Tush, tush, 'twill not appear. |
| Barnardo | Sit down a while, |
|  | And let us once again assail your ears, |
|  | That are so fortified against our story, |
|  | What we have two nights seen. |
| Horatio | Well, sit we down, |
|  | And let us hear Barnardo speak of this. |
| Barnardo | Last night of all, |
|  | When yond same star that's westward from the pole |
|  | Had made his course t'illume that part of heaven |
|  | Where now it burns, Marcellus and myself, |
|  | The bell then beating one – |
|  | *Enter the Ghost* |
| Marcellus | Peace, break thee off. Look where it comes again. |
| Barnardo | In the same figure like the King that's dead. |
| Marcellus | Thou art a scholar. Speak to it, Horatio. |
| Barnardo | Looks 'a not like the King? Mark it, Horatio. |
| Horatio | Most like. It harrows me with fear and wonder. |

## Frame and schema theory

*Frame theory* is a theory about the structuring of discourse. It argues that we use past experience to structure present usage. Goffman (1974) and Minsky (1974) were early exponents of frame theory, followed by Gumperz (1982). The latter's theory of conversational inference suggests that as we talk we pick up contextualisation cues (or frames) enabling us to recognise the situation and structure our responses appropriately. These mental frameworks help us to interpret the current situation and anticipate what is going to happen. Thus 'going to see the doctor' and 'asking to see a range of products in a shop' have particular frames leading to particular discourse structures.

*Schema theory* is associated with frame theory. The term schema means a mental model or knowledge structure in the memory, which has its own patterning of expectations, frames and assumptions. Tannen (1993) linked frame theory with schema theory, and in a fascinating case study demonstrated how *conflicting frames* produced miscommunication between different groups/individuals involved (paediatrician, child patient, mother, audience of doctors watching video). The frames were examination frame (medical register/medical audience); paediatric consultant frame (informal, friendly register/child patient); and consultant frame (more formal register/mother of patient). Each frame should create – and fulfil – its own discourse expectations. In Tannen's example the paediatrician slipped up and used medical register when addressing the child patient (Doctor: 'Is your spleen palpable here?' Child: 'No.')!

Similarly, mismatched schema can also cause problems, which Tannen demonstrated in the same case study. The mother, in whose mental schema wheezing meant illness, was concerned about the child's noisy breathing at night. The paediatrician, however, knew that the noisy breathing was normal for the child's condition (different mental schema and diagnosis). To reassure the mother the paediatrician had to not only adjust schemas but also shift from examination frame to consultation frame. To read a transcript of this exchange, see page 24.

*What is useful about frame and schema theory* is that together they offer explanations of how people seem to 'know' how to interact in a variety of contexts, adjusting and shifting frameworks and schemas as required.

## Activity 19  Identifying the use of frames and schema

1  Listen to either a radio phone-in, a radio discussion (such as *Any Questions?*) or a television discussion (such as *Question-time*). Is there any evidence that participants are adjusting their frames in the course of the discussion?

2  Read the following extract from a *Monty Python* television comedy sketch. The basic schema here is the service encounter, which the script-writers have deliberately disrupted/inverted to achieve their desired comic effect. Identify as many of these disruptions as you can (there are at least five!).

| | |
|---|---|
| Praline (John Cleese) | Hello, I wish to register a complaint… Hello? Miss? |
| Shopkeeper (Michael Palin) | What do you mean, Miss? |
| Praline | Oh, I'm sorry, I have a cold. I wish to make a complaint. |
| Shopkeeper | Sorry, we're closing for lunch. |
| Praline | Never mind that, my lad, I wish to complain about this parrot what I purchased not half an hour ago from this very boutique. |
| Shopkeeper | Oh yes, the Norwegian Blue. What's wrong with it? |
| Praline | I'll tell you what's wrong with it. It's dead, that's what's wrong with it. |
| Shopkeeper | No, no sir, it's not dead. It's resting. |

## Pragmatics

Unlike discourse analysis, pragmatics focuses less on structures in spoken and written language, and more on the contexts and purposes of people communicating with each other. A good description is provided by David Crystal (1987): 'pragmatics studies the factors that govern our choice of language in social interaction and the effects of our choice on others'. Linguists in the field of pragmatics include Grice, Levinson (1983), Brown and Yule (1987) and Schriffrin (1994). The importance of Grice's conversational maxims of quality, quantity, relevance and manner has already been discussed, as well as his theory of implied meanings in talk (conversational implicatures). However, making sense of what we hear also depends on the context of the conversation, our experience of analogous contexts and an assumption that the speaker's utterances are coherent, even if the conversational maxims are flouted. Sometimes flouting is inevitable: a teacher needs to explain a topic in detail, so the maxim of quantity is overridden, or someone telling an elaborate shaggy-dog story cheerfully flouts the maxims of relevance and quantity. In both situations, communication remains successful because both speakers and hearers know why the maxims are being flouted, and the co-operative principle is sustained.

What is useful about pragmatics is that it takes into account everything about speakers and hearers, from the intentions of speakers to the effects of utterances on the hearer, from their assumed 'knowledge, beliefs and presuppositions about the world' (Crystal 1987) to the effect of situation/context and individual psychological factors upon what they say and how they interpret each other's talk.

| Activity 20 | Investigating the pragmatics of family conversation |
| --- | --- |
| **Class work** | |

Record a mealtime conversation in your family (or a friend's family if this is more convenient to arrange). Don't worry about the observer's paradox (people speaking awkwardly if they know they're being recorded) – any effect will wear off after 10 minutes or so. Listen carefully to your recording and note

- who speaks the most
- who interrupts the most
- whether the conversational maxims are being followed or flouted
- whether adults point out conversational rules to younger family members ('say please')
- whether there are any conversational implicatures.

You will notice the effect of context and purpose on all the speakers. Share your findings with the rest of the class.

## Conversation analysis

Conversation analysis provides an additional dimension to discourse analysis in that it focuses primarily on conversation structure. This approach derives from sociology and is known as ethnomethodology. Sacks, Schlegoff and Jefferson (1978, 1984) are major theorists in the area. They focus on the way society affects spoken interaction, proposing that conversation itself constructs a sense of social order, because we all know the 'rules' of everyday conversation intuitively. In other words, naturally occurring spoken language has its own dynamic structure and rules deriving from social interaction, not from the rules of grammar and syntax.

Conversation analysis investigates features in spoken language like

- turn taking
- adjacency pairs
- preferred/dispreferred responses
- discourse markers indicating openings and closures
- phatic communion
- topic shifts
- topic management
- change of speaker
- repair sequences
- conversational inferences
- contextualisation cues
- insertion sequences
- transition relevance points (TRP)
- overlaps
- interruptions.

All these features can be found in successful conversation. If certain conversation 'rules' and expectations are not followed, then conversation is unsuccessful and miscommunication ensues. For example, linguists studying the effects of gender on language have found that men and women sometimes fail to understand each other because they follow different conversational rules and hence misconstrue each other's meanings. Deborah Tannen has published extensively in this field for the general reader as well as for specialists (*That's not what I meant!* 1994; *Gender and Discourse,* 1994; *You're Wearing That? Understanding Mothers and Daughters in Conversation,* 2006). Further miscommunication can occur if one or both participants misjudge or ignore the social situation (context).

The contribution made by conversation analysis to discourse analysis has been summarised by Schriffrin (1994): '[it] consider[s] the way participants in talk construct systematic solutions to recurrent organisational problems of conversation'.

*What is useful about conversation analysis* is that it recognises where the responsibility for the ordering, organisation and dynamic of talk lies – with the people doing the talking.

| Activity 21 | Identifying characteristic features used in conversational analysis |
| --- | --- |

Identify within any transcript some of the features characteristic of conversational analysis listed on page 177. You may like to choose a section from the transcript in Activity 14 (page 167), or to work with your own transcribed material.

| Activity 22 | Observing how speakers adjust their conversational style to suit context or situation |
| --- | --- |

Listen to a radio phone-in programme and note down examples of phatic communion, opening and closing strategies, topic shifts and politeness strategies.

Collect anecdotal evidence within your group about the kind of situations/contexts in which miscommunications tend to occur. Do you agree with the often argued view that male and female students 'don't understand' each other?

The following examples, one non-literary, one literary, demonstrate this male/female miscommunication. Text A is from Deborah Tannen's book *You Just Don't Understand: Women and Men in Conversation* (1992). Text B is an extract from Sylvia Plath's novel *The Bell Jar* (1963) in which the anxious heroine tries to make sense of her boyfriend's unexpected question.

**Text A**

He    I'm really tired. I didn't sleep well last night.
She  I didn't sleep well either. I never do.
He    Why are you trying to belittle me?
She  I'm just trying to show you I understand.

**Text B**

'I want to ask you a question.' He had a disquieting new habit of boring into my eyes with his look as if actually bent on piercing my head, the better to analyse what went on inside it.

'I'd thought of asking it by letter.'

I had a fleeting vision of a pale blue envelope with a Yale crest on the back flap.

'But then I decided that it would be better if I waited until you came up, so I could ask you in person.' He paused. 'Well, don't you know what it is?'

'What?' I said in a small, unpromising voice.

Buddy sat down beside me. He put his arm round my waist and brushed the hair from my ear. I didn't move. Then I heard him whisper, 'How would you like to be Mrs Buddy Willard?'

I had an awful impulse to laugh.

I thought how that question would have bowled me over at any time in my five- or six-year period of adoring Buddy Willard from a distance.

# Ethnography of communication

Ethnography of communication is another sociological approach to discourse which describes the patterns of spoken communication as part of cultural understanding and behaviour. Dell Hymes is a key theorist in the area. An alternative term for 'cultural knowledge' is communicative competence. This means that the speakers of any given language will intuitively know its norms and variations, its cultural and linguistic constraints. Each speech act is part of a speech event which in turn is part of a sequenced interaction defined by context and participants. For example, an ethnographic approach to discourse would use the findings about a particular speech act to learn about the nature of a specific speech event, basing this on cultural knowledge of the exchange; in other words, an example of communicative competence (Schriffrin 1994). Whatever we say or do is meaningful only in the framework of our cultural knowledge, and the way in which we make sense out of our experience within our specific communities. This simple example of an interview based on Schriffrin shows in its structure the shared cultural knowledge of both participants.

| | | |
|---|---|---|
| **Sociologist** | How old was that respondent? | *seeks information* |
| **Respondent** | He's over a hundred! | *provides information* |
| **Sociologist** | He looks twenty years younger! Are you sure? | *information check* |
| **Respondent** | Oh yes – it's all been properly checked. | *affirms information* |

Both participants recognised what was expected of them in the exchange, and performed it.

*What is useful about the ethnographical approach to discourse* is that it locates speech events within the wider framework of the discourse community where we all do our talking.

---

**Activity 23** | ## Investigating examples of communicative competence

Record yourself interviewing an older friend or family member about their childhood and/or schooldays. Listen to the recording several times and assess

- the communicative competence of your interviewee
- the effectiveness of your own questioning to elicit information.

Be aware of how your own experience may differ from that of your interviewee.

---

# Characteristic features/realisations of spoken language

In this section so far we have explored a range of approaches to discourse. Next we focus on how features of spoken language *realise* (enact) these discourse functions through speakers' choices of lexis and grammar in relation to context and purpose.

**Grammar** in the context of *spoken* language means the relationships between the words in an utterance and its structure. (In *written* language the sentence is the basic grammatical unit.) There are different expectations and assumptions about grammatical usage in talk, and current research in corpus linguistics confirms that there are significant differences between the grammar of written and of spoken language.

Some examples of grammatical and syntactical features typical of spoken language are

- use of contracted verb forms – 'Don't be late!', 'Let's hope not!'
- active rather than passive voice – 'The train is running late', 'I hate waiting.'

- frequent use of imperative and interrogative verb forms – 'Fetch the post please', 'Do you know when the next train's due?', 'Shall we go into town this evening?'
- phrases (not clauses or sentences) and especially noun phrases standing for complete utterances – 'Why were you so late?' 'Traffic jam.' or 'Where's the newspaper?' 'In the study.'
- simple and usually short clauses, without much embedding in noun clauses
- high proportion of co-ordinating clauses
- frequent use of 'and' as a continuation marker
- unusual clause constructs – 'That film it's really brilliant'
- tendency to ellipt grammatical features – 'Do you mind if we go home early?' 'Of course not [we don't mind]'
- use of deictics like 'this' and 'here' or 'there' – 'This cake is yummy', 'You take this here, and I'll put that there.'

**Lexis or vocabulary** in spoken language is determined by the context, the purpose of the talk and the people who are talking. These factors will affect the register and the semantic field. General features which tend to characterise the vocabulary of spoken language include

- tendency to use more concrete, less abstract vocabulary
- tendency to use simpler and more generalised vocabulary
- low lexical density (number of words per utterance)
- higher proportion of function words over content words
- context-determined lexical choice (determined by the topic of the exchange)
- use of vague language such as fillers or hedging devices – er, erm, like, you know, sort of, whatsit, thingummyjig, thingummybob, oojah
- use of terms of address – Your Honour, Mum, Miss Smith, Jim, sir, madam
- frequent use of phatic language (polite expressions fulfilling the function of 'social lubrication'), particularly in casual encounters or telephone conversation – 'How do you do?', 'How are you?', 'Fine thanks', 'See you!', 'Well, must be getting on', 'It was nice to meet you.'

**Discourse features** are those structural or interactive features of talk (neither lexical nor grammatical) which reflect the nature of the exchange between speakers (there will be at least two) – how they relate to each other, how they express attentiveness, interest, attitude, emotion, etc. Some commonly used discourse features are

- use of discourse markers indicating interpersonal nature of exchanges – tag questions, overlaps, interruptions, incomplete clauses
- repetitions and echoing between speakers – 'She said she'd never speak to him again!' 'Never again? I can't believe she said never again.'
- reformulation of utterances by speakers – 'You mean that you have a problem, not that you'll never take a plane again. Be honest – say you have a problem with flying.'
- back-channel features (sometimes called monitoring devices, minimal responses or sympathetic circularity); that is, terms indicating that a hearer is paying attention to the speaker – sounds (mm, ah-ha) or short words (yeah, right, really, sure, yes, no)
- use of disjuncts (comments on style or truth/value of what is being said – frankly, honestly, confidentially)
- use of comment clauses (expressing speaker's feelings) – for example, tentativeness (I think, I suppose, they say), certainty (I know, I'm sure, I must say, there's no doubt), emotional attitude (I'm delighted to say, I'm afraid, Heaven knows, to be honest, frankly speaking, with all due respect).

**Activity 24** | Identifying selected discourse features in spontaneous interaction

Listen to a radio phone-in programme and attempt to identify the following discourse features: tag questions, reformulations, back-channel features and comment clauses. You may prefer to record an extract to study in detail, or you may want to listen to several similar programmes to get a wider view.

Fluency (literally, 'flowing') in talk is a metaphoric term, and has come to mean the ease by which spoken communication is managed. Even so, there is some ambiguity about easy communication – to call someone a smooth talker is no compliment! Fluency in talking might be represented as a cline or continuum, with minimal evidence of non-fluency at one end, and virtual incoherence at the other. Most spoken interaction shows a balance between the two extremes, a kind of 'fluency norm', fluctuating according to who the speakers are and what they are talking about. Fluency is desirable to most of us and hence is the unmarked norm of talking. Because non-fluency features deviate from this norm, they are marked. Some typical non-fluency features which can be found in most people's talking to a greater or lesser degree include

- hesitation – particularly those longer than a few seconds: very frequent hesitations can have a serious effect on the listener, who may lose patience and stop attending
- false start – this is when the speaker starts an utterance, then stops and either repeats it, or reformulates it
- high proportion of fillers or other kinds of vague language like hedging devices
- repetition – not the speech dysfunction of stuttering, but an over-frequent use of the same word or phrase
- excessive use of overlap (when one speaker starts before another finishes)
- excessive use of interruption (when a speaker starts to speak whilst another is talking)
- failure to identify and repair miscommunication
- failure to use such strategies as clarification, shifting frames, adjusting schema, code switching, conversational maxims and other politeness strategies in order to improve communication.

However, it should be noted that the degree of fluency in talking is not in itself evidence of success or failure within an interaction. In literature we are all familiar with the stereotype of the smooth-talking villain and the stammering, hesitant hero (to be transformed into eloquence by the love of a good woman?). Successful communication can take place with a substantial degree of non-fluency if the participants are comfortable with the situation, and if the language choices and the discourse strategies (conscious or unconscious) are all functioning effectively.

**Activity 25** | Investigating levels of fluency in different contexts

**Individual**

First investigate fluency in casual conversation. Select a number of occasions when friends or family are talking informally and try to identify the person who uses the most non-fluency features and the person who uses the fewest. Take into account the influence of context (personality, situation, topic of conversation, other participants) on levels of fluency. You may be able to construct a fluency profile of each subject by noting the frequency and kind of non-fluency features used. Report back your findings to the group.

Now investigate fluency levels in classroom interaction. Ask permission to record all or part of a teaching session, preferably without the class being aware of the recording. Select an extract to study in detail and note down the kind of non-fluency features appearing in the exchanges between the participants. Tabulate your findings and present them to the group.

## Review

In this section, you have been given the opportunity to

- examine key theories of discourse analysis
- practise applying these theories in the analysis of spontaneous and crafted speech
- consider different contexts and purposes of communication through pragmatics
- investigate the presence of the characteristic features of spoken language in spontaneous talk.

# Talk and identity

We all have a sense of individuality, of identity, of difference, of uniqueness which is expressed in the way we speak (and write). In the first section (page 151) we looked briefly at the creation of individual idiolect. Having explored the theoretical basis of spontaneous and crafted talk, we shall now focus on two key factors which create linguistic identity and hence the way we use spoken language: age and gender. (Other factors, such as family position, class, education, occupation and ethnicity, though important, are less germane to the current purpose.)

## When and how does the sense of self emerge?

One of the most dramatic changes in a baby's development is at the age of approximately 12–13 months. Suddenly he or she becomes aware of being an individual, and separate, not attached to mother/father/care-giver. This is terrifying! The friendly, jolly baby who 'will go to anyone' hides away from strangers, refuses to leave the security of a friendly lap, and cries when their parent leaves the room. But this is a crucial moment in the child's psychological and linguistic development because it marks the dawning of a sense of self.

As we mature, our sense of identity also develops through a variety of means. Family and friends present us with their image (real or ideal) of who we are. The media presents us with images of who they think we'd like to be. The way other people act and react towards us can also provide a mirror for the self. Exploring our own identity is an ongoing process throughout life. Because our idiolect reflects individual identity, we shall look at two crucial factors in its creation, age and gender. How we speak is – to an extent – what we are!

## Activity 26

### Pair work

## Investigating what aspects of an individual creates his or her identity

In pairs, each person should write down six things about the other person which make them unique (possible categories include appearance, age, gender, family background, temperament, likes and dislikes). Compare notes.

# Identity and age

There is a tendency when we use the word 'age' to associate it with the last stages of human life, which in Western industrial society usually means post-retirement. But logically speaking, the term can apply to any stage in life, from infancy to adulthood and beyond. Moreover, chronological age is not necessarily in step with social and biological development, although we expect it to be. Indeed, if people's behaviour differs from *expected* age norms, there will be disparaging comments – 'Don't be such a baby', 'She's behaving like a teenager', 'He's middle-aged already at sixteen!', 'You're such an old woman!' A further interesting question – does each person's idiolect change in the course of a lifetime, as his or her speech community changes, or does linguistic individuality remain the same throughout life?

## Attitudes to age

'Age group' is a term used to refer to everyone at a similar chronological stage in life, from babies learning the rudiments of speech to elderly people with problems of language dysfunction. Each age group has its own (often stereotyped) language characteristics. For example, in Britain today, elderly people may remember not only the Second World War, but also the wartime slang of their youth. And the 1960s generation – now thoroughly middle-aged – may even retain the vocabulary of the so-called 'permissive society' (flower power, drug culture, the Swinging Sixties). Similarly, teenagers today are likely to be highly computer-oriented and at ease with the language of multimedia. Perhaps unsurprisingly, people can be intolerant of the characteristic language of other age groups. At home, where different age groups have to communicate, the older generation tends to demand that the younger conform to their language usage – 'Don't use bad language to me!', 'Talk properly!', 'I don't know what you're talking about', 'Why don't you speak up?'

## Age and linguistic theory

Age can be viewed as a sociolinguistic variable associated with language change or language variation. It can equally be seen as a source for ethnographic research concerned with age as a process affecting norms of behaviour. For example, attitudes to age are often reflected in spoken language by talking down to children or (the reverse) infantilising elderly people. Most age research has focused on child language development, with a few important studies on adolescent language (Labov 1972, Cheshire 1982, Romaine 1984); there has been very little research into old people's spoken language until the landmark publication of Coupland and Giles' *Language, Society and the Elderly* (1991) and Penelope Eckert's article 'Age as a sociolinguistic variable' (1998).

## Spoken language and adolescence/young adulthood

The language of adolescents often reflects their need to define themselves as separate from the adult world, and to create their own social group by preferring non-standard language, especially slang, taboo and anti-language. Labov (1972) was one of the first linguists to investigate the language of adolescents (the Jets, the Cobras and the Thunderbirds, all black youth groups in New York); more recently, Jenny Cheshire (1982) also investigated the language of teenagers in Reading, Berkshire.

## Activity 27 | Analysing spontaneous and crafted narratives

**Pair work**

Work together to compare the two narratives on pages 184–185, one spontaneous, one crafted, about teenager fights. Look particularly at lexis, non-standard usage and taboo language.

Text A is from Labov's *Language in the Inner City* (1972). Text B is an extract from William Golding's *Lord of the Flies*.

## Text A

I What was the most important fight you remember?
J Well, one (I think) was with a girl.
  Like I was a kid, you know,
  And she was the baddest girl, *the baddest girl in the neighbourhood*
  If you didn't bring her candy to school, she would punch you in the mouth:
  And you had to kiss her when she'd tell you
  This girl was only about 12 years old, man, but she was a killer.
  She didn't take no junk;
  She whupped all her brothers.
  And I came to school one day
  And I didn't have no money.
  My ma wouldn't give me no money.
  And I played hookies one day,
  She put something on me [*hit me hard*]…
  So I go to school
  And this girl says 'Where's the candy?'
  I said, 'I don't have it.'
  She says, powww!
  So I says to myself, 'There's going to be times my mother won't give me money
  because [we're] a poor family
  And I can't take this all, you know, every time she don't give me any money.'
  So I say, 'Well, I just gotta fight this girl.
  She gonna hafta whup me.
  I hope she don't whup me.'
  And I hit the girl: powww!
  And I put something on it.
  I win the fight.                                                    I = interviewer
  That was one of the most important.                                 J = interviewee

## Text B

Jack shouted above the noise.

'You go away, Ralph. You keep to your end. This is my end and my tribe. You leave me alone.'

The jeering died away.

'You pinched Piggy's specs,' said Ralph, breathlessly. 'You've got to give them back.'

'Got to? Who says?'

Ralph's temper blazed out.

'I say! You voted for me for Chief. Didn't you hear the conch? You played a dirty trick – we'd have given you fire if you'd asked for it – '

The blood was flowing in his cheeks and the bunged-up eye throbbed.

'You could have had fire whenever you wanted. But you didn't. You came sneaking up like a thief and stole Piggy's glasses!'

'Say that again!'

'Thief! Thief!'

Piggy screamed. 'Ralph! Mind me!'

Jack made a rush and stabbed at Ralph's chest with his spear. Ralph sensed the position of the weapon from the glimpse he caught of Jack's arm and put the thrust aside with his own butt. Then he brought the end round and caught Jack a stinger across the ear. They were chest to chest, breathing fiercely, pushing and glaring.

'Who's a thief?'

'You are!'

Jack wrenched free and swung at Ralph with his spear. By common consent they were using the spears as sabres now, no longer daring the lethal points. The blow struck Ralph's spear and slid down, to fall agonizingly on his fingers....

Both boys were breathing very heavily.

'Come on then –'

'Come on – '

### Spoken language and old age

Linguists who study the language of old people group their subjects either in decades (60–70, 70–80, etc.) or in 'life experience' groups (such as people who shared wartime experience, as either a child or an adult). Coupland *et al.* (1991) differentiate between 'young-old' people (up to mid-70s) and 'old-old' people (75 plus). They focus on inter-generational communication, noting that ageism can be a problem, reflecting negative attitudes held by younger people and the elderly themselves (decremental). In fact, research suggests that elderly people's spoken-language skills are relatively unaffected by age ('only modest ...evidence of suppressed performance skills'). Look back at pages 167–168 and 173 and compare the interview with the 103-year-old man and Lewis Carroll's poem 'You are old, Father William' for a clear refutation of ageism.

# Identity and gender

Researchers at Birkbeck College, University of London, have investigated gender attitudes among a group of secondary schoolboys aged 11–14 to see how they established their sense of masculine identity. The boys' top priority was to define themselves in direct opposition to any human quality that they perceived as feminine. The result was that quieter boys, or those who had girls as friends, or who showed any glimpse of 'feminine qualities', experienced homophobic name-calling (poof, wuss, wimp, queer). It was concluded that boys lack cultural permission to value in themselves the qualities of empathy and sensitivity which they admire in girls. The research team felt that this was a serious problem, because 'boys take umbrage at girls' burgeoning self-confidence and academic success by retreating still more deeply into machismo'. Moreover, male homophobia at school is both a cause and a consequence of boys 'lacking the full emotional repertoire [they feel] is off limits for them'.

## New representations of gender

Today in the adult world of work and family, social change has produced significant adjustments in gender roles, leading to some gendered role reversal, reflected in neologisms like 'house husband' or 'glass ceiling' (describing the promotion barrier often met by ambitious and/or able women). So powerful are these role-reversal images that we have new expectations of media representations of gender. For example, in some television advertising women are shown as intelligent, assertive and caring, while men appear the reverse. How long such an ambiguously ironic position will be sustained is unclear!

Interestingly, social judgements continue to be made about the male and female vocal sounds, and as usual, stereotypes exist. A recently published study by the linguist Deborah Cameron (*Good to Talk*, 2000) points out that 'Women's voices are judged in a different way from men's', and although her comment is specifically related to accent in men and women, there is evidence to suggest that similar judgements are made on vocal quality and pitch. Because of these social attitudes, according to a voice-training consultant, 'Women make more effort than men to change their voices; they are more driven to adapt'. The classic example of this is former Prime Minister Margaret Thatcher, who 'went through the most rigorous training to get that deep voice', suggesting confidence and authority.

---

**Activity 28** | ## Investigating the link between vocal pitch and power

**Individual**

1   Record *either* an episode from a soap opera *or* a news broadcast *or* a discussion programme. Can you find any direct correlation between gender, vocal pitch and conversational dominance in the interaction?

**Pair work**

2   Read the following passage from *Gender Voices* (ed. Graddol and Swann, 1989). Identify the male/female vocal stereotypes used by the author. How effective are the metaphors used to describe each voice?

> 'I don't care how many women you make love to in this room,' she lashed, scarcely recognising the high pitched voice as her own.
>
> 'Don't expect me to apologise for it.' His resonant voice had gone slightly hard.
>
> 'I hate you!' There was an unmistakeable tremor in her voice.
>
> 'Kate.' His voice was incredibly low and deep, his eyes dark and sensuous. He had never spoken her name before and the speaking of it made her aware of the deep, slightly grating timbre of his voice. It was the kind of voice suited to him, holding the gritty depths of his nature.
>
> [She] gave a husky laugh.
>
> 'Love you?' he grated. 'Of course I love you.'
>
> 'What is love?' she sighed.
>
> 'Lyle,' she croaked, and was unaware that her voice came out as a wordless whisper.
>
> He gave his gravelly laugh.

---

## Gender, politics and linguistic theory

The link between gender and politics became clearer as the 60s turned into the 70s and 80s, and 'women's lib' or 'the women's movement' emerged. Betty Friedan wrote *The Feminine*

*Mystique* (1963) and Kate Millett wrote *Sexual Politics* (1971). Feminism became linked with political activism (American Civil Rights, Vietnam anti-war protest movements). Concepts such as patriarchy (male-owned power), consciousness-raising and political correctness came into the public domain. Questions were asked on both sides of the Atlantic about women's position in society, their domestic role, female education and their political, legal and economic status. These challenges (unsurprisingly) produced substantial opposition, not all of it from men. More important in this context, two books were published which (for the first time) linked sexual politics, gender and spoken language, namely *Language and Women's Place* by Robin Lakoff (1975) and *Man Made Language* by Dale Spender (1980). From then onwards, interest in the field developed exponentially. Indeed, most research was on women's spoken language until relatively recently.

What is fascinating is that there has been in the 90s and early twenty-first century a 'seismic shift' in our understanding of gender. No longer perceived as a set of binary categories, gender is conceptualised as plural and performative. Never static, 'it is produced actively and in interaction with others every day of our lives' (Coates in Llamas *et al.* 2007). In 1996 Deborah Cameron noted that 'gender... has turned out to be an extraordinarily intricate and multi-layered phenomenon – unstable, contested, intimately bound up with other social divisions'. Researchers now look at speech patterns of men and women in a variety of cultures; they recognise areas of overlap between male and female speech, and emphasise the fact 'that gender is constructed locally, and that it interacts with race, class, sexuality and age'. In other words, we have moved a long way from the perceived norm of the first twenty years of gender studies as 'white, middle-class, anglocentric' women. This 'seismic shift' can be better understood by surveying the history of research into gender and spoken language.

### The deficit approach

In *Language* (1922) the Danish linguist Otto Jespersen described typical female language as using unfinished sentences and avoiding complex syntactic structures. Robin Lakoff (1975), describing male language as stronger, more prestigious and more desirable, implied that women's language lacks these features. On the basis of anecdotal evidence she suggested that

- female style is co-operative, apologetic and hence subordinating
- women use more tag questions (such as 'isn't it?') indicating tentativeness
- women use more intensifiers (so), hedges (sort of), 'empty' adjectives (nice, lovely, charming)
- women use exaggerated intonation
- women are more precise than men at describing colour.

Hence women's spoken language is deficient; to be taken seriously they must learn to speak like men.

*Limitations of approach:* Not based on research findings, hence subjective and anecdotal. Nevertheless flags up some recognisable features of some women's spoken language.

### The dominance approach

This approach derives from the deficit approach but sees the problem in terms of power and lack of power. The speech of men and women directly reflects male dominance and female oppression (Ardener 1975, Spender 1980). Male power is enacted through linguistic practices and men and women collude 'in sustaining and perpetuating' the power imbalance. Male and female speech behaviour can be described in binary terms (competitive/co-operative, hostile/supportive, factual/emotional).

*Limitations of approach:* Over-emphasis on power/lack of power in gendered language behaviour: deterministic.

### The difference approach

In the 80s researchers investigated gendered language behaviour within its social context (for example, the development of girls' and boys' language skills). Deborah Tannen's book on conversational miscommunication (*You Just Don't Understand Me: Women and Men in Conversation*, 1992) was a runaway bestseller, with its implication that men and women belong to different sub-cultures. The issue of power was not forgotten, but the new argument was that women and men are differently socialised, so differences in their spoken language are predictable.

*Limitations of approach:* Valuable emphasis on difference outside power framework, though studies of mixed gender talk can't ignore this aspect.

### The social constructionist approach

Gender identity in this approach is seen as a social construct rather than a 'given' social category. Speakers 'do gender' rather than being passively labelled as a particular gender (see Byng and Bergwall in Coates's *Language and Gender,* 1996). By avoiding gender polarisation and recognising individual differences, this approach insists on the importance of social context as a way of understanding gendered language behaviour.

*Limitations of approach:* Developments from this approach have already been described above. Gender is seen as fluid and performative and not categorisable.

## Activity 29 — Exploring theories on gendered speech

**Group work**

1 **Deficit approach:** Describe any social situation when you have observed someone struggling to express themselves clearly (not hearing clearly, asking a difficult question, etc.). Try to account for their difficulty (situation, other participants, personality of speaker, emotion, etc.). Was there any question of their language being in any way inadequate? What might have been the reasons?

2 **Dominance approach:** Have you ever felt powerless or dominated in a conversation or exchange? (With strangers, at an interview, at a party?) How would you explain this? (Context, gender, personality, expectations?)

3 **Difference approach:** What do you think are the differences between male and female spoken language? Write down two lists of characteristic features and compare your findings.

4 **Social constructionist approach:** How many social situations can you think of where gender difference is not a significant factor? Does the speech behaviour of the individuals involved differ in any way from situations where gender is a significant factor? Compare your experience with that of other people in the group.

## Looking at gender in action: men and women talking

According to the Labovian view of gender and spoken language, speech reflects social attitudes. He and Trudgill (1972, 1983) both linked gender with standard and non-standard grammatical usage and with regional/non-regional pronunciation. Both noted female preference for standard forms across all social classes, and lower-middle-class women's tendency to hypercorrect. This has been perceived as class-based linguistic insecurity, though it might equally be gender based. The Milroys (1981–7) identified more complex patterns of male and female usage. Women opted predictably for standard forms, men for non-standard. But whilst women had freer linguistic choices, men were under strong group pressure to use the vernacular, and especially so in economically stable communities.

# Applying the theory: gender and discourse structure

First, a health warning!

- Don't assume that individual research findings apply to all women and men!
- Be aware of assumptions that male language is the norm (unmarked form) and female language the deviation (marked form).
- Use of mainly middle-class subjects means the findings have built-in limitations.

## Overlaps and interruptions

Zimmerman and West (1975) studied same-sex and male/female speech and found that in same-sex speech overlaps and interruptions were evenly balanced, but in mixed talk the balance was extremely uneven. Interruptions were much more frequent than overlaps, and much more frequently initiated by males. The total interruptions ratio was men 96%/ women 4%. Parent–child interaction has a similar interruptions ratio (parent 86%/child 14%).

## Turn taking

Coates suggested (in Johnson and Meinhof's *Language and Masculinity,* 1997) that whilst men in same-sex conversation follow one-at-a-time turn-taking structure, women adopt collaborative, 'shared floor' structure, using overlapping/simultaneous speech in supportive and non-threatening ways.

## Topic shift

Topic choice and topic shift – holding the floor or keeping the topic – is a way of retaining control in a conversation. Evidence suggests that in mixed talk men hold the floor and initiate topic shifts more than women. In domestic contexts women do initiate new topics, but can be 'silenced' by no response from male partners.

## Tag questions

Tag questions ('You understand, *don't you*?') can express linguistic insecurity. Janet Holmes (1995) showed that there are several different kinds of tag questions

- Questions which invite the next speaker to respond – 'Let me introduce Mary – she's an architect too, aren't you?' These facilitative tags are used mainly by women; however, if men and women are talking co-operatively, both use them.
- Questions which express uncertainty ('The train leaves at 8.30, doesn't it?', 'I suppose I'll have to sort out this problem, won't I?'). These epistemic modal tags are used more by men.
- Questions which set a challenge ('You do realise this is a punishable offence, don't you?'). These are called challenging tags.
- Questions which make something more acceptable ('Never mind, you didn't mean to spill the milk, did you?'). These are called softening tags.

## Questions/interrogatives

Questions are power related because they require the addressee to respond. Overall, women use questions more than men: in same-sex conversation this is a supportive strategy; in mixed talk women use questions to maintain conversation or seek information.

## Directives/imperatives

These speech acts are associated with power and aim to make people do something. West (1990) compared the use of directives by male and female doctors. Men used aggravated directives ('Lie down', 'Get undressed', 'Take off your shoes and socks'), whereas female doctors used mitigated directives ('Let's see what the problem is', 'Maybe we should try you on a different medication'), thus minimising the power imbalance. Patients were more inclined to comply with the female doctors' directives!

**189**

### Conversation structures

The structure of mixed conversation can vary from short simple utterances with a single finite verb, often incomplete ('Did you get some milk?''I thought I'd – no, sorry…'), to linked clauses or parataxis ('I forgot but I'll pick some up later and I promise not to forget again'), to embedded clauses or hypotaxis ('The milk I really want is the green top – semi-skimmed.'). According to Jesperson, women prefer parataxis, men hypotaxis.

### Grammar

Lakoff thought that women use more extreme intensifiers and boosters in conversation (terribly, awfully, disgustingly, amazingly, etc). Fictional and stereotypical representations of women certainly suggest this.

Women seem to like to use modal auxiliaries in directives ('Would you answer the door?'), declaratives ('I'd just like to say…') and compound requests ('When you've finished those case-notes, would you like to look at this, and then could I possibly ask you to contact his GP?'). This could indicate politeness, be context-related – or just imply linguistic insecurity.

### Lexical choice

Evaluative words are ones which in one way or another express an opinion. Women are thought to use more strongly positive and negative evaluative lexis ('That's a really great outfit – you look fantastic!', 'It's such a bad idea to go for that option'). This usage may, however, be dependent on social context as well as class and age.

There are stereotypical assumptions (Jesperson 1922, Lakoff 1975) about male and female usage (men swear more than women and use more taboo language, women prefer euphemisms, etc.). Coates (1993), however, notes that these opinions were based not on evidence but on what the researchers thought ought to be true! De Klerk's study 'The role of expletives in the construction of masculinity' (in *Language and Masculinity* 1997) links male expletive use with issues of masculine identity. She suggests that the increase of female swearing is challenging for men, that the gap in taboo usage between men and women is closing, and that expletive use is associated more with power than with gender.

## Politeness strategies and gender

### Facework

We have already discussed politeness: what is relevant here is that research suggests that women are better at facework than men and use more positive politeness strategies (Holmes 1995). Because of their different socialising experience, women are more concerned to be involved and make connections, whereas men are more detached and autonomous.

### Terms of address

Social distance determines politeness strategies like terms of address. Men have little choice (Mr or first name – FN); for women there is some choice (Miss, Mrs, Ms, FN), though marital status is a factor.

Social context also determines terms of address: using FN can be friendly (between equals) or face-threatening (implying a put-down). The research of Poynton (1985) and West (1990) revealed that when men held the power (as employer, boss, doctor), women were addressed by FN or using terms of endearment (love, my dear). Similarly, in a simple service encounter (at a petrol station) male employees would address men as 'sir' and women as 'sweetheart', 'lovey', 'dear'. In America men use the more neutral 'ma'am' for women they don't know, and women address men they don't know as 'sir'. Some terms of address are purely male (Australian 'mate', 'sport'). In the UK there are neutral regional variants which address men and women the same (East Midlands 'duck', 'me duck'; Bristol 'my lovely'; Yorkshire 'love'; Geordie 'hen' or 'hinny').

## Activity 30 — Investigating the links between terms of address and power

**Individual**

1 Choose three women you know well of different generations (26–40, 41–55, 56–70) and ask them the following questions, keeping brief notes on their replies.

- Have you ever been addressed as 'my dear' by a male speaker in a position of power? (1 never, 2 occasionally, 3 frequently, 4 all the time.) Could you give examples of situations in which this occurred?
- Have you ever been addressed by a male speaker in a position of power who used your first name repeatedly? (1 never, 2 occasionally, 3 frequently, 4 all the time.) Did this make you feel childish and/or disempowered or did it not affect you? Give examples of situations where this happened.

Report your findings to the group, making sure that you correlate age group and frequency of reported usage.

**Group work**

2 Now read the following short passage from *Hamlet* in which Ophelia, daughter of the courtier Polonius, tries to return the love tokens given to her by Prince Hamlet. He has alarmed her by his strange behaviour since the sudden death of his father, the King.

| | |
|---|---|
| Ophelia | My lord, I have remembrances of yours<br>That I have longed long to re-deliver.<br>I pray you now receive them. |
| Hamlet | No, not I.<br>I never gave you aught. |
| Ophelia | My honoured lord, you know right well you did,<br>And with them words of so sweet breath composed<br>As made the things more rich. Their perfume lost,<br>Take these again. For to the noble mind<br>Rich gifts wax poor when givers prove unkind.<br>There, my lord. |
| Hamlet | Ha, ha! Are you honest? |
| Ophelia | My lord? |
| Hamlet | Are you fair? |
| Ophelia | What means your lordship? |

Identify the terms of address in this passage. What dramatic effect might Shakespeare be seeking by using them here?

### Compliments

Compliments are positive politeness strategies which refer (directly or indirectly) to some good quality of the person addressed (appearance, ability or skill, possession, personality). For example, a direct compliment might be paid to someone about their skill ('You're so good at tennis') or it might be an indirect compliment ('Superb acting!' addressed not to the actor, but to the director). According to Holmes (ed. Coates 1997), women perceive and use compliments 'to establish, maintain and strengthen relationships', whereas compliments face-threaten men, in just the same way that stranger compliments (remarks and wolf-whistles from building-site workers) face-threaten women.

### Apologies

Apologies are negative politeness strategies which address the face needs of a person who has in some way been injured. Holmes identifies six categories of offence: space offence (bumping into someone – 'Sorry, I didn't see you!), talk offence (interrupting, talking too much), time offence (keeping people waiting, taking too long), possession offence (damaging or losing someone's property), social gaffes (burping, coughing, laughing inappropriately), inconvenience (inadequate service, giving wrong item).

She concludes that women and men seem to regard apologies differently. Women see them as positive politeness strategies supporting face needs (especially of female friends); men seeing them as face saving (to be used only when not apologising would cause more offence).

### Back-channel behaviour

Predictably, in mixed-talk situations, women use more back-channel behaviour or minimal responses (mmm, mhm, yeah) than men, since the function of minimal responses is to encourage a speaker by indicating interest and attention, thus fulfilling face needs. Delayed minimal responses show that the listener's attention is receding!

### Hedges

As we saw earlier, hedges enable speakers to avoid being definite (I mean, sort of, kind of, maybe, perhaps, probably, you know, kind of thing, and stuff). Other hedging strategies include modal verbs (could, should, might) and verbs of state (seem, become). The effect of hedges is to weaken or reduce the force of an utterance. Lakoff regards hedges as expressions of weakness and tentativeness in women's speech, whereas Holmes (1995) and Coates (1997) associate hedging with positive politeness strategies and with confidence and truth. In mixed talk women use 'you know' more frequently than men if they feel confident; if not confident, they use it less.

---

**Review**

In this section, you have been given the opportunity to

- explore two key factors which influence an individual's speech – age and gender
- test out different theoretical approaches to gendered speech
- consider links between terms of address and power in spontaneous and scripted speech.

---

# Talk in literature

The previous section has focused much more on talk in life rather than talk in literature. It is, however, important for you to be aware of recent developments in the theory of discourse and the relationship of speech and personal identity, in order to understand how complicated it is for writers to re-create or craft speech! The literary genres we shall look at include poetry, drama and prose fiction.

Why is it necessary to craft or represent speech in any literary genre? The reason is that the author has a literary purpose, or purposes, to fulfil that is quite different from the purposes of ordinary conversation, which will vary depending on the literary genre in question. For example, in fiction the author's purpose is usually to create character, to further the plot, to describe situation and mood, and to establish themes.

In poetry there may be similar purposes if it is a narrative poem. In a lyric poem, however, the poet's purpose is to be expressive, to convey ideas and emotions through images, or through the description of a scene. The nature of the genre may mean that the poet has to be more selective than the fiction writer, who has chapters available for imaginative expansion! In drama the purpose of the dramatist is also to create character and further the plot, in this case using dialogue or monologue to create mood and describe context.

In other words, all three major literary genres have similar artistic purposes, with some proportional adjustment, depending on the individual genre.

## Talk in poetry

This genre can include everything from the ballad to the epic poem, the dramatic monologue, the sonnet and the ode. Every poem has its own voice, whether it is that of the poetic persona, or a character involved in a narrative, or even the poet speaking directly. Although direct speech or dialogue may not be involved, there will be some representation of the human voice. As it is crafted, it will inevitably differ from natural spontaneous speech.

What poetry also possesses that talk lacks is a high level of musicality and patterning. A poet will use a wide range of sound patterns as well as metrical variation to support the communication of ideas, emotions and themes to a reader. (For more on these aspects, see pages 17–20.) For example, alliteration, assonance, consonance, dissonance and onomatopoeia all derive from the actual sounds or phonemes in the words of the poem. Puns, rhyme, half-rhyme and end rhyme represent the slightly wider sound structure of the phrase or line. Iambic pentameter, heroic couplets, the refrain, the quatrain are larger sound structures/poetic forms – and the caesura occurs when there is no sound, when it stops briefly, within the poetic line, to make a literary point.

So the patterned musicality of poetry is where crafted speech has to find its place. In the contrasting poems that follow we can hear the created voice or voices of speakers.

### Waiting Gentlewoman

If Daddy had known the setup,
I'm absolutely positive, he'd never
Have let me come. Honestly,
The whole thing's too gruesome
For words. There's nobody here to talk to
At all. Well, nobody under about ninety,
I mean. All the possible men have buggered
Off to the other side, and the rest,
Poor old dears, they'd have buggered off
Too, if their poor old legs would have
Carried them. HM's a super person, of course,
But she's a bit seedy just now,
Quite different from how marvellous she was
At the Coronation. And this doctor they've got in –
Well, he's only an ordinary little GP,
With a very odd accent, and even I
Can see that what HM needs is
A real psychiatrist. I mean, all this
About *blood*, and *washing*. Definitely Freudian.
As for Himself, well, definitely

Not my type. Daddy's got this thing
About self made men, of course, that's why
He was keen for me to come. But I think
He's gruesome. What HM sees in him
I cannot imagine. *And* he talks to himself.
That's so rude, I always think.
I hope Daddy comes for me soon.

This poem by U.A. Fanthorpe (1986) uses the imagined voice of one of Lady Macbeth's waiting-women to present a twentieth-century view of the Elizabethan/medieval tragedy. The choice of a waiting-woman's voice is rather like Stoppard's choice of Rosencrantz and Guildenstern (see page 238). An unexpected angle is provided on a familiar story. Ironically, Fanthorpe imagines the speaker as a modern upper-class girl who has taken a job without the least idea of what will happen. Fanthorpe uses linguistic features including social variables like class ('ordinary little GP') and gender (hedges – 'I mean', 'I always think'; intensifiers – 'too gruesome', 'marvellous') to create character, as well as terms of address, slang and informal register. And there is more to be discovered. Look back to the previous sections for further pointers on discourse structure, politeness strategies, etc.

## Activity 31    Investigating poetic voice

How many voices can you identify in this poem written in 1818 by Percy Bysshe Shelley? Are some more significant than others and how is this signalled? Analyse any patterns created by sound and metre which help to establish these voices.

Compare your views with the commentary on page 200.

### Ozymandias

I met a traveller from an antique land,
Who said – 'Two vast and trunkless legs of stone
Stand in the desert... Near them, on the sand,
Half sunk a shattered visage lies, whose frown,
And wrinkled lip, and sneer of cold command,
Tell that its sculptor well those passions read
Which yet survive, stamped on these lifeless things,
The hand that mocked them, and the heart that fed;
And on the pedestal these words appear:
My name is Ozymandias, King of Kings,
Look on my Works, ye Mighty, and despair!
Nothing beside remains. Round the decay
Of that colossal Wreck, boundless and bare
The lone and level sands stretch far away.'

## Talk in drama

Plays of whatever genre – romantic comedy, tragedy, satire, comedy of manners – are crafted versions of talk with particular purposes, as we have noted. Bear in mind too, as you analyse a drama text, that the discourse involves not only the characters within the play, but also the audience watching outside the action. The dramatist will always be conscious of how an audience responds to the dramatic effects being created by their literary and linguistic choices.

In the examples that follow, notice the ways in which dialogue reveals character via discourse structure and power relations, as well as via rhetorical and politeness strategies and figurative language. The first extract is from Shakespeare's *Henry V*.

> King Henry   Once more unto the breach, dear friends, once more,
> Or close the wall up with our English dead!
> In peace there's nothing so becomes a man
> As modest stillness and humility:
> But when the blast of war blows in our ears,
> Then imitate the action of the tiger;
> Stiffen the sinews, conjure up the blood,
> Disguise fair nature with hard-favoured rage;
> Then lend the eye a terrible aspect;
> Let it pry through the portage of the head
> Like the brass cannon; let the brow o'erwhelm it
> As fearfully as doth a galled rock
> O'erhang and jutty his confounded base,
> Swilled with the wild and wasteful ocean.

Henry is urging on his troops at the siege of Harfleur. Shakespeare is keen to show a contrast between the frivolity of his past life as Prince Hal and his present nobility and courage as king. Terms of address ('dear friends') and possessives ('our English dead') suggest empathy with his soldiers; the major image is of a face which is normally peaceable being transformed into fearsomeness in time of war – again, a personalised touch. Other images (tiger, stormy seas, weaponry) convey a sense of violent threat. The use of the rhetorical device of hyperbole (piled-up bodies filling the breach in the wall) is supported by the fierce unmitigated directive 'close'.

## Activity 32 — Investigating dramatic discourse (1)

**Pair work**

In this horrifying scene Othello has been convinced by the villainous Iago that his new wife has betrayed him. Mad with jealousy and grief, he determines on her death. Examine the nature of this exchange between Shakespeare's Othello and his wife, Desdemona. Look in particular at the structure of the lines, the use of sound patterning, images and politeness strategies.

Compare your views with the commentary on page 200.

> Othello   I saw the handkerchief.
> Desdemona       He found it then.
> I never gave it him. Send for him hither.
> Let him confess a truth.
> Othello       He hath confessed.
> Desdemona   What, my lord?
> Othello   That he hath used thee.
> Desdemona       How? Unlawfully?

| | |
|---|---|
| Othello | Ay. |
| Desdemona | He will not say so. |
| Othello | No, his mouth is stopped: |
| | Honest Iago has ta'en order for't. |
| Desdemona | O, my fear interprets! What, is he dead? |
| Othello | Had all his hairs been lives, my great revenge |
| | Had stomach for them all. |
| Desdemona | Alas, he is betrayed, and I undone. |
| Othello | Out, strumpet! Weep'st thou for him to my face? |
| Desdemona | O banish me, my lord, but kill me not! |
| Othello | Down, strumpet! |
| Desdemona | Kill me tomorrow: let me live tonight! |
| Othello | Nay, if you strive – |
| Desdemona | But half an hour! |
| Othello | Being done, there is no pause. |

## Activity 33  Investigating dramatic discourse (2)

Written less than a century after *Othello*, Wycherley's comedy of manners, *The Country Wife* (1675), satirises the corruption of Restoration society through the story of the newly married country girl arrived in London. How do the representations of language variation and dialect serve to develop character and engage the audience in this extract?

Read the commentary on page 200 for one view.

| | |
|---|---|
| Mrs Pinchwife | Pray, sister, where are the best fields and woods to walk in, in London? |
| Alithea | [aside] A pretty question! [Aloud] Why, sister, Mulberry Gardens and St James's Park; and, for close walks, the New Exchange. |
| Mrs Pinchwife | Pray, sister, tell me why my husband looks so grum here in town, and keeps me up so close, and will not let me go a-walking, nor let me wear my best gown yesterday. |
| Alithea | O, he's jealous, sister. |
| Mrs Pinchwife | Jealous! What's that? |
| Alithea | He's afraid you should love another man. |
| Mrs Pinchwife | How should he be afraid of my loving another man, when he will not let me see any but himself? |
| Alithea | Did he not carry you to a play yesterday? |
| Mrs Pinchwife | Ay; but we sat amongst ugly people. He would not let me come near the gentry, who sat under us, so that I could not see them. He told me none but naughty women sat under there, whom they toused and moused. But I would have ventured, for all that. |
| Alithea | But how did you like the play? |
| Mrs Pinchwife | Indeed I was weary of the play; but I like hugeously the actors. They are the goodliest properest men, sister! |

Finally, here is an exchange between two characters from the opening scene of Harold Pinter's *The Birthday Party* (1958).

| | |
|---|---|
| Meg | What time did you go out this morning, Petey? |
| Petey | Same time as usual. |
| Meg | Was it dark? |
| Petey | No, it was light. |
| Meg | [beginning to darn] But sometimes you go out in the morning and it's dark. |
| Petey | That's in the winter. |
| Meg | Oh, in the winter. |
| Petey | Yes, it gets light later in winter. |
| Meg | Oh. [pause] What are you reading? |
| Petey | Someone's just had a baby. |
| Meg | Oh, they haven't! Who? |
| Petey | Some girl. |
| Meg | Who, Petey, who? |
| Petey | I don't think you'd know her. |
| Meg | What's her name? |
| Petey | Lady Mary Splatt. |
| Meg | I don't know her. |
| Petey | No. |
| Meg | What is it? |
| Petey | [studying the paper]. Er, a girl. |
| Meg | Not a boy? |
| Petey | No. |
| Meg | Oh, what a shame. I'd be sorry. I'd much rather have a little boy. |
| Petey | A little girl's all right. |
| Meg | I'd much rather have a little boy. |

This extract introduces Meg and Petey, an elderly couple who run the seaside boarding-house where their lodger Stanley will experience a nightmare birthday party. Their conversation is patterned triviality, particularly Meg's, making use of phatic expression, colloquialism ('what a shame') and cliché to create a sense of bland banality and greyness.

## Talk in prose fiction

The literary purposes of the writer of the novel or short story are even more focused on creating character, furthering the plot, describing situations and conveying mood. Talk is central to these purposes, whether it is the first-person narrative voice of the eponymous hero in *Huckleberry Finn* and *The Catcher in the Rye* or direct conversation between characters as in an Austen, Dickens, Hardy or McEwan novel. Writers do experiment with narrative voice as in *Mrs Dalloway* or Molly Bloom's soliloquy in *Ulysses*, where the technique of narrating thought as speech is called stream of consciousness. In fiction you can also have the voice of the omniscient narrator who comments on events, such as George Eliot in *Middlemarch* or the central figure in *Tristram Shandy*. In other words, there is even more flexibility for the writer in the way talk is represented in this literary genre of prose fiction.

| Activity 34 | Investigating talk in prose fiction (1) |

Consider the interplay between direct speech and narrative voice in the following extract from *Northanger Abbey* by Jane Austen (1818).

The heroine, Catherine, staying in Bath for the first time, has become firm friends with a fashionable young woman, Isabella. Both girls are devoted readers of fiction, but Catherine is unused to intrigue and romance in real life.

Isabella now entered the room with so eager a step, and a look of such happy importance, as engaged all her friend's notice. Maria was without ceremony sent away, and Isabella, embracing Catherine, thus began: – 'Yes, my dear Catherine, it is so indeed; your penetration has not deceived you. – Oh! that arch eye of yours! – It sees through every thing.'

Catherine replied only by a look of wondering ignorance.

'Nay, my beloved, sweetest friend,' continued the other, 'compose yourself. – I am amazingly agitated, as you perceive. Let us sit down and talk in comfort. Well, and so you guessed it as soon as you had my note? – Sly creature! – Oh! my dear Catherine, you alone who know my heart can judge of my present happiness. Your brother is the most charming of men. I only wish I were more worthy of him. – But what will your excellent father and mother say? – Oh! heavens! when I think of them I am so agitated!'

Catherine's understanding began to awake: an idea of the truth suddenly darted into her mind; and, with the natural blush of so new an emotion, she cried out, 'Good heaven! my dear Isabella, what do you mean? Can you – can you really be in love with James?'

This exchange reveals the character of both speakers – Catherine's innocence and Isabella's egotism and folly. The latter is reflected in her extravagant language, full of intensifiers ('sweetest friend'), exaggeration ('amazingly agitated'), fashionable cliché ('Sly creature') and exclamation ('Oh! heavens'). Austen pokes fun at both young women, especially Isabella's praise of Catherine's 'penetration', rather contradicted by her 'look of wondering ignorance'!

| Activity 35 | Investigating talk in prose fiction (2) |

Examine this extract from the short story 'The Stranger' by Katherine Mansfield. It is an exchange between a middle-aged husband and wife in their hotel room. How does Mansfield show signs of increasing lack of understanding between them?

Compare your views with the commentary on page 200.

"Oh, it wasn't anything the least infectious!" said Janey. She was speaking scarcely above her breath. "It was heart." A pause. "Poor fellow!" she said. "Quite young."

And she watched the fire flicker and fall. "He died in my arms," said Janey.

The blow was so sudden that Hammond thought he would faint. He couldn't move; he couldn't breathe. He felt all his strength flowing – flowing into the big dark chair, and the big dark chair held him fast, gripped him, forced him to bear it.

"What?" he said dully. "What's that you say?"

"The end was quite peaceful," said the small voice. "He just" – and Hammond saw her lift her gentle hand – "breathed his life away at the end." And her hand fell.

"Who else was there?" Hammond managed to ask.

"Nobody. I was alone with him."

Ah, my God, what was she saying! What was she doing to him! This would kill him! And all the while she spoke:

"I saw the change coming and I sent the steward for the doctor, but the doctor was too late. He couldn't have done anything, anyway."

"But – why you, why you?" moaned Hammond.

At that Janey turned quickly, quickly searched his face.

"You don't mind, John, do you?" she asked. "You don't – it's nothing to do with you and me."

## Activity 36     Investigating talk in prose fiction (3)

**Pair work**

In this extract from *A History of the World in 10½ Chapters* how does Julian Barnes (1989) create a convincing and original narrative voice? What discourse strategies, registers and conversational features does he use to achieve this?

Read the commentary on page 201 for one view.

As far as we were concerned the whole business of the Voyage began when we were invited to report to a certain place by a certain time. That was the first we heard of the scheme. We didn't know anything of the political background. God's wrath with his creation was news to us; we just got caught up in it willy-nilly. *We* weren't in any way to blame (you don't really believe that story about the serpent, do you? – it was just Adam's black propaganda), and yet the consequences for us were equally severe: every species wiped out except a single breeding pair, and that couple consigned to the high seas under the charge of an old rogue with a drink problem who was already in the seventh century of his life.

So the word went out; but characteristically they didn't tell us the truth. Did you imagine that in the vicinity of Noah's palace (oh, he wasn't poor, that Noah) there dwelt a convenient example of every species on earth? Come, come. No, they were obliged to advertise, and then select the best pair that presented itself. Since they didn't want to cause a universal panic, they announced a competition for twosomes – a sort of beauty contest cum brains trust cum Darby-and-Joan event – and told contestants to present themselves at Noah's gate by a certain month. You can imagine the problems. For a start, not everyone has a competitive nature, so perhaps only the grabbiest turned up. Animals who weren't smart enough to read between the lines felt they simply didn't need to win a luxury cruise for two, all expenses paid, thank you very much. Nor had Noah and his staff allowed for the fact that some species hibernate at a given time of year; let alone the obvious fact that certain animals travel more slowly than others. There was a particularly relaxed sloth, for instance – an exquisite creature, I can vouch for it personally – which had scarcely got down to the foot of its tree before it was wiped out in the great wash of God's vengeance. What do you call that – natural selection? I'd call it professional incompetence.

**Review**

In this section, you have been given the opportunity to

- consider how talk is represented in different literary genres
- explore how writers use conversational features, including sound patterning, to create particular effects in a wide range of literary texts.

**Commentary**

**Activity 31**

This sonnet uses two main voices – the poet/poetic persona who starts to tell us the story ('I met a traveller...') and the traveller himself, whose account of the shattered statue in the desert concludes only at the end of the final line. However, other voices are also heard: the voice of the 'shattered visage' which 'tells' more; the inscription carved by the sculptor at the command of Ozymandias, and Ozymandias himself ('Look on my Works...'). This is a poem which could be analysed as a narrative (see Labov) and as an example of temporal and spatial deixis in poetry ('from an antique land' does both!). Shelley's own accent even appears in the flawed rhyme (to modern ears) of 'stone'/'frown'.

**Commentary**

**Activity 32**

The exchange between Othello and Desdemona (still technically in blank verse) reflects the violent fragmentation of their marriage and of Othello's former greatness in the half lines, incomplete sentences, exclamatives, hyperbole, use of imperatives and verbal variation. It is a most painful scene for an audience to watch.

**Commentary**

**Activity 33**

The audience would have been much entertained by Mrs Pinchwife's naivete and openness to temptation. Her more sophisticated sister-in-law Alithea tries to help. Their difference in character is reflected via lexical choice and grammar (Standard English – 'a pretty question'; non-Standard English – 'grum', 'hugeously', 'toused and moused', 'properest').

**Commentary**

**Activity 35**

Janey has been away from Hammond for ten months, visiting their married daughter in Europe. They are finally alone together, after a delayed disembarkation from the ocean liner because a passenger had died the previous night. Mansfield uses free indirect thought and direct speech to convey Hammond's shock. Janey is equally (but differently) shocked and persists in describing the death in detail. The longed-for reunion is tainted and the last line of the story will be: 'They would never be alone together again'.

**Commentary**

**Activity 36**

This extract is taken from the first chapter in Barnes' remarkable novel. The dominant tone of irony is immediately established as the unidentified narrator (the Stowaway) tells the story of Noah's Ark from an insider's point of view. We have an omniscient narrator who adopts an ironic, post-modernist stance to the Genesis myth, reflected by off-the-cuff comments on Adam and Eve and Noah. He also uses tag questions ('do you?'), rhetorical questions ('What do you call that – natural selection?') as well as direct address ('you don't really believe that story', 'You can imagine the problems', 'Come, come.' ) together with cliché from the world of contemporary culture ('I can vouch for it personally') and slang ('the grabbiest turned up'). Barnes also juxtaposes modern usage with biblical echoes ('there dwelt…', 'God's vengeance', 'God's wrath'). Through this rich mixture of discourses, registers, conversational features and rhetorical strategies, Barnes has created an extraordinarily convincing and original narrative voice.

# Producing Your Own Texts

5

## At the end of this chapter you should be able to

- select and apply relevant concepts and approaches from integrated linguistic and literary study, using appropriate terminology and accurate coherent written expression (AO1)

- demonstrate detailed critical understanding in analysing the ways in which structure, form and language shape meanings in a range of spoken and written texts (AO2)

- use integrated approaches to explore relationships between texts, analysing and evaluating the significance of contextual factors in their production and reception (AO3)

- demonstrate expertise and creativity in using language appropriately for a variety of purposes and audiences, drawing on insights from linguistic and literary studies (AO4).

For a more student-friendly version of these Assessment Objectives, turn to page vii in the Introduction.

This chapter will offer suggestions for writing in different genres. Each section will provide you with model texts, examples of tasks and guidance for creating your own texts. Some sections include questions and brief commentaries. You could use the questions either to guide your own reading of the texts or in group discussions.

There are some key points that you should remember when creating any text. You will need to

- identify your target audience
- be clear about the purpose of your writing
- research the conventions of the genre you have chosen to write in
- be aware of the implications of the mode of your text – written or spoken, for a reading or a listening audience
- choose topics that are of genuine interest to you.

# Writing a review

Here are two examples of reviews by non-professional writers. Text A is a review of an Amy Winehouse concert published in the *Independent* newspaper in February 2007. Text B is a review of a novel written for a teenage audience published in *Mslexia* magazine in Spring 2007.

## Activity 1   Analysing reviews

What are the features of Texts A and B that identify them as being in the genre of reviews?

What do you consider to be the purposes of a review (there may be more than one) and how well do you think these reviews fulfil those purposes?

Turn to page 231 for a commentary on this activity.

**Text A**

# AMY WINEHOUSE

**Astoria London.** Amy Winehouse's appearance at London's Astoria in January ended one song in when she was taken ill, so there is palpable unease as the frail-looking singer takes the stage.

When she peers into the crowd searching for her dad early on, and then makes a theatrical dash to the rear of the stage, people suspect the worst.

However, it's all an elaborate tease. She is clearly in control tonight. Dressed casually in a T-shirt and jeans, she plays for about an hour; drawing mainly from her *Back to Black* album.

*Back to Black* represents a significant improvement on her first album, Frank. Her debut was rambling and veered too close to the bland crooning typical of modern R&B, but *Back to Black* features a more distinctive sound.

Her lyrics are revealing: here, brassy and confident; there, vulnerable and confessional. The song 'Back to Black' sees the narrator abandoned by her lover and returning to a state of black depression.

Her rendition is masterful: a hip-swaying Motown beat changes to a weary tone, as she resigns herself to her fate.

Winehouse is backed by a tightly-competent group: sax and trombones and two sharp-suited male backing vocalists. The eye is drawn towards her as she regally extends her arms on high notes and affects a strange, twitchy dance reminiscent of Ska's running-on-the spot movements. She delivers 'Tears Dry on Their Own' in a finger-clicking frenzy that is at odds with the subject matter of the song (making the wrong romantic choices).

The final two songs are signature tunes. On 'I'm No Good', she warns her fella, 'I told you I was trouble', before recounting a complex web of infidelity and unsatisfactory, hurried liaisons. This is her voice at its very best. The way she savours the word 'trouble', leaves no doubt that she is, indeed, trouble.

The last song is 'Rehab', an anthemic cry celebrating her refusal to seek rehab therapy. The song asserts that she will confront her demons on her own terms. It's an exquisite, up-yours gesture to society sung in a Ronnie Spector voice that is extraordinary for a young north Londoner.

Winehouse returns for two covers: the Specials' 'Monkey Man', followed by what she says is her favourite song of last year, the Zutons' 'Valerie'.

This ends a triumphant gig that exorcises any lingering Astoria ghosts and leaves everyone wanting more.

**Andrew Byrne**
Bank employee: London

**Text B**

*Ophelia* by Lisa Klein: Bloomsbury £5.99

Having devoured this book at the steady speed of one page per minute while at the same time willing the story never to end I can tell you that *Ophelia*, by Lisa Klein, is a novel you will finish with teary eyes. The story is written from the viewpoint of Ophelia, sister of Laertes, and Hamlet's lover, and follows her journey from a child to a woman, complete with love, loss and treachery along the way. If you are prone to tears or are particularly squeamish, do not let the fact that the novel is based on one of Shakespeare's four major tragedies put you off. Lisa Klein shows immense skill, conveying murder, revenge and madness just as vividly as she does Ophelia's carefree childhood and romantic young love.

As a reader who becomes, if possible, overly attached to book characters, I particularly enjoyed discovering Ophelia through observing her experiences. My favourite scenes were therefore those taking place in Queen Gertrude's household, as it is here that we witness Ophelia's transformation from girl to woman, and are also treated to an insider's view of Elsinore: the gossip, rivalry and romance. Kleenex at the ready, another of my favourite parts of the book was its ending. Indeed, finishing this book upset me on two counts, one of which I dare not reveal for fear of ruining your enjoyment of the book, and the other being that I would now have to find some other occupation for my bus journey to and from school.

I think that the book could have been improved by seeing a little more of Ophelia's childhood, such as is described in the first few chapters. These chapters were a particular favourite segment of mine. Another improvement could have been to develop the character of Horatio, with whom I did not feel so well-acquainted despite his leading role. Despite this, I would definitely recommend *Ophelia* as an original and satisfying side dish to your traditional *Hamlet*. Personally, I've started again at page one.

Dawn Kanter
student

## Writing tasks

## Write a review

1 Write a 500-word review of any arts event or book of your choice. Decide the type of audience and publication you are going to write for. For example, a concert/album review could be for a specialist music magazine, or for a non-specialist glossy lifestyle magazine aimed at young people, or for a magazine aimed at a teenage audience. A book review could be for the review section of a magazine, newspaper, free newspaper for commuters or Sunday supplement.

2 Write a web review for an event or book of your choice – for example, an on-line music magazine or a reading-group website. Some key points:

- think about readability – remember that your text will be read on screen
- your text must be easy to navigate: incorporate some simple layout features, e.g. subheadings, different font sizes, strategic use of white space
- your language should be accessible, direct and lively
- don't be afraid to use some specialist language – your target audience will probably have some knowledge of the subject.

3 Write a script for a presentation on a text of your choice (this could be based on one of your set texts or a text for wide reading). Some key points:

- remember that your audience will be *listening*
- think about the clarity and sequencing of your text
- establish a rapport with your audience with a friendly opening
- identify the key points that you would like your audience to remember
- you could conclude with a reference back to your starting point.

Remember to make a note of your decisions and planning as this will help you in writing a commentary on your own work (see the section 'Writing the commentary', pages 230–231).

# Writing interviews

Choose a suitable person to interview. You will read many interviews with celebrities and well-known people in the national press but interviews with ordinary people can be equally interesting, absorbing and thought provoking.

There are different ways of conducting and presenting your interview.

## Step 1: the interview

The first stage is to interview your subject face to face. It would be a good idea to tape the interview and transcribe it later although you may also wish to record some notes on a note-pad.

● Prepare a series of questions based on a specific list of topics. Start with 'easy' warm-up questions then move to more detailed ones.

● Phrase questions so that the interviewee needs to reply at some length (not just 'yes' or 'no'). You will get fuller answers if you ask questions starting with 'Who', 'When', 'Why', 'What' or 'Where'.

● Follow up on any points the interviewee has made. Ask them to give examples. Remember to listen carefully and to allow them plenty of time to respond.

Good interviews are personality pieces and tell the audience what a person is like. They may even guide the audience's response to the person.

## Step 2: writing up the interview

Make some notes from your tape-recording or transcript. Organise them under loose headings until you have found a logical sequence.

There are two main ways of presenting interviews.

● **Question and answer:** This format is easier to write and has a feeling of speed and immediacy. It is popular with publications aimed at young people, music and film magazines, and is used by national newspapers to emphasise the importance of the subject – when interviewing politicians, for example.

● **Integrated approach:** This approach is much freer and less restrictive, giving the writer the opportunity to set the scene and convey atmosphere. It involves rewriting the interview in continuous prose from a third-person perspective with quotes from the interviewee.

To see examples of these two approaches, look at the interviews with Andy Warhol and Beth Ditto on pages 80–81. In the Warhol interview, which was broadcast on television, the interviewer asked a series of questions and returned to topics when he felt that Warhol had not given a full enough answer. The interview with Beth Ditto is strikingly different. It has been deliberately crafted by the journalist to be appropriate for a newspaper article.

Your choice of approach could depend on your choice of mode – for example, a spoken text for radio/television or a written text for a publication.

Here are two more examples of these different approaches. Text A is an extract from an interview with Mary Phillip, footballer for Arsenal and England, which appeared in a national newspaper (*Guardian*, 2007). As a contrast, Text B was written in response to an interview with the model Kate Moss in 1993.

## Text A

### The Close-up
Mary Phillip
Interview by Imogen Fox

**What are you wearing today?**
An Arsenal top, an England tracksuit and some jewellery that my kids bought for me.

**Are you allowed jewellery on the pitch?**
No, we used to be allowed wedding rings but it is very strict – even though you still see the male players wearing their big chains and rings. We have to take out tiny stud earrings and even hairclips. I don't know what injury you can inflict with a hairclip.

**Do you like wearing a tracksuit?**
I don't like going down to the park in a tracksuit with Arsenal or England written all over it. It is just not me to be labelled like that – I prefer to fade away in the background. My other tracksuits only have tiny sports logos on them, which no one would really notice. On non-sporty stuff I would never buy something that had a big D & G on it even if I like the cut of it. When I go away with England I have to wear the official tracksuit all the time, even if we go to the cinema together as a team but it takes a load off your shoulders in terms of packing, and it raises the profile of the team, so it makes sense not to dress in your own stuff.

**Are you happy with the way you look?**
Yes, I am content with how I look and I don't take much notice of my shape. We have to watch what we eat and not eat too much fat, but if I fancy a kebab or fish and chips I'll have it. If you have a mix of fruit and veg as well, it doesn't matter too much.

**Have you got a lucky shirt to play in?**
No, but I will only tuck my shirt in as I am walking out to the field. Even when officials tell me to tuck it in beforehand, I will have to pull it out and re-tuck it. I've done that for ever.

**Do you have any tattoos?**
Not big ones, but I have a rose on my ankle and a little angel on my back with my kids' names on it. But I got mine before Beckham, about 11 years ago.

## Text B

### STILL ONLY 19, AND ENDEARINGLY POLITE
Angela Lambert meets Kate Moss

She is an ordinary, grimacing evasive teenager – until the photographer says 'would you go and stand against that blank wall?' She goes, she stands, and as the lens focuses upon her, Kate Moss is instantly transformed from her own gawky self into a pretence of gawkiness.

Her hands furl awkwardly inwards, her limbs droop as if too long and slender to support her. She assumes a mask of shyness, changing her pose fractionally with each click of the shutter. It is a brilliant pretence of innocence, and I see at once why this slip of a girl commands anything from £1,000 to £10,000 an hour as one of fashion's tiny band of supermodels.

The camera stops clicking and at once the embarrassed clumsiness returns. 'Can I have a cigarette?' she asks, 'Do you have a light? Oh, God, I've only got four fags left!' She perches on the edge of my sofa and draws desperately on the cigarette. She is wearing a much-washed, white sleeveless T-shirt (no logos), a frayed pair of denim shorts and a pair of grubby running shoes. Oh, and a couple of silver rings. Nothing else. She looks artless, careless, hapless. She is already very rich but she is not in any way spoilt or arrogant and, once she overcame her initial shyness, was not monosyllabic either. When I finish preparing lunch, she offers to carry things into the dining room, and does so.

At the age of 19, after barely two years of professional modelling, Kate Moss rents apartments in Paris and New York and is looking to buy a base in London: something around the quarter million pound mark. She surveys my flat. 'It's nice and light and airy, innit? I'd like to live in London in a house somewhere like Little Venice so you're not bang in the middle of everything. I did get a house finder, but I'm never in London to look at what she finds.'

## Writing tasks

### Write an interview

You are now ready to choose your subject and write your own interview. Decide which approach you would like to adopt and think carefully about your target audience. You will need to have a specific audience in mind and some idea of the type of publication that you feel would suit your style.

# Writing biography

In this section you will explore approaches to writing biography. To prepare yourself, look at the extracts from biographies written by professional writers in Chapter 2 (page 61) and the commentary on page 89.

Below are some suggested tasks and guidance on how to get started.

## Writing tasks

### Write a biography

1   Write an extract from a biography of a literary character. To do this you will need to use details from a chosen text and use them to form the basis for your interpretation of that fictional character's life. It might be a good idea to choose one of the minor characters rather than one of the main protagonists as this will give you more scope for creating original work.

2   Choose a famous historical personality who interests you in some way – perhaps because their life is connected with adventure, romance or discoveries. Write an extract from a biography for an audience of children or teenagers. This will involve doing some research into the person's life but you will also need to shape your material to interest a specific age range. If you choose a personality who fascinates you, you should be able to share your enthusiasm with your audience.

3   Write an extract from an autobiography of a living person. Choose as your subject someone known to you rather than a celebrity as you will need to use original material.

One way to approach this task is to begin by interviewing your subject to get the raw data (see page 205). As an example of how this data can be used, read the following two accounts of the first meeting between Diana, Princess of Wales, and Prince Charles. Text A is an extract from a taped interview with Princess Diana made by the biographer Andrew Morton. Text B is Morton's reworking of the material for the published biography.

## Text A

I've known her [the Queen] since I was tiny so it was no big deal. No interest in Andrew and Edward – never thought about Andrew. I kept thinking 'Look at the life they have, how awful' so I remember him coming up to Althorp to stay, my husband, and the first impact was 'God, what a sad man'. He came with his Labrador. My sister was all over him like a bad rash and I thought 'God, he must really hate that'. I kept out of the way. I remember being a fat, podgy, no make-up, unsmart lady but I made a lot of noise and he liked that and he came up to me after dinner and said: 'Will you show me the gallery?' and I was just about to show him the gallery and my sister Sarah comes up and tells me to push off and I said 'At least, let me tell you where the switches are to the gallery because you won't know where they are', and I disappeared. And he was charm himself, and when I stood next to him the next day, a 16 year old, for someone like that to show you any attention – I was just so sort of amazed. 'Why would anyone like him be interested in me?' and it *was* interest.

That was it for about two years. Saw him off and on with Sarah and Sarah got frightfully excited about the whole, then she saw something different happening which I hadn't twigged on to, ie when he had his 30th birthday dance I was asked too.

## Text B

It was during her sister's romance that Diana first came into the path of the man considered then to be the world's most eligible bachelor. That historic meeting in November 1997 was hardly auspicious. Diana, on weekend leave from West Heath School, was introduced to the Prince in the middle of a ploughed field near Norbottle Wood on the Althorp estate during a day's shooting. The Prince, who brought along his favourite Labrador, Sandringham Harvey, is considered to be one of the finest shots in the country so he was more intent on sport than small talk on that bleak afternoon. Diana cut a nondescript figure in her checked shirt, her sister's anorak, cords and Wellington boots. She kept in the background, realising that she had only been brought along to make up numbers. It was very much her sister's show and Sarah was perhaps being rather mischievous when she said later that she 'played Cupid' between her sister and the Prince.

If Charles's first memories of Diana on that fateful weekend are of 'a very jolly and amusing and attractive 16 year old – full of fun', then it was no thanks to her elder sister. As far as Sarah was concerned, Charles was her domain at that time and trespassers were not welcomed by the sparky redhead who applied her competitive instincts to the men in her life. In any case Diana was not overly impressed by Sarah's royal boyfriend. 'What a sad man', she remembered thinking. The Spencers held a dance that weekend in his honour and it was noticeable that Sarah was enthusiastic in her attentions. Diana later told friends: 'I kept out of the way. I remember being a fat, podgy, no make-up, unsmart lady but I made a lot of noise and he liked that.'

| Activity 2 | Comparing biographical texts |

What would you say are the main differences between Texts A and B?

Can you find examples of where Morton has used material from the taped interview and reshaped it in the biography?

Which of the two texts do you consider to be more effective and why?

Turn to page 232 for a commentary on this activity.

# Writing news stories

In this section you will find out how to write news stories and make reports. As a starting-point it would be helpful to look at the 'Reportage' section in Chapter 2 (pages 65–74). The texts provided as examples in that section are all concerned with global events and issues like war, but reportage can also focus on more-local issues and can cover a range of topics.

You can give an account of an event from a third-person perspective or you can write from the point of view of a participant. You must be secure in your knowledge of your subject so you will need to do some research. Choose either a local event or issue or a topic which has ongoing appeal. The following texts provide you with some examples.

- Text A is a story about the topical issue of space burials. This article on popular science (from *Metro* newspaper, 2007) is written in a very accessible, reader-friendly style.

- Text B is an extract from an article about rubbish disposal, written as an eye-witness account by a journalist who joined a refuse collection team. The issue of pollution is very much in the media. This article (from *Financial Times Weekend*, 2007) also features an insight into the lives of the people who work to dispose of our refuse, adding a human-interest dimension.

- Text C is a transcript of a BBC news programme (broadcast in 2005) on measures to deal with truancy in schools: a topic which would be of interest to many people, but this article adopts a new angle on the subject.

- Text D is a human-interest story (from *The Times*, 2007) – a story that concerns ordinary people and offers an insight into aspects of modern life. The topic is an example of an ongoing issue rather than one that will quickly become out of date.

**Text A**

## METROFOCUS

**SPACE BURIALS – If you're thinking of giving a family member a special send-off, the sky's the limit, says Ed West**

It's your final countdown
Ever since our ancestors first gazed at the night sky it's been mankind's dream to visit the moon. And almost 40 years after Neil Armstrong took that first giant leap, Earth's satellite is finally in reach of anyone with £20,000 to spare. Providing they're dead, that is.

Space burials are the ultimate in 21st century send-offs: it's thought that some 150 people have already been 'buried' in space and a further 400 have signed up to have their remains shot into the sky. The first to boldly go, where no dead man had gone before were the 24 men and women, including *Star Trek* creator Gene Roddenbury and LSD guru Timothy Leary, whose remains travelled aboard Earthview 01: the founders' flight which was launched on April 21 1997.

## Who'd have thought?

Space Services Inc, based in Houston, Texas, is currently the only company that offers space burials.

SSI spokeswoman Susan Schoenfeld says 'Funeral options such as this have become much more mainstream over the past five or six years: we now have distributors all over the world. Back in the 1980's, did you ever think you'd see a rocket in a funeral home?'

This Spring, SSI launches the Legacy Flight from Spaceport America, near Las Cruces in New Mexico, in which a space probe will carry the remains of 129 people, among them James Doohan (Scotty from the original *Star Trek*), who died in 2005. Naturally such a high-profile posthumous astronaut has increased interest in space funerals.

## A return ticket to ride

At the moment, most missions do not leave Earth's orbit. Instead, a portion of cremated ashes is sent into the outer atmosphere, from where they ultimately return at some point due to gravity. Doohan and Company will be on an earth-return service, meaning their ashes will drop back down 24 hours after being ceremonially buried.

## Religious opposition

Naturally, the world's most adventurous nation is getting in on the act; at least seven Britons have signed up already. But while the Soviets were the first to consider the idea, Russia has so far failed to get onboard and it's not just due to a lack of money.

Dimitri Grioriev, an Orthodox priest at St Nicholas Cathedral in Washington, recently said, 'Burying people in space has nothing to do with Christian traditions. Some argue Christian remains shouldn't be separated at all'.

There are other options for the religious infidels: for about £7000 Starburst Memorials in Toronto can send an entire urn-load up into the upper atmosphere using a high velocity gun launcher. This will also please anyone who's always wanted to be at one with nature. Starburst's Richard Graf says: 'The finer particles get picked up by the jetstream and form the nucleus of raindrops'.

That way, your ashes will either help Mother Nature replenish her seed – or they'll ruin Wimbledon once again, whichever thought makes you happier.

**Text B**

# The Waste Land

## As he joins the binmen on their dawn rounds and visits the monstrous furnaces of a London recycling centre, **Andrew O'Hagan** ponders the pressing morality of rubbish

High above the Brent Reservoir a fringe of red, trailing light was spread across the sky at 5.30am. It was still dark on the road and the houses slept as the lorries pulled into the depot. In the artificial brightness of 'the office' – a huddle of Portakabins – the binmen were gathered around a newspaper.

Les said he liked the early start and the afternoons off. He has worked in Harrow for more than 12 years, up early every day and out clearing the bins before anyone is awake. He now drives the truck and considers that a significant upgrade. 'I'm the gaffer', he said, 'but not really'. Les and I tried to make jokes but tiredness got to us and the laughter came slower as we progressed along the route. Every few yards I jumped down and joined the lifters as they rolled the bins from people's yards. That morning the crew were only responsible for collecting organic rubbish.

'It's a nightmare', said Joshi, whose parents were born in Bangladesh. 'No matter how many times you give them information, or mark their card, they still contaminate the bloody recycling bins'. They hide all sorts of stuff at the bottom of the organic bins – like machine parts. There's no telling them.' He showed me one of the bins outside a large house; it had grass on the top and Tesco bags full of paper underneath.

It took the best part of six hours for the team to do their round, emptying the bins and marking the contaminators. Half an hour later, we were beyond the suburban countryside, heading at speed for the composting site at the extremity of North-West London.

The place smelt powerfully of rotting Christmas trees. There was smoke rising from the composting area; the process takes ten weeks from the delivery of vegetable matter to the maturation of compost.

When we arrived on the site Les's vehicle was weighed on a weighbridge. I stood at the side of the tipping shed as other trucks arrived and dropped their loads into a large hangar, where it was scooped up for shredding.

Les was shaking his head. The inspector who examines the material in the back of the bin lorries before it is off-loaded was not happy. 'No', said the man with the clipboard, 'Contaminated', and then he signed a sheet and handed it to Les. Despite their efforts, the team had allowed too much non-organic rubbish to be tipped into the back of the lorry.

'What about this load?' I asked.

'It's not good enough', he said. 'We'll take it to Ruislip tip and Harrow will have to pay to dump it there'.

'That's a pity', I said, 'a long morning too'.

'Never mind', Les said, turning the wheel and smoothing his hair in the rearview mirror. 'We won't be saving the world today'.

211

**Text C**

Key

| | |
|---|---|
| MP | male studio presenter |
| NP | Nick Parrott (interviewer) |
| FP | female teacher |
| (.) | micropause |
| (1.0) | timed pause (in seconds) |
| (?) | indecipherable |
| **bold type** | indicates a strongly stressed word |

........................................................................................................................

| | |
|---|---|
| Voice-over | Text alerts tackle school skivers |
| MP | Bilton School in Rugby has been sending text messages to parents when their children haven't turned up to school (.) the school says truancy rates have dropped by half since the system was introduced (.) Neil Parrott has been to see how it works [*Video footage of classroom at registration*] |
| FP | morning James (.) |
| NP | nothing out of the ordinary **here** until this happens |
| James | Vincent's not here today |
| NP | unauthorised absences here are tracked by computer (.) once registration is over the form is taken to the school office (.) there it's fed into a computer which logs every child who has failed to turn up (.) if the school don't know why they send a message to the parents [noise of text message being sent] |
| Headmaster | since we've had it (.) three years now (.) we've improved our attendance by four percent (.) well above the national average (.) and we've reduced our (.) er (.) our number of truants |
| NP | the system has had mainly positive but mixed reception |
| FP | I don't like it (.) because when my mum finds out about it (.) I get in trouble |
| James | when they send one home (.) if you're not in registration (.) they send a message home (.) and it's good because you get in deep trouble (.) and if you're truanting (?) |
| NP | but it doesn't stop there |
| Headmaster | the system is designed to reach a wider range of parents through text messages in different languages (.) Arabic Urdu Welsh (.) this latest multi-language version will allow parents to access the system. |
| NP | only five percent of schools have text messaging technology but Bilton School has been demonstrating and installing for others (.) so (.) it might not be long before it comes to a school near you |

**Text D**

# Get dressed, head tells the pyjama mamas

## Mothers do school run in nightwear
## Trend sets a bad example to children

**David Sharrock** Ireland Correspondent

So many women in Belfast take their children to school while still dressed in their pyjamas that a headmaster has appealed to them to show some respect.

Joe McGuiness, principal of St Matthew's primary in Short Strand, a Roman Catholic working class enclave of East Belfast, was moved to action after seeing as many as 50 mothers arriving at the school gates in their nightwear.

In a bulletin to parents, Mr McGuinness wrote: 'over recent months the number of adults leaving children at school and collecting children from school dressed in pyjamas has risen considerably.

'While it is not my position to insist on what people wear or don't, I feel that arriving at the school in pyjamas is disrespectful to the school and a bad example to set to children'.

Women walking round Belfast estates in all-day pyjama gear is a phenomenon that has been well documented by Robin Livingstone, a columnist in the *Anderstown News*.

Mr Livingstone said he first identified all-day pyjama syndrome (ADPS) in 2003. He knows a student at Belfast Institute for Further and Higher Education who is writing a dissertation on the subject.

The women are colloquially known as 'pyjama mamas' or 'Millies'. Their pyjama ensembles are often complemented by large, gold hoop earrings known as 'budgies' – because such cage birds could swing from them. They also sport 'scrunchies' to create the 'Turf Lodge facelift' in which the hair is scraped so tightly to the back of the head that it pulls the facial skin taut.

There is even a dress hierarchy in those suffering from ADPS: the wearing of silk-effect baggy pyjamas with fluffy, mule-type slippers contrasts, for example, with the traditional dressing gown and hair rollers.

Mr McGuinness told the *Anderstown News* 'There used to be about 15 to 20 pyjama-wearing parents, but there are anything up to 50 now, and they are all women.

People don't go to see a solicitor, bank manager or doctor dressed in pyjamas so why do they think it's OK to drop their children off at school dressed like that? It's about respect and setting children a bad example.

'There is an old word called slovenliness, which means messy and lazy. I think this can be applied to people who spend the day dressed in pyjamas.'

The *Anderstown News* supported Mr McGuinness's stand in an editorial. Those people who wear pyjamas as they go about their daily business will argue it is their right to do as they choose and they are breaking no law. Perhaps they do not care what the rest of us think. If so, then they should seriously ask themselves what message they are handing to their children.

| Activity 3 | Investigating news stories |

Read Texts A–D and try to identify what it is about them that makes them good stories.

You will probably conclude that they all provide information relevant to modern life while involving a strong element of human interest; that is, making reference to people and places and using quotations from real sources.

These examples should have given some ideas about the variety of content and approaches that are available to you.

### Finding your audience
Writing a news story can be a real-life task where you try to have your work published. Think local: most cities have evening newspapers and free newspapers which are distributed in urban areas for commuters to read while travelling to work. Most towns have weekly local newspapers and may also have local radio stations operating, for example, from schools, colleges or hospitals.

### Researching the market
Read a variety of local and evening newspapers to discover the types of news stories they feature. As space is usually limited you will need to write concisely and with a clear focus.

Here are some of the types of stories that appear in local and evening newspapers

- profiles of local people who have made a particular achievement
- opinions on local environmental issues
- articles on fund-raising/charity events
- reports of exhibitions, shows, carnivals and sporting events
- promotion of local facilities and places of interest
- animal stories.

| Writing tasks | Write a news story |

Aim to write approximately 1500 words for whichever option you choose.

1  Choose a topic or event of local interest and write a news report for a weekly or evening newspaper. If specific personalities are involved you may wish to arrange to interview them and incorporate their comments into your report.

2  Choose a topical issue in which you have an interest and write an article suitable for a free morning newspaper. Try to find a new angle on the topic.

3  Write a news report on an issue of immediate interest to be broadcast on a local radio station.

There are, of course, many other areas of journalism and you may prefer to write in a different sub-genre – for example, features, letters, reviews, articles on specialist subjects.

If you are interested in writing features see the section 'Writing features for magazines' (pages 224–226).

# Writing advisory or instructional texts

For this type of writing you will need to draw upon your own experiences or knowledge to share with others. Texts that advise and instruct tend to follow certain linguistic and structural conventions. The most obvious example is a text whose only purpose is to offer a clear set of instructions, like the following extract from a set of instructions aimed at the general public (from an insurance document issued by More Than insurance company).

---

### What to do if you break down on a motorway

- Pull onto the hard shoulder as far away from the inside lane as possible.
- Turn your front wheels towards the hard shoulder.
- Try to stop near an emergency phone.
- Switch on your hazard warning lights.
- Keep your sidelights on if it is dark or visibility is poor.
- Get out of your car on the passenger side.
- Keep passengers away from the motorway and keep children under control.
- Keep pets safe in the car, or, in an emergency, keep them under proper control on the verge.
- Walk to an emergency phone on your side of the motorway. The phone call is free and connects to the police, who can work out where you are.
- Face oncoming traffic while you are on the phone.
- If you are travelling alone and feel at risk you may want to wait in the front passenger seat with the doors locked. If someone approaches, wind down the window a little to talk to them. Only unlock the door once you are sure they are genuine.

---

This text is a bullet-pointed list in chronological order explaining what to do in this situation. Prominent language features are

- use of the present tense
- imperative verb forms
- use of conditionals – if
- use of adverbs to sequence the order of actions – after, before
- direct address to the reader – you.

You will have noticed that the register is formal and distant and that the writer does not offer personal opinion.

But this type of text will obviously not offer you the opportunity to demonstrate your writing skills so you need to explore texts which combine instruction with advice. In order to make it interesting for the audience this genre of text will involve an element of persuasion, either subliminal or with the views/opinions of the writer more prominently featured.

---

**Activity 4** ## Appealing to the target audience

Texts A and B on page 216 are extracts from *The Rough Guide First-Time Europe* (2005), which offers advice to young people thinking of travelling around Europe as an extended holiday or as a gap-year project. Read both texts and then consider how they might appeal to their target audience.

Compare your response with the commentary on page 232.

## Text A

### FAQ

**Will I manage travelling around Europe only speaking English?**
Better than you'll manage only eating at McDonald's. English, and, when necessary a few hand gestures will get you by just fine in most situations. Remember to keep your speech slow and basic, skip the slang and don't take a puzzled look as a sign to speak louder. That said, if you make the effort to pick up a language, that will enrich your experience tenfold. At the very least take twenty minutes to learn 'please', thank you', 'excuse me', 'where', 'toilet', 'how much', and 'eight euros for a beer!' in the local languages.

**I've got £500 saved up. Will that be enough?**
No problem. The question is for what kind of trip and for how long? To figure out a daily budget that suits your comfort level turn to the *'Costs and Savings'* section for some tips.

**How do I figure out where to sleep each night and what to see during the day?**
Easy. Carry a guide book. There are extensive lists of places to stay at various price ranges in each city, with short descriptions to help you narrow down your selection. They even have maps to help you navigate your way there.

In peak periods you may want to find an internet café and book a few hostels in advance.

At most tourist offices they'll call around and find an available room for you once you've arrived. Of course, you can always just show up at the front door with your pack.

> **Why even the rich travel cheap**
> There's a trend shift under way, a return to the old-fashioned style of travelling where people actually seek out the foreignness of a place. No matter how nice the room, people are waking up to the fact that no four walls make up a complete (or very real) travel experience. It's what happens outside the hotel, your connection with your immediate surrounds and your interaction with the local people that enables you to embrace travel with the intensity it deserves.

## Text B

### The benefits of travelling solo

You learn about yourself. You'll find out what your likes and dislikes are. And you'll be able to act on them. Often travellers spur each other on to tick off a 'to-do' list. With no one looking, perhaps you'll give that famous museum a miss and rent a bike and head for the countryside instead. You'll be less distracted and more likely to notice the small things happening around you. With more time to reflect you'll get better writing in your journal, more thoughtfully composed photos, more reading time and greater insights from studying the culture – in short, you'll absorb more of the country you're travelling in. Plus, you're less likely to attract attention by speaking English with your partner. Instead, you'll be approached by more locals and other travellers eager to make conversation.

> I first went to Europe after I graduated from college. I bought a Volkswagen right from the factory in Germany and drove around the continent – drank wine in Pamplona during San Fermin and downed beers in Munich's Hofbrau Haus.
>
> I learned that you learn far more during your travels if you go alone. You spend time with the locals and find out what's important to them. It's moments like that that provide the reason for travel.
>
> **Tim Cahill**
> Author of ***Lost in My Own Backyard***

Try to adopt the same approach as the one suggested for writing news stories (page 209), finding a real-life task and audience. As with other genres, instruction/advice texts may also be produced as spoken texts to deliver to a listening audience.

Here are some ideas for possible tasks. Your choice will depend on your own personal interests, experiences and knowledge.

**Writing tasks**

## Write an advisory or instructional text

1 Write an extract from a guide aimed at young people which offers advice and instruction on, for example, leaving home to go to university, seeking part-time jobs or work experience, travelling and/or working abroad.

2 Produce the text in Task 1 as a speech to be delivered to an audience of your peers at a student council meeting, for example.

3 Produce a leaflet or handout which gives advice on an area where you have some expertise or personal involvement – for example, advice on personal safety or advice on how to join an organisation concerned with environmental or human-rights issues. This task offers the opportunity to address a wider audience than Tasks 1 and 2 but you must still have a specific target readership in mind.

4 Give a talk on the kind of topic suggested in Task 3 to a peer-group audience – for example, in a student conference or as part of a Personal and Social Education or Tutorial programme.

# Writing short stories

There are many different genres of short stories so you have a wide range to choose from. The main genres are

- psychological thriller
- detective/mystery
- horror
- ghost stories
- historical
- love/romance
- fantasy
- realistic stories (sometimes referred to as 'slice of life')
- stories which feature a particular setting or geographical location
- magic realism (this involves blending realistic elements with more surreal aspects: stories by Angela Carter are a good example).

These genres are, of course, not necessarily distinct and one story may blend features of different genres. The factors you need to consider when planning your story are

- genre
- audience
- narrative perspective.

You should identify a specific audience for your story – for example, it could be included in a particular type of magazine, newspaper supplement or anthology. Do you want to write for a general adult audience, for young teenagers or for children? Remember that stories can be written to be read aloud – to children, for example, or to be listened to on CD or radio.

Whether you choose to write for a reading or a listening audience, the voice of your story is important. (For an explanation of 'voice', see page 15.) This is linked with narrative perspective – the point of view from which the story is told, which involves the position of the person narrating the story and how this affects the position of the reader or listener.

There are three main types of narrative perspective.

- **The** omniscient **author** – Here the writer stands back from the scene and makes observations about the characters and their behaviour. The writer is distanced from the action and has an overview.
- Third-person **narrative** (using the pronouns 'he' and 'she') – Similar to the omniscient author but the writer can interpret the events from the viewpoint of one of the characters so that the reader is invited to share the experience and possibly empathise with that character.
- First-person **narrative** (using the pronoun 'I') – Here the narrator is one of the characters and the reader is given their perspective of the events. This means that the reader is positioned to adopt the narrator's total view of life and of other characters. The reader may be manipulated into identifying with a character who is, for example, a criminal or who is subversive in some way.

If you choose to write in the first person do try to avoid writing about yourself, as the story may become autobiography. Instead you need to adopt a persona – a character that you have created. An interesting idea is to choose for your narrator someone of a different age and gender from yourself. For more on narrative perspective, see pages 36–37.

## How to structure a short story

From your reading of short stories you will be aware that they tend to follow a particular structure which looks something like this

- **Exposition** – sets the scene and introduces the characters
- **Disruption** – introduces a problem, an issue or a type of conflict
- **Development** – the story unfolds
- **Resolution** – the conclusion. This does not necessarily have to tie all loose ends together and does not have to have a 'twist' at the end, but you should try to leave the reader with something to think about.

The extracts that follow are from different short-story genres which also adopt a variety of narrative perspectives.

- Text A uses third-person narrative and is from a mystery/thriller (*The Room* by David Karp).
- Text B uses third-person narrative and is from a crime story/psychological thriller (Val McDermid's *Stranded*, 2005).
- Text C has a first-person narrator and is a type of interior monologue, with the reader invited to view through the character's eyes (from Ian McEwan's *First Love, Last Rites*, 1997).
- Text D has a first-person narrator and is from a contemporary love story (Deborah Moggach's *Changing Babies*, 1996).
- Text E uses an omniscient author and mixes the genres of horror/magic realism (from Angela Carter's *The Bloody Chamber*, 1996).
- Text F uses third-person narrative but events are seen from the perspective of the main character; the genre is urban realism (from Michel Faber's *The Fahrenheit Twins*, 2005).

### Text A

Burden's first awareness was that he was naked and the room was cold. He opened his eyes and saw only the grey light. He thought for an instant that he was lying naked on the floor of the corridor. It was not the corridor, nor his room in the hospital section. It was a bare, enormous room. Perhaps two storeys tall. And it was so huge that it curved almost out of sight. There were no windows in it, not a stick of furniture, nothing but the soaring monotony of rough concrete. The floor was smooth and cold to his bare feet. Burden rose and walked slowly. There was enough light for him to see the room in its entirety. It was perhaps twenty feet in width and fifty feet in height and it curved with the building. Cautiously Burden followed the wall, looking for a door, a window, a break in the concrete. But there was none.

## Text B

The woman strolled through the supermarket, choosing a few items for her basket. As she reached the display of sauces and pickles, a muscle in her jaw tightened. She looked around, willing herself to appear casual. No one watched.

Swiftly she took a jar of tomato pickle from her large leather handbag and placed it on the shelf. She moved on to the frozen meat section.

A few minutes later, she passed down the same aisle and repeated the exercise, this time adding two more jars to the shelf. As she walked on to the checkout, she felt tension slide from her body, leaving her light-headed.

She stood in the queue, anonymous among the morning shoppers, another neat woman in a well-cut winter coat, a faint smile on her face and a strangely unfocused look in her pale blue eyes.

## Text C

I saw my first corpse on Thursday. Today it was Sunday and there was nothing to do. And it was hot. I have never been so hot in England. Towards midday I decided on a walk. I stood outside the house, hesitating. I was not sure whether to go left or right. Charlie was on the other side of the street, underneath a car. He must have seen my legs for he called out.

'How's tricks?' I never have ready answers to questions like that. I fumbled in my mind for several seconds, and said,

'How are you, Charlie?' He crawled out. The sun was on my side of the street, straight into his eyes. He shielded them with his hand and said,

'Where you off to now?' Again, I did not know. It was Sunday, there was nothing to do, it was too hot….

'Out', I said. 'A walk….' I crossed over and looked at the car's engine, although it meant nothing to me. Charlie is an old man who knows about machines. He repairs cars for the people in the street and their friends. He came round the side of the car carrying a heavy tool kit in two hands.

'She died, then?' He stood wiping a spanner with cotton waste for something to do. He knew it already, of course, but he wanted to hear my story.

'Yes', I told him. 'She's dead'. He waited for me to go on. I leaned against the side of the car. Its roof was too hot to touch. Charlie prompted me.

'You saw her last…?'

'I was on the bridge. I saw her running by the canal'.

'You saw her…'.

'I didn't see her fall in'.

## Text D

It all started when this chap came in one day. He was older than me, mid-forties, and what I liked was the mess he was in. I mean, he was covered with plaster dust. His eyebrows and everything. He was wearing army trousers and an old jacket and was powdered all over. He was a big bloke, nice-looking, with huge hands which I watched when he paid. The cassette-tape looked so trivial in his palm. Outside he had an old van, crammed with planks from the timber yard opposite, and there he was buying a cassette tape of *Cosi Fan Tutte*.

Somehow I had never connected builders with opera.

He came in the next week. It was pouring with rain. The shop was empty and I was eating coleslaw from a tub. He was scanning the classical M-P and he gave me a wink, so I pointed to the tub with my plastic fork and said 'The trouble with some things is, you go on eating and eating them and they never seem to get any less'.

He came over and looked in the tub. 'The trouble with coleslaw is that it's coleslaw'.

He went out from the shop and in a moment was back with a carrier bag he had got from his van. He fished about inside and produced some bread and Parma ham. 'Even got some tomatoes', he said, taking out a pocket knife and slicing one.

That's how it all started, over crumbs and tomato pips and cassettes: and that's how it went on. I fell in love with him, helplessly, that first day when we sat on my desk with the rain sluicing down outside. His name was Hamish.

### Text E

It is a northern country; they have cold weather, they have cold hearts.

Cold; tempest; wild beasts in the forest. It is a hard life. Their houses are built of logs, dark and smoky within. There will be a crude icon of the virgin behind a guttering candle, the leg of a pig hung up to cure, a string of drying mushrooms. A bed, a stool, a table. Harsh, brief, poor lives.

To these upland woodsmen, the Devil is as real as you or I. More so; they have not seen us nor even know that we exist, but the Devil they glimpse often in the graveyards, those bleak and touching townships of the dead where the graves are marked with portraits of the deceased in the naïf style and there are no flowers to put in front of them, no flowers grow there, so they put out small, votive offerings, little loaves, sometimes a cake that the bears come lumbering up from the margins of the forest to snatch away. At midnight especially on Walpurgisnacht, the Devil holds picnics in the graveyards and invites the witches; then they dig up fresh corpses, and eat them. Anyone will tell you that.

### Text F

The view from Jeanette's window was, frankly, shite.

Outside lay Rusborough South. There was no Rusborough North, West or East, as far as Jeanette knew. Maybe they'd existed once, but, if so, they must have been demolished long ago, wiped off the map, and replaced with something better.

Jeanette's house was right opposite the local shop, which had its good and bad side. Not the shop itself: that had four bad sides, all of them grey concrete with graffiti on.

But having your house right near the shop: there was a good side to that. Jeanette could send Tim out for a carton of milk and a sack of frozen chips and watch him through the window in case he got attacked. The bad side was that the shop was a magnet for the estate's worst violence.

'Look, Mum: police!', Tim would say almost every evening, pointing through the window at the flashing blue lights and the commotion just across the road.

'Finish your supper', she would tell him, but he would keep on watching through the big dirty rectangle of glass.

'What are police for?' Tim had asked her once.

'They keep us nice and safe, pet', she'd replied automatically. But deep down, she had no faith in the boys in blue, or in the zealous busybodies who tried to get her interested in Neighbourhood Watch schemes. It was all just an excuse for coffee mornings where other powerless people just like herself complained about their awful neighbours and then got shirty about who was paying for the biscuits.

Positive action, they called it. Jeanette much preferred to buy lottery scratchcards, which might at least get her out of Rusborough South, if she was lucky.

For more on narrative structure, see pages 37–40

## Getting started

It is a good idea to do some warm-up activities before starting on your short story. A good way to practise and develop your skills is to begin with flash fiction.

Flash fiction or micro fiction means short pieces of writing, usually less than 500 words, that give a snapshot and create a scene or atmosphere. Flash fiction can be in any genre and can blend genres. If you experience something which makes an impact on you, you can capture it in flash-fiction form. The word limit means that you will have to select carefully.

## Activity 5 | Writing flash fiction

Practise writing flash fiction of between 250 and 500 words. Your market would probably be a magazine or even a newspaper. In many cities free newspapers are distributed for commuters to read while travelling to work. Your flash fiction could be included for a quick and easy read.

## Activity 6 | Choosing a title

**Pair work**

The title of your short story is important and this needs to intrigue the audience immediately. Below are the titles of the stories from which Texts A–F were taken but they are in a random order. Try to connect the titles to the stories: this could involve a brief analysis of the extracts.

- The Eyes of the Soul
- The Werewolf
- The Room
- Butterflies
- Getting Him Taped
- A Wife in a Million

## Activity 7 | Developing a short story

Choose one or more of Texts A–F and consider how it might develop. Try to write in the style and keep to the narrative perspective of the original text you have chosen. You could add another one or two paragraphs.

# What makes a short story successful?

It has to grip the reader or listener immediately. It needs pace. It needs some of these ingredients

- immediately recognisable characters
- a strong sense of place/location
- an element of conflict
- realistic dialogue.

In the words of crime-writer Ian Rankin,

'A short story should unsettle, provoke and explore. It has to convince that it would have happened, or might be happening right now.'

Now you should feel ready to tackle a more substantial piece of writing. Begin by reading the following extract. It is from a short story which features an interesting approach to narrative perspective (from Deborah Moggach's *Changing Babies*, 1996).

Duncan was only little, but he noticed more than they thought. He knew, for instance, when the phone rang and it was his Dad on the other end, because his mother always got out her cigarettes. She only smoked when his Dad phoned up.

He knew Christmas was coming, but everybody knew that. In the shops tinsel was strewn over microwave cookers. There was a crib at school, with a black baby in it.

It was his Granny who told him the Christmas story. She said that the birth of Jesus was a miracle, and that Joseph wasn't his real father. God was.

He liked being with his Granny. She watched TV with him, sitting on the sofa; and she wasn't always doing something else. She kept photos of him in a proper book, with dates under his name, instead of all muddled loose in a drawer. She smelt of powder. She wasn't always talking on the phone. Nowadays, she came to his house a lot to babysit. Before he went to bed, she made him say his prayers.

His Mum didn't pray; she did exercises. Once he went into her bedroom and she was kneeling down. He thought she was praying for his Dad to come home but she said she was tightening her stomach muscles. He often got things wrong; there were so many big, tiring adjustments he had to make. Anyway, she didn't want his Dad back. She was always on the phone to her friends. 'He never thought of *my* needs', she said.

'He's so cut off from his feelings, so bloody self-absorbed. It would take a miracle to change him'.

But Christmas was a time of miracles, wasn't it? That was the point.

His Dad had moved into a flat with a metal thing on the door which his voice squawked through. His mother would stand there in the street, shouting at its little slits. She never came in. The hall smelt of school dinners. The flat smelt of new paint.

Duncan visited his Dad twice a week. He slept on the sofa. Its cushion had a silky fringe which he sucked before he went to sleep. His Dad talked on the phone a lot, too.

When he had finished he would take him out. If it was raining they went to the swimming baths. If it wasn't raining, they went to the Zoo. Duncan knew every corner of the Zoo, even the places hardly anyone ever went, like the cages where boring brown birds stayed hidden.

Christmas was getting nearer. He went shopping with his Dad and they bought a very small Christmas tree. They walked past office buildings. Old men sat in the doorways, their heads poking out of cardboard boxes. 'Huh, they've been thrown out too', said his Dad. Duncan kept quiet. He wanted to ask his Dad if he was coming back for Christmas but he didn't dare.

They stood at the bus stop. When he was with his Dad they were always waiting for things. For a waitress to come when they sat in a café. For the bus, because his Dad didn't have a car.

'At school', Duncan said, 'we've got a black baby Jesus'.

'Very p.c.' laughed his Dad, whatever that meant. Pee-see?

'Last Christmas there was a pink one'. He was suddenly conscious of the stretch of time, since a year had passed. What had happened to the pink baby? It couldn't have grown older like he had. It was just pretend. Had they thrown it away? But it was supposed to be Jesus.

The bus came at last. They got out at the late-night supermarket. It was called Payless but his Dad called it Paymore. They bought some Jaffa cakes. Back in the flat, the phone was ringing. It wasn't his mother; his Dad didn't turn his back and lower his voice. He spoke quite normally.

'… they've had to re-edit the whole damn thing', he said. 'Nobody told them at Channel Four. It'll take another four weeks. Frank's incensed'.

Frankincense! The word billowed out, magically.

His father was still talking. Duncan had sucked the chocolate off his Jaffa cake. He dozed on the sofa. To tell the truth, it was way past his bedtime, but he wasn't saying anything. He closed his eyes.

His father, wearing a flowing robe, knocked on the door on Christmas Day. He would come and visit, carrying gold and frankincense. He would come.

The next morning he was back home. After lunch his mother took him swimming.

At the pool they had a struggle with his water wings. He said he was too old for them now. She liked him to wear them because he could bob around in the water while he swam to the deep bit, up and down for miles. She said she had to do a unit of exercise a day, which meant twenty minutes. She told somebody on the phone it was part of her Cosmopolitan Shape-Up Plan. 'I'm going to take care of my body', she said.

'It's had years of neglect. It's like one of those old churches nobody's been into for years'. She laughed loudly at this, but he didn't see why it was funny.

He bobbed up and down in the water. A sticking plaster floated nearby. He liked collecting sticking plasters and lining them up at the edge of the pool. In fact, he loved everything about the pool. When he came with his parents they used to laugh together and splash each other. They mucked around like children. There was a shallow, baby's bit and an elephant slide. In the deeper bit a whistle blew and the waves started, which was thrilling. He liked wearing the rubber band with the locker key on it; this made him feel important. There was a machine where you could buy crisps.

He loved going there. That was why it was so terrible, what happened.

This particular day he had got dressed. His mother was drying her hair. In the corner of the changing room he saw something he hadn't seen before: it was a big red plastic thing, on legs, like a crib. He nudged his Mum and pointed. 'What's that for?' he shouted. She switched off the dryer. 'What's what for?'

'That', he pointed. 'Oh, it's for changing babies', she said and switched on the dryer again.

That night his Mum went out and his Granny came to babysit. She tut-tutted around the house as usual. She opened the fridge and wrinkled her nose. 'Jiff and a J-cloth', she said. 'That's all it needs. But they're all too busy nowadays, aren't they?'

Then she sat with him while he ate his supper. 'You're very quiet', she said. 'I know what you're thinking about! All the things you'd like for Christmas!' He didn't reply.

'Come on, poppet, aren't you going to eat up your lovely fish fingers?'

Later she washed up. Usually the clatter comforted him. Tonight it didn't work. He was thinking about the red plastic crib. Which babies did it change? Any baby that climbed into it? If his mother put him there, what would happen? At school they had taken away the old baby and put in another one. His mother was always changing things. Granny's presents, for instance. Granny gave her clothes and she took them back to Harvey Nichols. And only last week she had looked at her bed as if she had never seen it before. 'Paisley's so seventies', she said. She had yanked off the duvet cover and squashed it into a rubbish bag.

His head spun. When his Granny was getting him ready for bed he said. 'Tell me about Jesus in the manger again'.

Undressing him, she told him the story. He squeezed his eyes shut. 'Virgin Mary', he heard 'wrapped him in swaddling clothes and laid him in a manger'.

She took him to the bathroom to brush his teeth. He suddenly saw the carrier bag, from swimming. It sat slumped in the corner, bulging with his damp towel and swimming trunks. The bag had big letters on it. VIRGIN MEGASTORE. He stared at it, hypnotised. Swaddling clothes ... Virgin Mary. He tried to work it out but it was all so difficult. What was wrapped up in swaddling clothes, lying in the Virgin bag? Did he ever dare unwrap it?

His mother tried to make him go swimming on Tuesday after school, but he refused to go. He knew exactly what she was planning. She was going to wrap him up in a towel and put him in the crib. Jesus had no father, just like him.

He heard his mother on the phone, talking to one of her friends.

'I know why Duncan doesn't want to go swimming', she whispered. 'It's because his father goes and we sometimes see him there. When he sees his father unexpectedly, he gets really upset.'

She had got it all wrong, of course, about swimming. Grown-ups got everything wrong. But he couldn't possibly tell her. He started crying so she took him out to buy a Christmas tree instead. It was much bigger than Dad's. They decorated it with tinsel and bags of chocolate money but when she switched the lights on they didn't work. She shouted a rude word. Then she muttered. 'First the washing machine, then the guttering, now the bloody lights. Christ, I need a man!' She looked as if she was about to cry too. She went to the phone and dialled a number. 'Is Mr Weisman home yet?' she asked. 'I've been phoning him for two days'.

Duncan stopped peeling a chocolate coin. He sat bolt upright. Mr Wise Man?

## Writing tasks

### Write a short story

1   The story about Duncan is told from the point of view of a child: we are shown the adult world through his eyes and we share his misunderstandings and fears. We leave the story where Duncan is scared and is unable to explain his fears to the adults in his life. There are many different ways in which the story could end.

    Write the rest of the story.

2   Write a short story in any genre that would appeal to young adults.

3   Write a short story to be read to young people. If you choose this option you will need to think carefully about phonological techniques and choice of lexis.

# Writing features for magazines

Features are different from news stories as they deal with ongoing issues rather than immediate reporting of an event which has just taken place. Features appear in magazines and newspaper supplements. People who choose to read features are prepared to spend more time on a more detailed read.

The grid on page 225 summarises some of the differences between news stories and features.

| News stories | Features |
| --- | --- |
| immediate | ongoing and planned in advance |
| informative | discursive |
| quick paced and economical | longer paragraphs |
| limited space | more space for texts and visuals |
| for skim reading | for more detailed, concentrated reading |

## Activity 8

Read the following feature which appeared on a 'Your opinion' website aimed at an audience of 16–21 year olds. What do you think are the characteristics of the article that would appeal to its target audience?

Compare your ideas with the commentary on page 233.

### MOSQUITO MENACE
### Buzz off if you're under 25

What's all the fuss in the media about the mosquito device?

The device, which makes a persistent high-pitched whine, is only audible to those under the age of 25. It's used to disperse groups of young people who have gathered in a public place – the idea being that this will lessen opportunities for noisy, anti-social or criminal behaviour. However, some people are now objecting to the device on the grounds that it infringes human rights. The Children's Commissioner for England, Sir Albert Aynsley-Green, has called for it to be banned and he is supported by the human rights group, Liberty. Liberty's director, Shami Chakrabarti, called it 'a sonic weapon directed against children and young people'.

### SHOULD WE BE CONCERNED?
Yes. You might be surprised to know that this device has been installed at approximately 3,500 locations across the country. So watch out – there may be one coming to a shopping street near you!

What it means in practice is that anyone in the under-25 age-group is vulnerable and will be affected by the noise, regardless of who they are or what they are doing.

So imagine you are a young parent pushing your baby through your local shopping centre where one of these 'mosquitos' is installed – you will be able to hear the noise and so will your baby. Surely the use of this device could create a division in our society by demonising young people. Imagine what would happen if a similar device was invented to target all people over 60, all people of one gender or all people with red hair.

### KIDS FIGHT BACK
An ironic twist to the story is that the mosquito sound can be downloaded as a ringtone onto mobile phones. As it is teacher-proof (apart from those young enough to be straight from Uni) it causes confusion and disruption in the classroom.

**YOUR OPINION**

Why are we being stereotyped in this way? I am not a hoodie or a hooligan but I do want to walk through the streets of my local town without being subjected to a form of torture. Society needs to come up with ways of confronting and tackling those who litter, loiter and terrorise rather than introducing tactics reminiscent of Orwell's '1984'.

Mark, 19, Birmingham

## Writing tasks

## Write a magazine feature article

As an alternative to writing a news story you could choose a current topic of interest about which you feel strongly and write an article similar to the example in Activity 8. You will need to research the market to choose a suitable publication for your writing.

This suggested structure for a feature article should help you with your planning.

■ **Introduction** – sets the scene or introduces the topic quickly.

- **Development** – paragraphs are linked together to develop different ideas and aspects.
- **Argument and counter-argument** – opposing viewpoints are explained to provide different perspectives.
- **Conclusion** – ideas are consolidated or brought together. If possible, try to finish your article with a reference back to the starting-point to give your text a more cohesive, cyclical structure.

# Writing popular-science articles

## What is popular science?

To remind yourself of this genre look back at page 71 and reread the extract from David King's speech on climate change (on page 72). Popular science is concerned with discussing contemporary or historical global issues. It should be accessible to the non-specialist and should employ strategies to intrigue and interest a wide general audience.

**Activity 9** **Identifying characteristics of popular science**

Read the following extract from *Almost Like a Whale* (2001), which is a new, updated version of Darwin's *Origin of Species* (1859). The book's jacket blurb claims that it 'Explains the workings of evolution as they are understood with beautiful clarity and, naturally, with a lot more fun and jokes than Darwin ever allowed himself'. How far would you agree with this description?

What is it about this text that would make it of interest to the ordinary reader? What would make it 'popular'? You should consider

- the choice of topic
- the tone or voice of the writer
- the strategies used to involve the reader.

Compare your response with the commentary on page 233.

### Variation Under Domestication
Man has a strange relationship with his domestic animals.

The Victorian explorer William Burchell found himself unable to eat zebra when he was near starvation in Africa, because of its resemblance to his favourite mare. The French government, alarmed by the waste of good protein, had managed in the 1860s to persuade its citizens to feed on horse, but in London, the Society for the Propagation of Horse Flesh as an Article of Food failed in the endeavour, in spite of a launch banquet of Salmon with Racehorse Sauce, Filet of Pegasus, and, to follow, a *Gateau Veterinaire*.

Even so, at about that time, the 'Live Stock Journal and Fancier's Gazette' complained that 'in some parts of England cats are not wholly despised as an article of diet' and that a notorious gang of cat eaters in West Bromwich meant that fanciers 'cannot keep a favourite a week'.

Animals, as they become domestic, enter an uncertain domain between the real and the artificial. They persuade man to accept the living world as part of himself, promoted from food to member of the family. In the Middle Ages pigs were tried and hanged for murder, and only forty years ago a female rhinoceros was elected, by a large majority, to the Sao Paulo City

Council. In an equal confusion today, a third of all dog owners are happy to identify their pet as closer to their heart than is anyone else in the household.

As the wilderness creeps into the home, boundaries that were once distinct become blurred. Greeks, Egyptians and Icelanders each had sacred gods – Cerberus, Anubis and Garm – to guard the entrance to the next world. In them, and in William Burchell's mare, the wild undergoes a spiritual transformation beyond the reach of science.

## Activity 10    Making science popular

Now that you have established some of the characteristics of the popular-science genre, read the following text and identify the strategies used to involve and interest the reader. This text is a 'MetroCosmos' article: a regular feature on science and discovery which appears in a daily newspaper distributed free to commuters.

Compare your findings with the commentary on page 233.

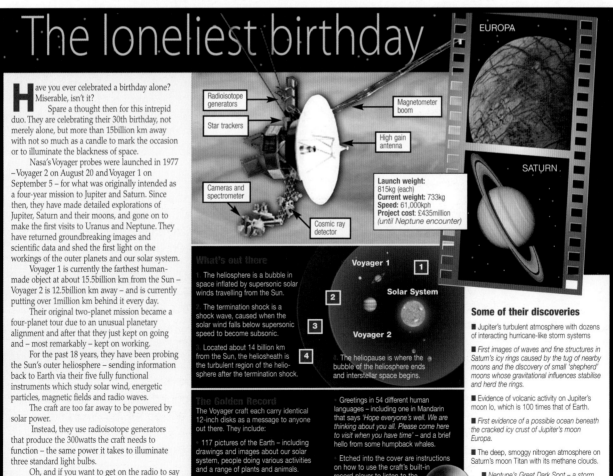

# The loneliest birthday

Have you ever celebrated a birthday alone? Miserable, isn't it?

Spare a thought then for this intrepid duo. They are celebrating their 30th birthday, not merely alone, but more than 15billion km away with not so much as a candle to mark the occasion or to illuminate the blackness of space.

Nasa's Voyager probes were launched in 1977 – Voyager 2 on August 20 and Voyager 1 on September 5 – for what was originally intended as a four-year mission to Jupiter and Saturn. Since then, they have made detailed explorations of Jupiter, Saturn and their moons, and gone on to make the first visits to Uranus and Neptune. They have returned groundbreaking images and scientific data and shed the first light on the workings of the outer planets and our solar system.

Voyager 1 is currently the farthest human-made object at about 15.5billion km from the Sun – Voyager 2 is 12.5billion km away – and is currently putting over 1million km behind it every day.

Their original two-planet mission became a four-planet tour due to an unusual planetary alignment and after that they just kept on going and – most remarkably – kept on working.

For the past 18 years, they have been probing the Sun's outer heliosphere – sending information back to Earth via their five fully functional instruments which study solar wind, energetic particles, magnetic fields and radio waves.

The craft are too far away to be powered by solar power.

Instead, they use radioisotope generators that produce the 300watts the craft needs to function – the same power it takes to illuminate three standard light bulbs.

Oh, and if you want to get on the radio to say happy birthday it will take the signal 13.8 hours – at light speed –to get there.

EUROPA

Radioisotope generators

Star trackers

Magnetometer boom

High gain antenna

Cameras and spectrometer

Cosmic ray detector

**Launch weight:** 815kg (each)
**Current weight:** 733kg
**Speed:** 61,000kph
**Project cost:** £435million
*(until Neptune encounter)*

SATURN

### What's out there

1. The heliosphere is a bubble in space inflated by supersonic solar winds travelling from the Sun.

2. The termination shock is a shock wave, caused when the solar wind falls below supersonic speed to become subsonic.

3. Located about 14 billion km from the Sun, the heliosheath is the turbulent region of the heliosphere after the termination shock.

Voyager 1

Solar System

Voyager 2

4. The heliopause is where the bubble of the heliosphere ends and interstellar space begins.

### Some of their discoveries

■ Jupiter's turbulent atmosphere with dozens of interacting hurricane-like storm systems

■ *First images of waves and fine structures in Saturn's icy rings caused by the tug of nearby moons and the discovery of small 'shepherd' moons whose gravitational influences stabilise and herd the rings.*

■ Evidence of volcanic activity on Jupiter's moon Io, which is 100 times that of Earth.

■ *First evidence of a possible ocean beneath the cracked icy crust of Jupiter's moon Europa.*

■ The deep, smoggy nitrogen atmosphere on Saturn's moon Titan with its methane clouds.

■ *Neptune's Great Dark Spot – a storm with 1,600kph (1,000mph) winds.*

### The Golden Record

The Voyager craft each carry identical 12-inch disks as a message to anyone out there. They include:

• 117 pictures of the Earth – including drawings and images about our solar system, people doing various activities and a range of plants and animals.

• Sounds from Earth – ranging from storms and volcanoes to rocket launches and animals.

• Greetings in 54 different human languages – including one in Mandarin that says 'Hope everyone's well. We are thinking about you all. Please come here to visit when you have time' – and a brief hello from some humpback whales.

• Etched into the cover are instructions on how to use the craft's built-in record player to listen to the recording and how to decipher the images.

Your exploration of the texts in this section should have helped you to see how scientific topics and issues can be made accessible by using effective literary, linguistic and structural techniques. This genre can be made relevant, interesting and intriguing for the non-scientist and the casual reader through a careful balance of the informative, educational and entertaining aspects.

## Writing tasks

### Write a popular-science article

Choose a topic that is of interest to you and about which you feel that you have some knowledge and enthusiasm – for example, inventions, space exploration, the solar system, or environmental and global topics such as climate change, ecological issues and pandemics.

1 Write a short article for publication in a newspaper or magazine aimed at a specific target readership – for example, young adults, people travelling to work. Aim to write approximately 300 words.

2 Write the script for a presentation to either a group of students and tutors at a college or a class of primary-school children aged 9–10.

3 Design your own task by choosing your own target audience and mode – for example, spoken presentation, radio item, extended news item, article in specific publication.

Remember that the quality of your writing will be assessed according to the way that you present the scientific facts and information in an accessible manner.

You will need to

- write concisely
- decide how to create a short, cohesive text
- use strategies to interest and involve your readers/listeners in some way.

## Review

The first seven sections of this chapter have given you some ideas about writing in different genres and should help you to choose suitable writing tasks for your coursework folder. Some popular examples have been featured but there are others that could be considered. Look back at Chapter 2 (pages 49–96) if you need further ideas.

Do read a range of texts in the genres in which you choose to write. They should stimulate your imagination and may give you good ideas about approaches, style and topics, but the work you produce must, of course, be original and should have your own special voice.

### Coursework tips

- Avoid any tasks that are too formulaic and easily replicated.
- If you are asked to include more than one piece in your coursework folder, you will need to ensure that there is variety in your choice of audiences, purposes and topics.
- Don't be afraid to try out ideas and then leave them if they don't work – this may take time but any writing you do is useful practice.
- Be patient until you have found something you really want to write about.

# Drafting and editing

Drafting and editing are essential processes for any original work or creative writing. No writer is ever completely satisfied with their first attempt and you will find that you will need to redraft your work.

There are three stages in text production

1 planning
2 writing a draft
3 reading, redrafting and editing.

## Drafting

The number of drafts you are asked to produce will depend on the particular examination specification that you are studying: your tutor will advise you about this.

When you have completed your first draft you need to reread it, approaching it as if you are doing an analysis by asking yourself questions about it. It is important that you read the text from the perspective of a totally new reader: if possible, allow a short time gap between finishing your first draft and rereading it. You need to imagine that you have never seen it before.

You will no doubt have some feedback from your tutor but you can prepare yourself by asking yourself the following questions.

- Does your text fulfil your original purpose?
- Does it have a logical structure with signposts for the reader or listener to lead them through the text?
- Have you chosen an appropriate register to address your target audience and is it consistent?
- Have you established the type of relationship with your reader or listener that you were trying to achieve?
- Have you incorporated any good ideas about effective stylistic approaches that you gained from your reading of stimulus texts?
- Is your writing technically accurate with clear paragraphing, well-constructed sentences and accurate punctuation and spelling?

You are really asking yourself

- Does your text work?
- Do you like your text and find it interesting to read?

Next test the market. If possible try out your text on a member of the target audience and incorporate their comments into your redrafting.

To help you with the redrafting process you should now have

- feedback from your tutor
- your own reflections on your work in response to the questions above
- some suggestions from a member of the target audience.

Keep copies of your drafts as they will provide a record of the changes you have made – you will need this information when writing up your commentary. You can track the changes by using the tools option on your computer

- click on the tools option
- highlight 'track changes'.

You could then classify the changes into

- lexical
- syntactical
- orthographical
- rhetorical (changing the impact on the audience).

## Editing

You will be given an approximate word count for each piece of original writing. Students often find it difficult to keep within the word count but editing is an important practical skill and the following guidance will help you make decisions about how and where to edit. Often, this does not have to mean cutting sections of content but involves looking at your work critically to see how it can be rewritten more concisely and precisely.

Be concise.

- Avoid irrelevant material or unnecessarily lengthy explanations.
- Avoid repetition unless it is used deliberately as a rhetorical device.
- Avoid vague and pointless words like 'quite' and 'almost'.

Check that you have used varied vocabulary and if you have used the same word too frequently look for alternatives.

Watch your style.

- Don't be tempted to make excessive use of exclamations and rhetorical questions – instead think of effective words and phrases to convey your mood.
- Don't use clichés – these are overworked phrases which have lost all impact, such as 'slowly but surely', 'last but not least'.

It is important to ensure that your work has pace.

# Writing the commentary

You will be asked to write a commentary on your own texts. However satisfied you are with your original writing it is important to produce a successful commentary. The purpose of the commentary is to explain the process of your writing and how you made your decisions. It is, in fact, an analysis of your own work but you will be adopting a different perspective as you will be writing from the viewpoint of the author rather than the reader or listener.

It is important to produce a coherent, structured commentary but you must avoid using a rigid checklist as this will restrict you. You could organise your work under the following headings but be flexible and introduce other headings and subheadings where they are needed.

- **Purpose** of your text
- **Intended audience**
- **Genre** – newspaper, magazine, radio, speech, etc.
- **How you attempted to establish a relationship with your audience** – any use of involvement strategies such as personal pronouns, direct address, questions and imperatives, intertextual references or assumption of shared knowledge
- **Lexical choices and their** connotations – words chosen to have a particular effect, use of specialist or context-bound lexis
- Grammatical **choices** – sentence types and their functions, use of foregrounded conjunctions for emphasis, minor sentences, present tense to create immediacy.
- **Phonological and rhetorical devices** (for both spoken and written texts) – repetition, alliteration, assonance, parallel structures, use of rhetorical questions,

interrogatives, imperatives, imitation of speech features, colloquial language, idiomatic phrases, use of quoted speech.

- Cohesion/**structure** or how you guide the reader through your text – paragraphing, use of discourse markers like adverbials to act as time markers.

Use frequent, brief quotations from your text to exemplify the points that you make.

Make use of linguistic and literary terminology when appropriate but take care to ensure that you are being precise and accurate. You should use technical terms too because they enable you to make your points in the clearest way possible so you need to be confident about their meaning. The glossary at the end of the book should be helpful.

## Commentary don'ts

- Do not make negative comments by writing about what you did not do.
- Avoid repetition and over-lengthy quotations.
- Do not simply list or label features but explain their precise purpose and intended effect – what you wanted the audience to think or feel or how you wanted them to respond.
- Avoid the temptation to include technical terms purely as a demonstration of knowledge – they must be relevant to your analysis of your own work.
- Do not evaluate your own work by saying how good you think it is or by pointing out the defects, although you may wish to comment on problems that you encountered and how you dealt with them.

To assist you in writing your commentary, keep a record in note form of the decisions and the changes that you make while you are planning, writing and revising your text.

And a final point: although you will be writing your commentary in the first person, this is a formal piece of work so you will need to write in an appropriate style.

**Review**

In this section you have explored

- the purpose of your commentary
- how to classify and organise your material for the commentary
- how to present your commentary.

You have also been given advice on good practice.

**Commentary**

**Activity 1**

Both texts highlight important features of their subject (the concert and the book). They offer a personal response but they also evaluate the quality of the performance or writing – they look at both good and less successful parts.

There is an assumption that the audience will share some of the writers' knowledge – for example, the specialist lexis and references to album names in Text A and references to characters in *Hamlet* in Text B.

The enthusiasm of both writers for their subject is also obvious.

These two reviews have the following purposes

- to provide information clearly and concisely
- to evaluate
- to offer personal opinions and feelings
- and, of course, to entertain their readers.

**Commentary**

**Activity 2**

This table provides a quick comparison of the two texts.

| Text A | Text B |
|---|---|
| Spoken | Written |
| First person | Third person |
| Colloquial, elliptical style – 'Saw him off and on with Sarah' | Formal register |
| Vague and inexplicit – 'just so sort of amazed' | Some lengthy sentences – 'The Prince, who brought along his favourite Labrador...' |
| Pronoun 'he' to refer to Prince Charles | Lengthy noun phrase – 'the world's most eligible bachelor' |
| Personal idiolect – 'frightfully excited', 'twigged on to' | Professional and detached |
| Lots of quoted speech | Some quoted speech used selectively |
| Self-critical | More distanced and objective |
| 'Saw him off and on with Sarah' | '...it was noticeable that Sarah was enthusiastic in her attentions' |

**How effective are Texts A and B?**

Text A would work well as part of a television programme where the viewer would have visual cues. It has a lively, engaging and intimate tone but it is far less effective for a reading audience as it has some vague, inexplicit references, elliptical statements and shifts in register (which are all natural features of spontaneous speech).

Text B is much more structured and has clearly been edited and rewritten. It provides all the necessary grammatical links and cues needed by a reading audience.

Your study of these two texts should have demonstrated how raw data can be shaped and crafted to produce an interesting and readable biography.

**Commentary**

**Activity 4**

Text A has a clear structure in a question/answer format with each topic paragraph starting with an emboldened question which is then answered below.

The writer adopts a conversational tone and establishes an informal relationship with the reader by employing language features such as minor sentences, elision and parenthetical structures to include more information economically.

The tone is direct, reassuring and somewhat persuasive in suggesting that problems can be dealt with.

Text B develops this into continuous prose, although maintaining the friendly nature of the relationship with the reader. The persuasive element can be seen in the enthusiastic voice of the writer in providing encouragement to the reader to travel alone. This is supported by an 'expert' case study which gives a first-person experience.

**Commentary**

**Activity 8**

The subject chosen here is topical, controversial and relevant to a young audience. The writer introduces it, outlines the issues and includes a reader's response. Use of expert evidence adds authority, with quoted speech from the Children's Commissioner and the Director of Liberty, and factual details are integrated.

The writer uses several strategies to involve the reader, e.g. rhetorical questions, second-person direct address, putting the reader into an imaginary scenario. The literary reference to '1984' and the subversion of the popular-culture reference 'coming to a cinema near you' assume shared knowledge. The register is relatively informal, particularly in the sub-heading 'Kids Fight Back', and there is humour in the account of the subversive use of the ringtone. The 'Your Opinion' section adds the dimension of immediate audience response.

**Commentary**

**Activity 9**

These are the features of the text which identify it as popular science

- a potentially complex topic is related to familiar situations
- animals are personified, suggesting manipulation of man – 'They persuade man'
- it subverts the reader's expectations by introducing elements of the absurd – 'pigs were tried and hanged'
- the mock French menu is incongruous as it is a departure from the reader's preconceptions
- it appeals to popular European culture and sentiment – 'dog owners are happy to identify their pet as closer to their heart'
- use of lexis from the Ancient World evokes a sense of mystery – 'Pegasus'
- it implies intriguing and strange concepts – 'beyond the reach of science'.

**Commentary**

**Activity 10**

Strategies used in the 'MetroCosmos' article to interest the reader are

- the topic of the solar system is one of general interest
- the reader is immediately involved with a personal question – 'Have you ever celebrated a birthday alone?'
- the text establishes cohesion with the use of the extended metaphor of the birthday
- the Voyager probes are personified with lively human qualities – 'this intrepid duo'
- scientific fact is made accessible by being embedded in a type of human-interest story
- a relaxed, familiar tone is maintained throughout
- lengthy sentences and parenthetical statements are made more accessible with the use of dashes, avoiding the more formal brackets, commas and colons: this gives the impression of pacier reading
- hyphens are used to link pre-modifiers – 'two-planet mission', 'four-planet tour'
- graphological and layout features complement the main text with the use of pictures, captions, numbered and bullet-pointed fact files
- the article concludes with a reference back to the birthday motif, providing an effective cyclical link and returning to the tone of light humour used in the introduction.

Although this is a written publication the material could easily be reshaped to make it suitable for an item on a morning or evening television news bulletin.

# Creating New Texts from Old

6

**At the end of this chapter you should be able to**

- demonstrate detailed critical understanding in analysing the ways in which structure, form and language shape meanings in a range of spoken and written texts (AO2)

- use integrated approaches to explore relationships between texts, analysing and evaluating the significance of contextual factors in their production and reception (AO3)

- demonstrate expertise and creativity in using language appropriately for a variety of purposes and audiences, drawing on insights from linguistic and literary studies (AO4).

For a more student-friendly version of these Assessment Objectives, turn to page vii in the Introduction.

## What is text transformation?

In this chapter, we are going to look at some of the most interesting ways in which you can respond to your reading of literary texts. This will build on much of what you have already learnt about how readers react to and think about texts; at the same time it will show how you can use your knowledge of language and genre to respond creatively to what you have read and enjoyed. You will learn how to produce pieces of original writing that are not only pleasurable to read in their own right, but which also give illuminating insights into some familiar (and some not so familiar) works of fiction, drama and poetry. You will learn how to transform literary texts into different genres and, in the process, show readers more about the original text through the interaction and interplay between what you have written and the original. Some Language & Literature specifications refer to this as text transformation.

| Activity 1 | Imitation: the sincerest form? |
|---|---|
| Group work | Read these two texts. Text A is the very familiar Christmas story, taken from the Gospels of St Luke and St Matthew in the King James version of the Bible, published in 1611. Text B is a reworking of the story as it might have been reported in the *Sun* on 28 December AD 1. |

## Text A

And it came to pass in those days, that there went out a decree from Caesar Augustus, that all the world should be taxed. (And this taxing was first made when Cyrenius was governor of Syria.) And all went to be taxed, every one into his own city. And Joseph also went up from Galilee, out of the city of Nazareth, into Judaea, unto the city of David which is called Bethlehem; (because he was of the house and lineage of David:) to be taxed with Mary his espoused wife, being great with child. And so it was that, while they were there, the days were accomplished that she should be delivered. And she brought forth her first-born son, and wrapped him in swaddling clothes, and laid him in a manger; because there was no room for them at the inn. And there were in the same country shepherds abiding in the field, keeping watch over their flock by night. And, lo, the angel of the Lord came upon them, and the glory of the Lord shone about them: and they were sore afraid. And the angel said unto them, Fear not: for behold, I bring you tidings of great joy, which shall be unto all people. For unto you is born this day in the city of David a Saviour, which is Christ the Lord. And this shall be a sign unto you; Ye shall find the babe wrapped in swaddling clothes, lying in a manger. And suddenly there was with the angel a multitude of the heavenly host praising God and saying, glory to God in the highest, and on earth, peace, good will toward men. And it came to pass, as the angels were gone away from them into heaven the shepherds said one to another, Let us now go even unto Bethlehem, and see this thing which has come to pass, which the Lord hath made known unto us. And they came with haste and found Mary and Joseph, and the babe lying in a manger. *(St Luke's Gospel)*

Now when Jesus was born in Bethlehem of Judaea in the days of Herod the king, behold, there came wise men from the east to Jerusalem, saying Where is he that is born King of the Jews? For we have seen his star in the east, and are come to worship him. When Herod the king had heard these things, he was troubled and all Jerusalem with him. And when he had gathered all the chief priests and scribes of the people together, he demanded of them where Christ should be born. And they said unto him, in Bethlehem, in the land of Juda: for thus it is written by the prophet, 'And thou Bethlehem, in the land of Juda, art not the least among the princes of Juda, for out of thee shall come a Governor, that shall rule my people Israel.' Then Herod, when he had privily called the wise men, enquired of them diligently what time the star appeared. And then he sent them to Bethlehem, and said, 'Go and search diligently for the young child; and when ye have found him, bring word to me again, that I may come and worship him also.' When they had heard the king, they departed; and, lo, the star, which they saw in the east, went before them, till it came and stood over where the young child was. When they saw the star, they rejoiced with exceeding great joy. And when they came into the house, they saw the young child with Mary his mother, and fell down, and worshipped him: and when they had opened their treasures, they presented unto him gifts; gold, and frankincense, and myrrh. And being warned of God in a dream that they should not return to Herod, they departed into their own country another way. *(St Matthew's Gospel)*

**Text B**

# A STAR IS BORN

## Messiah claim as virgin has baby in stable By FRANK INCENSE

A BABY born to a virgin mother was last night claimed to be the Son of God and the saviour of mankind.

He was discovered in a lowly cattle shed by three Wise Men who said an unusually bright star led them there.

They were so overwhelmed when they found the tot, named Jesus, they bowed down and handed him gold, frankincense and myrrh.

The baby was wrapped in cloth and lying in a manger, which his mum Mary and dad Joseph were using as a makeshift cot.

The stable was at the back of an inn in Bethlehem, Judaea. It is believed the couple had to deliver the child there because the inn was chock-a-block with people in town for a census the Romans ordered.

**SWADDLING**

The baby was first found by a group of shepherds who said an angel tipped them off to his whereabouts when they were watching over their flocks by night.

The angel told the terrified men: 'Fear not – I bring you great joy. For unto you is born this day in the city of David a Saviour, which is Christ the Lord.

'Ye shall find the babe wrapped in swaddling clothes, in a manger.'

The Wise Men behind yesterday's claims were sent to track down the baby by King Herod after he heard a new King of the Jews had been born. He is privately terrified of being ousted.

***Herod: My Nightmare*** Pages 4 and 5

---

Now discuss these questions.

1　Which parts of the story as told in the Bible have the writers of the *Sun* version retained? Which have been discarded? Can you suggest any reasons for these decisions? (NB The reference to Mary being a virgin, which is not in this extract from the Bible, is found in earlier verses in St Matthew's Gospel.)

2　What changes to the order of events as narrated in the Bible have the writers of the *Sun* version made? Why do you think the order has been changed?

3　What changes to the biblical language have been made in the *Sun* version? What is the effect of these changes? Why do you think the writers chose to retain some of the original language of the angel to the shepherds?

4　What other features of the transformed text are typical of the *Sun*? You may need to check these genre features that the writers have included by looking at the front page of a recent edition.

Turn to page 281 for a commentary on this activity.

You should now be in a position to do some *Sun* writing of your own. You could write Herod's 'My Nightmare' that is to appear on pages 4 and 5 or transform your own choice of Bible story into a *Sun* version. If you choose the Herod story, you will find it useful first to read the continuation of the story in St Matthew's Gospel, chapter 3, verses 13–16.

## Refocusing

We can now move on to examine a different type of transformation. In this excerpt from Act 2, Scene 2 of *Hamlet*, the King asks Hamlet's old friends Rosencrantz and Guildenstern to find out why Hamlet's manner has changed. The King, Claudius, has swiftly married Hamlet's mother, Queen Gertrude, following the death of the previous King, who was Hamlet's father and Claudius' brother.

> **King** Welcome, dear Rosencrantz and Guildenstern!
> Moreover that we much did long to see you,
> The need we have to use you did provoke
> Our hasty sending. Something have you heard
> Of Hamlet's transformation; so call it,
> Since nor th'exterior nor the inward man
> Resembles that it was. What it should be,
> More than his father's death, that thus has put him
> So much from th'understanding of himself,
> I cannot dream of. I entreat you both,
> That, being of so young days brought up with him,
> And since so neighboured to his youth and haviour,
> That you vouchsafe your rest here in our court
> Some little time; so by your companies
> To draw him on to pleasures, and to gather
> So much as from occasion you may glean,
> Whether aught, to us unknown, afflicts him thus,
> That, opened, lies within our remedy.
>
> **Queen** Good gentlemen, he hath much talked of you;
> And I am sure two men there are not living
> To whom he more adheres. If it will please you
> To show us so much gentry and good will
> As to expend your time with us awhile,
> For the supply and profit of our hope,
> Your visitation shall receive such thanks
> As fits a king's remembrance.
>
> **Rosencrantz** Both your majesties
> Might by the sovereign power you have of us,
> Put your dread pleasures more into command
> Than to entreaty.
>
> **Guildenstern** But we both obey,
> And here give up ourselves, in the full bent,
> To lay our service freely at your feet,
> To be commanded.
>
> **King** Thanks, Rosencrantz and gentle Guildenstern.
> **Queen** Thanks, Guildenstern and gentle Rosencrantz.
> And I beseech you instantly to visit
> My too-much-changed son.

The next extract is from Tom Stoppard's play *Rosencrantz and Guildenstern Are Dead,* written in 1967. The two 'spies', having failed to speak to Hamlet as he passed by, decide to role play to see if they can get to the bottom of his 'transformation' and 'too-much-changed' state. Guildenstern is pretending to be Hamlet, responding to Rosencrantz's quick-fire questioning.

Ros  Am I pretending to be you, then?
Guil  Certainly not. If you like. Shall we continue?
Ros  Question and answer.
Guil  Right.
Ros  Right. My honoured lord!
Guil  My dear fellow!
Ros  How are you?
Guil  Afflicted.
Ros  Really? In what way?
Guil  Transformed.
Ros  Inside or out?
Guil  Both.
Ros  I see. *[Pause].* Not much new there.
Guil  Go into details. *Delve.* Probe the background, establish the situation.
Ros  So – so your uncle is the king of Denmark?!
Guil  And my father before him.
Ros  His father before him?
Guil  No, my father before him.
Ros  But surely–
Guil  You might well ask.
Ros  Let me get it straight. Your father was king. You were his only son. Your father dies. You are of age. Your uncle becomes king.
Guil  Yes
Ros  Unorthodox.
Guil  Undid me.
Ros  Undeniable. Where were you?
Guil  In Germany.
Ros  Usurpation, then.
Guil  He slipped in.
Ros  Which reminds me.
Guil  Well, it would.
Ros  I don't want to be personal.
Guil  It's common knowledge.
Ros  Your mother's marriage.
Guil  He slipped in.
Ros  *[lugubriously]* His body was still warm.
Guil  So was hers.
Ros  Extraordinary.
Guil  Indecent.
Ros  Hasty.
Guil  Suspicious.
Ros  It makes you think.
Guil  Don't think I haven't thought of it.
Ros  And with her husband's brother.
Guil  They were close.

| Ros | She went to him— |
|------|------------------|
| Guil | Too close— |
| Ros | —for comfort. |
| Guil | It looks bad. |
| Ros | It adds up. |
| Guil | Incest to adultery. |
| Ros | Would you go so far? |
| Guil | Never. |
| Ros | To sum up: your father, whom you love, dies, you are his heir, you come back to find that hardly was the corpse cold before his young brother popped onto his throne and into his sheets, thereby offending both legal and natural practice. Now why exactly are you behaving in this extraordinary manner? |
| Guil | I can't imagine. |

Clearly, this is a very different type of transformation than the one that the writers of the *Sun* version of the Nativity produced. So, just what has Tom Stoppard done to achieve this transformation? If you know *Hamlet*, then you will remember that the characters Rosencrantz and Guildenstern play a relatively small, if quite important, part in the play. They cannot, however, be regarded in any way as central characters. At best, they are 'on the fringe' of the action. In Tom Stoppard's play, this marginal pair of characters take centre stage. Stoppard, as you can tell from this extract, has transformed Rosencrantz and Guildenstern into temporary members of the Danish royal court who have too much time on their hands and are frequently trying to work out exactly what it is they are supposed to be doing. In this extract, following some comical role play, they stumble on the reasons for Hamlet's 'too-much-changed' state. One of the additional effective stratagems of the new play is that Stoppard weaves many of Shakespeare's familiar lines and some of the action into his own version, though there are no examples of this in the extract.

Tom Stoppard has shifted the centre of interest of the base text, *Hamlet*, to two minor characters. By doing this, not only has he produced a highly witty and entertaining new text that has been extremely successful both in the theatre and on film, but he has offered some stimulating new insights into the original text. If you watched or read *Hamlet* after having seen *Rosencrantz and Guildenstern Are Dead*, then it would be almost impossible to respond to Shakespeare's play in the same way as before. You would most likely be imagining Rosencrantz's and Guildenstern's inner thoughts and feelings even when they are on the edges of the main action and not speaking. It would be radically underplaying Stoppard's achievement to suggest that what he has done is to produce a piece of text transformation that would be most suitable for A level (though rather long!), but this is indeed the case. The writing of a new text that can stand on its own feet by being entertaining in its own right, whilst at the same time providing new and illuminating insights into the text on which it was based, is the essence of text transformation.

## Activity 2  Links and new perspectives

Can you find any direct verbal links between the *Hamlet* and *Rosencrantz and Guildenstern Are Dead* extracts?

What makes the exchanges between Rosencrantz and Guildenstern comic? What other genre do the exchanges remind you of?

If you know *Hamlet* well, choose another fringe character (or characters) to make the centre of the action – for instance, the Gravediggers in Act 5 or the soldiers from the first scene of the play, Bernardo, Francisco and Marcellus. You need not write a play, but could consider other possibilities and genres – for example, an e-mail or text to his girlfriend from Francisco (or perhaps a blog) after the night watch or the dialogue from a novel when the Gravediggers are discussing their day's work over a pint in the pub. Or you could choose minor characters from any play that you know well by Shakespeare or, indeed, by any other dramatist.

The two examples you have been working on illustrate two different types of text transformation. The first involved rewriting a familiar story in an incongruous and anachronistic new genre and the result was great fun, whilst at the same time providing a critically affectionate new look at the original. The second involved recentring the concerns of the base text and producing an entirely new dramatic genre, presenting audiences with new insights into the original.

## In good company

In producing pieces of text transformation for your A-level English Language & Literature course, you are following plenty of famous precedents. Text transformation is something that writers have been doing since, at least, the days of Chaucer in the fourteenth century. For example, some of his *Canterbury Tales* are reworkings of stories told by the Italian poet Boccaccio. Even Shakespeare was not averse to transforming original source material into his dramatic successes. *Antony and Cleopatra*, for instance, was based in part on a Tudor translation of the writings of a Roman historian, Plutarch.

Modern authors, too, transform texts. The poet Ted Hughes transformed some Latin originals in his *Tales from Ovid* (1997). Carol Ann Duffy retold some famous stories from the woman's point of view in *The World's Wife* (1999). For example, there is 'Pilate's Wife', in which the wife of the Roman Governor involved in the Crucifixion story gives her version of events. Or 'Frau Freud', in which the wife of the Austrian psychoanalyst tells her story. Novelists also write books which are transformations of earlier works. William Golding's famous *Lord of the Flies* is his take on R.M. Ballantine's boys' adventure story *Coral Island.* Jean Rhys told the story of Mr Rochester's first wife in *Wide Sargasso Sea,* her prequel to *Jane Eyre.* The South African novelist J.M. Coetzee rewrote Daniel Defoe's *Robinson Crusoe* in his novel *Foe* and introduced a woman into the story, adding a new dimension to the original. So you clearly are in good company when you embark on your own text transformation.

**Activity 3**  **In others' words**

**Group work**

Can you think of any other examples of text transformation by famous poets, novelists or playwrights?

**Review**

In this section you have been given the opportunity to
- become familiar with the principles of text transformation
- analyse text transformations of two famous texts
- learn that many famous authors use transformation techniques.

# Intertextuality

You may have come across this term before as it has become increasingly common in criticism. What does it mean and what is its relationship to text transformation?

Intertextuality is often said to occur when writers deliberately refer to other well-known (and not so well-known) texts in their own writing. Here, for example, is the text on the title page and the very beginning of one of the most famous poems of the twentieth century.

> ## *The Waste Land*
> ### *1922*
>
> 'Nam Sibyllam quidem Cumis ego ipse oculis meis
> vidi in ampulla pendere, et cum illi pueri dicerent:
> Σίβυλλα τί θέλεις; respondebat illa: ἀποθανεῖν θέλω.'[1]
>
> For Ezra Pound
> *Il miglior fabbro.*[2]
>
> ### *I. The Burial of the Dead*[3]
>
> April is the cruellest month, breeding
> Lilacs out of the dead land, mixing
> Memory and desire, stirring
> Dull roots with spring rain.[4]

*The Waste Land* by T.S. Eliot is famous (notorious?) for its use of quotations, allusions, references to and echoes of other works. For instance, in this brief excerpt there is

1. a quotation from the Roman writer Petronius, which translates as 'for once I myself saw with my own eyes the Sibyl at Cumae hanging in a cage, and when the boys said to her "Sibyl, what do you want?" she replied, "I want to die"'
2. a quotation (meaning 'the better craftsman') from the medieval Italian poet Dante as a tribute to Eliot's editor, the poet Ezra Pound
3. a quotation from the burial service of the Anglican Church
4. a reworking of the opening of Chaucer's *Canterbury Tales.*

There is not the space here to explain the significance of these allusions to Eliot's meanings in the poem, but they are clearly intended to add an extra dimension for readers who can pick up on them. Also, when someone who knows Eliot's poem rereads, say, *The General Prologue to the Canterbury Tales,* they will be unable to do so without thinking of *The Waste Land*. It's almost as if the two texts are having a dialogue with each other.

Not all uses of intertextuality are as mysterious as Eliot's, you'll be pleased to know. Here, for instance, is the opening of J.D. Salinger's novel *The Catcher in the Rye*:

> 'If you really want to hear about it, the first thing you'll probably want to know is where I was born, and what my lousy childhood was like, and how my parents were occupied and all before they had me, and all that David Copperfield kind of crap….'

The reference to Dickens' novel *David Copperfield,* which is, like *The Catcher in the Rye,* a first-person account of a young man's life, is a clear signal to readers that they should expect a very different type of story and narrator from the one encountered in Dickens.

The irreverence and world weariness signalled by 'crap' demonstrates this. Again, readers not familiar with *David Copperfield* will miss the full force of this intertextual reference.

So, you can see that though intertextuality has similarities to text transformation, they are not the same thing. Whereas intertextuality usually manifests itself through brief references, allusions and connections between texts, text transformation is more developed and sustained. The links with and changes to the source text in text transformation are present in order to throw light on and provide a new perspective on it (like intertextuality) but text transformation usually works on the whole of a source text or, at least, a substantial portion of it. The aim of text transformation is not only to demonstrate sophisticated interplay between the texts, but also to produce a new text that can both stand on its own feet and be entertaining in its own right.

## Text transformation: a definition

So, we have arrived at a definition of text transformation.

- A source text is chosen in order to undergo significant change.
- The transformed text must retain identifiable links with the original text.
- An aspect (or aspects) of the source text is changed and re-presented.
- The new text must provide a new insight into or perspective on the source text.
- The new text must be able to stand alone and be enjoyable for the reader.

Various aspects of a source text offer opportunities for transformation. The writer may, for example, change the following.

- **Genre** – a novel may be presented as a TV soap opera, like *Coronation Street* or *EastEnders*; a Bible story may be retold in the style of a tabloid newspaper (as on page 236).

- **Plot** – an alternative ending might be provided (as in John Fowles' novel *The French Lieutenant's Woman* or the happy ending to King Lear written in the eighteenth century by Nahum Tate in which Cordelia does not die); a text could be extended before the events represented (as in *Wide Sargasso Sea*, Jean Rhys' 'prequel' to *Jane Eyre*).

- **Mood** – a 'tough' text could be rewritten 'tenderly' or a humorous text more seriously; a text could be retold in the manner of another author. For example, *Macbeth* could be rewritten in the style of, say, Raymond Chandler.

- **Perspective** – parts of a story could be retold from another character's point of view. For example, parts of *Great Expectations* could be narrated from Magwitch's point of view, not Pip's.

- **Characterisation** – central characters could be given different personalities. For example, Jack in *Jack and the Beanstalk* could be depicted as a ne'er-do-well rather than as a lucky idiot. Fringe characters could be given central roles, as in *Rosencrantz and Guildenstern Are Dead* (see page 238).

However, the transformation must not be so great or so radical that all sight of the original is lost. To recognise the original text in the transformation is part of the pleasure for the listener or reader. Young children take delight in retellings or reworkings of familiar fairy stories or nursery rhymes, and this pleasure or delight is not lost when the child becomes an adult. There are adult equivalents of the child's fun and excitement on hearing 'Now I'm going to tell you the story of "Goldilocks and the Four Bears"' or 'Let's listen to *The Three Billy Goats Cheery*'.

# Fairy stories – new perspectives

Everybody knows the
story of the Three Little Pigs.
Or at least they think they do.
But I'll let you in on a little secret.
Nobody knows the real story,
because nobody has ever heard
*my* side of the story.

I'm the wolf. Alexander T. Wolf.

You can call me Al.

I don't know how this whole Big Bad Wolf thing got started, but it's all wrong.

Maybe it's because of our diet.

Hey, it's not my fault wolves eat cute little animals like bunnies and sheep and pigs.
That's just the way we are. If cheeseburgers were cute, folks would probably think you were Big and
Bad, too.

But like I was saying, the whole Big Bad Wolf thing is wrong.

The real story is about a sneeze and a cup of sugar.

This is the real story.

Way back in Once Upon a Time time,
I was making a birthday cake
For my dear old granny.
I had a terrible sneezing cold.
I ran out of sugar.

So I went next door to ask if I could borrow a cup of sugar.
Now the guy next door was a pig.
And he wasn't too bright, either.
He had built his whole house out of straw.
Can you believe it? I mean who in his right mind would build a house of straw?

That was the opening of *The True Story of the 3 Little Pigs by A Wolf* (as told to Jon Scieszka, 1989). If you haven't read it, you have missed out on one of the most delightful of modern children's books. The familiar story is retold by the wolf, 'Alexander T. Wolf', but, in the words of the Paul Simon song, 'You can call me Al. I don't know how this whole Big Bad Wolf thing got started, but it's all wrong', he says. The wolf gives his very plausible version of events and by the end of the story has persuaded us that he was framed. We won't spoil it by telling you how he was framed, but this children's story is a very good example of a text transformation. A new perspective is offered on a familiar story and because the audience will know the original source, enjoyment in this new version is increased. There are, too, added pleasures for sophisticated adult readers that a child may not pick up. 'You can call me Al' (after a famous pop song) is one of these.

**Activity 4** | **Transforming the tradition**

Transform a traditional story (fairy story, folk tale or nursery rhyme, for example) by changing one or more of genre, plot, mood, perspective or characterisation. Your transformation should be written for today's children, but the original tale must be kept firmly in mind. Here are ten suggested titles, but you are, of course, free to choose your own.

- The Frog Prince Continued
- The Secret of Snow White
- Revenge of the Ugly Sisters
- Whatever Happened to Humpty Dumpty?
- Little Miss Muffet Strikes Back
- The Confessions of Goldilocks

- The Return of the Pied Piper
- I Married Robin Hood
- Sleeping Beauty: The Nightmare Continues
- The Strange Case of Hansel and Gretel

**Review** | In this section you have been given the opportunity to

- learn how writers can use intertextual references
- learn which aspects of texts can be transformed
- transform a traditional tale.

# Planning your transformation

Many exam specifications require you to choose a literary text as your source. Indeed, one specification provides a list of authors from which you must choose your source text. Most of the examples in this section are, therefore, based on texts by authors on this list. There are three main types (or genres) of literary text: drama, poetry and prose fiction, which includes both novels and short stories. The majority of successful transformations are based on texts from these main genres so this is what you should try to do.

What are the steps that you must take in order to produce your transformation?

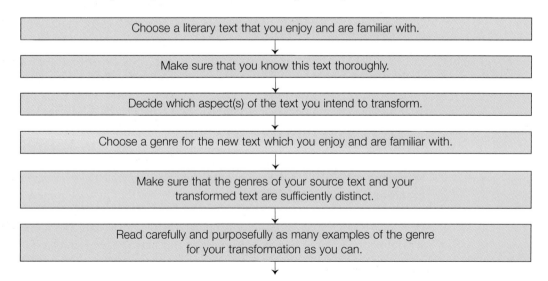

Choose a literary text that you enjoy and are familiar with.

↓

Make sure that you know this text thoroughly.

↓

Decide which aspect(s) of the text you intend to transform.

↓

Choose a genre for the new text which you enjoy and are familiar with.

↓

Make sure that the genres of your source text and your transformed text are sufficiently distinct.

↓

Read carefully and purposefully as many examples of the genre for your transformation as you can.

↓

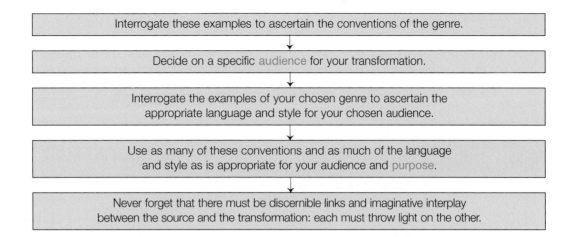

To give you an idea of the type of transformation that can prove successful, here is a list of recent examples submitted by students. They might provide you with some inspiration!

| Source text(s) | Transformation |
|---|---|
| *Macbeth* – Shakespeare | A short story about a corporate takeover in the world of international finance and business |
| *Porphyria's Lover* – a dramatic monologue by Robert Browning | A psychiatrist's report on the murderer of Porphyria |
| *A Streetcar Named Desire* – a play by Tennessee Williams | An extract from a 1920s-style Soviet Socialist realistic novel |
| A selection from the war poems by Wilfred Owen | A 'Hitchhiker's Guide to the First World War', written in the style of Douglas Adams |
| *Twelfth Night* – Shakespeare | A Japanese graphic novel |
| 'To His Coy Mistress' – a poem by the seventeenth-century writer Andrew Marvell, MP for Hull | A play set in twenty-first-century Hull told from the point of view of a seventeen-year-old girl |
| 'The Laboratory' – a poem by Robert Browning | A chapter from a new Harry Potter novel |
| 'The Journey of the Magi' – a poem by T.S. Eliot | A travelogue written in the style of Bill Bryson |
| *Hamlet* – Shakespeare | Ophelia's account of events told in the style of *Bridget Jones' Diary* |
| *The Great Gatsby* – a novel by the American writer F. Scott Fitzgerald | An article in *Hello* magazine based on an interview with Gatsby |
| *A Hitchhiker's Guide to the Galaxy* – a comic science-fiction novel by Douglas Adams | Articles in the *Galactic Gazette*, a newspaper similar to the *Daily Mail* |
| *Gulliver's Travels* – a satiric work by the eighteenth-century writer Jonathan Swift | A travel article about Lilliput (one of the countries visited by Gulliver) from a newspaper colour supplement |
| 'The Wife of Bath's Tale' – one of Chaucer's *Canterbury Tales* | A modern short story focusing on political and feminist issues |
| *Romeo and Juliet* – Shakespeare | A series of letters from Philip Marlowe (hard-bitten detective hero of Raymond Chandler's novels) to Romeo and to Juliet |
| *The Catcher in the Rye* – a novel by J.D. Salinger about an American teenager – and *A Doll's House* – a play by the Norwegian dramatist Henrik Ibsen | A spoof *Big Brother* programme featuring the two main characters from the source texts |

You can see from this list not only the wide range of literary source texts that students have chosen, but also the imaginative and enjoyable transformations that have ensued. In every case, the reader would clearly be able to see the links and the interplay between the transformation and the source text (or texts) and, of course, get pleasure from reading the new text. The next two activities will give you an opportunity to see if you can match or even surpass some of these imaginative ideas for transformations.

## Activity 5 — Familiarising yourself with a source text

**Pair work**

Here is a poem by the seventeenth-century writer John Donne. Most of the spelling has been modernised. Read it carefully.

### The Flea

Mark but this flea, and mark in this,
How little that which thou deny'st me is;
It suck'd me first, and now sucks thee,
And in this flea, our two bloods mingled be;
Thou know'st that this cannot be said
A sin, nor shame, nor loss of maidenhead,
    Yet this enjoys before it woo,
    And pamper'd swells with one blood made of two
    And this, alas, is more than we would do.

Oh stay, three lives in one flea spare,
Where we almost, yea more than married are.
This flea is you and I, and this
Our marriage bed, and marriage temple is;
Though parents grudge, and you, w'are met
And cloistered in these living walls of Jet.
    Though use make you apt to kill me,
    Let not to that, self murder added be,
    And sacrilege, three sins in killing three.

Cruel and sudden, hast thou since
Purpled thy nail, in blood of innocence?
Wherein could this flea guilty be,
Except in that drop which it suckt from thee?
Yet thou triumph'st, and saist that thou
Find'st not thy self, nor me the weaker now;
    'Tis true, then learn how false fears be;
    Just so much honour, when thou yield'st to me,
    Will waste, as this flea's death took life from thee.

This, believe it or not, is an attempt at seduction, though it doesn't give a good impression of seventeenth-century hygiene conditions! The speaker is using the flea and its blood-sucking habits to try to achieve the desired outcome of successful seduction.

In pairs, discuss these questions, which should enable you to gain a clear understanding of the poem.

1 Is the speaker male or female? How do you know?
2 Where do you think the two people are?
3 What has the flea done in the first verse?
4 How does the speaker use the flea's actions to further his/her argument?
5 What is his/her partner threatening to do at the start of the second verse?
6 How does the speaker use this threatened action to again further his/her argument?
7 What has happened between verses two and three?
8 How does the speaker attempt to turn this to his/her advantage?
9 Do you think the attempt at seduction will succeed?

You are now in a position to think about transforming this text: you have, in this case, had a literary text chosen for you and are now completely familiar with its meaning. The next stages are to decide whether you are going to transform the whole text or just some aspects of it and to decide what genre you are going to use. But first, words of warning!

Two essential features of transforming a text, as you have already learnt, are that there should be discernible links between the source text and your transformation of it and that your transformation must throw light on the source text. This new light has earlier been referred to as 'insight', 'interplay' or 'perspective', but if it is not shining brightly, then however well written and enjoyable your new text might be, it will not be a text transformation.

If there is no discernible connection with the source text, then it's as if you have used it merely to 'springboard' into a new one. You will have used your source text simply as a stimulus for some creative writing. This can happen if you take just the setting, a theme or a type of character from the source text and produce a transformation that focuses on one of these without ensuring that the link with the original is apparent. So, if you use *The Flea* merely as an excuse to write a story about a girl and her boyfriend because a boy and a girl feature in the original poem, then you won't have produced a true transformation. Two other examples should help to make clear this important distinction between transformation and creative writing.

*The Rime of the Ancient Mariner* is a well-known poem by Coleridge which tells the story of a doomed sea voyage. It contains many haunting descriptions of being stranded at sea on a ship that is full of dead and dying sailors. If your 'transformation' were a short story set on board a ship, but without any links with the themes, atmosphere or the characters of Coleridge's original, then it might be an interesting short story, but it wouldn't be a transformation. Similarity of setting is not sufficient.

*The Catcher in the Rye,* by J.D. Salinger, has already been mentioned. It is a popular novel about adolescent angst set in New York in the 1950s. If you simply 'transformed' this into a radio play about teenagers you would not be fulfilling the requirements. There must be connections with the themes and ideas of Salinger's original work; all you would have done would have been to take the age of the characters from the novel and think that this is adequate. It isn't.

For success you must ensure that readers can always perceive the links between your two texts.

**Activity 6**

## Transforming *The Flea*

In small groups, brainstorm some possible transformations of *The Flea* from page 246. Here are three suggestions to start you off

- a 'Bridget Jones' type 'diary' in which the girl gives her account of the day
- an article in *Loaded* (or similar magazine) giving a reader's account of his successful seduction techniques (for example, chat-up lines, arguing, false logic)
- a letter and the reply published in the problem pages/advice section of a teenage girls' magazine (for example, 'Should I sleep with this guy with a good line in chat-up?').

What others can you come up with?

## The importance of genre

In Chapters 2 and 5, which explore genre, you will have had plenty of practice in identifying and analysing the characteristics of a number of different genres, both written and multi-modal. You will also have had the opportunity both in your A-level courses and on countless other occasions in your school or college career to have written in a variety of genres. You will be able to draw on this valuable experience when deciding how to transform or rewrite a particular literary text. Indeed, one of the most important aspects that your new text will be judged on is how well you have replicated the characteristics of the genre you have chosen to write in. It is no use, for instance, claiming to have written a piece that was intended to appear in *Cosmopolitan* if it shares none of the genre characteristics of articles that do appear in the real magazine. So your work on genre is essential in helping you prepare for this part of your course. For more on individual genres and their conventions, see pages 49–96.

**Activity 7**

## Choosing a new genre

This activity will give you further practice in choosing a new genre for a source text that is to be transformed. The list that follows consists of twenty different genres, some literary, some non-literary and some multi-modal. The characteristic that they all share is that each one has been chosen by at least one student (and in many cases by more than one) as the new genre for their text transformation.

- Sequence of sonnets
- Short story
- Jerry Springer TV show script
- Screenplay
- Article in *OK* magazine
- Script for an audio-tape guide
- Additional chapter for a Harry Potter novel
- School prospectus
- Lyrics for a musical
- Travel writing for a glossy magazine
- Material for a series of web pages
- Young girl's scrapbook
- Psychiatrist's report
- Fairy story
- Graphic novel
- Newspaper article
- Weblog
- Series of text messages
- Popular history book for children
- Dramatic monologue

The next list contains twenty texts that were used as the basis for these students' transformations. In groups, discuss which you think would be the most suitable genre from the list above for each of these texts. If you are unfamiliar with any of the source texts, first assign the ones that you know to an appropriate genre then try to fill in any gaps with texts with which the group is unfamiliar. Remember, there is no right answer for this activity, as source texts can be changed in a multitude of ways, using a multitude of different genres.

- *Jane Eyre* – Charlotte Brontë
- *Romeo and Juliet* – William Shakespeare
- *The Great Gatsby* – F. Scott Fitzgerald
- *Dr Jekyll and Mr Hyde* – Robert Louis Stevenson
- 'Dulce et Decorum Est' – Wilfred Owen
- *Macbeth* – William Shakespeare
- *The Curious Incident of the Dog in the Night Time* – Mark Haddon
- *The Handmaid's Tale* – Margaret Atwood
- *Gulliver's Travels* – Jonathan Swift
- *Lord of the Flies* – William Golding
- *Little Women* – Louisa May Alcott
- Selection of poems by Simon Armitage
- *Pride and Prejudice* – Jane Austen
- *Animal Farm* – George Orwell
- *Educating Rita* – Willy Russell
- *The Color Purple* – Alice Walker
- 'The Journey of the Magi' – T.S. Eliot
- *Of Mice and Men* – John Steinbeck
- *Blood Brothers* – Willy Russell
- 'The Raven' – Edgar Allan Poe

Turn to page 281 for a commentary on this activity. For more on writing in different genres, see pages 202–233.

**Review**

In this section you have been given the opportunity to
- learn the importance of knowing your source text thoroughly
- understand how important it is to know the conventions of your new genre thoroughly.

# Imitation revisited

Because of the huge variety of potential transformation genres and source texts, it isn't possible in one short chapter to deal with every one, so we will have to restrict ourselves to considering just two that have proved popular and effective. The first one that we will consider has been called imitation. This is when the source text is recast or rewritten in the style and manner of another author (or sometimes in the style and manner of, say, another film or theatre director). This type of transformation isn't just a matter of unquestioning imitation of a writer's style (though this is an important part of the process), but involves taking into consideration such things as significant issues and themes, together with settings and context of the two writers. Once you start to rewrite or transform, for example, Jane Austen as she might have been written by Thomas Hardy or by J.R.R. Tolkien, then it becomes obvious that you are recreating a world, not merely a style.

| Activity 8 | Analysing a writer's style |

Read this extract from the beginning of Raymond Chandler's *Farewell, My Lovely*. Chandler was an American writer of classic detective fiction and had a very distinctive style. His novels are set in Los Angeles and the southern California region and his detective hero, Philip Marlowe, became the prototype for many subsequent hard-bitten fictional investigators.

The doors swung back outwards and almost settled to a stop. Before they had entirely stopped moving they opened again, violently, outwards. Something sailed across the sidewalk and landed in the gutter between two parked cars. It landed on its hands and knees and made a high keening noise like a cornered rat. It got up slowly, retrieved a hat and stepped back onto the sidewalk. It was a thin, narrow-shouldered brown youth in a lilac coloured suit and a carnation. It had slick black hair. It kept its mouth open and whined for a moment. People stared at it vaguely. Then it settled its hat jauntily, sidled over to the wall and walked silently splay-footed off along the block.

Silence. Traffic resumed. I walked along to the double doors and stood in front of them. They were motionless now. It wasn't any of my business. So I pushed them open and looked in.

A hand I could have sat in came out of the dimness and took hold of my shoulder and squashed it to a pulp. Then the hand moved me through the doors and casually lifted me up a step. The large face looked at me. A deep soft voice said to me quietly:

'Smokes in here, huh? Tie that for me, pal.'

It was dark in there. It was quiet. From up above came vague sounds of humanity, but we were alone on the stairs. The big man stared at me solemnly and went on wrecking my shoulder with his hand.

'A dinge,' he said. 'I just thrown him out. You see me throw him out?'

He let go of my shoulder. The bone didn't seem to be broken, but the arm was numb.

'It's that kind of place,' I said, rubbing my shoulder. 'What did you expect?'

'Don't say that, pal,' the big man purred softly, like four tigers after dinner. 'Velma used to work here. Little Velma.'

He reached for my shoulder again. I tried to dodge him but he was as fast as a cat. He began to chew my muscles up some more with his iron fingers.

'Yeah,' he said. 'Little Velma. I ain't seen her in eight years. You say this is a dinge joint?'

I croaked that it was.

'Dinge' was American slang for a Black person when this novel was published in 1940.

Some characteristic features of Raymond Chandler's style are
- detailed concrete description
- short sentences
- dynamic verbs (verbs of action)
- unusual similes
- first-person narrative point of view

- terse conversation
- verbless sentences
- ironic humour
- synecdoche (use of part to signify the whole)
- laconic voice
- slang
- sustained metaphors.

Look closely at the extract from the novel and find examples of each of these features.

Your work on this extract from *Farewell, My Lovely* will have given you a detailed and secure knowledge of one of the most individual styles of writing of the last century. It should also have equipped you to write in imitation of it. But remember that when rewriting a source text in imitation of another author, it is not just their style that you will be using, you will also be adapting their context to an entirely different one. It is not just the manner you will be employing, but the subject-matter as well. Here, for example, is a well-known story rewritten as it might have been told by Raymond Chandler.

It was a Thursday morning and I had lots to do, like stare out of my window. I heard my outer office door open, and turned to see a blonde girl, maybe twenty-five years old.

'You can come right in,' I called.

She straightened her skirt and walked in very quickly. She was tall and composed, with a perfect nose, absolutely perfect.

'You're Marlowe?'

'Who wants me?'

'My man Jack needs your help.'

I couldn't have cared less. I cared more when she crossed her legs.

'I hardly know where to begin, Mr Marlowe.'

'Try the beginning. It's been a slow week.'

'Jack and I are co-starring in *The Grand Old Duke of York*. We were shooting the hill scene. You know he's a big star, but he's been drinking more lately. He's got something on his mind.'

'Blackmail?' Her open blue jacket revealed a tight sweater that was being stretched to its limits.

'That's for you to find out. He's playing the king and he was real tipsy last night. When it got to the bit when we had to fetch a pail of water, he fell down and broke his crown. And I just fell right down there with him.'

For more on the genre of crime writing, see pages 98–110.

## Activity 9
**Pair work**

## 'Jack and Jill' by Raymond Chandler

It will not have proved too difficult for you to have recognised the source text for this transformation – the nursery rhyme 'Jack and Jill'. But which elements of Raymond Chandler's 'hard-bitten' style has the writer imitated?

In pairs, discuss the following questions.

- In this version of 'Jack and Jill', what examples are there of the characteristic features of Chandler's style listed in Activity 8?
- Are there any that the writer has not used?
- Are there any stylistic features not included in the list in Activity 8 that the writer has used?
- What impression do you gain of the character of Marlowe from this new text? And of Jill?
- Why has the writer said that Jack and Jill are co-starring in *The Grand Old Duke of York*?

You probably don't need reminding of the original version of the story but, nevertheless, here it is.

Jack and Jill went up the hill
To fetch a pail of water;
Jack fell down and broke his crown,
And Jill came tumbling after.

Up Jack got, and home did trot,
As fast as he could caper,
To old Dame Dob, who patched his nob
With vinegar and brown paper.

A gender question: whatever happened to Jill? Why aren't we told! You might not know that there are other versions of the nursery rhyme. Here, for instance, is one from the early nineteenth century that is considerably longer than the familiar version. It does give an account of Jill's fate.

### The Adventures of Jack and Jill and Old Dame Gill

Jack and Jill
Went up the hill,
To fetch a pail of water;
Jack fell down,
And broke his crown, and Jill came tumbling after.

Then up Jack got, And home did trot,
As fast as he could caper;
Dame Gill did the job,
To plaster his nob
With vinegar and brown paper.

Then Jill came in,
And she did grin
To see Jack's paper plaster;
Her mother, vexed,
Did whip her next,
For laughing at Jack's disaster.

This made Jill pout,
And she ran out,
And Jack did quickly follow;
They rode dog Ball
Till Jill did fall,
Which made Jack laugh and halloo.

Then Dame came out
To enquire about,
Jill said Jack made her tumble;
Says Jack, I'll tell
You how she fell,
Then judge if she need grumble.

Dame Gill did grin
As she went in,
And Jill was plagued by Jack;
Will Goat came by,
And made Jack cry,
And knocked him on his back.

Though Jack wasn't hurt,
He was overall dirt;
I wish you had but seen him,
And how Jill did jump
Towards the pump, and pumped on him to clean him.

Which done, all three
Went in to tea,
And put the place all right;
Which done, they sup,
Then take a cup,
And wish you a good night.

## Activity 10  Jack and Jill: a second look

On pages 254–256 are five extracts from the work of well-known writers. Each writer is recognised as having a distinctive style.

- Text A is from Mark Haddon's *The Curious Incident of the Dog in the Night Time* (2004).
- Text B is from Lewis Carroll's *Alice's Adventures in Wonderland* (1865).
- Text C is from Arthur Conan Doyle's story 'The Beryl Coronet' from *The Adventures of Sherlock Holmes* (1892).
- Text D is from Mark Twain's *Adventures of Huckleberry Finn* (1884).
- Text E is from Rudyard Kipling's 'How the Camel got his Hump' from *Just So Stories* (1902).

Choose one of these extracts and identify the characteristics of the style. To start you off, one of the main characteristics is pointed out at the end of each extract. There are others, of course!

Rewrite some or all of the story of Jack and Jill in imitation of the manner and matter of the writer of the extract you selected.

## Text A

Then the police arrived. I like the police. They have uniforms and numbers and you know what they are meant to be doing. There was a policewoman and a policeman. The policewoman had a little hole in her tights on her left ankle and a red scratch in the middle of the hole. The policeman had a big orange leaf stuck to the bottom of his shoe which was poking out from one side.

The policewoman put her arms round Mrs Shears and led her back towards the house.

I lifted my head off the grass.

The policeman squatted down beside me and said, 'Would you like to tell me what's going on here, young man?'

I sat up and said, 'The dog is dead.'

'I'd got that far,' he said.

I said, 'I think someone killed the dog.'

'How old are you?' he asked.

I replied, 'I am 15 years and 3 months and 2 days.'

'And what precisely were you doing in the garden?' he asked.

'I was holding the dog,' I replied.

This extract uses grammatically simple sentences.

## Text B

'Your hair wants cutting,' said the Hatter. He had been looking at Alice for some time with great curiosity, and this was his first speech.

'You should learn not to make personal remarks,' Alice said with some severity: 'it's very rude.'

The Hatter opened his eyes very wide on hearing this; but all he *said* was: 'Why is a raven like a writing-desk?'

'Come, we shall have some fun now!' thought Alice. 'I'm glad they've begun asking riddles – I believe I can guess that,' she added aloud.

'Do you mean that you think you can find out the answer to it?' said the March Hare.

'Exactly so,' said Alice.

'Then you should say what you mean,' the March Hare went on.

'I do,' Alice hastily replied: 'at least – at least I mean what I say – that's the same thing, you know.'

'Not the same thing a bit!' said the Hatter. 'Why, you might just as well say that "I see what I eat" is the same thing as "I eat what I see"!'

'You might just as well say,' added the March Hare, 'that "I like what I get" is the same as "I get what I like"!'

'You might just as well say,' added the Dormouse, which seemed to be talking in its sleep, 'that "I breathe when I sleep" is the same thing as "I sleep when I breathe"!'

'It *is* the same thing with you,' said the Hatter, and here the conversation dropped, and the party sat silent for a moment, while Alice thought over all she could remember about ravens and writing-desks, which wasn't much.

This extract uses repeated grammatical structures.

## Text C

'Holmes,' said I, as I stood one morning in our bow-window, looking down the street, 'here is a madman coming along. It seems rather sad that his relatives should allow him to come out alone.'

My friend rose lazily from his arm-chair, and stood with his hands in the pockets of his dressing gown, looking over my shoulder. It was a bright, crisp February morning, and the snow of the day before still lay deep upon the ground, shimmering brightly in the wintry sun. Down the centre of Baker Street it had been ploughed into a brown crumbly band by the traffic, but at either side and on the heaped-up edges of the footpaths it still lay as white as when it fell. The grey pavement had been cleaned and scraped, but was still dangerously slippery, so that there were fewer passengers than usual. Indeed, from the direction of the Metropolitan station no one was coming save the single gentleman whose eccentric conduct had drawn my attention.

He was a man of about fifty, tall, portly, and imposing, with a massive, strongly marked face and a commanding figure. He was dressed in a sombre yet rich style, in black frock-coat, shining hat, neat brown gaiters, and well-cut pearl-grey trousers. Yet his actions were in absurd contrast to the dignity of his dress and features, for he was running hard, with occasional little springs, such as a weary man gives who is little accustomed to set any tax upon his legs. As he ran he jerked his hands up and down, waggled his head, and writhed his face into the most extraordinary contortions.

'What on earth can be the matter with him?' I asked. 'He is looking up at the numbers of the houses.'

'I believe he is coming here,' said Holmes, rubbing his hands.

This extract includes precise descriptions.

## Text D

When it was daylight, here was the clear Ohio water in shore, sure enough, and outside was the old regular Muddy! So it was all up with Cairo.

We talked it all over. It wouldn't do to take to the shore; we couldn't take the raft up the stream, of course. There warn't no way but to wait for dark, and start back in the canoe and take the chances. So we slept all day amongst the cotton-wood thicket, so as to be fresh for the work, and when we went back to the raft about dark the canoe was gone!

We didn't say a word for a good while. There warn't anything to say. We both knowed well enough it was some more work of the rattle-snake skin; so what was the use to talk about it? It would only look like we was finding fault, and that would be bound to fetch some more bad luck – and keep on fetching it, too, till we knowed enough to keep still.

By and by we talked about what we better do, and found there warn't no way but to just go along down with the raft till we got a chance to buy a canoe to go back in. We warn't going to borrow it when there wasn't anyone around, the way pap would do, for that might set people after us.

So we shoved out, after dark, on the raft.

This extract uses non-standard grammar.

## Text E

Presently there came along the Djinn in charge of All Deserts, rolling in a cloud of dust (Djinns always travel that way because it is Magic), and he stopped to palaver and pow-wow with the Three.

'Djinn of All Deserts,' said the Horse, '*is* it right for anyone to be idle, with the world so new-and-all?'

'Certainly not,' said the Djinn.

'Well,' said the Horse, 'there's a thing in the middle of your Howling Desert (and he's a Howler himself) with a long neck and long legs, and he hasn't done a stroke of work since Monday morning. He won't trot.'

'Whew!' said the Djinn, whistling, 'that's my Camel, for all the gold in Arabia! What does he say about it?'

'He says "Humph!"' said the Dog; 'and he won't fetch and carry.'

'Does he say anything else?'

'Only "Humph!"; and he won't plough,' said the Ox.

'Very good,' said the Djinn. 'I'll humph him if you will kindly wait a minute.'

The Djinn rolled himself up in his dust cloak, and took a bearing across the desert, and found the Camel most 'scruciatingly idle, looking at his own reflection in a pool of water.

'My long and bubbling friend,' said the Djinn, 'what's this I hear of your doing no work, with the world so new-and-all?'

'Humph!' said the Camel.

The Djinn sat down, with his chin in his hand, and began to think a Great Magic, while the Camel looked at his own reflection in the pool of water.

'You've given the Three extra work ever since Monday morning, all on account of your 'scruciating idleness,' said the Djinn; and he went on thinking Magics, with his chin in his hand.

'Humph!' said the Camel.

'I shouldn't say that again if I were you,' said the Djinn; 'you might say it once too often. Bubbles, I want you to work.'

And the Camel said 'Humph!' again; but no sooner had he said it than he saw his back which he was so proud of, puffing up and puffing up into a great big lolloping humph.

'Do you see that?' said the Djinn. 'That's your very own humph that you've brought upon your very own self by not working. Today is Thursday, and you've done no work since Monday, when the work began. Now you are going to work.'

'How can I,' said the Camel, 'with this humph on my back?'

'That's made a-purpose,' said the Djinn, 'all because you missed those three days. You will be able to work now for those three days without eating, because you can live on your humph; and don't you ever say I never did anything for you. Come out of the Desert and go to the Three, and behave. Humph yourself!'

This extract uses repeated lexical items.

Of course, you need not restrict yourself to imitating these writers nor to Jack and Jill. You have the whole range of literature written in English at your disposal!

**Review**

In this section you have been given the opportunity through examining the work of a number of different authors to put into practice some of the important skills involved in imitation. These include

- choosing a writer for your source text who has a distinctive style and subject-matter
- ensuring that your new text is not merely an imitation of that writer's style, but places their attitudes and values in a new and probably unexpected context.

Doing this will have helped you to fulfil two of the main requirements of a successful text transformation

- writing an entertaining new text
- guaranteeing that there will be enlightening interplay between your new text and its source.

# Adaptation

The second popular type of transformation that we will consider is known as adaptation. The principles behind adaptation are very similar to those we have looked at already. A source text and a new genre are chosen, but in this case the new text is not always for a written medium. Most of the examples of transformations in the list on page 245 are of written texts being transformed into another written genre: *Gulliver's Travels* into a travel article, for instance, or *Porphyria's Lover* into a psychiatrist's report. However, texts can be adapted for another medium – the visual (film or television), the aural (radio) or even mixed media (a web page, for example).

Some of the most popular television programmes in recent times have been adaptations of classic novels, sometimes into a one-off play or, more usually, into a four- or six-episode serial. The nineteenth-century novels *Middlemarch* by George Eliot, *Vanity Fair* by William Makepeace Thackeray and *Diary of a Nobody* by George and Weedon Grossmith have all been very successfully adapted and transformed into television serials. Jane Austen's and Charles Dickens' novels are forever being transformed and televised. And it's not just the classic nineteenth-century 'blockbuster' novels that are used. Highly successful have been Evelyn Waugh's *Brideshead Revisited* (published in 1945), Paul Scott's *Jewel in the Crown* (1973), David Lodge's *Nice Work* (1988) and Jeanette Winterson's *Oranges Are Not the Only Fruit* (1991). You will be able to think of many others that you have seen. Detective fiction, too, has provided a rich source for adaptation for television: Sherlock Holmes, Hercule Poirot, Miss Marple, Lord Peter Wimsey, Brother Cadfael, Inspector Morse, Dalziel and Pascoe, Chief Inspector Wexford and a host of others all began life in the pages of novels or short stories.

Nor is it just for television that novels are adapted. Film-makers have mined novels to provide them with the sources for some of the most successful movies of all time. You only have to think of *The Godfather, Jaws, Carrie, The Postman Only Rings Twice,* Alfred Hitchcock's *The Birds* and *Strangers on a Train* and a host of other movies to realise how important the adaptation of novels is for them. Think, too, of genres other than prose fiction: the numerous film versions of Shakespeare's plays are a good example. Kenneth Branagh's *Henry V* and *Much Ado About Nothing,* Roman Polanski's *Macbeth* and Franco

Zefferelli's *Romeo and Juliet* are just some recent ones. And just a little further back in time, Laurence Olivier's *Richard III* and *Henry V* are rated amongst the very best films.

Shakespeare himself was a great adapter of texts, as you have already seen. Very few of his plays, even the most famous ones, have entirely original plots. For example, his history plays, such as *Richard II, Henry IV (Parts I and II)* and *Henry V*, have their source in his reading of an Elizabethan history book called Holinshed's *Chronicles*. This also provided some of the source material which Shakespeare transformed into two of his greatest plays, *Macbeth* and *King Lear*. We have already mentioned that his reading of an Elizabethan translation of a Roman history book led to *Antony and Cleopatra* and also to *Julius Caesar*. Italian stories provided the source of *Romeo and Juliet*, Elizabethan poetry the source of *As You Like It* and a Roman comedy by Plautus the source of *The Comedy of Errors*.

| Activity 11 | Shakespeare the transformer |
|---|---|

**Pair work**

This activity will provide you with some insight into Shakespeare's skill as a text transformer.

■ Text A, the source text that Shakespeare transformed, is an extract from Raphael Holinshed's *Chronicles of England, Scotland and Ireland*, written in 1587. This was intended to be a 'universal' history, but it remained, not surprisingly, unfinished.

■ Text B is the opening scene of *Macbeth*, in which Macbeth and Banquo, returning from their recent victory over the Norwegians, meet three witches on a heath.

Read the two texts carefully and discuss, in pairs, the questions on page 260.

### Text A

Shortly after happened a strange and uncouth wonder, which afterward was the cause of much trouble in the realm of Scotland, as ye shall after hear. It fortuned as Makbeth and Banquho journeyed towards Fores, where the king as then lay, they went sporting by the way together without other company save only themselves, passing through the woods and fields, when suddenly in the middest of a laund, there met them three women in strange and ferry apparel, resembling creatures of an elder world, whom when they attentively beheld, wondering much at the sight, the first of them spake and said: 'All hail Makbeth, Thane of Glammis' (for he had lately entered into that dignity and office by the death of his father Sinell). The second of them said: 'Hail Makbeth, Thane of Cawder.' But the third said: 'All hail Makbeth, that hereafter shalt be King of Scotland.'

Then Banquho: 'What manner of women (saith he) are you that seem so little favourable unto me, whereas to my fellow here, besides high offices, ye assign also the kingdom, appointing forth nothing for me at all?' 'Yes' (saith the first of them), 'we promise greater benefits unto thee than unto him; for he shall reign indeed, but with an unlucky end; neither shall he leave any issue behind him to succeed in his place, where contrarily thou indeed shalt not reign at all, but of thee those shall be born which shall govern the Scottish kingdom by long order of continual descent.' Herewith the foresaid women vanished immediately out of their sight.

**Text B**

*Enter Macbeth and Banquo*

| | |
|---|---|
| Macbeth | So foul and fair a day I have not seen. |
| Banquo | How far is't called to Forres? What are these, |
| | So withered and so wild in their attire, |
| | That look not like the inhabitants o'the earth, |
| | And yet are on't? Live you? Or are you aught |
| | That man may question? You seem to understand me |
| | By each at once her choppy finger laying |
| | Upon her skinny lips. You should be women; |
| | And yet your beards forbid me to interpret |
| | That you are so. |
| Macbeth | Speak if you can! What are you? |
| First Witch | All hail, Macbeth! Hail to thee, Thane of Glamis! |
| Second Witch | All hail, Macbeth! Hail to thee, Thane of Cawdor! |
| Third Witch | All hail, Macbeth, that shalt be king hereafter! |
| Banquo | Good sir, why do you start, and seem to fear |
| | Things that do sound so fair? – I'the name of truth, |
| | Are ye fantastical, or that indeed |
| | Which outwardly ye show? My noble partner |
| | You greet with present grace, and great prediction |
| | Of noble having and of royal hope |
| | That he seems rapt withal. To me you speak not. |
| | If you can look into the seeds of time |
| | And say which grain will grow and which will not, |
| | Speak then to me who neither beg nor fear |
| | Your favours nor your hate. |
| First Witch | Hail! |
| Second Witch | Hail! |
| Third Witch | Hail! |
| First Witch | Lesser than Macbeth, and greater. |
| Second Witch | Not so happy, yet much happier. |
| Third Witch | Thou shalt get kings, though thou be none. |
| | So all hail, Macbeth and Banquo! |
| First Witch | Banquo and Macbeth, all hail! |
| Macbeth | Stay, you imperfect speakers! Tell me more! |
| | By Sinell's death I know I am Thane of Glamis; |
| | But how of Cawdor? The Thane of Cawdor lives |
| | A prosperous gentleman. And to be king |
| | Stands not within the prospect of belief – |
| | No more than to be Cawdor. Say from whence |
| | You owe this strange intelligence; or why |
| | Upon this blasted heath you stop our way |
| | With such prophetic greeting? Speak, I charge you! |

*Witches vanish*

1 Is the order of the events the same?
2 Has Shakespeare added anything to Holinshed's account?
3 Has he removed anything? If so, why do you think he did this?
4 How has he transformed the speech and dialogue that Holinshed wrote?
5 What has Shakespeare decided to retain of Holinshed's version? Why do you think he has done this?
6 What makes Shakespeare's version more dramatic and theatrically effective?

## Activity 12    Be your own Shakespeare

Here you have the opportunity to see if you can out-Shakespeare Shakespeare! As you have already learnt, he transformed a variety of source texts in the writing of his plays. One of the most important was Sir Thomas North's translation of the Roman historian Plutarch's *Lives of the Noble Greeks and Romans*, which was published in 1579. This was a collection of biographies of ancient Roman and Greek men (not women!). What must have appealed to Shakespeare the dramatist was that Plutarch the historian was interested not just in the events in these men's lives but also wrote subtle analyses of their characters as well.

The extract that follows is from Plutarch's *Life of Marcus Antonius*, which Shakespeare used as one of his sources for *Antony and Cleopatra.* Here Plutarch tells of the death of Cleopatra, the Queen of Egypt and Antony's lover. Antony has just committed suicide after his defeat in the battle which led to Octavius Caesar's conquest of Egypt. Cleopatra no longer wishes to go on living. Iras and Charmian are her attendants.

Transform this extract into a scene (or scenes) from a play. If you want to compare your version with Shakespeare's, you should read Act 5, Scene 2 of *Antony and Cleopatra* from line 240 to the end of the play.

Nowe whilest she was at dinner, there came a contrieman, and brought her a basket. The souldiers that warded at the gates, asked him straight what he had in his basket. He opened the basket, and tooke out the leaves that covered the figges, and shewed them that they were figges he brought. They all of them marvelled to see so goodly figges. The contrieman laughed to heare them, and bad them take some if they would. They beleved he told them truely, and so bad him carie them in. After Cleopatra had dined, she sent a certaine table written and sealed unto Caesar, and commaunded them all to go out of the tombes where she was, but the two women, then she shut the dores to her. Caesar when he received this table, and began to read her lamentation and petition, requesting him that he would let her be buried with Antonius, founde straight what she ment, and thought to have gone thither him selfe: howbeit he sent one before in all hast that might be, to see what it was. Her death was very sodaine. For those whom Caesar sent unto her ran thither in all hast possible, and found the souldiers standing at the gate, mistrusting nothing, nor understanding of her death. But when they had opened the dores, they founde Cleopatra starke dead, layed upon a bed of gold, attried and araied in her royall robes, and one of her two women, which was called Iras, dead at her feete: and her other woman called Charmion halfe-dead, and trembling, trimming the diademe which Cleopatra ware upon her head. One of the souldiers seeing her, angrily sayd unto her: Is that well done Charmion? Verie well sayd she againe, and meete for a Princes discended from the race of so many noble kings. She sayd no more, but fell downe dead hard by the bed. Some report that this Aspicke was brought unto her in the basket with figs, and that she had commaunded them to hide it under the figge leaves, that when she shoulde thinke to take out the figges, the Aspicke shoulde bite her before she should see her: howbeit, that when she would have taken away the leaves for the figges, she perceived it, and said, Art thou here then? And so, her arme being naked, she put it to the Aspicke to be bitten.

Aspicke – asp (a poisonous snake)

# Radio daze

We won't be able to cover all the possible ways of adapting texts in this short chapter, so we are going to concentrate on the ways that writers adapt texts for just one medium – radio. You may well be surprised at the variety of ways in which texts are adapted for radio, especially if you are not a frequent radio listener. For example, in just one week, BBC radio broadcast

- 3 stage plays – adapted for radio
- 2 short stories – adapted and abridged
- 2 novels – adapted as drama serials
- 3 novels – adapted and abridged for serial reading
- 1 novel – adapted as a comedy series
- 1 novel – adapted as a one-off play
- 1 poem – adapted for serial reading.

Now, this may well have been an exceptional week, but you can see from this list that the practice of adapting a source text is alive and well in just this one medium. And we haven't even considered the TV output!

## Activity 13 | Counting the adaptations

Look in the current issue of *Radio Times* and compile a list of the text adaptations

- for radio
- for television.

Note also how many films, not specifically made for television, are based on original literary texts.

You'll probably find that many of these adaptations are of novels or short stories. This isn't, of course, always an easy task to undertake. One of the most successful adaptations was the radio serialisation of J.R.R. Tolkien's *The Lord of the Rings* which was broadcast before the film version that you may have watched. Those of you who have read Tolkien's novel will realise just what a massive undertaking this radio adaptation was. The three-volume novel is over a thousand pages long and has a huge number of characters, so the problems for the adapter, Brian Sibley, were legion. This is what he has written about some of the problems he had to solve.

Here are just a few facts about the first appearance in the book of some of the major characters (page numbers refer to the one-volume paperback edition): Frodo does not speak until p. 46: ('Has he [Bilbo] gone?'); Sam and Frodo do not appear together until the eavesdropping scene on p. 76; Merry has only two sentences until he meets his companions at the ferry on p. 110; and Gollum does not speak – apart from his reported exchange with Déagol – until p. 638! In order to resolve such difficulties – which would clearly be more of a problem for listeners who did not know the book – it seemed necessary to invent some passages of dialogue. A scene was written in which Sam delivers replies to the party invitations to Bilbo and Frodo at Bag End, and another in order to establish Merry before he sets out for Crickhollow. And as no-one can have failed to notice, the first episode began with the arrest of Gollum on the borders of Mordor and his subsequent interrogation in Barad-Dûr (an event reported by Gandalf and referred to in *Unfinished Tales*).

## Activity 14

**Group work**

## Adapting *The Lord of the Rings*

Read the next two extracts. Text A is from the book and Text B from the radio adaptation of *The Lord of the Rings*. Both tell of Merry's departure for Crickhollow.

In small groups, discuss

- What information is given in the radio script that is not found in the extract from the book?
- How does the adaptation establish Merry's light-hearted personality?

Turn to page 282 for a commentary on this activity.

### Text A

On September 20th, two covered carts went off laden to Buckland, conveying the furniture and goods that Frodo had not sold ... The thought that he [Frodo] would so soon have to part with his young friends weighed on his heart. He wondered how he would break it to them...

The next morning they were busy packing another cart with the remainder of the luggage. Merry took charge of this, and drove off with Fatty... 'Someone must get there and warm the house before you arrive,' said Merry. 'Well, see you later – the day after tomorrow, if you don't go to sleep on the way!'

### Text B

Frodo   Well, Merry, is everything ready?

Merry   Yes: two cart-loads yesterday, full to overflowing, and now another one. I'm beginning to wonder if your new home will be big enough!

Frodo   Well, I've sold everything I could bear parting with to Lobelia, but some things I just had to take to remind me of Bilbo and Bag End.

Merry   Well, I'd best be off ... If I leave now I can get to Crickhollow and warm the house before you arrive – that is, if you're quite sure you want to walk rather than go by cart...

Frodo   Quite sure.

Merry   Then I'll see you the day after tomorrow – if you don't go to sleep on the way!

Frodo   [*laughing*] I'll try not to!

> *Cart starts off, then stops*
>
> **Merry** [*calling back*] I'll tell you one thing, Frodo, you had better settle when you get to Buckland, because I for one am not helping you to move back again!
> **Frodo** What on earth makes you think Lobelia would ever sell Bag End back to me?
>
> *Cart starts off once more*
>
> **Merry** She might – at a profit! Farewell, Frodo – and good walking!
>
> *Cart drives off*
>
> **Frodo** [*to himself*] Poor Merry, what will you say when you learn the truth of all this!

## How do you start to adapt a text for radio?

Perhaps the most important thing to get clear in your mind is the angle that you are going to take on the text. Some of the questions that you will need to answer in order to ascertain this angle are

- What makes me want to work on *this* text? What is *my* idea about it? What is *my* artistic purpose in wanting to adapt it?
- Will I include all the events/episodes of the original?
- Will I maintain the order of the events/episodes as narrated in the original?
- From whose point(s) of view is the story going to be told?
- Am I going to maintain the mood of the original?
- Will I include, adapt or jettison any sub-plot(s)?
- Will I combine or jettison any of the characters from the original?
- Will I need to bring anything up to date for a modern audience?

You could summarise these by ensuring that you know the answers to

- How will the story be told?
- In what way is it suited to radio?

There are therefore some important things you need to have clear before you begin to work on adapting your source text. You should

- know the characteristics of the radio programme you are writing for as it will be aimed at a particular audience
- have a thorough knowledge of the text you are adapting
- know the techniques of writing for radio.

We will look at each of these, but remember that we are dealing with only one genre for one medium here and that if you choose to adapt your source text for a medium other than radio you will need similarly thorough knowledge of that medium and genre.

## The characteristics of radio programmes

You can find out comprehensive information on BBC radio programmes from the BBC website (bbc.co.uk). This provides details of the type of content they want for particular radio programmes or series and the make-up of the audience that usually listens to them. The ones that are of most interest to you as a text adapter are the commissioning guidelines for drama.

We are going to see what an excerpt from some earlier BBC guidelines for the *Classic Serial* programme broadcast on Radio 4 has to say. This is highly relevant to the work you will do as a text adapter.

This slot is exclusively for dramatisations of works of narrative fiction that have achieved classic status. 'Classic' should mean that the work has won acclaim from succeeding generations of readers. Books that are cult successes, famous for their 'kitsch' element or not part of the mainstream, would not be appropriate. Beyond this, the definition of 'classic' should be as wide as possible to include works from around the world, from the 20th century and neglected writing. Offers might range from the popular British works of the 19th century, e.g. the recent successes of *North and South* by Elizabeth Gaskell or *Tom Jones* by Henry Fielding, to contemporary international masterpieces from authors such as Gabriel Garcia Marquez or Gunter Grass.

If a fairly recent novel is dramatised there should be some feeling that it is a very important or seminal one and that the dramatisation is helping to make the book into a 'classic' in its own right.

Sometimes the source text may not be a novel – it could be, say, a collection of short stories (e.g. *Dubliners* by James Joyce), epic work (e.g. *The Iliad*) or traditional tales (e.g. Aesop's *Fables* or the fairy stories written by the Brothers Grimm).

Imaginative and creative treatments of the texts are welcome though it is best that these are reserved for very well-known books. For example, an unusual adaptation of a little-known novel would not be a good idea, because listeners would not be familiar enough with the book to appreciate the changes.

A strong, clear story is important, as is a plot structure that would work well when abridged – too many flash-backs, time-shifts or changes in narrative point of view are not likely to work well.

There are a number of important points to note here. Not only can writers choose to transform a variety of modern and nineteenth-century novels: they are not restricted to the novel alone. Short stories, epic poems and traditional tales are also potential candidates for transformation. The editors welcome 'imaginative and creative treatments' and we will examine one of these later in this section. Note, too, the need for a strong story line in the adaptation and also the likelihood that the story would need to be abridged. It's obvious that you must do a great deal of planning and preparation before you begin the actual writing of the transformation.

Your work as an adapter of source texts is not necessarily restricted to classic works of literature. There are opportunities for adapters to work on many other genres of source texts. This, for instance, is a brief extract from the BBC's commissioning guidelines for the *Afternoon Play*.

The *Afternoon Play* is about storytelling. It may be called the *Afternoon Play*, but it is a slot with a huge scope and licence in both subject matter and form.

### What is broadcast in this slot
Listeners want, above all, a good story. So it's vital that that's what the adaptation has: a strong narrative line. The strength of the *Afternoon Play* is its variety – anything and everything can go in this slot – modern and historical plays, comedy, biography, plays dealing with important issues and concerns of the day, drama documentaries, family plays, crime dramas and thrillers, even poetry, fantasy, etc. It can be a free-standing play, a dramatisation (of short stories, letters, memoirs or even non fiction), a dramatised feature, a narrative poem such as Chaucer's *Canterbury Tales*, or a sequence of short plays on the same theme or featuring the same characters.

But: remember that you must have a good story!

Obviously we have to consider that our main aim is to entertain a large number of afternoon listeners, but there is no drama slot within broadcasting with as much editorial freedom as the *Afternoon Play*. Find new ways to tell stories and we will broadcast them; be imaginative.

**We** are looking for three crucial things:

- Story
- Story
- Story

Three things from this brief for the *Afternoon Play* should interest you as a text adapter. First, the repeated emphasis on telling a good story; second, the invitation to be as imaginative as you like in your adaptation (stressed in the brief for the *Classic Serial* as well), and finally, the great variety of texts that can be transformed for radio: it's not just classic novels, but 'short stories, letters, memoirs and even non fiction' that are welcomed. You, of course, will be able to think of many more.

## Knowing the text

It almost goes without saying that you must know any text that you wish to adapt very thoroughly indeed. If it's a novel or short story that you are going to be working on, then these are some of the features of the text that must become almost second nature to you

- the structure of the plot (whether there is just one plot or a number of sub-plots and how these relate to each other)
- those scenes which are key and those which are less central
- the setting(s) and period(s) in which the action takes place
- the point of view from which the story is narrated
- the language style of the narrative
- the characters: what they do; how they relate to each other; they way they speak; what happens to them; which ones develop and change and which ones remain static; which ones are central and which peripheral to the plot.

There's quite a lot to consider here and we've only looked at one genre! (We'll be looking at some others on the website that accompanies this book.) It's obvious you can't begin the work of adapting a source text without this detailed knowledge and understanding. How you obtain it is a matter of choice, but you're unlikely to gain it through just a very quick and sketchy reading of the text. You really need to immerse yourself in the work. Andrew Davies, who has adapted many classic novels for television, including *Vanity Fair, Pride and Prejudice* and *Wives and Daughters*, follows this method.

If it's been recorded unabridged by 'Cover to Cover' or one of those things, I try to avoid sitting down in front of it. I buy the cassette and go for long drives in the car and listen to it because that way you can't skip ... so that's the first step anyway ... either by reading or by listening to it. I listen to it two or three times until I'm pretty well soaked in the thing.

Then I start dividing it into chunks. I suppose the first thing I do when I'm soaking myself in it is also putting myself into it as well ... thinking, 'What do I think of this?' 'Do I have a particular angle on it?' or 'Am I just trying to present it as it is?'

You'll notice that Andrew Davies stresses the need to have a 'particular angle' on the text.

Whether you follow Andrew Davies' method or one of your own, you can see that thorough preparation is essential. Again, there is a bonus for you in that not only will your thorough preparation mean a successful transformation, but you'll also have important insights to communicate in your commentary.

## The techniques

Not only do you need to know the text you are adapting thoroughly, but you also have to be very familiar with the techniques and characteristics of the radio genre you will be using. You must ensure that your work conforms to its conventions. In other words, your adaptation must work as a radio dramatisation, not as one for the stage!

You can find some very helpful and detailed advice given by Tim Crook on how to write radio drama at www.irdp.co.uk/scripts.htm. These are some of the things that he says are essential if you want your adaptation to be successful. You should, of course, try to read the whole piece.

- Have a strong, arresting beginning.
- Your plot must have plenty of twists and turns.
- Make sure there are elements of surprise for the listener.
- Have a main character that your audience can identify with.
- Make sure your characters are easily distinguishable from each other.
- Make sure that there's some conflict or struggle in your dramatisation.
- Maintain tension.
- There must be a satisfying climax.
- Your dialogue must be both dramatic and believable.
- Use sound effects, music (and silence, too) to create atmosphere and setting.
- Balance character and plot: don't let one or the other dominate.
- *Everything* you write must have a dramatic purpose in terms of character or plot development.

---

**Activity 15**  **How not to do it!**

Here's the opening of a radio play *The Gun that I Have in My Pocket is Loaded* by Timothy West. Read it carefully and list as many things as you can that would make it very unsuccessful as radio drama. What are the 'creaky' bits?

Turn to page 282 for a commentary on this activity.

---

*Bring up music then crossfade to traffic noises. Wind backed by ship's sirens, dog barking, hansom cab, echoing footsteps, key chain, door opening, shutting*

| | |
|---|---|
| Laura | [*off*] Who's that? |
| Clive | Who do you think, Laura, my dear? Your husband. |
| Laura | [*approaching*] Why, Clive! |
| Richard | Hello, Daddy. |
| Clive | Hello, Richard. My, what a big boy you're getting. Let's see, how old are you now? |
| Richard | I'm six, Daddy. |

| Laura | Now Daddy's tired, Richard, run along upstairs and I'll call you when it's supper time. |
| Richard | All right, Mummy. [*Richard runs heavily up wooden stairs*] |
| Laura | What's that you've got under your arm, Clive? |
| Clive | It's an evening paper, Laura. [*paper noise*] I've just been reading about the Oppenheimer smuggling case. [*effort noise*] Good gracious, it's nice to sit down after that long train journey from the insurance office in the City. |
| Laura | Let me get you a drink, Clive darling. [*lengthy pouring, clink*] |
| Clive | Thank you, Laura, my dear. [*clink, sip, gulp*] Aah! Amontillado, eh? Good stuff. What are you having? |
| Laura | I think I'll have a whisky, if it's all the same to you. [*clink, pouring, syphon*] |
| Clive | Whisky, eh? That's a strange drink for an attractive auburn-haired girl of twenty nine. Is there ... anything wrong? |
| Laura | No, it's nothing, Clive, I – |
| Clive | Yes? |
| Laura | No, really, I – |
| Clive | You're my wife, Laura. Whatever it is, you can tell me. I'm your husband. Why, we've been married – let me see – eight years, isn't it? |
| Laura | Yes, I'm sorry Clive, I ... I'm being stupid. It's ... just ... this. [*paper noise*] |
| Clive | This! Why, what is it, Laura? |
| Laura | It's ... it's a letter. I found it this morning in the letter box. The Amsterdam postmark and the strange crest on the back ... it... frightened me. It's addressed to you. Perhaps you'd better open it. |
| Clive | Ah ha. [*envelope tearing and paper noise*] Oh, dash it, I've left my reading glasses at the office. Read it to me, will you, my dear. |
| Laura | Very well. [*paper noise*] Let's see. 'Dear Mr Barrington. If you would care to meet me in the Lounge Bar of Berridge's Hotel at seven-thirty on Tuesday evening the twenty-first of May, you will hear something to your advantage.' |

## Activity 16    Writing the wrongs

Rewrite Timothy West's script so that it becomes an effective opening to a radio play.

## Activity 17    Dramatic Dickens

**Pair work**

Charles Dickens was always aware of the dramatic potential of his novels. Indeed, he himself toured the country exhaustively giving sell-out dramatised readings from his works, rather like the mega-tours that some singers and bands make nowadays. His novels have always been popular choices for radio adaptation. We are going to look in detail at a recent radio dramatisation of *David Copperfield*.

Text A is the opening of the first episode of Radio 4's dramatisation of *David Copperfield*. Text B is the passage from the novel on which it is based. The extract from the radio programme lasted 87 seconds on air. Read the two passages carefully and discuss the questions on page 268.

1 The novel is written in the first person. How does the adapter deal with this in the dramatisation?
2 Precisely what material from the first five paragraphs of Text B (up to 'My mother went') is used in the dramatisation?
3 What material from these first five paragraphs is omitted?
4 How does the dramatisation provide information about the speakers' identity and circumstances?
5 What narrative material is transformed into dialogue?
6 Not all of Dickens' dialogue is used, presumably because of pressures of time. What is omitted? Is anything of significance lost?

Turn to page 283 for a commentary.

## Text A

*Wind blowing. Knock at door. Door opens.*

| | |
|---|---|
| Betsey | Mrs David Copperfield? |
| Mrs C | Yes. |
| Betsey | Miss Trotwood, your late husband's aunt. You have heard of her, I dare say? |
| Mrs C | I, I have had that pleasure. |
| Betsey | Now you see her. |
| Mrs C | Yes. Please come in here, Miss Trotwood. [*wind stops*] There is a fire. |
| Betsey | Thank you. |
| Mrs C | [*cries*] |
| Betsey | Don't do that. Come, come. Take off your cap and let me see you. Why, bless my heart, you're a baby. |
| Mrs C | I'm afraid I'm but a childish widow and I'll be but a childish mother, if I live. |
| Betsey | Why Rookery in the name of heaven? |
| Mrs C | Do you mean the house, ma'am? The name was Mr Copperfield's choice. When he bought the house he liked to think there were rooks in it. |
| Betsey | And where are the birds? |
| Mrs C | There haven't been any since we lived here. We thought it was a rookery, but the nests were very old ones. |
| Betsey | David Copperfield all over. Takes the birds on trust because he sees the nests. |
| Mrs C | [*sobs*] Mr Copperfield is dead, if you dare to speak unkindly of him, I'll …[*sobs*] |
| Betsey | Come, child. Sit down. You've gone pale. There. When do you expect? |
| Mrs C | I can't stop trembling. I don't know what's the matter. I shall die. |
| Betsey | No you won't. Have some tea. |

## Text B

My mother was sitting by the fire, but poorly in health, and very low in spirits, looking at it through her tears, and desponding heavily about herself and the fatherless little stranger, who was already welcomed by some grosses of prophetic pins in a drawer up-stairs, to a world not at all excited on the subject of his arrival; my mother, I say, was sitting by the fire, that bright, windy March afternoon, very timid and sad, and very doubtful of ever coming alive out of the trial that was before her, when, lifting her eyes as she dried them, to the window opposite, she saw a strange lady coming up the garden.

My mother had a sure foreboding at the second glance, that it was Miss Betsey. The setting sun was glowing on the strange lady, over the garden-fence, and she came walking up to the door with a fell rigidity of figure and composure of countenance that could have belonged to nobody else.

When she reached the house, she gave another proof of her identity. My father had often hinted that she seldom conducted herself like any ordinary Christian; and now, instead of ringing the bell, she came and looked in at that identical window, pressing the end of her nose against the glass to that extent that my poor dear mother used to say it became perfectly flat and white in a moment.

She gave my mother such a turn, that I have always been convinced I am indebted to Miss Betsey for having been born on a Friday.

My mother had left her chair in her agitation, and gone behind it in the corner. Miss Betsey, looking round the room, slowly and inquiringly, began on the other side, and carried her eyes on, like a Saracen's Head in a Dutch clock, until they reached my mother. Then she made a frown and a gesture to my mother, like one who was accustomed to be obeyed, to come and open the door. My mother went.

'Mrs. David Copperfield, I think,' said Miss Betsey; the emphasis referring, perhaps, to my mother's mourning weeds, and her condition.

'Yes,' said my mother, faintly.

'Miss Trotwood,' said the visitor. 'You have heard of her, I dare say?'

My mother answered she had had that pleasure. And she had a disagreeable consciousness of not appearing to imply that it had been an overpowering pleasure.

'Now you see her,' said Miss Betsey. My mother bent her head, and begged her to walk in.

They went into the parlour my mother had come from, the fire in the best room on the other side of the passage not being lighted – not having been lighted, indeed, since my father's funeral; and when they were both seated, and Miss Betsey said nothing, my mother, after vainly trying to restrain herself, began to cry.

'Oh tut, tut, tut!' said Miss Betsey, in a hurry. 'Don't do that! Come, come!'

My mother couldn't help it notwithstanding, so she cried until she had had her cry out.

'Take off your cap, child,' said Miss Betsey, 'and let me see you.'

My mother was too much afraid of her to refuse compliance with this odd request, if she had any disposition to do so. Therefore she did as she was told, and did it with such nervous hands that her hair (which was luxuriant and beautiful) fell all about her face.

'Why, bless my heart!' exclaimed Miss Betsey. 'You are a very Baby!'

My mother was, no doubt, unusually youthful in appearance even for her years; she hung her head, as if it were her fault, poor thing, and said, sobbing, that indeed she was afraid she was but a childish widow, and would be but a childish mother if she lived. In a short pause which ensued, she had a fancy that she felt Miss Betsey touch her hair, and that with no ungentle hand; but, looking at her, in her timid hope, she found that lady sitting with the skirt of her dress tucked up, her hands folded on one knee, and her feet upon the fender, frowning at the fire.

'In the name of Heaven,' said Miss Betsey, suddenly, 'why Rookery?'

'Do you mean the house, ma'am?' asked my mother.

'Why Rookery?' said Miss Betsey. 'Cookery would have been more to the purpose, if you had had any practical ideas of life, either of you.'

'The name was Mr. Copperfield's choice,' returned my mother. 'When he bought the house, he liked to think that there were rooks about it.'

The evening wind made such a disturbance just now, among some tall elm-trees at the bottom of the garden, that neither my mother nor Miss Betsey could forbear glancing that way. As the elms bent to one another, like giants who were whispering secrets, and after a few seconds of such repose, fell into a violent flurry, tossing their wild arms about, as if their late confidences were really too wicked for their peace of mind, some weather-beaten ragged old rooks'-nest burdening their higher branches, swung like wrecks upon a stormy sea.

'Where are the birds?' asked Miss Betsey.

'The–!' My mother had been thinking of something else.

'The rooks – what has become of them?' asked Miss Betsey.

'There have not been any since we have lived here,' said my mother. 'We thought – Mr. Copperfield thought – it was quite a large rookery; but the nests were very old ones, and the birds have deserted them a long while.'

'David Copperfield all over!' cried Miss Betsey. 'David Copperfield from head to foot! Calls a house a rookery when there's not a rook near it, and takes the birds on trust, because he sees the nests!'

'Mr. Copperfield,' returned my mother, 'is dead, and if you dare to speak unkindly of him to me–'

My poor dear mother, I suppose, had some momentary intention of committing an assault and battery upon my aunt, who could easily have settled her with one hand, even if my mother had been in far better training for such an encounter than she was that evening. But it passed with the action of rising from her chair; and she sat down again very meekly, and fainted.

When she came to herself, or when Miss Betsey had restored her, whichever it was, she found the latter standing at the window. The twilight was by this time shading down into darkness; and dimly as they saw each other, they could not have done that without the aid of the fire.

'Well?' said Miss Betsey, coming back to her chair, as if she had only been taking a casual look at the prospect; 'and when do you expect–'

'I am all in a tremble,' faltered my mother. 'I don't know what's the matter. I shall die, I am sure!'

'No, no, no,' said Miss Betsey. 'Have some tea.'

## Activity 18 | Adapting David Copperfield

This activity will give you an opportunity to see whether you can put into practice what you have learnt about adapting classic literary texts for radio.

The following extract is the passage from *David Copperfield* that comes immediately after the extract from the novel in Activity 17 (Text B). Write a script for this extract. Your script should last for 90 seconds of air time (the length of the Radio 4 dramatisation).

'Oh dear me, dear me, do you think it will do me any good!' cried my mother in a helpless manner.

'Of course it will,' said Miss Betsey. 'It's nothing but fancy. What do you call your girl?'

'I don't know that it will be a girl, yet, ma'am,' said my mother innocently.

'Bless the Baby!' exclaimed Miss Betsey, unconsciously quoting the second sentiment of the pincushion in the drawer up-stairs, but applying it to my mother instead of me, 'I don't mean that. I mean your servant.'

'Peggotty,' said my mother.

'Peggotty!' repeated Miss Betsey, with some indignation. 'Do you mean to say, child, that any human being has gone into a Christian church, and got herself named Peggotty?'

'It's her surname,' said my mother, faintly. 'Mr. Copperfield called her by it, because her Christian name was the same as mine.'

'Here Peggotty!' cried Miss Betsey, opening the parlour-door. 'Tea. Your mistress is a little unwell. Don't dawdle.'

Having issued this mandate with as much potentiality as if she had been a recognised authority in the house ever since it had been a house, and having looked out to confront the amazed Peggotty coming along the passage with a candle at the sound of a strange voice. Miss Betsey shut the door again, and sat down as before; with her feet on the fender, the skirt of her dress tucked up, and her hands folded on one knee.

'You were speaking about its being a girl,' said Miss Betsey. 'I have no doubt it will be a girl. I have a presentiment that it must be a girl. Now, child, from the moment of the birth of this girl–'

'Perhaps boy,' my mother took the liberty of butting in.

'I tell you I have a presentiment that it must be a girl,' returned Miss Betsey. 'Don't contradict. From the moment of this girl's birth, child, I intend to be her friend. I intend to be her godmother, and I beg you'll call her Betsey Trotwood Copperfield. There must be no mistakes in life with this Betsey Trotwood. There must be no trifling with her affections, poor dear. She must be well brought up, and well guarded from reposing any foolish confidences where they are not deserved. I must make that my care.'

There was a twitch of Miss Betsey's head, after each of these sentences, as if her own old wrongs were working within her, and she repressed any plainer reference to them by strong constraint. So my mother suspected, at least, as she observed her by the low glimmer of the fire: too much scared by Miss Betsey, too uneasy in herself, and too subdued and bewildered altogether, to observe anything very clearly, or to know what to say.

'And was David good to you, child?' asked Miss Betsey, when she had been silent for a little while, and these motions of her head had gradually ceased. 'Were you comfortable together?'

'We were very happy,' said my mother. 'Mr. Copperfield was only too good to me.'

'What, he spoilt you, I suppose!' returned Miss Betsey.

'For being quite alone and dependent on myself in this rough world again, yes, I fear he did indeed,' sobbed my mother.

'Well! Don't cry!' said Miss Betsey. 'You were not equally matched, child – if any two people can be equally matched – and so I asked the question. You were an orphan, weren't you!'

'Yes.'

'And a governess!'

'I was nursery-governess in a family where Mr. Copperfield came to visit. Mr. Copperfield was very kind to me, and took a great deal of notice of me, and paid me a good deal of attention, and at last proposed to me. And I accepted him. And so we were married,' said my mother simply.

'Ha! Poor Baby!' mused Miss Betsey, with her frown still bent on the fire. 'Do you know anything?'

'I beg your pardon, ma'am,' faltered my mother.

'About keeping house, for instance,' said Miss Betsey.

'Not much, I fear,' returned my mother. 'Not so much as I wish. But Mr. Copperfield was teaching me—'

('Much he knew about it himself!') said Miss Betsey in a parenthesis.

## Review

In this section you have been given the opportunity to look in detail at

- the characteristics of radio drama
- the techniques you need to master when writing plays for radio
- the types of texts that can be adapted as a radio programme
- the importance of knowing your source text thoroughly
- the decisions you need to make about how you will treat your source text
- the specific techniques used in writing radio adaptations of classic literary texts.

We have had time and space to deal with only one of the media and only one of the genres found within that medium. If you decide that you wish to adapt your source text for a different medium or a different genre within a particular medium, you will need a similar amount of knowledge about and expertise in it. It should go without saying, of course, that you will need the same degree of familiarity with your chosen source text. Further help can be found on our associated website.

# Writing the commentary

In most cases, when you have produced a piece of original or creative writing for your A-level work in English, you are asked to provide a commentary on what you have done and this can be worth just as many marks as the piece itself. Text transformation or adaptation is no exception. In this section, we will look at what is required for such a commentary.

A commentary gives you an opportunity to reflect on what you have achieved in your transformation or adaptation – your intentions in choosing a particular text and choosing to transform or adapt it in this or that specific way. You are likely to write about the processes you went through in producing it: the planning, drafting, writing and rewriting that is likely to have been involved and all the decisions that you made.

There can be no blueprint or formula for commentaries on text transformation. No 'one size fits all'. The reason for this, of course, is that the transformations themselves are so diverse. What is appropriate to include or to emphasise in one commentary may not be appropriate for another: the source text will be different; the genre for the transformation will be different, as will be the intentions of the writer. It would be futile therefore to insist that each commentary follows the same pattern or contains the same observations. That said, it is possible to indicate the main areas that commentaries can cover. These are

- the relationship between the source text and the transformation or adaptation
- the genre, audience and purpose(s) of the transformation or adaptation
- the form, structure and language of the transformation or adaptation.

You can see from this list that there is much that you could include in your commentary. If you were to write about every aspect of your work, then it is very likely that you would exceed any stipulated word limit. However, you are not expected to write about everything. What you should focus on are the essential, significant aspects of your transformation or adaptation. Of course, the secret of a good commentary is to decide what is significant or essential in your own work. What were you trying to achieve? How did you set about this? What decisions did you make as you worked towards the production of your final piece?

We will now examine some of the important areas that can be included in a commentary. Others will be considered on the associated website.

## Choice of source text

You will have good reasons for your choice of source text. Your teacher may have introduced you to a text that you enjoyed reading or perhaps there was a particular text that you yourself had discovered and enjoyed. Naturally, the main reason for your choice should be that the text will provide some profitable opportunities for transformation or adaptation. If you are working for an exam specification that allows you a complete free choice of source text rather than one where you have to choose one from a prescribed list of authors, then there are some types that it is best to avoid. This is because they may not offer you enough challenging opportunities for transformation or because you are too familiar with them with the result that you already have very fixed views about them. Such texts can include

- favourite childhood books
- texts that you have studied at GCSE
- insubstantial texts that are briefly fashionable.

Remember that, though you are being judged ultimately on the quality of your transformation and commentary, the choice of your source text can have a crucial bearing on whether your transformation will be successful. You may want to include in your commentary, therefore, some indication as to why you chose your source text and the opportunities it provided for transformation.

---

**Activity 19**

Group work

## Commentary: choosing a source text

On page 274 are extracts from four commentaries in which students review the reasons for their choice of source text. They are placed in ascending order of quality. Discuss them to ascertain what are their strengths and weaknesses.

### Student's commentary A

I've always been interested in current affairs and reading about the lives of famous people. That's why I chose to do my text transformation on this subject. I had decided on the base text before I had actually decided on the genre of my transformation. I had seen the film of *The Great Gatsby* and thought it was great. My mum said that I ought to read the book if I liked the film so much and I thought this was a good idea. As I had never come across the novel before, I decided that I would start to find some information on it and then read the novel itself. When I first started reading it, I found the whole concept and language of the novel to be quite complex, but as I carried on reading it I found myself more and more interested in the famous characters, the story and the whole idea that surrounded it. I felt that I had to definitely use this as my base text.

### Student's commentary B

My aim was to transform a chapter from the William Golding novel *Lord of the Flies* into a radio play that would be beneficial for studying the piece at GCSE. I proposed to do this because I had studied the novel at GCSE and I felt that something like a radio play would help provide a greater understanding of the text and to give my audience a more personal insight into the main characters such as Ralph, Piggy and Jack. In the original text certain aspects about Jack, Piggy and Ralph seemed to stand out more than any other of the characters. That is why I focused on them in my radio play.

### Student's commentary C

I chose to use *Not Waving but Drowning* by Stevie Smith as my base text as it offered me endless options for transformation. This is due to the ambiguity involved in the poem. I could have taken the idea of drowning literally (the subject could have been physically drowned) or metaphorically (mentally drowning with emotion). I found myself imagining a character and a situation to fill out the elusiveness of the poem. This allowed me to exploit the character I had created and the apparent misinterpretation of the situation by the people around the character.

### Student's commentary D

I used *Gulliver's Travels* for my transformation. I had previously read storybooks about the adventures of Lemuel Gulliver, and had a fairly naïve outlook on Jonathan Swift's text, regarding it essentially as a children's story. When I read the original, however, I changed my mind very quickly. I found the use of extended metaphor a subtle and immensely powerful piece of satiric writing and thus I sought to be a latter day Swift by taking the whip to contemporary figures and institutions, as he had done in 1726. The first edition of *Gulliver's Travels* was published in response to endemic corruption surrounding British rule in Ireland, but the scope of the attack centred on almost all contemporary aspects of human culture.

## Aims and intentions

You will have noticed that in the extracts above, three of the writers in explaining their choice of source text also give some indication of what they intended to do with it in the transformation. For example, we learn that Student C wished to 'fill out the elusiveness of the poem' and that Student D 'sought to be a latter day Swift by taking the whip to contemporary figures and institutions'. The choice of source text and your aims and intentions in choosing it are, of course, inextricably linked, but it is as well to point out clearly to the readers of your commentary exactly why you chose it and to be unambiguous as to your purposes.

Students C and D both developed this aspect of their work in more detail later in their commentaries. One of the important reasons for doing this is to reassure the reader that you are not merely producing a piece of creative or original writing, but that your new text is a genuine reworking or transformation of a source text. There are opportunities elsewhere in your course to produce pieces of original writing, but here the emphasis must be on the interplay between two texts – the source text and your reworking of it. If the connection between the two is not evident to a reader (perhaps through unfamiliarity with the source text), then the commentary is your opportunity to demonstrate exactly what this connection is. You should do this if for no other reason than the very practical one that you will lose marks if the reader considers that you have produced a piece of original writing rather than a transformation or adaptation!

## Genre and discourse features

One of the most useful areas to cover in a commentary is that of the genre of the new text. Comments that not only illuminate the reasons for your wanting to chose a particular genre or style model for your transformation or adaptation but also show your understanding of the codes and conventions of the new genre can be especially helpful to people who read your work. They want to be able to confirm that what you wrote in your transformation was the result of a deliberate choice rather than merely a lucky (or unlucky!) chance. Indeed, it is often a good idea to include an example of your chosen genre or style model with your work so that it can be seen how effectively you have used or replicated it.

Remember, the best transformations or adaptations are the ones in which there is a clear distinction between the genres of the original text and your reworking of it. Genres that are too similar (say, a part of a novel transformed into a short story or a play into a film script) are generally less successful because they will not have made enough demands on you.

**Activity 20**

**Group work**

## Commentary: genre characteristics

Here are excerpts from four commentaries in which the writers try to explain the reasons for their choice of genre and how they intended to use its characteristics. The four excerpts are followed by a moderator's evaluation of each of them. Discuss them in order to match each evaluation with the appropriate commentary.

### Student's commentary A
For my text transformation I decided to transform my source text into an article that would feature in the Sunday supplements of a newspaper. The article being an interview with the real life character from the book. I decided to create a retrospective article looking back on her childhood, based around a modern day interview with her. I decided that the article would therefore have to be part of a Sunday review supplement, as it is not based around any actual new or current affairs. It is therefore a general interest article based around social history – this also meant that the story was not going to be investigative or sensationalist in any way,

just a true life account of a person's childhood. I therefore decided that the kind of paper that would be most suited to running a story like this would be *The Mail on Sunday* as it comes under the quality tabloid umbrella. There are certain conventions I have tried to follow in replicating the style of writing used in a more upmarket tabloid such as in the opening paragraph containing 'and as part of *The Mail on Sunday*'s features celebrating this event'. This is a common feature where they write about themselves in the third person in the article. I have tried to structure the piece as it would appear in the newspaper – with the writing in columns and quotations scattered through the article in a large italic font. The opening paragraph is also in a bold font and sets out the content of the article and puts it into context – i.e. the reason the piece has been written.

## Student's commentary B

My basic genre theme is based on love, betrayal, and honour killing portrayed as a key element of murder. I have chosen to write my transformation as a dramatic monologue, which is from the father's point of view. Finding a style model for this genre theme was quite difficult, because I wanted a style model that would follow the same theme, e.g. killing someone and then regretting it, so I researched on the internet and found two different style models that I liked, and thought they would help me with my transformation.

## Student's commentary C

I chose to transform the text into a detective short story based on the style model of Raymond Chandler. I chose this because I thought it could shed new light on the play and its characters through taking a different angle and setting it in a more recent time and place. The angle I chose was one through which the attitudes and values of the Inspector can be transmitted directly and just as effectively whilst conforming to a new set of conventions. I did this by making the detective the narrator and putting my story into the first person. I felt that this angle could provide further insight into the Inspector's character. I also hoped that by this I could create a slight sense of the Inspector's motivation which in the play is kept a mystery. The generic conventions of the play would obviously have an effect on my own story as I had to change features to fit in with the conventions of a detective story. One of these features is the need for there to be an actual crime in a detective story whereas in the play the death is a suicide. I did keep it as a suicide but I gave an indistinct comment: 'Apparent suicide, but in this part of town that could always be disputed' so I could keep with the generic features of detective fiction.

## Student's commentary D

I chose to transform *Hamlet*, taking the basic characters and plot line and turning it into diary entries in the style of Helen Fielding's *Bridget Jones Diary*. I have chosen to focus on Ophelia's point of view, as I wanted a female voice telling the story, mirroring that in Fielding's book. I wanted to tell the story from the point of view of a character that doesn't have such a significant role within the play … Research into this type of novel helped me to understand the basics which characterise the genre. Often referred to as 'chick-lit', many of the books are centred around women and the various relationships in their lives. One thing that did particularly stand out was the strong female voice which carried each story … As I continued to study the fundamentals of the *Bridget Jones* novel I found increasing similarities between the two texts. The dysfunctional family dynamic is found in both plot lines, as well as the struggle over who the central characters are able to trust. I was unable to depict every character as the diary entries are from one person's point of view. Due to this fact I had to note what Ophelia knew/was aware of, so as not to misrepresent her within the plot. Stylistic features I decided to include were… .

## Moderator's evaluation 1
There is confusion in this commentary as to what a style model actually is and how it should be used. Having already decided on her new genre, the candidate, instead of exploring what are its stylistic and structural features, seems to think that all she needs to do is to find works that contain the same themes to inform her transformation. This is a very poor commentary.

## Moderator's evaluation 2
This commentary goes into considerable detail about the reasons for his choice of genre, some of which are convincing; others, perhaps, a case of special pleading, as he does not supply enough evidence from an example of the genre itself to justify his claims. When he writes about his use of the genre's conventions he assumes, as do many average candidates, that conventions merely mean layout and presentation, rather than a more detailed and exemplified examination of the discourse structure of the genre.

## Moderator's evaluation 3
An exemplary and intelligent commentary. The candidate demonstrates detailed knowledge of the conventions of her chosen genre and the unexpected links between her two very different texts. She provides cogent reasons for her choice and is fully aware of both the limitations and the opportunities her choice of new genre provides.

## Moderator's evaluation 4
This is a good commentary that shows awareness both of some of the important conventions of his chosen genre and also how he needed to adapt his source text to fit in with these conventions. He furthermore gives some clear indication of the reasons for his choice of genre, which directly reflects the interplay between the two texts.

We have dealt with two important areas that you may wish to cover in a commentary, but there are, of course, others. You are likely to want to comment on some of the changes you have made between the texts. These might include, in addition to the ones already mentioned, changes in time, sequence of events, setting, narrative point of view and so on. Any change you have made should be related to your aims and intentions and your comments should be focused on these. Your moderator will be looking for some clear and informed comments on the purpose and effects of some of the most important changes. Why, for instance, did you change the formal style of *Pride and Prejudice,* the order of events in *Oliver Twist,* the narrative point of view in *My Last Duchess* or the political perspective in *Animal Farm*? It is to these sorts of question that your commentary should provide quite detailed answers.

# Language choices

You may have noticed that no mention has yet been made of comments on any specific language changes in your transformation. You may think this odd in a Language & Literature course, especially when you will clearly have made some changes from the grammar, lexis and register of the source text. It is not that such changes are unimportant, but there is a danger of overemphasising them to the exclusion of others. The commentary on your transformation or adaptation is not really the place for the close linguistic or stylistic analysis of a text, whether written by yourself or another writer.

We have already discussed what can be the main focus of a commentary and you will have realised that these issues are comparatively large ones connected with your aims and intentions or with aspects of discourse or genre. In writing about these features, it will have been almost impossible for you to ignore some of the language choices and changes you made. It is here, when considering the larger discourse issues of your new text, that you will be writing in some detail about language, but you will be writing about it in support of these other, wider features. You will be commenting on some aspects of your language in support of these wider points. If you begin a commentary by immediately analysing minor aspects of your language choices then the danger is that you will lose focus on the other, arguably more significant, areas. This is not to say, of course, that there shouldn't be any comments on the decisions you have made about language. Clearly it would be a very odd commentary indeed that did not make any reference to the lexical, grammatical and stylistic choices you made in writing. Marks schemes make this clear.

## Activity 21 — Commentary: language choices

Here are the ways that one mark scheme describes the quality of the comments that candidates make on their language choices. They are quoted in ascending order, beginning with the description for the least successful.

- Imprecise and inaccurate comments on language choices
- Comments show basic understanding of language choices
- Comments show awareness of the significance of language choices
- Comments show reliable and perceptive awareness of the significance of language choices
- Comments show consistently perceptive and sensitive awareness of the significance of language choices.

**Pair work**

There follow a number of extracts from students' commentaries in which they refer to their language choices. Discuss each extract with a partner and decide which descriptor from the list best fits the extract. Remember that there may be some disagreement as to which descriptor is the most appropriate. If you find yourselves disagreeing, you should argue through the disagreement until you reach a final decision. This, you may be pleased to know, is exactly the process that your teachers go through when they are deciding how to grade your work!

### Student's commentary A
Examples of the lexical choices that had to be made in order to update the text include the following: 'It would be endearing if it weren't so bloody annoying!' I used words like 'bloody' in reference to today's culture where these types of phrases and comments are very common.

Other examples of modern lexical choices are 'TV's broke so expect it will be a night of comparing whose bloke is the worst'. By mentioning television it immediately brings the story and its characters into the modern world, without having to state when it is set ... To add drama to the piece I used short staccato sentences, this coupled with specific punctuation gave the text a sense of urgency, e.g. 'Motive! ... I trusted him!'

## Student's commentary B

In terms of sentence structure, the format I used in my text varied. On the front page, I used mainly simple sentences, as on the front page of a newspaper its purpose is to draw the audience in to a story, without them struggling through complex sentence structures.

## Student's commentary C

Bathos is used frequently. In the second paragraph, I employed the semantic field of historical images 'cheerful barons in smocks', before contrasting it with modern profane lexis 'piss off to the suburbs'. This served the purpose of maintaining a humorous atmosphere, and not committing myself to a definite tone, thus making the style less forceful.

## Student's commentary D

I have used various techniques throughout my piece when conveying a character's distress or confusion through their language. For example, near the beginning, Clive lets out an exclamation 'Oh Mike, please don't drop me!' showing his anxiety and he frequently uses interrogatives 'What if she's been hurt? What kind of boyfriend am I?' for the same reason.

## Student's commentary E

The article then goes on with the questions that are asked to Tom: 'So Tom, being extremely wealthy and perceived the way that you are, what do you think is the biggest misconception about you?' 'OK, well, moving on then, I'm sure our readers would love to know what your day to day lifestyle consists of you doing?'

## Student's commentary F

When adding extra dialogue into my piece, I had to make sure I had a firm grasp of the language that is apparent through the original text. Although I was not working with an archaic text it is over 50 years old and therefore I had to make sure that I included some of the colloquialisms that would have been apparent in that time but not necessarily in modern times. What also had to be taken into account was the different classes of the characters and therefore clearly show how their class is represented through speech.

## Student's commentary G

To maintain this tone, my transformation also features dialect but with more complex dialect since it is aimed at a Jamaican audience and also because it is based in Jamaica where the

> dialect will be much stronger. For example 'Ahy, afternoon Lucy, call you mada de fi me ask her if she want no fish di afternoon'. This imperative features many complex dialects such as 'fi' and 'de' and 'ahy' which are explained in the glossary. The grammar in my transformation is deliberately non-standard as dialect doesn't feature many plural nouns nor is there much differences with the tense. For example 'My god, you girls must be tired carrying them bag.' This quote shows how the word 'bag' isn't pluralized but instead takes on the word 'them' before it.

## Comments to avoid

There are a number of areas that are best avoided in commentaries as they gain no marks and give a bad impression of the folder overall. The three main ones are considered here.

### Self-congratulation

As you draft and redraft your transformation, you will be given lots of help and advice from your teacher and, no doubt, you will ask other people, classmates, friends and family, to read it and offer their comments on your work. Most students want to submit their very best work and will therefore be likely to act on this advice. The transformation will be of the highest standard you can achieve. But it is others – your teachers and moderator – who will make the final judgement and award a mark. There is nothing to be gained by your saying how well you think you have done or how successful you think the final version of your transformation is. Such comments will not influence your teachers or moderator at all. Comments of this nature or even of 'My mum read it and enjoyed it' should be avoided!

### If only I had more time!

This is the opposite of self-congratulation. The reader of your commentary is not interested in which source text you wish you had chosen; nor is he or she interested in any changes or improvements you wanted to make to the final version, but time ran out! The judgement on your work is made on what your teacher or moderator has in front of them, not on what might have been there, if only you had had that extra week to perfect it. One of the rationales behind coursework is that you do have plenty of time in which to produce your best work and therefore moaning about what you would have done is going to be read unsympathetically with negative thoughts about your time-management skills.

### Describing what you have done

The heart of any commentary should be the analysis and evaluation of your transformation together with relevant and succinct supporting evidence for your observations. No one wishes to read an anecdotal account of what you did in the preparation and execution of your work nor to read a description or summary of its contents. They will have just finished reading it and therefore do not require a summary of what they read only a few minutes previously.

---

**Review**

In this section you have been given the opportunity to look in detail at the requirements for a successful commentary. These include

- reflecting on your choice of source text
- explaining your aims and intentions in writing your transformation

- discussing the interaction of genre, style and discourse between your texts
- commenting on some of your significant language choices.

By following the advice and completing the activities in this chapter, you should have been equipped to write a successful text transformation and its associated commentary whichever of the exam specifications you are studying.

## Commentary Activity 1

We hope that you found this slightly irreverent *Sun* text interesting and amusing. That was certainly the intention of its authors. The new text is probably entertaining in its own right, but the imitation (or parody) of the tabloid-newspaper genre as represented here by the *Sun* adds an extra dimension to its impact.

Your discussion of the questions should have focused your attention on the nature of the changes the writers had to make to ensure a successful transformation of the biblical text. Changes were made to the content of the original in that some details were removed (the information about Caesar Augustus and Cyrenius or the details of the prophecy that so alarmed Herod, for example); the order and structure of the events of the story were altered so that the most important (the nature of this particular baby and the role he was to play) begin the newspaper's coverage and, of course, the biblical language of the early seventeenth century was both modernised and made more informal, so that instead of the angel who 'said unto' the shepherds, his modern counterpart 'tipped them off'. You should also have noticed the use made of recognisable tabloid-newspaper conventions, such as the 'joke' in the headline, with its anachronistic reference to the title of a 1954 classic film musical.

The relationship between these two texts will have focused your attention on one form of text transformation. What the writers of the *Sun* piece have done is to take a well-known story, select those parts of it that are relevant to their purpose and rewrite it in the style of a different genre or text type. They will have carefully researched the codes and conventions of tabloid journalism and used them to re-present the Nativity story in an unexpected manner. In so doing, they will not only have amused and entertained (and, hopefully, not have offended any readers), but may even have brought new life to a familiar story through the interplay between the texts. Modern retellings of the Bible have exactly that aim – to bring the Bible to life for readers who may be put off by more traditional versions.

## Commentary Activity 7

During your discussion, you may well have recommended many other possibilities for transforming the list of texts that we provided. Indeed, we are not suggesting that this is a definitive list of genres, nor that there is a finite number of source texts. What is likely to have emerged from your discussion are the myriad ways of transformation that are feasible and, indeed, the number of texts other than the ones suggested that offer equally rich potential for transformation. When you come to choose your own source texts and genres, you should try to consider as many different ways of transforming a text as possible, so that you find one that not only offers you enjoyment and satisfaction in creating this new text, but also provides the enlightening interplay between the source and the transformation that is the essence of the activity.

281

A variety of information is conveyed by the dramatisation that is not found in the extract from the book. We learn that Merry and Frodo are going to Crickhollow, that Bag End has been sold to Lobelia and we are also given a reminder of the existence of Bilbo Baggins. The adapter has not invented this information (though he has had to invent the dialogue that conveys it); he has merely transferred it from another point in the novel, since he thinks it would be more effective here. Merry is given invented dialogue that reflects his name. For example, he stops the cart and calls back to Frodo: 'I'll tell you one thing, Frodo, you had better settle when you get to Buckland, because I for one am not helping you to move back again!'

You'll be relieved to know that the play is a send-up of the conventions of radio drama. To see just what has gone wrong with this play, these guidelines for aspiring radio writers issued by the BBC should prove illuminating.

GEOFF, CAROL, ALICE, ROGER AND RICHARD ARE IN A CROWDED PUB WITH SOME OTHER FRIENDS – *NO!*
The only means of establishing a character's presence is to have them speak or be referred to by name. If there are too many characters in a scene the listener will lose track.

GEOFF (LOOKING ANGRILY AT IRENE, HIS PALE FACE FLUSHED) "I WILL NOT" – *NO!*
'Stage directions' for the producer's or actor's benefit are to be avoided. If it is important it should be there in dialogue.

A CAR PULLS UP. ENGINE OFF. DOOR OPENS AND SHUTS. FEET WALK TO THE FRONT DOOR. KEY IN THE LOCK. DOOR OPENS. FEET WALK DOWN THE HALL TO THE KITCHEN. "I'M HOME DARLING". – *NO!*
Sound effects should be used sparingly. They should work with the dialogue. Out of context they will mean little. Effects are useful in setting a scene, but the signpost must be subtle.

GEOFF'S BREATHING IN THE 'PHONE BOX BECOMES MORE LABOURED. PAINFUL. BEHIND HIM A SYMPHONY ORCHESTRA, AT FIRST QUIETLY, PLAYS MAHLER'S FIFTH. BRING UP INTERIOR ALBERT HALL. – *YES. THINK IN SOUND!*
A variety of sound is essential for holding the listener's attention and engaging their imagination. This variety can be achieved by altering the lengths of sequences, number of people speaking, space of dialogue, volume of sound, background acoustics and location of action. On radio, one room sounds very much like another if they're about the same size, but the difference between an interior and an exterior acoustic is quite considerable. The contrast between a noisy sequence with a number of voices and effects and a quiet passage of interior monologue, is dramatic and effective.

Obviously, the best way to become familiar with the conventions and the possibilities of radio dramatisations is to listen to as many of them as you can.

**Commentary**

**Activity 17**

Though Text A is the beginning of the radio dramatisation, Text B is not the very beginning of the novel. There have already been three pages in which David Copperfield reflects on the peculiar circumstances of his birth, tells of the earlier death of his father and introduces his great-aunt, Betsey Trotwood. You'll remember that abridging the text is one of the skills stressed and we can see it in operation throughout this extract from the radio dramatisation. A short part of the first paragraph of the novel is used a little later in the dramatisation, but again, you have learnt that too many time shifts are to be avoided. It can be quite awkward, though not impossible, to rely on a first-person narrator in a dramatisation. The adapter overcomes this potential difficulty here by deciding to use no narrator at all. Later, David Copperfield does narrate parts of his own story.

Text A begins with Betsey Trotwood's knock on the door. Her first words indicate the identity of David's mother-to-be. Note, too, how the adapter has to add 'your late husband's aunt' to Betsey's announcement of her own name. You'll have noticed that other sound effects are employed to convey 'that bright, windy, March afternoon' but that some incidents are ignored: 'my mother had left her chair in her agitation, and gone behind it in the corner'. Some of Dickens' descriptions and comparisons are impossible to convey on radio – 'she came walking up to the door with a full rigidity of figure and composure of countenance that could have belonged to nobody else' and 'she seldom conducted herself like any ordinary Christian' – though the distinctly different voices of the two actors playing Betsey Trotwood and Mrs Copperfield do suggest the differing characters and ages of the two women. The decision to dispense with the services of a narrator at this point means that some incidents must be conveyed through invented dialogue. There is an example of this when David's mother-to-be 'sat down again very meekly, and fainted' and 'Miss Betsey had restored her'. The dramatisation covers this by 'Come, child. Sit down. You've gone pale. There.' before picking up Dickens' dialogue with 'When do you expect?'

# Glossary

**Accent** usually refers to characteristic features of regional pronunciation or social class. It also refers to deviations from Received Pronunciation in the speech of people whose first language is not English. The term can also be used to denote emphasis on a particular word or syllable. In written French, for example, it refers to signs added to individual letters to indicate their pronunciation. *pp 16, 151*

**Acoustic modelling** computer modelling of sounds we produce, a process involved in creating artificially produced voices, e.g. for voice-activated computers. *p 150*

**Acoustic phonetics** analyses the physical properties of all the actual speech sounds. *p 157. See also Phonetics.*

**Acronym** refers to the use of the initial letters of a group of words or a phrase as shorthand for the words themselves. When said aloud an acronym makes a new word, e.g. Acquired Immune Deficiency Syndrome becomes AIDS, Anti Social Behaviour Order becomes ASBO. *p 8*

**Active voice** *pp 15, 179. See Voice.*

**Adaptation** when a text is rewritten or changed to make it suitable for another medium. For example novels can be adapted for showing on television as serials or one-off plays or broadcast on radio. *p 257*

**Adjacency pairs** feature of a conversation where there is a regular sequence of utterances by two different speakers, e.g. question and answer. Adjacency pairs can be separated by insertion sequences (one or more intervening utterances). *pp 60, 172, 173*

**Affect** emotional force of a word or words. *p 42*

**Affixation** addition of a prefix or suffix to a word or morpheme to make a new semantic or grammatical form (e.g. **re**turn, **in**formal, sing**ing**, walk**ed**). *p 8*

**Alliteration/alliterative** repetition of the same initial sound within a group of words, e.g. **s**ing a **s**ong of **s**ixpence. *pp 18, 59, 145, 161, 230*

**Allophone** one of two or more different pronunciations of the same phoneme. *p 16*

**Ameliorative change** change in meaning of a word from negative/unpleasant to positive/pleasant associations. *p 8*

**Analogy** as a general term means that there is a similarity between two objects or ideas. In linguistic terms it refers to one of the methods for creating new words by finding a similarity with an object or idea that already exists. For example, a crane (for building) is tall and thin like the bird. A computer window is like the window in a building – in shape and in function. As a process analogy also works for other changes in language. For example, the plural of 'hippopotamus' is 'hippopotami' if it follows the Greek pattern of making plurals but by analogy with other English plural formations 'hippopotamuses' can also be used. *p 34*

**Anaphoric reference** cohesive device by which a pronoun is substituted for and *refers back* to a previous noun or noun phrase to avoid clumsy repetition. *pp 40, 41*

**Anthropomorphism** literary device of giving human characteristics to animals. The word combines two elements adopted from Greek – *anthropo*, meaning 'human', and *morpho*, meaning 'change'. George Orwell's *Animal Farm* is a good example of a story in which animals are presented as having human personalities and behaviour. *p 119*

**Antithesis/antithetical** rhetorical term referring to the use of contrasting ideas or words. *pp 45, 89*

**Antonym** word with opposite meaning to another word. *p 8*

**Archetypal** in its strictest sense refers to the 'first' or 'original'. In the creation of artefacts, it might refer to the first piece made, which then serves as a model for all subsequent pieces. In literary criticism, it is used to describe a character whose qualities and actions have an impact beyond the limits of the immediate story and remind the reader of some earlier figure in literature or myth. For example, Brecht's creation Mother Courage can be seen as a type of Earth Mother, suffering and making sacrifices for her children. *p 119*

**Articulatory phonetics** analyses the way sounds are produced by the vocal organs when we speak. *p 157. See also Phonetics.*

**Aspect** verb form which conveys information about the duration of an action, and whether it was completed or continuous. *p 13*

**Assonance** repetition of the same vowel sound with different consonants, e.g. feel, heap, chief. *pp 18, 161, 230*

**Asyndetic listing** listing items separated by commas without conjunctions, e.g. 'roses, lilies, freesias'. *p 69. See also Syndetic listing.*

**Audience** the specific category of reader or listener that a text is intended for. Audiences can be categorised in a number of different ways, e.g. by age, gender, specific interest group, level of expertise. *pp 2, 55, 113, 170, 202, 245*

**Auditory phonetics** analyses the way speech sounds are received when we hear them. *p 157. See also Phonetics.*

**Authorial voice** implied author (rather than 'real' author) of fictional text who comments directly on character and action to the reader. *p 36*

**Autobiography** account of a person's life written by him/herself. *pp 35, 49, 53, 207*

**Back formation** process of forming a new word, usually a verb, from a noun that already exists. The noun will sound as if it ends in 'er', and this phoneme is removed to form the verb, e.g. 'burglar' becomes 'to burgle', 'editor' becomes 'to edit'. This type of word formation is relatively rare. *p 9*

**Back-channel features** alternative (rather clumsy) term for response tokens. *p 180*

**Bathos** term used in rhetoric for a ludicrous anticlimax. A famous example is 'For God, for country and for Acme Gasworks'. *pp 89, 279*

**Beast fable** style of narrative in which animals are the central figures and are presented as having interests and lifestyles that reflect the human world in a way that ignores probability and realism. The stories are told for their moral message and for their value as instructive criticism of the virtues and follies of humans. *p 119*

**Biography** account of a person's life written by someone else. *pp 35, 49, 53, 207*

**Blending** word formation process where two words are 'blended' or merged together to form a new word, e.g. blending 'breakfast' and 'lunch' produces 'brunch'. *p 8*

**Blog/Weblog** consecutive entries posted on the internet, e.g. a personal diary or entries by a group of people on a particular subject such as politics or global issues. *p 52*

**Booster** has a similar meaning to intensifier, a word that strengthens other terms, e.g. really, hugely, massively. *p 190*

**Borrowing** describes the process where the English language appropriates a word from another language, usually because no English word exists to describe the concept, activity or thing to be described, e.g. déjà vu, karaoke, pizza, Schadenfreude. *p 8*

**Branching** a left-branching sentence opens with a number of subordinate clauses, and *ends* with a main clause; a right-branching sentence *opens* with a main clause, and ends with a number of subordinate clauses. *p 12*

---

**Caesura** pause in poetic line for dramatic or emphatic effect. *pp 30, 161*

**Cataphoric reference** cohesive device whereby a pronoun is used to substitute for and *refer forward* to a noun or noun phrase in the next clause or sentence. *pp 40, 41*

**Cautionary tale** story with a warning, like the tale of the shepherd boy who regularly pretended that a wolf was attacking his flock, crying, 'Wolf! Wolf!' When the wolf really did attack, his fellow shepherds ignored his frantic cries for help. The tale's warning: those who needlessly 'cry wolf' will get no help in times of real danger and will have no one to blame but themselves. *p 119*

**Challenging tags** *p 189. See Tag questions.*

**Cliché** overused or stereotyped phrase. *pp 10, 87, 197, 230*

**Clipping** process of forming a new word by removing a morpheme from an existing word. The existing word is shortened or 'clipped', e.g. 'telephone' becomes 'phone', 'omnibus' becomes 'bus'. *p 9*

**Closure** in a work of literature refers to a satisfying ending in which all the threads of the story are neatly tied. Having followed characters through the story, the audience enjoys the assurance that admirable characters are rewarded, villains are punished, mysteries have been solved and families or lovers are reunited. *pp 122, 177*

**Code switching** describes how speakers can change between the languages of different language groups. Almost everyone can switch automatically, for example, when conversing with two speakers who might require different levels of formality or when changing accent or lexis according to the person you are talking to. *p 181*

**Coherence** refers to the overall sense and meaning of a text. *pp 8, 40*

**Cohesion** refers to the way a text fits together via grammar, syntax, lexis and sound patterning. Specific instances of cohesion are called cohesive devices. *pp 8, 40, 55, 231. See also Anaphoric reference and Cataphoric reference.*

**Collocation** phrase or group of words habitually used together. *pp 10, 135*

**Colloquial language/colloquialisms** everyday, informal vocabulary and grammar, e.g. 'yeah'. *pp 9, 55, 197, 231, 279*

**Commissive** illocutionary speech act when the speaker is committed to a course of action, e.g. 'I promise...', 'I agree...'. *p 171*

**Communicative competence** is similar to code switching. It describes how a speaker has command of a variety of communicative styles. It expresses the proficiency or competence with which a speaker communicates with other speakers. *p 179*

**Compounding** process of forming new words by adding two existing words together, e.g. black + board = blackboard. *p 8*

**Conative function** refers to language which is focused on the addressee with the intention of exerting influence. *p 21*. *See also* **Persuasive function** *and* **Function of language**.

**Connotations** associations aroused by certain words, e.g. danger, terrorist, darkness. *pp 69, 119, 230*

**Connoted meaning** associated meaning. *p 4*

**Consonance** repetition of final consonant or consonant group. *pp 18, 161*

**Consonants** in English (24) are produced by air being expelled at the front of the mouth with the positioning of the lips, teeth, tongue and alveolar ridge (bone behind the teeth) changing the sound produced. *pp 17, 157*

**Content words** grammatical units (parts of speech) conveying semantic meaning, e.g. nouns, adjectives, verbs, adverbs. *pp 9, 180*

**Context** parts of a text preceding or following a particular passage; (more generally) a situation or event within its temporal, social, locational or cultural setting. *pp 2, 27, 98, 151, 249*

**Conversation analysis** approach to discourse analysis that focuses primarily on conversation structure, investigating features like turn taking, discourse markers and non-fluency features. Conversation analysis derives from sociology and is known as ethnomethodology. Theorists focus on the way society affects spoken interaction, proposing that conversation itself constructs a sense of social order, because we all know the 'rules' of everyday conversation intuitively. In other words, naturally occurring spoken language has its own dynamic structure and rules deriving from social interaction, not from the rules of grammar and syntax. *pp 170, 177*

**Conversational implicature** implicit rather than explicit meaning of an utterance, e.g. 'I'm cold' really meaning 'Shut the window'. *pp 24, 163*

**Conversational maxims** four 'rules' for successful conversation described by H.P. Grice (1975). The first is 'be relevant – don't wander off the topic' (maxim of relevance). The second is 'be truthful and have enough evidence for what you say' (maxim of quality). The third is 'speak appropriately – don't talk too much or too little' (maxim of quantity). The fourth is 'speak in a clear, coherent and orderly way' (maxim of manner). These maxims remain valid today, and are built into our everyday exchanges as unrecognised but basic assumptions about talk. *pp 23, 163, 164*

**Corpora** is the plural form of 'corpus' and refers to computer-based 'banks' of twentieth- and twenty-first-century spoken and written language held at various universities, where researchers and publishers often share resources and expertise. **Corpus (or computational) linguistics** researches language data collected in corpora. *pp 9, 150*

**Creative function** is associated with productivity in language and has links with the imaginative function of children's language. *p 21*. *See also* **Function of language**.

---

**Declaration** illocutionary speech act when the speaker alters a situation by their action, e.g. 'I dismiss you, 'I pronounce you man and wife', 'The court sentences you to ten years in prison'. *p 171*

**Declarative** describes a sentence that makes a statement, e.g. 'The dog is sitting on the chair.' *pp 69, 190*

**Deficit approach** term used in gender theory of language to describe the view that women's spoken language is deficient, and that to be taken seriously women must learn to speak like men. *p 187*. *See also* **Difference approach**.

**Deictic** denotes a word whose reference (what it refers to) in a utterance is determined by the context of the utterance, e.g. 'here' or 'there' in 'I'll meet you

there' and 'We're over here'. Deixis refers to use of deitics. *pp 59, 60, 180*

**Demotic** from the Greek *demos*, meaning 'people', describes language which uses everyday vocabulary and grammar, as distinct from poetic and literary crafting or specialised vocabulary and formal structures that might be used in such places as parliament or law courts. *p 136*

**Denoted meaning** 'dictionary' definition giving precise meaning. *p 4*

**Descriptive function** can either be a factual and informative account or be associated with the representational function of language whereby the writer or speaker re-creates and constructs an imagined version of the real world. *p 21*. *See also* **Function of language**.

**Diachronic change** change over time; historical change. *pp 1, 129*. *See also* **Synchronic change**.

**Dialect** describes the particular words, phrases or grammatical structures associated with a particular region or group. These will be consistent enough to form a distinctive variation in the common language. Regional dialects are the most familiar but there are also social, cultural and occupational dialects. *pp 16, 121, 196, 279*

**Dialogic** adjective from 'dialogue'. In relation to Bakhtin, it refers to the interactive nature of all language, whether spoken or written. *p 34*

**Diary** personal daily record of events. *p 52*

**Didactic** describes texts one of whose primary purposes is teaching or instruction about morals, attitudes and values. For example, the aim of Dickens' *Great Expectations* is didactic in using the story of Pip to teach the dangers of excessive materialism. The term is not generally applied to texts which are functionally instructive, e.g. a car manual. *p 119*

**Difference approach** is used in gender theory of language. It describes the view that male and female language use is simply about difference in language choices. It was developed in contrast to the deficit model: the view that women's language is deficient in some way. A third model is the dominance model: the theory that difference in language use between genders is more to do with power relations because in society the male dominates the female. *p 188*

**Dimeter** verse line of four syllables, of which two syllables are stressed. *p 20*

**Diphthong** two vowels together. *pp 157, 158*

**Directive** in a linguistic context refers to a given order, like a command. An aggravated directive is a direct command, whereas a mitigated directive is softened by the use of hedges or modality. *pp 171, 189*

**Discourse** is used to describe text types. It refers to the structure of the text and the conventions or typical features. It is therefore used to classify specific types of text. So speech discourse is a type of text that has a specific structure and particular features. In written texts narrative will have a particular discourse, because it might have typical lexis, grammar, structure, etc. *pp 6, 169, 278*

**Discourse analysis** refers to 'the linguistic analysis of naturally occurring *connected* spoken and written discourse' (Stubbs 1983). A major area of focus is spoken language, which includes speakers in a wide range of social contexts from casual conversation, to service encounters and court-room exchanges, to answer-phone messages, classroom talk and transcribed texts such as interviews and talk in parliament. Some important theories of discourse analysis include speech act theory, exchange structure theory, pragmatics, ethnography of communication, conversation analysis, frame and schema theory. *pp 31, 150, 170*

**Discourse community** group of people using the same sorts of discourse, e.g. lawyers who are proficient in legal discourse. It is similar to a speech

community but discourse could include written as well as spoken discourse. *pp 7, 179*

**Discourse marker** lexical item that is specific to a particular discourse type. It is often used to describe terms that signpost the text, create cohesion and help the audience to follow the way the text works. For example 'well', 'so', 'as I said' are all discourse markers of speech that can signal a change of topic. *pp 10, 108, 177, 231*. *See also* **Tag questions**.

**Discourse structure** describes the way in which a particular type of text is structured. For example a narrative will often have a chronological structure. An argumentative essay will start with an introduction, present one view, then the opposite view and end with a synthesis of the various viewpoints. A conversation will be structured by the participants and will shift from topic to topic according to the contributions. It may have side-sequences, where a new, related topic is introduced before returning to the main topic. *pp 24, 122, 170, 277*

**Disjunct** comments on style or truth/value of what is being said, e.g. frankly, honestly, confidentially. *p 180*

**Dissonance** clashing consonant sounds. *pp 18, 161*

**Dominance approach** is a term in gender theory which links the differences in male and female language to the dominant roles males often have in society. It finds links between research into gender and power. It sees women's language use as created by asymmetric exchanges, finding that there is a similarity between women's language use and that of the less powerful participants. *p 187*

**Double negative** the use of two negative constructions within the same clause, e.g. 'Don't never do that', 'I don't know no-one'. Both Chaucer and Shakespeare used double negatives but, by the eighteenth century, influential grammarians dismissed them as 'illogical' given that two negatives mean a positive statement. Other views on language use see this as a way of accentuating the negative statement. Some dialects would consider a double negative as standard use but prejudice against its use in Standard English remains strong. *p 121*

**Dynamic verbs** describe action, e.g. running, singing, playing, lying. *pp 13, 250*. *See also* **Stative verbs**.

---

**Elision** speech feature where the speaker misses out sounds in a word, e.g. a final sound ('doin'' instead of 'doing'), an initial sound (''appen' instead of 'happen'), or a sound in the middle of a word ('don't' instead of 'do not'). *p 232*

**Ellipsis/ellipt/elliptical** refers to omission of whole words from an utterance or sentence because they are grammatically implied. For example, it is sufficient to reply 'Yes I can' to the question 'Can you cook?' The word 'cook' is redundant because it is implied. This is a normal feature of spoken English. *pp 40, 87, 180, 232*

**End rhyme/end stopping** *pp 19, 161*. *See* **Rhyme**.

**Enjambement** refers to smooth transition (without a pause) from one line of a poem to the next. *pp 30, 161*

**Epistemic modal tags** *p 189*. *See* **Tag questions**.

**Ethnography of communication** sociological approach to discourse which describes the patterns of spoken communication as part of cultural knowledge and behaviour. *pp 170, 179*

**Ethnomethodology** branch of sociology which studies social interaction. Because conversation (linguistic interaction) is central to most social interaction, close study of conversation is an important part of this field of study. *p 177*

**Etymology** study of the origins of words: how words are formed and how they acquire meaning. A good dictionary will give you the etymology of a word as well as its current meaning. *pp 5, 113*

**Euphemism** word or words which soften or even hide meanings, e.g. 'passed away' instead of 'die', 'killed by friendly fire' instead of 'killed by troops on the same side'. Euphemisms are also often used to avoid direct and explicit language referring to sex or sexual parts of the body. *pp 135, 190*

**Evaluative function** is associated with the expressive function in that it involves judgement and the communication of subjective attitude and opinion. *p 22*. See also *Function of language*.

**Evaluative lexis** way of expressing an opinion about the object or concept being discussed. Adjectives are often evaluative lexis, e.g. lovely, great, super. *p 190*

**Exchange structure theory** term originally derived from the study of classroom interaction, but now applied more generally. Exchange structure consists of an optional framing move (e.g. 'Right') followed by a three-part exchange: first the initiating move or opening move (e.g. 'Where is Shakespeare's birthplace?'); then the response (e.g. 'I think it was Stratford-on-Avon – I know he was baptised there.'); and finally feedback/evaluation/follow-up (e.g. 'Yes, that's right.'). Another kind of exchange structure is the two-part adjacency pair, which usually has a question/answer format (e.g. 'How are you?' 'Fine, thanks.'). *p 170*

**Exclamative** describes a sentence or utterance that conveys an emotion such as surprise or warning. In written texts exclamatives are marked with exclamation marks; in speech they are marked by intonation. They may not always be marked in transcripts. In terms of sentence structure they could be questions, statements or imperatives. *p 200*

**Expletive** swear word or exclamation in the form of an oath or vulgar word. *pp 78, 190*

**Expository function** function associated with argument and the communication of attitude and opinion. *p 21*. See also *Function of language*.

**Expressive** illocutionary speech act when the speaker expresses a personal attitude, e.g. 'I deplore...', 'I congratulate...'. *p 171*

**Expressive language** language which conveys emotion, attitude or opinion; creative language. *p 1*

**Fable** story with a moral. Some fables have been passed down through the oral tradition while others have been written as literary pieces. For example, Browning's poem *The Pied Piper of Hamelin* moralises about greed and broken promises. Fables share common characteristics. There are fantasy characters, both human and animal, and improbable happenings but the links to human experience are sufficient to support the moral and make the stories enjoyable and instructive. *p 119*

**Face** in linguistic terms relates to politeness theory and most people's desire to be approved of by others. This is comparable to its use in the idiom 'lose face', meaning be made to feel foolish in front of others. *pp 14, 163*

**Face needs** describes the need that most people have to feel they have a positive status in the company of others. *p 163*

**Face-threatening** describes the way in which some language use threatens the need to be seen positively by others and therefore threatens the sense of self-esteem. Face-threatening acts are actions or speech that impose on other people. *p 163*

**Facework** effort made so that others feel comfortable and maintain their positive face or self-esteem. *p 163*

**Facilitative tags** *p 189*. See *Tag questions*.

**Felicity conditions** *p 171*. See *Speech act theory*.

**Filler** refers to a sound or word that while it does not necessarily add to the conversation, maintains the speaker's turn, while they decide what to say next. A filler might be a word like 'so' or a sound like 'um' or 'er'. Pauses in conversation are referred to as silent/unfilled or voiced/filled. *p 152*

**Film noir** genre in the context of cinema. Coined in the 1930s to describe detective and gangster movies, *film noir* introduced a more realistic portrayal of crime and violence by comparison with the film industry's early tendency to present a sanitised or even glamorous aura. In *film noir*, characters and events are presented in ways that emphasise the dark side of human nature and of the modern world, together with a stark exposition of evil and often ineffectual attempts to rein it in. *p 104*

**First person** grammatical form which refers to the speaker or writer. The first person singular is indicated by the pronouns 'I', 'me', 'my', 'mine'. The first person plural uses 'we', 'our', etc. *pp 36, 59, 107, 218, 241*

**Flash/micro fiction** short pieces of spontaneous creative writing, usually no more than 150 words. *p 221*

**Focalisation** describes the way in which a writer uses different strategies to focus and communicate point of view, usually in prose fiction. *p 36*

**Focused comparison** requires exploration of specific textual features, usually stipulated by an examination question or coursework task. An open comparison of Tolstoy's *Anna Karenina* and Flaubert's *Madame Bovary* will show that one woman is Russian, the other is French (difference) but they both commit suicide (similarity) as a result of failed extra-marital love affairs (similarity) and so on. Whereas a focused comparison of these novels demands an analysis of how each writer presents themes of adultery and punishment. *p 137*

**Footing** refers to the way people align themselves with what they are saying (in other words, their stance). For example, someone's footing when talking to a university admissions tutor might be as a would-be participant and they would adjust their language appropriately. *p 163*

**Foregrounding** method of drawing attention to a particular linguistic item, e.g. beginning a sentence with 'And' or 'But'. *pp 72, 230*

**Fourteener** verse line of fourteen syllables, of which seven are stressed. *p 20*

**Frame** set of contextualisation clues enabling a speaker to recognise a situation. Frame and schema theory refers to a more advanced stage of recognition when the speaker already possesses a mental model (schema) of a situation. *pp 24, 111, 170, 175*

**Framing** term for the way in which a concept or phenomenon will be described. For example, you might frame a debate about immigration in terms of economic benefit or conversely in terms of invasion. Framing is linked to dominant discourses in the way it restricts and defines the language available to discuss an idea or presupposes the attitudes of the audience. *p 131*

**Framing move** *p 172*. See *Exchange structure theory*.

**Fronting** inverting normal word order for purposes of emphasis. *p 12*

**Function of language** The overall function of language is to communicate meaning through its systems and structures. Many distinguished linguists have listed and described the range of language functions, yet their accounts overlap at times. This entry lists 21 language functions and each has its own separate entry in the glossary. You are advised to look up each term as and when you need to, rather than trying to absorb and memorise them all at once. Be ready for some overlap in these functions. Commonly encountered descriptions of language function include the following: referential; descriptive; conative; expressive; phatic; metalingual; poetic; instrumental; informative; regulative; interactional; personal; heuristic; representational; pragmatic; creative; expository; persuasive; transactional; social; evaluative. *pp 20, 21*

**Function words** grammatical units or 'parts of speech' (e.g. pronouns, conjunctions, prepositions and determiners) which connect content words and create coherent meaning. *pp 9, 113*

**Functional language** language which communicates information and gets things done. *p 1*

**Genderlect** term used to describe the way in which genders speak, but more specifically how women speak. It is a way of viewing women's language choices as equivalent to a dialect or a sociolect. *p 6*

**Genre** way of classifying or describing texts that share content, function or form, e.g. diaries, letters, novels. Genres can be divided into sub-genres. For example, the genre of novels includes the sub-genres of adventure novels, mystery stories, romantic novels. *pp 13, 49, 98, 154, 202, 234*

**Ghost writer** someone who writes the biography of a living person as if they had written it themselves. *p 53*

**Gothic horror** centres on gruesome happenings in haunted houses, ruined castles, graveyards, deserted landscapes, in fact anywhere that gives added terror to foul deeds. The term alludes to the medieval style of architecture named 'Gothic'. A key ingredient in gothic narratives is the threat, either real or imagined, of malevolent supernatural powers at work. Ghostly and unnatural events create a macabre atmosphere to delight the reader. *p 99*

**Grammar** component or system of language which relates to form and structure, rather than to meaning and sound. *pp 1, 2, 103, 150, 278*

**Grapheme** smallest unit in the writing system of a language; letter or symbol which can be a visual representation of sound. In English there is no one-to-one relationship between grapheme and phoneme. *pp 2, 160*

**Graphology** refers to language as a semiotic system, creating meaning through textual design, signs and images. Or more simply, it refers to any aspect of the form and/or appearance of a text that modifies meaning in any way. *pp 87, 233*

**Hedge** refers to a feature found in spontaneous conversation when a speaker wants to soften what they are saying, e.g. 'I think', 'I guess', 'sort of'. Hedges can also function to get support from the listener, e.g. 'if you see what I mean'. *p 155*

**Heroic couplets** pairs of rhyming lines in iambic pentameter. *p 193*

**Heteroglossia** Greek word literally meaning 'different tongue'; term used by the Russian linguist Michael Bakhtin to describe the multivoiced nature of spoken and written language. *p 34*

**Heuristic function** language function identified by Halliday in young children's speech, e.g. 'Tell me why'. *p 21*. See also *Function of language*.

**Hexameter** verse line of twelve syllables, six of which are stressed. *p 20*

**Hyperbole** exaggeration intended to emphasise for effect, e.g. 'I've been waiting hours'. *pp 92, 195*

**Hyponym** Lexical meaning can be understood as a system of categories. The most generalised meaning is the hyponym (e.g plant), the next level of semantic refinement (e.g. flower) is the superordinate category and the most specific level of meaning (e.g. rose) is the subordinate category. *p 8*

**Hypotaxis** refers to use of embedded or subordinate clauses, e.g. 'Dave was hanging his washing on the line, until it started raining'. *p 190*. See also *Parataxis*.

**Iambic pentameter** verse line of ten syllables, five of which are stressed. Also referred to as 'blank verse'. *pp 19, 161*

**Idiolect** refers to the fact that each individual has a specific way of using language. Everyone has their own idiosyncratic way of speaking (idiolect) which is the sum of all the influences on their language. *pp 6, 55, 124, 151, 232*

**Idiom** phrase in a language that does not have a literal meaning (e.g. 'raining cats and dogs') or phrase that is used in a set way (e.g. 'tall, dark and handsome', where the language users would understand the meaning of the words as a set phrase). 'Idiom' is linked with the term 'idiomatic' as being particular to an individual situation. *pp 55, 124, 231*

**Illocutionary** refers to an act of speaking that 'performs' by making a promise, giving a warning, putting forward a request, offering a suggestion, predicting a result, etc. *p 171. See also Speech act theory.*

**Imaginative function** language function identified by Halliday in young children's speech, e.g. 'Let's pretend…'; later associated with the creative or productive function of language. *p 21. See also Function of language.*

**Imitation** occurs when writers deliberately write their own work in the style of another writer. This can be for a variety of purposes including parody, satire, tribute and illumination. *p 249*

**Imperative mood** verb form which expresses a command or instruction. *pp 14, 60, 180, 215, 280. See also Mood.*

**Indicative mood** verb form which conveys factual information. *pp 14, 146. See also Mood.*

**Indirect speech acts** are not simply a statement of fact but mean something quite different. For example, 'I'm boiling hot!' might mean 'Please open the window' or 'Why did you tell me to wear my coat?' *p 171. See also Speech act theory and Conversational implicature.*

**Informative** *p 171. See Speech act theory.*

**Informative function** language function identified by Halliday in young children's speech, e.g. 'I've got something to tell you'; later associated with the referential function of language and the ideational metafunction. *p 21. See also Function of language.*

**Initiating move** *p 172. See Exchange structure theory.*

**Insertion sequences** *p 173. See Adjacency pairs.*

**Instrumental function** language function identified by Halliday in young children's speech, e.g. 'I want…'. *p 21. See also Function of language.*

**Intensifier** word that strengthens the expression of another word, e.g. very, really, so. *pp 87, 187*

**Interactional function** language function identified by Halliday in young children's speech, e.g. 'Me and you'; later associated with the interpersonal metafunction. *p 21. See also Function of language.*

**Interactive** term used to describe discourses that allow exchange between the participants or allow the reader to manipulate the text. Text-messaging is interactive because there is an exchange between the two participants. Web pages may be interactive if they allow the reader to navigate around the site. *pp 87, 180*

**Interior monologue** literary representation of the feelings and thought processes of a character. *pp 36, 218, 282*

**International Phonetic Alphabet** *See IPA.*

**Interpersonal** usually contrasts with 'transactional'. It describes the type of communication that is largely focused on social functions, e.g. exchanging views, feelings, phatic conversation. *pp 21, 152*

**Interrogative mood** verb form which asks a question. *pp 14, 180, 231, 279. See also Mood.*

**Interruption** refers to a non-fluency feature found in spontaneous conversation and is simply when someone wants to butt into the conversation. *p 153*

**Intertextuality** describes the fact that all texts are 'in dialogue' with other texts via echoes, allusions, references or rewriting. *pp 34, 88, 230, 241*

**Intransitive verbs** *p 15. See Transitive verbs.*

**IPA (International Phonetic Alphabet)** was first developed in the late nineteenth century by the International Phonetic Association, the most recent revision being in 2005. It uses symbols (based on the Roman alphabet) to represent the sounds of any language in the world. Names are given to vowels, consonants and diphthongs according to where they are produced in the mouth. Other markers (diacritics) can be used to indicate sound variants. The most common vowel sound, as in pict**u**re, **u**nhappy, terr**o**r, has its own name (schwa) and is represented by an upside-down 'e' – ə. *pp 17, 150*

**IRF structure** describes the three-part exchange between two groups that is common in a teaching discourse but might also appear in child directed speech. The three parts are initiation, response, feedback. The dominant participant initiates exchange (e.g. by asking a question), gets a response from the other participant and gives feedback on how acceptable the response is. This is an asymmetric exchange where the dominant participant controls the discourse and the other participant's response. *p 172.*

**Irony** rhetorical figure of speech or trope in which a speaker or writer uses words which seem to contradict the actual context (i.e. saying the opposite of what is really meant), usually for comic or satiric or sarcastic purposes. *p 44*

---

**Journalese** style of writing that has been developed over time by newspaper journalists. In particular, the writing of headlines has become an art in itself, aiming to provide the reader with direct and engaging subject-matter, while putting over a viewpoint. Journalese does not limit its intentions to informing and entertaining. It is a powerful tool in public life and has social, political and financial agendas to push. *p 100*

---

**L1/L2 speakers** 'L1' refers to a speaker's mother-tongue; 'L2' refers to their second (learnt) language. *p 157*

**Latching** immediate follow-up from the previous speaker without overlap. *p 160*

**Left-branching sentence** *p 12. See Branching.*

**Lexical density** number of words per utterance. *p 180*

**Lexical field** vocabulary relating to a particular topic or category, e.g. the lexical field of transport – car, train, plane, bus. *p 55*

**Lexis** (origin: the Greek for 'word') refers to the vocabulary or word-stock of a language. *pp 1, 2 , 55, 103, 150, 224, 278.* **Lexicon** has a similar meaning, but can also refer to a dictionary. *p 8.* **Lexeme** and **lexical item** are interchangeable terms meaning 'word'. *pp 2, 10, 256.* **Lexical semantics** means the study of the meaning of words. *p 4*

**Linguistic modelling** computer modelling of sounds interpreted as words, a process involved in creating artificially produced voices, e.g. for voice-activated computers. *p 150*

**Literary fiction** is usually a work of prose, of some length, in which the writer has the freedom to construct a plot and characters which are entirely imagined. However believable these may be, there is no requirement for any factual basis in real life. The fiction or falsehood in the story is an accepted convention of writing for entertainment. The writer's skill in the style and management of the narrative give it the 'literary' quality. *p 97. See also Flash fiction.*

**Literary non-fiction** shares many of the presentation features of literary fiction, in that the reader follows a narrative describing characters and events in which they take part, but the source material for the narrative must be authentic and must be faithfully portrayed. People and events must be real. The writer is permitted to offer some interpretation and opinion, provided it is acknowledged as such. *p 97*

**Loan word** word borrowed from another language which becomes part of the new language, e.g. pizza (from Italian). *pp 8, 92*

**Locutionary act** *p 171. See Speech act theory.*

**Major and minor boundaries** in conversation are equivalent to commas, semi-colons, colons and full stops in punctuation. *p 160*

**Masterplot** basic plotline which is frequently reworked with variations in the form of new characters and situations. For example, Tom Wolfe's *Bonfire of the Vanities* charts the descent of a successful man from wealth and respectability into disgrace, largely as a result of his own arrogance. Experienced readers will recognise the link with earlier morality tales, while being open to the writer's new treatment. *p 119*

**Maxim of manner/quality/quantity/relevance** *p 164. See Conversational maxims.*

**Medium** *pp 106, 257. See Mode.*

**Metafunction** term used by the linguist Michael Halliday to describe the three key overarching functions of language. The ideational metafunction conveys information about everything that's happening in the world; the interpersonal metafunction represents the relationship between the addresser and the addressee; the textual metafunction refers to whatever spoken or written mode is used to enable communication to take place. *pp 21, 152. See also Function of language.*

**Metalingual function** function that focuses on the language itself. *p 21. See also Function of language.*

**Metaphor** figure of speech which is an implicit comparison based on certain shared attributes, e.g. 'He's a real wet blanket'. *pp 4, 45, 59, 135, 151, 233, 251.* Conceptual metaphor is applied by cognitive linguists to what they regard as basic 'life' metaphors which seem to be built into the human imagination, e.g. death is sleep, sport is war. *p 45*

**Metonymy** figure of speech or trope in which a single term stands for everything associated with it, e.g. 'the press' includes all newspapers. *p 44*

**Metre** regular patterning of stressed and unstressed syllables in verse. *pp 19, 161*

**Metrical patterns** variants or deviations from regular patterning in verse to create a particular effect. *p 19*

**Minor boundaries** *p 160. See Major and minor boundaries.*

**Minor sentence** unit of syntax conveying the meaning of a complete sentence but without the explicit inclusion of all the component parts. Missing parts are understood but not expressed, as in 'Not going to be finished', which omits the subject and finite verb. The whole sentence would be 'The job is not going to be finished '. In reply to 'Where's the cat?' the answer 'On the mat' omits both subject and verb. *pp 87, 125, 230*

**Miscommunication** feature of unsuccessful conversation, when participants fail to understand each other. This may happen if speakers are following different conversational rules. *pp 24, 175*

**Modality** describes state or mood and, in linguistics, is used to define modals which express the mood of a verb. These modal verbs are any of the group of English auxiliary verbs (can, could, may, might, shall, should, will, would, must) that are used with the base form of another verb to express distinctions of mood, e.g. 'Can I leave now?' compared with 'May I leave now?'. Modal auxiliaries can also function in politeness strategies to soften directives or express requests in a more formal register, e.g. 'Would you help?' *pp 13, 14, 94, 190*

**Mode** channel of communication within a text, e.g. spoken, written, visual. Multi-modal refers to a text (such as a film or web page) that communicates using more than one mode. *pp 21, 54, 149, 202, 248*

**Monophthong** single pure vowel, as in 'cat', 'hat'. *p 158*

**Mood** range of verb forms conveying information (indicative), giving commands (imperative), asking questions (interrogative) or allowing for the expression of actions which may not actually take place (subjunctive). *pp 13, 14. See also Indicative mood, Imperative mood, Interrogative mood and Subjunctive mood.*

**Morpheme** smallest grammatical unit in a language. A free morpheme is one that makes sense on its own; it is a word, e.g. 'hand'. A free morpheme cannot be broken down any further. A bound morpheme is one that needs to be 'bound' or attached to another to form a word, e.g. 'y', as in handy (= hand + y). Morphemes are used to change the grammatical functions of words, e.g. the morpheme 's' makes nouns plural, the morpheme 'ed' puts verbs into the past tense. *p 10*

**Morphology** study of the structure of words and their roots, stems and affixes (or morphemes). Morphology is an integral part of grammar. *p 10*

**Multi-modal** *pp 31, 248. See Mode.*

**Murder, mystery and suspense** phrase combining the key elements of the detective story in which murder has been committed by a person or persons unknown. Even while the mysterious circumstances are being investigated, further dangers lurk, with the distinct possibility of more unexpectedly sudden deaths. There are multiple variations on the formula but the writer must sustain the reader's interest by delaying revelations until the latest possible moment and keeping up the level of suspense. *p 98*

---

**Naming insight** term (introduced by Jean Aitchison) referring to a stage in acquiring language when early humans started to name objects and people around them, as young children do today. *p 151*

**Narrative** story or storytelling. *pp 10, 35, 97, 154, 250*

**Narrative perspective/voice** both refer to the angle or point of view from which a story is told. This may be autobiographical (first-person narrative voice) or told by an omniscient narrator or by a participating observer (third-person narrative voice). *pp 30, 36, 60, 197, 217, 218. See also Persona.*

**Narrative structure** the way in which a narrative is organised with relation to events, participants, time frame and voice. William Labov's narrative structure theory provides a useful methodology. *pp 37, 174*

**Neologism** word new to a language. New words are formed all the time in English in a variety of ways, including compounding, clipping, blending, back formation, affixation and acronyms. *pp 8, 77, 186*

**Non-fluency features** features of speech where the utterances or exchanges temporarily lose fluency, e.g. pauses, repairs, interruptions or repetition. They are common because speakers are thinking as they speak and so sometimes rephrase their comment as they are producing it. *p 152*

**Norm** in linguistics describes the accepted or expected way in which something would be said or written. *pp 36, 179*

**Observer's paradox** refers to the unnatural effect on speakers when being observed or recorded. The very act of observation produces the opposite effect of what is desired: natural speech/interaction. *pp 177*

**Onomatopoeia** phonological feature that mimics the sound it describes, e.g. 'bang' or 'buzz'. *pp 17, 161*

**Opposition** contrast between words, often used for dramatic effect, e.g. dark/light, good/evil. *p 233*

**Orthography** refers to the study of spelling and the writing system of a particular language. *pp 113, 230*

**Overlap** refers to a non-fluency feature found in spontaneous conversation. It is like an interruption but intended to support the speaker rather than butt into the conversation. *p 153*

**Over-stereotyping** fixed set of characteristics given to a type of person or concept which has been over-used, so that it is no longer effective. *p 55*

**Oxymoron** phrase that can be viewed as a contradiction in terms, e.g. 'an honest thief'. In rhetoric, it is a neat device for identifying conflicting but seemingly accurate judgements about people and situations, e.g. 'The wisest fool in Christendom'. *pp 69, 145*

---

**Parable** story providing a moral or told to teach a religious belief. The parables of the Bible illustrate important concepts about God and human behaviour, such as forgiveness and responsibility for others, e.g. the parables of the Prodigal Son and the Good Samaritan. *p 119*

**Paradigmatic and syntagmatic axes** represent (in diagrammatic form) the fact that all language users work within two frameworks – the words available for choice (paradigmatic axis) and the structure or form of the language into which these choices fit (syntagmatic axis). *p 2*

**Paralinguistic feature/paralinguistics** refers to body language, or features of speech which don't have any actual meaning, e.g. 'mm', 'uh'. *pp 80, 152*

**Parallel structures** patterning of words, sounds or sentences to create a sense of balance, e.g. 'It was the best of times, it was the worst of times'. *pp 92, 230*

**Paraphrase** means literally 'other words'. Paraphrasing a text means rewriting it in one's own words. A skilful paraphrase should aim to make the meaning more accessible, possibly by reducing the length and/or replacing challenging vocabulary and expressions, without sacrificing important aspects of meaning. Writing a paraphrase tests the writer's grasp of the meaning and significance of a text. *p 120*

**Parataxis** refers to use of linked and equal clauses. The clauses are linked by co-ordinating conjunctions such as 'and', 'but', 'or'. For example, 'Rob did the washing up and Jo did the shopping'. *p 190. See also Hypotaxis.*

**Parody** mocking imitation of a writer, speaker or genre. *pp 96, 281*

**Passive voice** *pp 15, 179. See Voice.*

**Pejorative change** change in meaning of a word from positive/pleasant to negative/unpleasant associations. *p 7*

**Performative** *p 171. See Speech act theory.*

**Perlocutionary** refers to the way in which a listener or addressee is affected by an utterance (or speech act). For example, is s/he frightened, delighted, annoyed, pleased, persuaded, dissuaded? *p 171. See also Speech act theory.*

**Persona** term used to refer to the adopted or assumed personality of a narrator as distinct from the true identity of the writer. Generally speaking the anonymous, omniscient narrator has no identifiable persona but some narrators address the reader directly and offer their own interpretation and opinion on events and characters. They are as much creations of the writer's imagination as the characters in the story. *pp 93, 132, 141, 193, 218. See also Narrative perspective/voice.*

**Personal function** language function identified by Halliday in young children's speech, e.g. 'Here I come'. *p 21. See also Function of language.*

**Personification** effect created when a non-human object or quality is given human characteristics, e.g. 'the weather was kind to us'. *p 89*

**Persuasive function** All language is persuasive to a greater or lesser degree, depending on the audience, purpose and context, ranging on a continuum or cline from a dictionary definition to posters on a shop front declaring 'Fire-damaged goods!! SALE!!!! EVERYTHING MUST GO!!!' *p 25. See also Function of language.*

**Phatic function** function that establishes social contact and maintains communication in any given interaction. Phatic tokens like 'Hi' and 'See you' are part of everyday speech. The term phatic communion was coined by an anthropologist to describe this kind of social behaviour. *pp 21, 177. See also Function of language.*

**Phonaesthesia** the expressive element in sound patterning. *p 17*

**Phoneme** smallest individual unit of sound in a language. There are 44 phonemes, or sounds, in English. They can be transcribed using the phonetic alphabet. *pp 2, 157. See also IPA.*

**Phonetics** recognised way of classifying the vocal sounds in a language. Writing something phonetically means using the alphabet and other symbols to indicate how a word was pronounced, e.g. 'gonna', 'cuz'. Within phonetics, there are specialised areas of study: articulatory phonetics analyses the way sounds are produced by the vocal organs when we speak; acoustic phonetics analyses the physical properties of all the actual speech sounds; auditory phonetics analyses the way speech sounds are received when we hear them. *pp 17, 150, 157. See also IPA.*

**Phonology** study of the sounds in language. As well as pronunciation, it includes the way sound patterning is used in written and spoken English. *pp 2, 103, 157.* Phonological features may include alliteration, repetition, rhyme. *pp 1, 55, 145, 224*

**Poetic function** function that incorporates the aesthetic, productive and creative functions of language, and is ultimately a development of the imaginative function Halliday identified in young children's speech. *p 21. See also Function of language.*

**Politeness**, in linguistics, is used to describe certain language forms and behaviours. Politeness forms soften requests and show respect for others. Robin Lakoff formulated this into her politeness principle, which suggests three 'rules' we follow in order to smooth interaction: don't impose, give options, make your receiver feel good. These principles form part of the politeness strategies, which also can involve adjusting your language to reduce the linguistic distance between yourself and another. Common politeness markers are 'please', 'thank you', 'I'm sorry to bother you but…', 'I'm afraid (you've got that wrong/you owe me some money, etc.)'. *p 163*

**Political correctness** describes a variety of language use that is deliberately constructed to avoid giving offence to particular persons or social groups. It was popularised in the USA and has been attacked for being overly sensitive and politically divisive. (Consider the banning of 'Baa Baa Black Sheep' in schools.) It is an important concept as it highlights the power of language to exclude. It was also responsible for raising societal awareness about language use. *p 187*

**Popular science** writing on a scientific topic which adopts a style similar to fiction to make it accessible to a wide audience, e.g. *Longitude* and *Galileo's Daughter*, by Dava Sobel. *pp 54, 209, 226*

**Post-modification** *p 77. See Pre-modification/post-modification.*

**Pragmatic function** general description of language used to achieve specific practical purposes, and associated with the transactional function. Much everyday communication is pragmatic in function and purpose. *p 21. See also Function of language.*

**Pragmatics** study of implied meaning and how social context affects the meaning of language. It has been defined as 'not what is said but what is understood'. This area of language study also includes assumed knowledge, politeness, taboo and 'reading between the lines'. When a teacher says 'You're late!' what do they really mean? *pp 23, 170*

**Pre-modification/post-modification** refers to the position of adjectives or adjectival phrases. When an adjective is placed before a noun, as in 'beautiful weather', the noun 'weather' is said to be pre-modified. In 'The weather, beautiful, warm and sunny, allowed us to walk outdoors', the noun 'weather' is said to be post-modified because the adjectives follow the noun. *pp 77, 145, 233*

**Prosody** describes the phonology or sounds of speech, including the rhythm and intonation. *p 157*

**Proxemics** communication by touch. *p 152*

**Pun** play on words that sound the same or similar. *pp 45, 161*

**Purpose** In terms of writing for A-level English Language, purpose within texts can be divided into the following broad categories: writing to entertain, writing to persuade, writing to inform and writing to advise/instruct. It should be noted, however, that texts rarely, if ever, have a single purpose, e.g. persuasion texts often contain elements of information and/or entertainment. It is often more helpful to regard texts in terms of their primary (most significant) purpose and their secondary (or less significant) purpose(s). *pp 2, 98, 202, 245*

**Quatrain** Four-line poetic stanza. *p 193*

**Rank order** is associated with Halliday's systemic grammar. The idea of a rank scale or order relates to larger units and smaller units in discourse, ranging from sentence, clause, phrase, to word and morpheme. *p 11*

**Reader-response theory** useful theory which explores the relationship between author, text and reader. The basic premise is that reading a text is a dynamic and complex experience in which the reader is active rather than passive, in a variety of ways. *p 37*

**Reading position/readerly text, writing position/writerly text** The differences here are between texts where the reader's expectations are matched and texts where the writer's desire to innovate leads to the reader's expectations of a text being (excitingly, one hopes) disrupted. *p 27*

**Received Pronunciation (RP)** describes an accent used by less than 3% of English speakers. It has traditionally been the accent of royalty and 'BBC' English, i.e. the accent of Prince Charles or the actors in the film *Brief Encounter*. *p 151*

**Referential function** *p 21. See Function of language.*

**Reformulation** feature of interaction often associated with non-fluency, when a speaker feels the need to rephrase what he or she has just said. *p 180*

**Refrain** repeated line or phrase appearing in the same position in each verse of a poem. *p 193*

**Register** describes variations in language according to the 'user' (defined by variables such as social background, geography, gender and age), and variations according to 'use' (in the sense that each speaker has a range of varieties and chooses between them at different times and in different contexts). *pp 8, 55, 109, 164, 215, 278*

**Regulative function** language function identified by Halliday in young children's speech, e.g. 'Do as I tell you'. *pp 21. See also Function of language.*

**Repair sequence** non-fluency feature of speech when speakers correct themselves in their utterance. *p 177*

**Reportage** journalist's interpretation of an event in the form of a spoken or written report. *p 54*

**Representative** illocutionary speech act when the speaker believes in the truth of the proposition, e.g. 'I believe...', 'I conclude...'. *p 171*

**Rhetoric** comes from the Greek *techne rhetorike*, meaning the art of speech. It acquired a more specialised meaning associated with persuasion and was later used in written as well as spoken language. *pp 17, 42, 122, 135, 154, 230*

**Rhyme** literally, a 'phonetic echo in verse'; regular repetition of selected sounds in verse. **End rhyme** is full rhyme at the end of a line. **Half-rhyme** is echoing of final consonants with different vowels. **Internal rhyme** is full rhyme within a line, rather than at the end. **Eye rhyme** is visual, not phonetic repetition, e.g. slough/ rough. **Feminine rhyme** refers to repetition of unstressed final syllables. **Masculine rhyme** refers to repetition of stressed final syllables. *pp 18, 19, 161*

**Rhythm** patterning of stressed and unstressed syllables, usually in poetry but sometimes in prose. *p 18*

**Right-branching sentence** *p 12. See Branching.*

**Schema** *pp 24, 170, 175. See Frame.*

**Scheme** name for a rhetorical device such as antithesis. *p 45*

**Semantic change** describes the process words undergo when they change their meaning over time. For example, the word 'wicked' has changed its meaning and is now often used to mean 'great' or 'good'. *p 7*

**Semantic field** group of words or terms related to the same area of meaning. The word 'net' belongs to the semantic field of computers, but also to the semantic fields of fishing and hair. If we can identify the context of a word we can pin down the 'field' to which it belongs. *pp 6, 93, 180, 279*

**Semantics** study of meaning connections between words. It may also include the study of meaning devices such as metaphor, allusion, connotation and juxtaposition. For example, the meaning of the word 'dress' changes as soon as we connect it with other words such as 'party' or 'wound' or 'down'. The meanings of words are not fixed but can change according to context. *pp 4, 45*

**Semiotics** study of the cultural signs and symbols used in text. It can refer to language use as well as the use of images. This is important to the way we 'read' text. We are influenced not only by what is written but the images and symbols that accompany it. *p 4*

**Service encounter** technical term for any occupational exchange that involves the role of service such as in shops or restaurants. Such exchanges generally have the same structure, e.g. a greeting, a question so that the customer can ask for what they want, then a closing. *pp 21, 160*

**Sibilance** sequence of repeated consonants which have a hissing sound, e.g. 's'. *p 77*

**Simile** extended metaphor in which the comparison between entities is explicit, e.g. 'The old man walks like a snail'. *pp 45, 90, 135, 250*

**Social constructionist approach** views gender as a social construct rather than a given social category. In other words, people do gender. This avoids polarisation and recognises individual differences, by emphasising social context as a way of understanding gendered language behaviour. *p 188*

**Social context** general term that describes any social situation that might influence language use. *p 5*

**Social function** function associated with the interactional and phatic functions of language, and also part of the interpersonal metafunction. *p 22. See also Function of language.*

**Sociolect** language variety linked to any sort of social group, e.g. the language of local football supporters, friendship groups or work-based associations. *p 6*

**Sociolinguistic** refers to language variation as a result of social context. *p 183*

**Softening tags** *p 189. See Tag questions.*

**Speech act theory** derives from the work of philosophers Austin and Searle (1962, 1969). Speech acts perform or act at three levels: the words themselves are a locutionary act; whatever the words are doing has illocutionary force; and the result of the speech act on the addressee is the perlocutionary effect. These speech acts can be informative (e.g. 'My eyes are blue') or performative (using performative verbs, e.g. 'I welcome you', 'I demand that...').To perform successful speech acts a speaker must have authority to speak, must be able to speak appropriately and must be sincere, thus achieving felicity conditions. *pp 170, 171. See also Illocutionary, Perlocutionary and Indirect speech act.*

**Standard English (SE)** variety of English recognised as the norm for spoken and written English. It is the predominant variety of English used in education. It grew out of the need for countrywide and later worldwide communication in English. *pp 121, 152, 200*

**Stative verbs** describe states of existence, of being, seeming or becoming. *p 13. See also Dynamic verbs.*

**Stream of consciousness** primarily a literary technique; can also be described as an interior monologue. *pp 36, 197*

**Sub-genre** category which is part of a wider genre, e.g. a travel journal is sub-genre of travel writing. *pp 53, 98, 214. See also Genre.*

**Subjunctive mood** verb form which allows for the expression of actions which may not actually take place. It is most commonly used with verbs of wishing, hoping and fearing and situations in which the action is unlikely to happen. For example, in the sentence 'When we marry next year, I will devote my life to you', both verbs are in the indicative mood, whereas in 'If we were to marry, I would make you happy', the subjunctive mood identifies the hypothetical nature of the action. *p 146. See also Mood.*

**Subliminal** refers to something which is under the surface and may be only subconsciously perceived. *p 215*

**Subordinate category** *p 8. See Hyponym.*

**Superlative** comparative adjective which describes the highest degree, e.g. biggest, best. *p 92*

**Superordinate category** *p 8. See Hyponym.*

**Syllabic verse** verse form where the metrical patterning depends on the number of syllables per line of verse, not on the balance and number of stressed and unstressed syllable. *p 20*

**Synchronic change** unlike changes in language and style which happen over a period of time (diachronic change), this refers to variations in language which are influenced by context and purpose. These are evident simultaneously and are attributable to cultural and logistical factors rather than historical influences. English usage varies from place to place with, for example, British English and American English demonstrating differences not only of pronunciation but also of lexis and grammar. *p 129*

**Syndetic listing** listing items separated by conjunctions, e.g. 'roses and lilies and freesias'. *p 69. See also Asyndetic listing.*

**Synecdoche** trope where a part stands for a whole, e.g. 'All hands on deck!' *pp 44, 251*

**Synonym** word with the same or similar meaning as another word. *p 8*

**Syntactic parallelism** pattern in language closely allied to contrasting pairs. Essentially it is when the order of words (syntax) is repeated close by. This is done for linguistic effect and can be a feature of good or persuasive writing. Often it is a feature of skilful and persuasive spoken language. For example, 'I came, I saw, I conquered' and 'This was not a terrorist attack against the mighty and the powerful. It was not aimed at Presidents or Prime Ministers. It was aimed at ordinary, working-class Londoners, black and white, Muslim and Christian, Hindu and Jew, young and old.' *pp 12, 89*

**Syntagmatic axis** *p 2*. See *Paradigmatic and syntagmatic axes*.

**Syntax** structure of the sentence, including word order and grammatical relationships. *pp 1, 2, 103, 152, 230*

**Synthesise** merge two or more texts into one comprehensive document so that the reader has a broad overview of the material. This requires judgement as to the extent of abbreviation, the elimination of redundant and irrelevant material and the foregrounding of focal points. *p 136*

**Synthetic personalisation** is used to describe the way some public texts manufacture a relationship with the audience. It can be created by the use of personal pronouns (particularly I/you/we), personal details, mitigation, and typical features of speech. *p 36*

**Taboo** describes any subject that a cultural or social group may consider beyond the realms of discussion. It is also used to refer to topics that people find it difficult to talk about. For this reason we develop ways of indirectly referring to taboo topics, e.g. euphemism. Taboo topics may include sex, money, death, disease. *pp 146, 151*

**Tag questions** discourse markers in the form of 'tagged on' questions like 'don't you?' Facilitative tags invite the next speaker to respond, e.g. 'Let me introduce Mary – she's an architect too, aren't you?' Epistemic modal tags express uncertainty, e.g. 'The train leaves at 8.30, doesn't it?' Challenging tags set a challenge, e.g. 'You do realise this is a punishable offence, don't you?' Softening tags make something more acceptable, e.g. 'Never mind, you didn't mean to spill the milk, did you?' *pp 180, 189*

**Tense** means of expressing time relations in the verb form. *p 13*

**Tetrameter** verse line of eight syllables, four of which are stressed; also called octosyllabic verse. *pp 20, 161*

**Text** passage of written or spoken language. This term can also refer to multi-modal extracts. *p 31*

**Text transformation** occurs when a writer takes a text (or a part of a text) and changes (or transforms) it in some way to produce a new text that can exist in its own right, yet illuminate some aspect(s) of the original. *p 234*

**Text type** refers to the genre of the text in question. *pp 22, 49, 103, 281*

**Theme** central topic, idea or concern. *pp 55, 98, 192, 247*

**Third person** grammatical form referring to others, e.g. he, she, him, her (third person singular) or they, their (third person plural). *pp 14, 60, 123, 209, 218, 232*

**Time marker** phrase used to give the reader a clearer picture of the speed of events and the order in which they occur. Time markers may be explicit, as in 'After two hours', or implicit, as in 'By now the sun had gone down and he was feeling cold'. *pp 87, 131, 231*

**Tone** term describing the way in which a writer's language choices are tailored to the requirements of genre, purpose, audience and situation. *pp 55, 108, 226, 279*

**Transactional function** language function associated with practical matters, getting things done, e.g. visiting the bank, shopping, going to the doctor. It is linked with pragmatic function of language. *pp 21, 153*. See also *Function of language*.

**Transcript** specific way in which speech is recorded in writing so that it can be studied. It has its own layout and notation. It is set out in a similar way to a play script with the speaker in the left margin. Everything that is spoken is written, including false starts, repairs, fillers, pauses, interruptions and simultaneous speech. A vertical line is used to show simultaneous speech or interruptions. Pauses are marked with brackets () with the time in seconds between them if appropriate, e.g. (1). *pp 22, 54, 160, 205*

**Transition relevance point (TRP)** moment in a conversation when the topic is about to shift and various cues (e.g. change in intonation) can be recognised. *p 177*

**Transitive verbs** have a grammatical subject and an object. Intransitive verbs have only a grammatical subject. According to Michael Halliday transitivity is an important part of the ideational metafunction of language, because it links people, actions and situations. *p 15*

**Triadic structure** list of three creating a rhythmic effect, e.g. 'Liberty, equality, fraternity'. This technique is often used in persuasive speeches. *p 94*

**Trimeter** verse line of six syllables, three of which are stressed. *pp 20, 161*

**Triphthong** three vowel quality, as in 'player', 'fire', 'tower'. *p 158*

**Trope** figure of speech in rhetoric. *p 43*

**Turn taking** feature of conversation. In a co-operative conversation the participants take turns to contribute an utterance. *pp 94, 157*

**Utterance** stretch of spoken language, brief or extended. *pp 2, 80, 87, 104, 153*

**Vague language** term used to describe words such as 'like', 'kind of', 'whatever'. *p 156*. See also *Hedge*.

**Variety** refers in linguistic terms to a type of written or spoken language use. There are endless varieties of language use. A variety is often associated with a particular context, e.g. formal language, slang, medical language, creole. *pp 6, 98*

**Vernacular** refers to plain, everyday, ordinary language, also to the standard native language of a country or locality, as opposed to learned or literary language. It is sometimes used to describe a variety of everyday language specific to a social group or region, e.g. the vernaculars of London. *p 174*

**Vocabulary** words a speaker of a language has at their disposal. We all have vocabularies that we use frequently. These are our active vocabularies. However we also know a lot of words that we do not use often, words that we understand but do not necessarily use. These are called latent or passive vocabularies. *pp 2, 55, 121, 151, 230*

**Voice** verb form which reveals whether or not the grammatical subject took action (active voice) or received/felt the action (passive voice). *pp, 13, 15, 55, 98, 193, 217, 251*

**Voiced** refers to the vocal chords being vibrated when a sound is produced. For example, in English 'b' is voiced, whereas 'p' is unvoiced. *p 157*

**Weblog** *p 52*. See *Blog/Weblog*.

**Writerly position** *p 27*. See *Reading position/readerly text, writing position/writerly text*.

**Writerly text** *p 27*. See *Reading position/readerly text, writing position/writerly text*.

# Acknowledgements

The publishers would like to thank the following for their kind permission to reproduce copyright material:

Monty Python Pet shop sketch © Python (Monty) Pictures Ltd; *The BFG* by Roald Dahl, Jonathan Cape Ltd & Penguin Books Ltd; 'Musée des Beaux Arts' from *Collected Poems of W.H. Auden*, Faber and Faber Ltd, © The Estate of W.H. Auden; 'Mrs Midas' from *The World's Wife* by Carol Ann Duffy, Pan Macmillan, London, © Carol Ann Duffy, 1999; 'I have a dream' from *The Penguin Book of Historic Speeches*, ed. Brian MacArthur, by permission of the Estate of Martin Luther King, Jr, Inc.; *The Cat That Could Open the Fridge* by Simon Hoggart, 2004, Atlantic Books; 'New York to Detroit' from *The Collected Dorothy Parker*, by permission of Gerald Duckworth & Co Ltd; 'Mind your language, critics warn BBC' by Anushka Asthana and Vanessa Thorpe, in the *Observer*, © Guardian News & Media Ltd 2007; *The Waste Land* by T.S. Eliot, Faber and Faber Ltd, © The Estate of T.S. Eliot; *White Teeth* by Zadie Smith, Hamish Hamilton, 2000, © Zadie Smith, 2000, reproduced by permission of Penguin Books Ltd; *Persuading People: An Introduction to Rhetoric*, 2nd ed. 2005, by Robert and Sue Cockcroft, Palgrave Macmillan; 'My Life in a Column' by Tracey Emin, © *The Independent*, 5 January 2007; 'My Boyfriend is a Twat' by Zoe from http://users.pandora.be/quarsan/zoe/; 'Weekends are being filled with parties' by Felicity Nicholls, © *The Independent*, 28 September 2006; 'Rock's Pied Piper' by Owen Adams, © *The Independent*, 2 October 2006; Extract from *Writing Home* by Alan Bennett, Faber and Faber Ltd; 'Forgive Us' by Yoko Ono; *Dickens* by Peter Ackroyd, published by Chatto & Windus, reprinted by permission of The Random House Group Ltd; *Mary, Queen of Scots* by Antonia Fraser, published by Weidenfeld & Nicolson, a division of The Orion Publishing Group; *Falling Leaves* by Adeline Yen Mah, Michael Joseph, 1997, © Adeline Yen Mah, reproduced by permission of Penguin Books Ltd; *Chinese Cinderella* by Adeline Yen Mah, Puffin, 1999, © Adeline Yen Mah, reproduced by permission of Penguin Books Ltd; Obituary of Sandy West by Pierre Perrone, © *The Independent*, 22 October 2006; 'The Grey Eminence' by Chris McGrath, © *The Independent*, 14 November 2006; 'Afghanistan front line' by Antony Loyd, *The Times*, London, © NI Syndication, London, 7 March 2007; *Imperial Life in the Emerald City* by Rajiv Chandrasekaran, Bloomsbury; *Panic Nation* by Stanley Feldman and Vincent Marks, John Blake; Speech on climate change by permission of Sir David King; *Rough Guide to New York* by Martin Dunford and Jack Holland, 2000 © Martin Dunford and Jack Holland, reproduced by permission of Penguin Books Ltd; *At Home and Abroad* by V.S. Pritchett, published by Chatto & Windus, reprinted by permission of The Random House Group Ltd; *Holidays in Hell* by P.J. O'Rourke, Pan Macmillan, London; © P.J. O'Rourke, 1989; 'Doggedly defiant' by Matilda Egere-Cooper, © *The Independent*, 12 October 2007; 'A Beacon to the World', speech by Tony Blair, reproduced by permission of Tony Blair's office, transcript © Guardian News & Media Ltd 1997; 'A Postcard from Iceland' by Gunnar Ragnarsson, © Guardian News & Media Ltd 2006; 'Life in the fast lane: M11 The mysterious one' by Stuart Jeffries, © Guardian News & Media Ltd 2007; *The Secret River* by Kate Grenville, Canongate, 2005; *In Cold Blood* by Truman Capote, © 1959 by Truman Capote, reproduced by permission of Penguin Books Ltd; Report of the Clutter murders in *New York Times*, by permission of United Press International; *The Big Sleep* by Raymond Chandler, © 1939 by Raymond Chandler, reproduced by permission of Penguin Books Ltd; *The Lost Continent* by Bill Bryson, published by Black Swan, reprinted by permission of The Random House Group Ltd; *The Beach* by Alex Garland, Viking, 1996, © Alex Garland, reproduced by permission of Penguin Books Ltd; *Bible Stories* by David Kossoff, Zondervan, 1968; *Oryx and Crake* by Margaret Atwood, Bloomsbury; *Congo Journey* by Redmond O'Hanlon, 1988, reprinted by permission of PFD on behalf of Redmond O'Hanlon; Extract reproduced from *A Passage to Africa* by George Alagiah with kind permission of Little, Brown Book Group, © George Alagiah 2001; *The Fatal Shore* by Robert Hughes, published by Harvill, reprinted by permission of The Random House Group Ltd; *The True History of the Kelly Gang* by Peter Carey, Faber and Faber Ltd; *Australia* by Philip Knightley, published by Chatto & Windus, reprinted by permission of The Random House Group Ltd;

*Molesworth* by Geoffrey Willans and Ronald Searle, Penguin Books, 1953; International phonetic alphabet reproduced by permission of the International Phonetic Association, Aristotle University of Thessaloniki, Greece; 'One Deaf Poet' by Walter Nash by courtesy of the author; *Analysing Talk* by David Langford, Palgrave Macmillan, 1994; *Top Girls* by Caryl Churchill, Methuen Drama, an imprint of A & C Black Publishers Ltd; *The Bell Jar* by Sylvia Plath, Faber and Faber Ltd, © The Estate of Sylvia Plath; *You Just Don't Understand* by Deborah Tannen, Little, Brown Book Group; *Lord of the Flies* by William Golding, Faber and Faber Ltd, © The Estate of William Golding; 'Waiting Gentlewoman' by U.A. Fanthorpe was first printed as one of a sequence of poems about Shakespeare's female characters titled 'Only Here for the Bier' in the long out-of-print collection *Standing To* (Peterloo Poets, 1982). It is now available only in *Collected Poems 1978–2003* by U.A. Fanthorpe (Peterloo Poets, 2005); *The Birthday Party* by Harold Pinter, Faber and Faber Ltd; *History of the World in 10½ Chapters* by Julian Barnes, published by Jonathan Cape, reprinted by permission of The Random House Group Ltd; Amy Winehouse review by Andrew Byrne, © *The Independent*, 27 February 2007; Dawn Kanter's review of *Ophelia*, in *Mslexia*, the magazine for women writers, Jan–Mar 2007; 'Mary Phillip, Footballer for Arsenal and England' by Imogen Fox, © Guardian News & Media Ltd 2007; 'Still only 19…' by Angela Lambert, in *The Indypendium*, Part 1, © *The Independent*, 2006; *Diana: Her True Story – In Her Own Words* by Andrew Morton, by permission of Michael O'Mara Books Ltd, © Andrew Morton 1992, 1998, 2003, all rights reserved; 'It's your Final Countdown' by Ed West, in *Metro* 29 March 2007, © Associated Newspapers; 'The waste land' by Andrew O'Hagan, *London Review of Books*; 'Text alerts tackle school skivers', transcribed from BBC News Online video clip; 'Get dressed, head tells the pyjama mamas' by David Sharrock, *The Times*, 8 June 2007, © NI Syndication, London; 'What to do if you break down on a motorway' by permission of MORE TH>N; *Rough Guide to First Time Europe* by Doug Lansky, 1996, 2005, © Doug Lansky, 2004, reproduced by permission of Penguin Books Ltd; 'A Wife in a Million' from *Stranded* by V.L. McDermid, © V.L. McDermid 1989; *First Love, Last Rites* by Ian McEwan, published by Jonathan Cape, reprinted by permission of The Random House Group Ltd; *Fahrenheit Twins* by Michel Faber, first published in Great Britain by Canongate Books Ltd, 14 High Street, Edinburgh, EH1 1TE; *The Bloody Chamber and Other Stories*, © 1980 Angela Carter, reproduced by permission of the author c/o Rogers, Coleridge & White Ltd, 20 Powis Mews, London W11 1JN; *Changing Babies*, © Deborah Moggach, permission granted by Curtis Brown Group Ltd; *Almost Like a Whale* by Steve Jones, published by Doubleday, reprinted by permission of The Random House Group Ltd; 'The Loneliest Birthday' by B. Gilliland, in *Metro*, 24 August 2007, © Associated Newspapers; 'A Star is Born', *Hold Ye Front Page*, *The Sun*, © News International Syndication Ltd, 1999; *Rosencrantz and Guildenstern Are Dead* by Tom Stoppard, Faber and Faber Ltd; *The Waste Land* by T.S. Eliot, Faber and Faber Ltd, © The Estate of T.S. Eliot; *The True Story of the 3 Little Pigs, by A. Wolf* by Jon Scieszka, Penguin Group (US) Inc © Jon Scieszka 1989; *Farewell, My Lovely* by Raymond Chandler, Hamish Hamilton, 1940, © 1940 by Raymond Chandler, reproduced by permission of Penguin Books Ltd; *The Curious Incident of the Dog in the Night-Time* by Mark Haddon, published by David Fickling/Jonathan Cape, reprinted by permission of The Random House Group Ltd; *The Lord of the Rings* by J.R.R. Tolkien, HarperCollins; Radio script for *The Lord of the Rings* by Brian Sibley, by courtesy of the adapter; *The Gun That I Have in my Right Hand is Loaded* by Timothy West, by courtesy of the author.

Images are reproduced by permission of the following:
John Lennon: image by © Bettmann/Corbis; 'Robinson Crusoe and his shipwreck' © 2007 Getty Images; 'Heart of Darkness': image by © Antar Dayal/Illustration Works/Corbis; Illustration from medieval manuscript: © 2008 The British Library Board, all rights reserved.

Every effort has been made to trace copyright holders of material reproduced in this book. Any omissions will be rectified in subsequent printings if notice is given to the publisher.